In Union There Is Strength

AMERICA IN THE NINETEENTH CENTURY

Series editors:
Brian DeLay, Steven Hahn, Amy Dru Stanley

America in the Nineteenth Century proposes a rigorous
rethinking of this most formative period in U.S. history. Books
in the series will be wide-ranging and eclectic, with an interest
in politics at all levels, culture and capitalism, race and slavery,
law, gender, and the environment, and regional and transnational
history. The series aims to expand the scope of nineteenth-century
historiography by bringing classic questions into dialogue with
innovative perspectives, approaches, and methodologies.

In Union
There Is Strength

Philadelphia in the Age
of Urban Consolidation

ANDREW HEATH

UNIVERSITY OF PENNSYLVANIA PRESS

PHILADELPHIA

Published by
University of Pennsylvania Press
Philadelphia, Pennsylvania 19104-4112
www.upenn.edu/pennpress

Printed in the United States of America
on acid-free paper
1 3 5 7 9 10 8 6 4 2

Library of Congress Cataloging-in-Publication Data

Names: Heath, Andrew, author.
Title: In union there is strength: Philadelphia in the age of urban consolidation /
 Andrew Heath.
Other titles: America in the nineteenth century.
Description: 1st edition. | Philadelphia: University of Pennsylvania Press, [2019] |
 Series: America in the nineteenth century | Includes bibliographical references
 and index.
Identifiers: LCCN 2018031786 | ISBN 9780812251111 (hardcover)
Subjects: LCSH: Philadelphia (Pa.)—History—19th century. | Philadelphia
 (Pa.)—Politics and government—19th century. | Philadelphia (Pa.)—Social
 conditions—19th century. | Urbanization—Pennsylvania—Philadelphia—
 History—19th century.
Classification: LCC F158.44 .H43 2019 | DDC 974.8/11—dc23
LC record available at https://lccn.loc.gov/2018031786

CONTENTS

ABBREVIATIONS

AHR *American Historical Review*
HSP Historical Society of Pennsylvania
JAH *Journal of American History*
JUH *Journal of Urban History*
LCP Library Company of Philadelphia
PMHB *Pennsylvania Magazine of History and Biography*

Philadelphia in an Age of Consolidation

In 1880, the pioneering social scientist Robert Ellis Thompson set out to explain the patterns of political growth. The "modern city," he argued with his own Philadelphia in mind, was "meant for a people whose social life takes place under the roof of home." For Thompson, this distinguished the ancients, who had privileged civic space over private comforts, from the men and women of an industrial age. But what twentieth-century critics would come to call the "fall of public man" appeared to him as a salutary change that brought peace, prosperity, and cohesion to a fractious metropolis.[1] His private city produced public benefits.

Even as Thompson charted the city's division into family homes, he showed how it had come together as an associated whole. Philadelphia, he insisted, illustrated the "growth of large social unities out of the union of smaller ones." Thompson was referring specifically here to Philadelphia's Consolidation Act of 1854: a measure that extended the territory of the two-square mile "city proper" across the entire county, more than doubled the metropolitan population, and made the municipality the largest by territory in the nation. Consolidation annexed two-dozen townships, boroughs, and districts to Philadelphia's metropolitan empire and marked one of the most ambitious urban reforms of the nineteenth century (see Maps 1 and 2). But he read the 1854 charter as more than a merely municipal matter; instead, it expressed a "fact of social science." "This is the natural method of growth the whole world over," Thompson explained, for "all great communities have been formed by this consolidation of smaller but older communities." With the Civil War no doubt in mind, he reminded his audience that the "revolution" could not go backward, as the "larger unity cannot again be sundered into its component parts." The law of association applied to nations as well as cities.[2]

Map 1. Philadelphia, pre-1854. Prior to Consolidation in 1854, independent districts, boroughs, and townships surrounded the two-square–mile city proper. Philadelphia's outlying suburbs outnumbered the city in population from 1820.

Map 2. Philadelphia after Consolidation. The 1854 charter erased the old district lines and divided the new city into twenty-four wards. At nearly 130 square miles, Philadelphia became the nation's largest city in territorial terms.

Thompson wrote at the end of an age of consolidation that stretched across the middle decades of the nineteenth century. Between the 1840s and 1870s, economic development, territorial conquest, and civil war transformed a divided republic into a national state. Further afield, loose federations and geographic expressions yielded to the integrative force of nationalism. And from the American West to Qing China, colonial powers forcibly incorporated peripheries into imperial systems. Municipal consolidation seemed to illustrate the same process on a metropolitan scale. Cities from Brooklyn to Paris joined Philadelphia by extending their borders around midcentury in pursuit of order, economy, and the prestige that came with a larger population; they embarked too on what contemporaries called "practical consolidation" by forging the institutional and infrastructural bonds to hold their metropolis together. The language of nation and empire helped to naturalize urban expansion: Philadelphians even talked about the "manifest destiny" of their city. But to see consolidation at any level as the inevitable working out of a natural law was a leap too far. Thompson's "large social unities" came out of conflict as much as consensus.[3]

This book explores battles over the metropolitan future in that age of consolidation by linking city, nation, and empire. The people who fill its pages confronted a fundamental question: How could power be brought to bear on a city in a manner that prevented growth from leading to disintegration? My story begins in the 1840s with the republic's "great cities" rolling back their own frontiers as the boundaries of the American republic leapt toward the Pacific. Philadelphia, despite falling behind New York in the race for urban supremacy, still doubled in size every twenty years, as meadows gave way to streets, factories, and homes. Boosters hoped to make it the London and Paris of the continent: a center of economic dynamism and cultural display that would profit from and proudly reflect the might of an American empire. But growth brought growing pains, as epidemics of riots, strikes, and disease ravaged its streets. Here, social strife in the antebellum city paralleled sectional struggles over slavery extension, and led citizens to wonder whether divisions would pull polities apart.[4]

In 1880, with Philadelphia a place of relative repose amid the tumult of Gilded Age America, Thompson cast consolidation as an inevitable and beneficial process that had remade metropolis and nation. Under the consolidationist impulse, a city of mobs had become a city of homes; *these* United States had become *the* United States. But the unionism that underpinned consolidationist schemes should not be read as a straightforward adjustment to the challenges posed by a complex and interdependent society. The entangled projects of city- and nation-building were far more fraught than Thompson implied. On the urban terrain, they involved drawing boundaries that left some out as they drew others in. They forced consolidators into confronting questions about citizenship, urban design, and the organization of social and economic life. They led them to question stark divisions between public and private. And they inspired opposition from Philadelphians who feared the financial and political effects of centralizing designs. Consolidation here provides a window onto the remaking of city and nation over the middle decades of the nineteenth century.

Over the following pages, I use "consolidation" in two ways. Consolidation with a capital "C" refers to the ten-year campaign that concluded in the passage of Philadelphia's 1854 city charter. In drawing 127 square miles of streets and fields under a single government, the Consolidation Act created a territorial and financial leviathan, and provided a precedent when cities like New York looked to expand their boundaries later in the century. When used in the lowercase, in contrast, "consolidation" pertains to a broader project of boundary-drawing and community-making that often took place beyond the sphere of the state. In this respect I follow nineteenth-century usage. Citizens at the time saw consolidation as the tightening of affective or associational ties: as any process that brought individuals or communities into closer communion. The Consolidation of 1854 marked just one expression of this impulse. Building internal improvements, forging class consciousness, or soothing social and sectional tensions could all count as consolidation too.

The men who battled over municipal Consolidation in the decade leading up to 1854 were consolidators in that wider sense. Consider, for instance, two figures who appear frequently over the following chapters. Morton McMichael (1807–1879) came to the city as a young man, and as a poet impressed Edgar Allan Poe. Before long, though, McMichael sacrificed his literary ambitions for a career in politics and publishing. As county sheriff, he failed to stop two vast riots in 1844, and thereafter turned his attention to consolidating the city across its social and spatial boundaries, using his talents as a public speaker and his command of the city's leading bourgeois newspaper, the *North American and United States Gazette*. A Whig and Republican in national affairs, he proved more loyal to class than party at the metropolitan level, and made it his mission to ensure the city's best men worked together in preserving order, building up the city, and holding together the nation. McMichael was among the leaders of the municipal Consolidation movement and helped to found the nationalist Union League a few years later. Few figures better exemplify Thompson's consolidationist impulse.[5]

Like McMichael, George Lippard (1822–1854) was a writer and newspaperman, who won plaudits from Poe, but his consolidationist ambitions took him in the direction of radical reform rather than civic boosterism. His 1845 novel, *The Quaker City*, was the best-selling work of American fiction prior to *Uncle Tom's Cabin*, and scandalized respectable Philadelphians with its thinly veiled caricatures of eminent citizens. Readers who dismissed the work as sensationalist drivel, though, ignored Lippard's social criticism. Influenced by Christian communitarianism, utopian socialism, and revolutions at home and abroad, the author imagined a consolidated city and federal union purged of injustice. Where McMichael looked to unite a bourgeoisie around the promise of an imperial metropolis, Lippard urged producers to combine in pursuit of social regeneration.[6]

For all their ideological differences, McMichael and Lippard had much in common. Each came of age in an antebellum world shaped by democratic opportunity, urban and national expansion, and social and sectional divisions. In Philadelphia they witnessed these forces playing out in battles at the ballot box, struggles on workshop floors, and riots over immigration and abolitionism. Shaped by such experiences, their manifestos for consolidation searched for ways to reap the fruits of economic and technological progress without the republic falling apart. They both joined projects to reconstruct society and space, which sought to channel the energies industrialization, urbanization, and imperial growth had unleashed. For their generation, the wrenching changes of the Jacksonian era, and the uncertainties that came out of upheavals at home and abroad, made the future seem more open-ended than perhaps at any other point in the American past. Looking forward from the 1840s, rather than backward, as Thompson did, from 1880, the age of consolidation brims with possibility.[7]

That midcentury generation has sometimes been missed by historians. Critic Lewis Mumford's indictment of the nineteenth-century industrial town, where freedom meant little more than the right to seek "unrestricted profits and private aggrandizement," might have been written with Philadelphia in mind.[8] One of the most influential works of American urban history, Samuel Bass Warner Jr.'s *Private City*, depicts a midcentury metropolis Mumford might have recognized: a Philadelphia scarred by a ubiquitous "privatism," which privileged individual enrichment over public needs. In the early national era, according to Warner, the leadership of civic-minded gentlemen limited the damage this capitalist ethic could do, but by the 1850s, the old elite had begun to give way to professional politicians. These political specialists brokered competing class and cultural interests, as Philadelphia's myopic working-class and nationally oriented businessmen lacked either the capacity or inclination to intervene. Consolidation itself appears as a belated and barely adequate response to rapid growth, which only served to hasten the rise of the party boss.[9]

Through tracing the careers of the men who fought over the terms of Philadelphia's consolidation, this book offers a different interpretation. Between that old elite and the machine politician stood a cohort who could hardly afford to retreat to the counting house. In their enduring engagement with civic life, cosmopolitan orientation that located Philadelphia in a world of "great cities," and belief in urban interdependence that stood at odds with laissez-faire, they sought an alternative to both an insular, individualistic privatism, and the late nineteenth-century bourgeois reform movement historians have termed "liberalism." That is not to say that I see virtue where previous historians saw vice. The people I write about usually expected to prosper individually and collectively from urban expansion. They were just unsure whether unbridled capitalism was the best way to do so.[10]

The consolidation cohort's doubts about privatism sprang too from an enduring attachment to the city. In charting the making of the modern world, historians have traced the subordination of self-governing cities to expanding national states. If their narrative has been tailored to the particularities of European state formation, a similar story can be told in the United States, where the nationalizing impulses of war and railroads reoriented loyalties from metropolis to nation. After 1865, the argument goes, victorious northern elites had less attachment to their locality: amor patriae and economic centralization trumped civic loyalties. Rather than focusing on city- and nation-building as rival processes in this era, however, the following chapters argue that as political, economic, and cultural projects, they were closely connected. Although municipal consolidators never had to face a problem as vexing as slavery, they grappled with many of the same difficulties that confronted their counterparts at the national level: not least, how to incorporate territory and people; how to balance central power and local control; and how to preserve order in a divided polity. The challenge

of spurring rapid growth in a manner that staved off the threat of dissolution became a burning question in both city and nation at around the same
time; the Philadelphia riots of 1844, indeed, coincided with fierce debates
over the extension of a slaveholders' empire into Texas. But more than
mere coincidence linked consolidationist designs for civic and national
union. Battles over the terms of municipal Consolidation were shaped by—
and in turn shaped—citizens' relationships to the nation.[11]

Across the midcentury decades, the city mattered as much as ever. For
rich and poor Philadelphians the metropolis was a site of work and play: a
place of collective consumption in which visions of social and spatial order
coalesced and clashed. Those who wanted to sell the city—to maximize the
exchange values of metropolitan property—often confronted defenders of
an urban commons. Those who wanted to save the city—to redeem it from
sin, riot, or "the crimes of Capital"—often tried to reshape the social organization of urban space in a way that would cultivate better citizens. In
the designs of park advocates, boulevard builders, and land reformers, we
encounter ideas of what the city might become. And over the course of the
period covered in this book—a moment before the "labor question" came
to dominate social thought in the North—space seemed, at least to some,
to exert a determinative influence in shaping society and politics. Whether
through cleansing "plague spots," laying out wide streets, or building the
small homes Thompson extolled on the metropolitan frontier, Philadelphians seemed to be molding the character of a city and its people.[12]

Even as citizens engaged in local battles, however, they looked far and
wide for inspiration. As an industrial hub producing largely for domestic
markets, nineteenth-century Philadelphia can appear less cosmopolitan
than the eighteenth-century port that preceded it; its foremost political
economists, indeed, preached a doctrine of economic nationalism over free
trade. Rapid urbanization, though, had convinced many residents by the
1840s that their metropolis belonged among the "great cites" of the Atlantic
World, and this sense of a shared destiny—and the new rivalries it opened
up—created the "common referents" for a series of halting attempts to
learn lessons from European capitals. When turning their eyes across the
ocean, Philadelphians chose what they wanted to see. For a radical like
Lippard, the National Workshops of the 1848 Revolution in Paris provided
a model of the social republic; for a booster like McMichael, on the other
hand, Baron Haussmann's debt-financed city-building seemed an intriguing experiment. But cosmopolitanism did not only find expression in

debates over which elements of Old World cities might be translated to the New. Promoters hoped that the steam power, military force, and industrial might that hastened American expansion in the 1840s would open up the opportunity for their metropolis to occupy a central place in a new global order. Philadelphia, they earnestly believed, could become an imperial node between the Atlantic and Pacific. The reconstruction of the city's interior arrangements would proceed apace with the reordering of its external relations: the annihilation of municipal borders in 1854, for example, was closely tied to railroads' annihilation of space. Here the city provides a prime vantage point to understand the interplay between local battles and global designs.[13]

As their cosmopolitan ambitions required fixating citizens' gaze on distant horizons and grand destinies, advocates of consolidation came into conflict with localism and tradition. Growth, consolidators feared, had fragmented the metropolis into dozens of tiny fiefdoms dominated by fire companies, street gangs, and ward bosses. Here, parochial needs were privileged ahead of the common good, and shortsightedness held back urban ascent. The exemplary figure was "King" William McMullen, an Irish American ward boss, who fought to defend his territory from meddling reformers. Elsewhere, especially among wealthy citizens with property and bonds to defend, consolidators encountered what they derisively referred to as "fogyism," a reluctance to take the financial and political risks required to make Philadelphia great. The attorney Horace Binney provides one of the best examples. Although he eventually embraced civic union, his conservative investments, wariness of growing state power, and reluctance to back railroad-building irritated self-styled modernizers. Politics sometimes became a matter of perspective: Could citizens see the city from a position that enabled them to comprehend its imperial future, or were their eyes trained only on immediate surroundings and personal portfolios? In boosters' telling, at least, battles over space, money, and government arrayed farsighted visionaries against myopic opponents.[14]

It also pitted consolidators against the disintegrative tendencies of individualism. Figures like McMichael and Lippard took "association" as a guiding principle. Like its close cousin, consolidation, "association" became a keyword of midcentury American politics. The French political scientist Alexis de Tocqueville used it to describe the Jacksonian city's flourishing civil society: the space between the individual and the state in which civic life takes hold. But "association" had a history that Tocqueville missed.

Philadelphians joined together well before 1776, and in the early national era, when wealthy Federalists were driven out of office, they turned to association to shield their power in cultural institutions and business corporations. By the 1830s, as urbanization frayed old communal bonds, associations proliferated. Although many Jacksonian-era associations crossed neighborhood boundaries, others accelerated the city's territorial balkanization, as fire companies, street gangs, and new municipal districts cut the metropolis up into dozens of jurisdictions and spheres of influence. Association here involved marking difference rather than promoting unity.[15]

Yet by 1850, association had acquired a wider meaning—as a principle as much as a practice—that tied it closely to consolidationist projects. For utopian socialists, it captured their ideal of a cooperative social order; for political economists, it held out the promise of a "harmony of interests" between labor and capital; for supporters of civic and national union, it served as a riposte to the claims of suburban districts or states' rights. Association in this regard moved easily between the politics of class, city, and nation. Indeed, the rallying cry "In Union There Is Strength" rang out in meetings of craft unions, municipal Consolidators, and defenders of the federal compact.[16]

Above all, association was a force multiplier: a "technology" that had the capacity to change the world through combined effort. Otherwise antagonistic advocates of association shared a suspicion of individualism. They took as their starting point the assumption that competition had to be tempered by cooperation and that citizens could achieve more by recognizing mutual interdependence than they could by denying the social character of human nature. Here the utopian community, labor union, business corporation, building society, consolidated city, and national state each became expressions of a type. Association could even be cast as a new epoch in historical development: a centripetal counterweight to the centrifugal forces of an earlier, individualistic era.[17]

In such respects, association provides an alternative perspective on the midcentury city to that of privatism. Where the former focuses our attention on collective organization, the latter directs us to the competitive marketplace. Yet the two were not necessarily in tension. In the history of American capitalism, the self-made man is more myth than reality, and Philadelphia's economic elite, like investors before and after them, proved adept at seeking public favors to pursue private ends. Both railroad-building and municipal Consolidation—schemes sold in the lofty language of the common good—lined the pockets of the boosters who backed them. But consolidators often saw privatism as a threat to their class vision. The same economic forces that enriched them as individuals frequently undermined their collective ideas about how Philadelphia (and indeed the nation) should look and function. How to balance capitalist growth with collective needs vexed the subjects of this book.[18] It led them to ponder the problem of power.

Producing Power

Morton McMichael, the so-called father of Consolidation Eli Kirk Price remembered after his death, "lifted up the city into power." Power fascinated consolidators. Although the word had rich meanings in American political thought, most would have recognized the German sociologist Max Weber's definition as the capacity to exert will over resistance. That resistance sprang from different sources. It could come from the "petty sovereignties" of fire companies, ward bosses, and suburban districts that had taken root in the age of Jacksonian Democracy. It could come from the rival cities that jostled with Philadelphia for command of seaborne commerce and western trade. And it could come too from the process of urban growth itself, which proved magnificent to behold but difficult to direct. How to control city government, capture remote markets, and manipulate the metropolitan form perplexed figures like McMichael.[19]

Consolidators saw power as both concentrated and dispersed. "The city, as one finds it in history," Lewis Mumford wrote in 1938, "is the point of maximum concentration for the power and culture of a community." Philadelphians intuitively understood as much; their claims to imperial status, they realized, would stand or fall on the condition of their metropolis. Yet within its bounds, the question of who ruled whom was by no means easy to answer. Power lay in the people and their politicians, in various branches of government, in quasi-public institutions like banks and railroads, and was even encoded in urban places and processes. To ask who controlled the city in this era and focus exclusively on electoral politics, then, misunderstands the character of American governance. Consolidators did not always seek to center decision-making in one place, yet men like McMichael continually looked for ways to produce power: to concentrate the means, that is, to reconstruct their city.[20]

Their first priority lay in seizing and shaping the local state. In this regard, the Consolidation of 1854 bore striking similarities to better-known state-building projects in the nineteenth century. Modernizing states aimed to expand their empires, build up bureaucracies, improve tax collection, provide public goods, and incorporate new ideas about the rights and responsibilities of citizenship. Simultaneously they sought to make an opaque social order legible through surveys, maps, and censuses. Consolidators turned to these tools in trying to transform Philadelphia's municipal regime into a powerful entity subject to their control: one capable of pursuing imperial ambitions.[21]

Such designs required command of finance as well as government. Histories of late nineteenth-century American cities are frequently filled with battles between profligate bosses and miserly reformers, but in the midcentury metropolis, the roles were often reversed. Boosters accused parsimonious politicians of muzzling the metropolis in its fight for supremacy with urban rivals. Debt, they argued instead, had the alchemical power to transform sleepy streets into bustling avenues of commerce and culture. And if Philadelphians were to seize the opportunities opened by technologies like railroads and sewers, then capital had to be mobilized. Yet borrowing came with risks, and it proved hard to persuade some bourgeois Philadelphians of its merits when their property served as a lien on any loan. Debates over debt-financed expansion reveal concerns over the capacity to reconcile growth, democracy, and order across the period.[22]

Citizens tried to produce power outside the channels of party politics. One of the most controversial measures I explore, the municipal financing of the Pennsylvania Railroad in 1846, inspired public meetings and petition drives that eventually fed into electoral battles. Popular agitation of this type, which was common across the era, sometimes pitted businessmen against the laboring classes. McMichael and Lippard, for instance, both believed class could serve as an axis of association, and sometimes tried to organize around the common economic interests of people they labeled "capitalists" and "producers." Class formation here became a project as much as a process: a means of popular mobilization that cut across the socially heterogeneous composition of political parties. But more often than not, movements from railroad-building to municipal consolidation tried to unite Philadelphians around a common commitment to growth through grandiose (and usually debt-financed) schemes. Indeed, McMichael, perhaps more than any other figure, aimed to construct a "growth regime" that sought to justify urban expansion as beneficial to all. Lippard and his allies continually challenged the claim that growth was good.[23]

Power sprang from cultural as well as economic mobilization. Where consolidators struggled to capture the state, they could turn to this sphere instead, shielding the cultural realm from democratic control, and using private institutions to reform behavior and reshape space. In league with evangelical reformers and secular organizations, they sought to sculpt streets, squares, and parks. If power lay in a citizen's capacity to leave an imprint on the city, though, it also lay in the city's capacity to leave its imprint on the citizen. By the 1850s, many consolidators took for granted the idea that the urban form could influence character and civilize the "barbarians" within their bounds. Here, parks, boulevards, and houses all acquired the power to determine Philadelphia's course, and had the potential, their advocates believed, to transform force into consent.[24]

Finally, power lay in the ability to project a vision that linked past, present, and future. McMichael, Lippard, and their respective allies moved back and forth between what city and nation had once been, what they were now, and what they might yet be. Looking ahead a century, McMichael imagined Philadelphia in 1950 as the empire city of the New World, while Lippard foresaw the remains of a ruined Independence Hall being ransacked to build a royal palace. Used in such ways, history and prophecy both became political interventions. Analogies to a mythical past inspired action in the present; predictions of the future, meanwhile, called on citizens to either forestall of fulfill what was to come.[25]

The following chapters show how, over the middle decades of the nineteenth century, citizens fought for the power to shape city and nation. My focus is more on McMichael's allies—the merchants, manufacturers, and professions who led the campaign for Consolidation—than on Lippard's producers, but because consolidation involved conflict and coalition-building, I pay close attention to radicalism too. Debates over property, design, and order entangle here as citizens battled over reconstruction.

The city Thompson lauded in 1880 was not just produced by a process of rapid urbanization or the logic of a liberal tradition of privatism. In the 1840s, as riots reminded onlookers of the French Revolution, citizens had questioned whether their republic really was exceptional. Four decades later, though, the "city of homes" appeared to offer an American alternative to the Paris Commune. In its imposing center, immense residential periphery, and skilled industrial workforce, Gilded Age Philadelphia became a symbol (rightly or wrongly) of how capitalism could work for ordinary people. In the tense climate of the Gilded Age, other cities latched onto its model. Thompson's Philadelphia, I argue, may have become an archetypal American city, but its consolidation had been inspired by surprising sources: European urban design, radical social thought, and an associational ethic at odds with individualism.

*   *   *

The following chapters are bookended by urban disorder: I begin in the riots and strikes of the Jacksonian era and conclude with labor conflict in the Gilded Age. Between these moments of crisis, though, a generation of consolidators linked the political organization of the city, the design of its built environment, and the shape of the nation as they struggled to reconstruct the metropolis.

The first five chapters, organized by theme, focus on the two decades before the Civil War. Chapters 1 and 2 explore how boosters and radicals tried to read the places and processes of the antebellum metropolis. Each fashioned distinct ideas about association and environment that shaped their urban vision. From there, I move in Chapter 3 to explore the making of growth politics, as citizens tried to put in place the building blocks to develop industry, railroads, and real estate: a project of urban empire-building that aimed to make the city the central place in an expanding United States. A new regime of urban capitalism left its mark on urban space, though not necessarily as boosters had envisaged. Chapter 4 therefore considers different plans for the built environment and the search for a method to set the metropolis's imperial pretensions in stone. Frustration at the failure of the city to look and behave as consolidators expected led some from the 1840s to question the merits of a broad suffrage, but as Chapter 5 contends, democratic doubts found expression more often in designs to incorporate the suburban frontier, gentrify politics through environmental reform, and strengthen "family government" in Philadelphia's homes.

The final two chapters look at the war years and after, as consolidation moved from a civic priority to a nation-building project. In alliance with the Republican Party, bourgeois citizens sought to harmonize sectional and social interests by reconstructing the center, expanding onto the rural frontier, and encouraging working-class property ownership. Philadelphia, they claimed, could be a city of boulevards and homes. Like the nation, boasted boosters, an imperial scale safeguarded republican government: the safety valve of suburbanization kept a permanent proletariat at bay. Philadelphia's consolidators here had helped to put in place the institutional foundations of a powerful defense of capitalism. Indeed, the political economy of urban growth they pioneered anticipates on a municipal scale the federally sponsored reconstruction of post–World War II American cities. In both cases, private enterprise, public power, and an ideology of class consensus spurred suburbanization and urban renewal. But like post-1945 city-building too, Chapter 7 shows, mid-nineteenth-century growth politics could divide as well as unite. Urban expansion raised rents, blighted avenues, and raised fears of spiraling taxes to meet a ballooning debt. After the Panic of 1873, these tensions threatened to pull growth politics apart. But by then, Philadelphia boasted the world's largest private corporation, the nation's most territorially extensive city, its biggest municipal park, and in its new city hall, what would become its grandest (and to some critics, its most grotesque) civic building. That urban inheritance was the product of a long-running struggle over the terms of a consolidation far less natural than Robert Ellis Thompson implied.

CHAPTER 1

"A Great City Is a Great Study"

In September 1854, just months after Philadelphia's political consolidation had extended the urban boundaries to encompass almost 130 square miles, Morton McMichael's *North American and United States Gazette* measured up the city and its people. The "vast multitudes" wandering the streets, the paper mused, embraced such a variety of "motives and men and actions" that the possibilities were "infinite." All that was known was Philadelphia's unknowability. "We who have lived from birth in the midst of this bustle know, comparatively, no more of the great city than the stranger who is within its gates," the paper concluded.[1]

European and American commentators over the middle decades of the nineteenth century observed the same disorienting effects of urban growth. In Manchester, the "shock city" of the Industrial Revolution, the liberal Alexis de Tocqueville and radical Friedrich Engels described "the disintegrating of society into individuals." Across the Atlantic in Philadelphia, an evangelical worried that the metropolitan masses lacked the mutual "sympathy" required for moral order. While their prescriptions ranged from reform to revolution to redemption from sin, each saw cities as solvents of community and tradition, as all that was solid melted into the air. Few captured this better than Edgar Allan Poe in his "Man of the Crowd." Set in London, but penned during the writer's sojourn in Philadelphia, Poe's narrator sorts the nameless people passing him by, before fixating on an inscrutable soul whose resistance to categorization hints at the anomie of "great cities."[2]

Poe's friend Morton McMichael had reason to share such pessimism. In 1844, soon after starting a term as county sheriff, he failed to stop the growth of two riots, which metastasized into the largest urban disorders in the history of the Union. Blamed for allowing the metropolis to fall apart, he made it his mission to put it back together. Consolidating the city across its divisions preoccupied him from the 1840s to the 1870s. Over decades in which federated republics, multiethnic empires, and geographic expressions converged as national states, McMichael set about building a nation in miniature. Philadelphia, having grown too big to know informally, needed imagining as a whole.

McMichael joined others in a quest for legibility. As the *North American* hinted in 1854, the more complex a society became, the harder it was to see. Nineteenth-century state builders tried to overcome their "partial blindness" by bringing territory and population into focus. The maps and censuses they produced helped incorporate colonial frontiers into national domains.[3]

One of those frontiers was the city. On both sides of the Atlantic, reformers, journalists, and novelists tried to illuminate the shadowy spaces of their cities and incorporate the urban wilderness. Gridironed Philadelphia may have looked the model of a transparent, modern metropolis, but in the courts and alleys that ran off the main thoroughfares and the unknown suburbs in which riot and disease held sway, it—like Poe's man of the crowd—defied the surveyor's gaze. McMichael, who wanted to sort the discordant phenomena of urban life, made the "great city" a "great study" for his paper. Scattered in Philadelphia's soil—his daily insisted—lay the seeds of metropolitan empire, but only knowledge could nourish their growth.[4]

The problems McMichael and his allies encountered in trying to make the city legible reveal the pitfalls of reducing the story to a linear tale of modernization. In contrast to most modernizing states, Philadelphia's pre-Consolidation municipalities evinced little interest in knowing their territory and people. Their inaction frustrated the *North American,* but when Philadelphians associated voluntarily to measure their metropolis, they struggled to make sense of what they found. "However we may con it over, we shall never know it thoroughly," McMichael's paper wrote of Philadelphia, "for continually some new phase . . . starts up to astonish and bewilder us." Rather than settle for still lifes of a place in perpetual motion, citizens searched for laws of cause and effect, asking not only what the metropolis was, but also what it might become. Their prophecies had the power to shape the city.[5]

In mapping Philadelphia's present and future, citizens imagined the city as an interdependent whole, while exposing its divisions. Here, the project of collecting, interpreting, and sharing knowledge of the city helped to consolidate an economic elite. At McMichael's urging, merchants, manufacturers, and professionals came together in counting the cost of riots and weighing up the productive power of the suburbs. Radicals, whose different take on Philadelphia I explore in Chapter 2, aimed to unite producers around their reading of the urban process. In doing so, each group grappled with questions of national import: Was the United States exceptional? Could a distended, divided republic endure? Did capitalism necessarily lead to an anomie the likes of which Tocqueville and Engels had seen in Manchester? The city here provided a laboratory for a "great study" with significance well beyond municipal boundaries.

A Divided City

J. C. Sydney's richly detailed 1849 cartography of the city hinted at Philadelphia's divisions. Like most maps from the 1830s onward, it portrayed the entirety of the built-up metropolis.[6] Philadelphia had grown phenomenally over preceding decades, but with land scarce in the center, the population pushed outward to the metropolitan frontier. Between 1820 and 1850, the inhabitants of the two-square–mile "city proper" nearly doubled from 63,802 to 121,376. The rest of the county, however, expanded almost fourfold to close to three hundred thousand. Yet as builders transformed farmland into streets, houses, and workshops, the boundaries of the two-square–mile city proper stayed fixed at their seventeenth-century limits, and by 1850, the boroughs and districts marked off by thick lines on Sydney's map included several of the largest municipalities in the United States. Spring Garden, the Northern Liberties, and Kensington, all north of the city center, ranked ninth, eleventh, and twelfth, respectively, in the nation in the midcentury census, with Southwark and Moyamensing to the south not far behind. Each of these subdivisions were more or less self-governing, and prior to 1850, only the Board of Health and county officers like the sheriff had metropolitan-wide powers. For most common functions of municipal government—maintaining order, regulating streets and markets, providing gas and water—the districts had independent jurisdiction. Sydney showed a city that looked like a miniature of the Holy Roman Empire.[7]

Advocates of municipal consolidation between 1844 and 1854 called these boundaries "imaginary lines," but the city proper and its suburban offspring had been growing apart for decades.[8] If it is easy to romanticize the "unity of everyday life" in the late colonial era, it is because the city could be traversed on foot, and differences of rank and status were more evident within households than across neighborhoods. The slow death of bound labor and the quick march of the Market Revolution, however, pushed the city outward and redrew its social geography. At midcentury, burgeoning suburbs varied in character, yet in general were poorer, more prone to disorder, and more dynamic than a center that had stagnated since the Panic of 1837.[9]

By the 1840s, the failure of the merchants of the city proper to arrest their decline as a national force had begun to tilt the economic balance of power toward the suburbs too, even if wealth continued to congregate in the center. For some time after 1787, Philadelphia remained the nation's foremost foreign port, but New York's superior harbor and Erie Canal enabled it to overhaul its rival. In the 1820s, Philadelphia boosters persuaded the Commonwealth to build its own route to the West, but the canals and railroads of the Main Line of State Works failed to deliver the promised benefits. The city's fortunes waned in finance too. Andrew Jackson's Bank War hurt Chestnut Street's institutions, which were then hit by panics in 1837 and 1841, the latter compounded by the state's default on its internal improvement debt. The crises saw Philadelphia lose $40 million in banking capital. One booster, surveying the wreckage from midcentury, compared the events to a "volcano" or "earthquake."[10]

While commerce and finance in the city proper declined, however, suburban manufacturing prospered. An ample supply of skilled and unskilled labor, power in the form of nearby anthracite coal, and a prosperous hinterland market spurred growth. In the suburbs, though, industry developed unevenly, creating a mixed metropolitan landscape in both scale and organization. Take for instance the two riot districts in 1844: Kensington and Southwark. In the western portion of the former, where Irish handloom weavers were fighting a rearguard action against mechanization, masters either put out work or consolidated production in small workshops; large mills were the exception rather than the rule. The district commissioner Hugh Clark was the wealthiest man in the vicinity, but the fortune he accumulated from the weavers' labor paled in comparison to industrialists elsewhere in the county.[11]

Southwark's iron manufacturers, in contrast, built big factories from the 1830s onward. On the block below Fourth and Washington, Sydney's map showed the sizeable foundry co-owned by Samuel Vaughan Merrick, a leader in the Consolidation movement. Philadelphia's typical manufacturer, if such a thing existed, looked more like the boss weaver Clark than the iron founder Merrick, and as most workshops only employed a dozen or so hands, proprietors often worked on the shop floor. Even some of the most prosperous proprietors like the Spring Garden locomotive builder Matthias W. Baldwin—a former jeweler who left his Market Street premises for a vast suburban lot—often started off as apprentices themselves.[12]

If Philadelphia's transformation into a manufacturing metropolis was well underway in the outlying districts by the 1840s, the pace and character of industrialization varied. Handloom weavers eked out a living from a preindustrial craft, while confronting the pressure of factory competition. Locomotive builders, on the other hand, owed their prosperity to the revolutionary technology of the era: the steam engine. Yet even these businesses—heralds of a new age rather than vestiges of handicraft production—were organized as proprietorships rather than business corporations, and employed skilled native labor, instead of assembly-line hands. The most common suburban workers, meanwhile, were neither artisans nor operatives, but laborers, stevedores, and servants. Irish immigrants and African Americans often found themselves forced into these poorly paid positions.[13]

Unskilled workers in both the city proper and suburbs tended to find shelter in the other divide discernible on Sydney's map: the interstices of the city's seventeenth-century grid. At a glance, Philadelphia looked far from opaque, as square after square stretched outward over the suburbs and into open countryside. Sydney's straight lines of unbuilt streets, reaching miles into the outlying county, provided a reference point for real estate developers and a prophecy of how the city would subdue its rural frontier.[14] But in Philadelphia's built-up districts, where Sydney captured present conditions rather than future prospects, the grid struck visitors, and not always favorably. The British visitor Frances Trollope conceded the plan made the metropolis "commodious to strangers," yet disliked its "almost wearisome regularity."[15] Dullness may have been the price of legibility. Indeed, James C. Scott, one of the most perceptive writers on modern statecraft, contrasts William Penn's transparent layout to inscrutable medieval towns.[16]

Initial impressions, though, can deceive. Looked at more closely, Sydney's map revealed the division of rectangular blocks into lanes, alleys, and courts, especially along the southern borderlands of the city proper. The practice was almost as old as Philadelphia itself, for while Penn—who grew up in a London ravaged by plague and fire—is often said to have pictured a "greene country towne" of evenly spaced houses, his settlers clung to the Delaware front. Responding to demand, landowners cut small streets through their property, which soon led to a distinct pattern of segregation: wealthier residents took houses on the main thorough-fares, while the poor clustered in claustrophobic warrens behind. In the city proper, this produced pockets of poverty hidden from the fashionable promenader; in the suburbs, it created neighborhoods known as early as the 1850s as slums.[17]

City and districts, streets and alleys: on the six plates of Sydney's map, the cartographer captured the metropolis as a whole, while hinting at its divisions. Those with the leisure time to move through its neighborhoods would have read in Sydney's lines and symbols the boundaries between wealth and poverty, commerce and industry, and virtue and vice, but no one would have experienced it all. Claims that the city was unknowable could therefore be read as a boast or a lament. On the one hand, they conveyed Philadelphia's vastness; but on the other, they conceded the dif-ficulty of comprehending something so big.

Philadelphia's political geography proved easier to plot. Partisan bound-aries proved far from impermeable, but citizens in the city proper tended to gravitate toward the pro-Bank Whigs, while suburban journeymen and laborers rallied in sufficient numbers to the Democratic flag to give that party control of most of the outlying districts prior to a nativist insurgency in 1844. All parties were coalitions. Democratic radicals coalesced around the antimonopoly, producerist creed of the Locofocos, while their allies, particularly in Irish neighborhoods, turned to politics to defend their turf from Protestants and blacks. Neither wing, however, had much time for the city proper's Whigs, who saw Andrew Jackson as the devil incarnate and held militant workers and Catholic immigrants in low regard. The city proper was known as the "Whig Gibraltar": a speck of rock menaced by the hostile and often Romish electorate beyond its borders.[18]

Prior to 1854, however, the street politics of the suburbs gave residents of the city proper greater cause for concern than anything that transpired at the ballot box. Conflicts over labor, race, religion, and politics all had the potential to spill over into violence. Crowd action in the city's "turbu-lent era" tended to conform to one of two types. The first, more frequent but less destructive, sprang from the "sporting male subculture" of the

antebellum city. Young men in the suburbs flocked to volunteer fire companies and street gangs that often reflected partisan, pietistic, or ethnic loyalties. Firemen and gangsters played a muscular role in suburban politics,
and commanded neighborhood respect, but their tendency to fight each
other rather than fight fires made nighttime battles with brickbats, stones,
and even pistols a familiar feature of urban life.[19]

The second form of violence, less common but more destructive, followed long-established patterns of popular action, in which a crowd would
demand redress for a particular grievance, with trouble escalating if the
authorities failed to respond. Rioters chose their targets carefully, striking
at African Americans (1834, 1842, and 1849), abolitionists (1836 and 1838),
and political rivals (1828 and many elections thereafter), and they often got
their way. When a mob reduced a new Garrisonian meeting place to a
smoldering ruin within days of it opening, for instance, the city authorities
blamed antislavery agitators for inciting trouble. A few years later, Moyamensing commissioners responded to a white supremacist pogrom by condemning a black temperance hall as a nuisance. Although such crowds
contained plenty of the sporting male "rowdies," who filled the ranks of
fire companies and street gangs, they sometimes had "gentlemen of property and standing" at their head.[20]

By the early 1840s, however, wealthy Philadelphians tended to look
down on mobs as counter to norms of reason and restraint, and anathema
to their booster aspirations. The two riots over the summer of 1844—the
biggest urban upheavals the republic had witnessed—consolidated elite
opinion against the crowd. Over the preceding months, rumors circulated
that Philadelphia's Catholic bishop wanted to banish the King James Bible
from the city's public schools, and the outrage proved a valuable recruiting
tool for a new political movement, the anti-immigrant American Republican Party. On May 3, and then again on May 6, the party tried to hold
meetings on an open lot in the northern suburb of Kensington's heavily
Irish third ward, but on each occasion Catholics fought them off. Gathering
in far greater numbers at Independence Hall on May 7, Protestants
marched back to the site, where they were met with a barrage of stones,
clubs, and gunfire. The fighting continued over the next two days, and once
natives wrested the initiative, they torched homes and churches, forcing
Irish residents to flee to nearby woods. With the rioters overwhelming Sheriff McMichael and the civil authorities, the governor reluctantly ordered
the state militia onto the streets and imposed martial law (see Figure 1).[21]

Figure 1. The Kensington "Bible Riot" of 1844. The frequency and severity of riots in Philadelphia during the 1830s and 1840s convinced many residents in the city proper that their fate was entwined with that of the suburban districts. Source: Reprinted from *A Full and Complete Account of the Late Awful Riots in Philadelphia* (Philadelphia: John B. Perry, 1844). Courtesy of The Library Company of Philadelphia.

The peace did not last long. A few weeks later, after injured veterans of the Kensington violence joined a large nativist parade on July 4, Protestants in the southern district of Southwark gathered outside the Catholic church of St. Phillippe de Neri, where the priest's brother had secured permission to stockpile arms in self-defense. This time, the militia quickly arrested some of the ringleaders, but on July 7, a group broke into the church to search for weapons and release the prisoners. Returning to the scene, where they were met with a barrage of missiles, General George Cadwalader's militia fired into the crowd. The volley killed two rioters, whose comrades retreated to the nearby riverfront, secured a pair of cannon, loaded them with scrap metal, and turned them on the troops. Their improvised grape-shot took out two militiamen, and over the following hours, artillery dueled on the district's streets. At least fifteen people died in the battle.[22]

In scale and substance, the 1844 riots were new. Commentators called them a "civil war," for what had begun in Kensington with the familiar spectacle of sectarian strife, concluded in Southwark with an armed battle between citizen and state.[23] For the first time, both sides had used firearms; for the first time, too, militiamen had poured fire onto the crowd. Unlike earlier riots, which usually petered out once the mob had meted out punishment to a few exemplary victims, the violence persisted for days, and left the county under military rule. Martial law, for a few weeks at least, consolidated the city.

Rioters' refusal to respect the political boundaries on the county map brought about this short-lived metropolitan union. Every major disturbance between 1828 and 1849 took place in the suburbs or on the borderlands between city and districts. The three biggest race riots occurred within about two hundred yards of one another, in an Irish and African American neighborhood that straddled the boundary between Philadelphia and the southern district of Moyamensing. But in 1844, Philadelphians could not rely on their frontier as a buffer. While the trouble in Southwark might have been contained within a few blocks, Kensington's arsonists soon turned to targets in Philadelphia proper. Rumors circulated that every Catholic church in the county would be torched.[24] Nowhere seemed safe.

Sydney captured the metropolis as a whole, but though his map gave clues about differences in government, economy, and space, his snapshot could not capture the divisions of class, color, and creed that manifested themselves in the endemic and episodic violence of the "great city." After 1844, mapping the causes and consequences of that violence, and finding ways to end it, helped to consolidate a divided economic elite. They would come together too in searching for a way out of the commercial and financial malaise that also threatened to relegate the metropolis to the second rank. Pacifying and promoting Philadelphia required understanding what the "great city" was and determining the laws that governed its behavior.

Consolidating Class

How to prop up Philadelphia's divided house at midcentury preoccupied citizens. What, they asked, made its foundations so unstable? When government failed to undertake the *North American*'s "great study," the economic elite took on the task themselves. They did so to advertise the metropolis to outsiders, while explaining its inner workings to citizens. The maps, censuses, and sketches they produced served the twin causes of boosterism and reform, and while these objectives sometimes jarred, they each tended toward reading the metropolis as a complex but interdependent whole.

Few enlisted in the project as eagerly as Philadelphia's press. The city's first penny paper, the *Public Ledger,* boasted a midcentury circulation in the tens of thousands, though most dailies, like McMichael's *North American,* catered to a far narrower audience. Though newspapers often served as party mouthpieces, even the most partisan editors claimed the higher ground of the "common good." Publishers stood as self-appointed—and self-important—stewards of the public interest. To the *Ledger,* no "moral, social and political engine" proved "half so powerful as the newspaper press."[25]

Their power knocked down municipal walls. Proprietors had good reason to portray their city as a whole. Claiming the entirety of Sydney's map as their purview enabled them to sell to the growing suburban market and portray the picaresque world of the outlying districts for citizens of the city proper. It also increased circulation further afield, where merchants relied on East Coast papers for commercial knowledge. In the golden age of local boosterism, the commitment of men like McMichael to the cause rivaled their counterparts in the upstart towns of the West. Philadelphia's press, a Boston journal noted in 1854, "constantly labors in behalf of the interests of the city."[26]

Newspapers self-consciously set out to reveal a Philadelphia that had outgrown any one individual's ability to comprehend. Only the press, the *Ledger* argued while reporting on suburban expansion, had the perspective to provide the public with "any definite idea of the progress that surrounds them."[27] Journals followed its lead in carrying news of metropolitan developments; printing copy from remote districts, which read as if it had been dictated by suburban speculators; and venturing into the courts and alleys that lay behind gridironed streets.[28]

The "great study" of the city in these respects bore similarities to the project of nation-building. Benedict Anderson has traced the link between print and patriotic sentiment, showing how the newspaper, by enabling people to consume events together, creates "that remarkable confidence of community in anonymity which is the hallmark of modern nations."[29] But in antebellum America, newspapers that carried national news catered primarily to city markets. From the 1840s, then, papers devoted columns to local affairs and lobbied in leader columns on behalf of their metropolis. In their pages, readers could grasp the city as a whole. The press profited from Philadelphia's fragmentation—a good riot surely did wonders for circulation—yet publishers provided a centripetal force. Unity came out of division.

Newspapers also helped to overcome social balkanization. McMichael in particular used print in pursuit of bourgeois consolidation. Philadelphia's wealthiest residents, his paper often declared, needed to speak with one voice.[30] It had a point. "Proper Philadelphians," as historical sociologists have sometimes termed the city's upper class, proved wary of arrivistes. The center's merchants and attorneys often held their noses when forced to interact with suburban manufacturers. When the scion of an old merchant family took the reins at a Southwark foundry in the 1830s, his decision, a friend remembered, involved "little less than social degradation."[31]

Old money's reluctance to intermingle with new has led some historians to conclude that a hereditary aristocracy held sway in antebellum society. Admiration for an aristocratic ethic ran deep. Sidney George Fisher, a gentleman tied by birth and marriage to several of the city's first families, saw land and breeding as the mark of a real elite, and in his company the taint of "bourgeois origin" proved hard to wash off. His diary gives the impression of a man continually circling the wagons against the rising "parvenu." Fisher's status-anxious snobbery, if extreme, was not uncommon. The first families of the city proper rarely married, worshipped in the same churches, or attended the same parties as suburban manufacturers. Socially and spatially they kept their distance.[32]

Such divisions, however, may have proved easier to surmount in Philadelphia than in other northern cities. In New York, the rift between merchant and manufacturing capital only healed once civil wars—in both the South and the streets—vindicated free labor ideology and reminded propertied citizens of the danger they faced from free laborers.[33] Before 1863, Manhattan merchants aligned with workers and proslavery Democrats, helping to build the alliance of planters, northern businessmen, and workingmen that determined national elections for much of the antebellum era. Insurgent manufacturers, who rejected the free trade and paternalistic ethos of the mercantile elite, turned to the Republican Party after 1854, albeit with more success nationally than locally. The story in Philadelphia, though, must give more emphasis to cooperation than competition. A tilt to manufacturing in the urban economy, the investment patterns of the city proper's elite, and boosters' ambition to reclaim from Manhattan the mantle of "Empire City" all drew wealthy industrialists into the orbit of old money; so too did the social crisis of the riots.

The charismatic and cosmopolitan McMichael played a vanguard role in the battle to unite a bourgeoisie.[34] Born to a gardener on the New Jersey estate of Napoleon Bonaparte's exiled brother in 1807, McMichael arrived in Philadelphia as a young man, where he trained in the law, worked for city newspapers, and wrote what Poe called "remarkably vigorous" poetry.[35] In the prosperous suburb of Spring Garden, politics soon drew his attention, and a brief flirtation with Jacksonian Democracy quickly gave way to a lifelong commitment to the Whig Party and its Republican heir. In 1843, he won election as county sheriff, though he could do little to stop the riots that ravaged the city a year later. Shaken by the experience of economic and social unrest, McMichael turned to the challenge of consolidation, and steadfastly adhered to the maxim "In Union There Is Strength." Over the course of a career that stretched from the Age of Jackson to the end of Reconstruction, he headed several reform efforts—from the battle for a new city charter to the foundation of the nationalist Union League—but he extended the principle to the economic elite itself, using his personal contacts and oratorical gifts to bully merchants, manufacturers, and professionals into cooperation. "His peculiar talents are so fitted for society and for public affairs," one of his friends later recalled, "that he rapidly became the representative man of the community."[36]

His main weapon, though, was his newspaper. In 1847, McMichael acquired the *North American*, which he soon merged with another Whig daily, the *United States Gazette*. On national questions, the journal followed the orthodox line of the Whig leader Henry Clay, but its first loyalty lay with class rather than party, and genteel Democrats found a warm welcome in the publisher's circle.[37] By the 1850s, the paper provided McMichael with a pulpit to preach unionist sermons to a bourgeoisie whose boundaries, he believed, needed enlarging. "The creation of a mutuality of interests," his paper argued, needed "that habit of constant and familiar intercourse among our merchants, capitalists, real estate owners, and trades people generally." One of its correspondents warned that a "community broken into isolated fragments" lacked "the rudimental principles which form the basis of great mercantile and metropolitan character."[38] The project of class consolidation for the publisher had the power to arrest the city's disorder and decline.

McMichael believed a ruling class could only rule if it understood its own interests—one reason he attached such importance to the great study of urban society. His newspaper tried to steer a divided economic elite on a common course. Like others in the age of consolidation, he saw individualism as disintegrative, and his paper rarely neglected to remind readers of the virtues of association. The daily floated above the fray of warring businessmen and disciplined a bourgeoisie that lacked the broad view to act in its own benefit. If McMichael used print as a weapon of social control, then he aimed it at Philadelphia's propertied as well as its poor.

The *North American* prodded propertied citizens toward a "concurrence of sentiment action." At ten times the price of the *Public Ledger*, only wealthy citizens subscribed, and the high-minded tone drew prosperous Democrats as well as Whigs to its pages. Meanwhile, as McMichael depended on businessmen for advertising and loans, he found himself at their beck and call. Radicals accused McMichael of being a slave to his bourgeois masters, but who controlled whom is hard to tell. Take for instance, Richard D. Wood, a Quaker merchant and "Proper Philadelphian," who visited McMichael in 1859 to sell him a pet railroad project, and recorded that the proprietor "assented to my views and promised to serve." A few years earlier, though, Wood had invested thousands in a canal, having "made up my mind, no doubt partly influenced by several articles published, for a few days past, in the North American."[39] His recollections hint at how the paper provided a forum for the circulation of ideas and information among Philadelphia's economic elite. By urging cooperation, boosting business, and reminding a bourgeoisie where its boundaries lay, the daily labored to produce a politically powerful class.

The urgency of McMichael's calls for bourgeois unity might be read as evidence of the rift between merchants and manufacturers. Yet even before he had taken control of the *North American*, wealthy citizens recognized the need to cooperate. During and after the 1844 riots, bourgeois Philadelphians worked together to comprehend what was happening to their city; over the following years, their alliance extended into railroad-building, real estate, and urban reconstruction. The project of consolidating a powerful class seemed to be making progress.

Measuring the Metropolis

Fear of what Philadelphia was and hopes of what it might become spurred bourgeois citizens to take up McMichael's "great study." Between the riots and the Civil War, boosters and reformers strove to map the social and economic life of the city and in doing so advanced the cause of urban and class consolidation. Disorder catalyzed prosperous Philadelphians into action, for the scale and substance of the 1844 violence troubled them more than earlier tumult. The seemingly indiscriminate destruction made it harder for the wealthy to indulge the crowd. *Every mob must be suppressed instantly,*" one observer of the Kensington battle insisted, "by using as much force as will put it down at once." "The duty of everyone," a meeting of prominent citizens resolved, "is to resist the rioters or to retire."[40]

The city proper's elite turned decisively against crowd action in 1844 and sanctified the state's monopoly on the use of force. Most of those at the meeting, which vindicated the militia's decision to fire, were merchants and lawyers, many of them with "Proper Philadelphian" names: Fisher, who had exacting standards, said the few dozen or so present were made up of the "better class of citizens."[41] Earlier, in the Kensington troubles, he joined associates from the Philadelphia bar to defend a Catholic church, having concluded that service alongside his fellow attorneys was preferable to the ward associations "in which one is thrown with a great many low people."[42] Fisher shared the anti-Catholic prejudices of the nativists but preferred the rule of law to the civil war unfolding on the streets. Nor was he alone. Thomas Pym Cope, a Quaker, councilman, and president of the Board of Trade, excused himself from debates over the use of force on religious grounds, but the agonized conclusion in his diary could have served as a motto for the city proper's elite: "order must [be] maintained."[43]

But could it be? Here the "great city" served as a laboratory. Was self-government possible in a polity made up of divided interests and property-less voters? Fisher thought he knew the answer. "I have long had an idea," he wrote a few weeks after the Kensington riot, "that the present civilization of the world, Europe & America, is destined to be destroyed by the irruption of the dark masses of ignorance & brutality which lie beneath it." If the "barbarians each country contain within itself," he continued, did not rise up in violent rebellion, they might capture the state at the ballot box and "destroy the fair fabric of knowledge, elegance, refinement & power."

For him, the Union's course had been foreshadowed in the fate of Rome. Republics died when they devolved too much power to the people.[44]

The depth of Fisher's antidemocratic conviction might have been rare, but rioting crystallized conservative fears about popular government. Philadelphians took comfort in the claim that the "ruffians" were a troublesome minority whose capacity to commit outrages rested on the supine ways of respectable citizens. Few, however, could deny that mobs enjoyed considerable support. After a long night of racial violence in 1849, for example, one correspondent to McMichael's paper conceded that "our worst riots have been sustained at the time by local popular sympathy."[45] If investing power in the people led to anarchy, then was the United States any different to the Old World, with its cycle of revolution and reaction?

Some citizens certainly learned from the riots that their "great city" had more in common than they hoped with the European metropolis. For the president of the Board of Trade, the sound of the State House Bell summoning volunteer firemen during the riots reminded him "of the awful tocsin of Revolutionary France." Over the following years, bourgeois Philadelphians used European markers to map the American metropolis. Inhabitants of courts and alleys sometimes became the "canaille," riots "emeutes," suburbs "faubourgs," and radical workingmen "red republicans." "The American and French people have many characteristics in common," argued one supporter of Consolidation after an 1849 riot. "They are both armed, brave, impulsive, and disposed to offer forcible resistance to real or fancied wrongs."[46]

Exceptionalism proved too strong for all the comparisons to stick, but the borrowing served its purpose. First, using "common referents" narrowed the gulf between the Old World and the New, making Atlantic exchange easier to imagine.[47] After Henry Mayhew's *Life and Labor of the London Poor* secured an American publisher, one Philadelphia paper concluded that the English capital "is only a type, on a large scale, of our great Atlantic cities," while a reformer in 1855 found "life among the lowly" was "equally true" in the New World and the Old. Second, the threat of revolutionary violence separated citizens into orderly and disorderly, reminded the economic elite of the danger lurking in the suburbs, and enforced the kind of class discipline the *North American* would push over the following decade. To sympathize with mobs was to succor Jacobinism.[48]

Indulgence also threatened the city's prosperity. Philadelphians were counting the "cost of riots" even before the militia stood down in 1844.

Pamphlets published in the months that followed tried to quantify the destruction, with early estimates putting the losses at a minimum of $250,000.[49] The burden of paying for the posse and militia fell on the county treasury, while the Catholic diocese sued the city proper for its failure to stop the mob from torching St. Augustine's, which stood a few yards inside the original corporate boundaries. But the economic consequences of the violence extended far beyond claims for compensation. During the Kensington riots, a New Yorker warned Board of Trade president Thomas Pym Cope that Philadelphia bonds would struggle to find a buyer in Manhattan, while a few days after the Southwark conflagration, a rumor reached him that shipbuilding on the Delaware had come to a halt in the face of demands for an all-native waterfront. Cope worried about the "great injury to our future prosperity." "Prudent men," after all, would "be afraid to place capital in manufactories in a place where the populace may at any time lay them waste."[50] A city still suffering from the financial aftershocks of the Panic of 1837 could hardly afford to drive away investors.

Both the scale of destruction and the threat it posed to prosperity demanded an energetic response. Respectable classes had to stand together regardless of social status. They had to stand together too regardless of where they lived and worked, for the riots offered a sanguinary lesson in metropolitan interdependence. In targeting creed rather than color, the mobs of 1844 proved less discriminating than usual. "It appears that though this was a riot against the Catholics," one writer noted, "the loss has also fallen heavily upon Protestant owners and tenants of property."[51] The "infected districts," as they quickly came to be known, may have stood in turbulent suburbs, but violence, like the epidemics that visited the antebellum city, proved hard to quarantine.[52] And strangers in distant markets paid no more heed to the lines on the county map than the rioters. As a result, the *Ledger* wrote of the city and districts in 1844, "all the parts suffer for the wrongs committed by one of them."[53]

Yet measured in economic terms, interdependence had its merits. The 1844 riots coincided with a long-awaited upturn in the city's fortunes. Suburban manufacturing, citizens assumed, had to play a leading role in any recovery. In the 1820s and 1830s, merchants invested heavily in developing the vast anthracite reserves of northern Pennsylvania, and the coal coursing into Philadelphia along canals and railroads fueled expansion. The city lacked an equivalent of the Boston Associates, but men from commercial backgrounds, like Merrick and Wood, branched into industry, while others lent to capital-hungry factory owners. Even in the 1830s, relations between the mechanics' Franklin Institute and the merchants' Board of Trade were cooperative rather than competitive. Members of both organizations broadly agreed on the need for a high tariff, a national bank, and government-sponsored internal improvements; and Frederick Fraley, a lawyer who later played a leading role in the Consolidation campaign, served as an officer on both bodies. Manufacturers may have lacked the social cachet of the largest merchants, but as the city fell further behind New York in the race for foreign trade, they became all the more important. With a national debate over protection raging in 1845, the Board of Trade stooped to notice manufacturing for the first time, announcing that "imperfect statistics" showed an advance in the city's industry, "which has astonished those whose attention has not been particularly called to this subject."[54] Over the next few years, the claim that Philadelphia would serve as the workshop of the New World became an article of dogma in promoters' creed.

How to preach that to the world vexed boosters. Philadelphia, they complained, had proved inept at "making her position and greatness . . . known." The Board of Trade blamed the city and commonwealth's destructive self-deprecation.[55] Such modesty probably owed less to Quaker humility than it did to New York's networks of finance, commerce, and publishing. Lingering resentment in Europe at Pennsylvania's default in 1842—which prompted William Wordsworth (a self-described "Surly Creditor") to pen a bitter sonnet on the state's "degenerate men"—hardly helped either. Others blamed the "insufficient experience" and "limited information" of leaders in city government. But whatever the cause, the sense that strangers in distant markets saw Philadelphia as a "speck on the horizon" spurred schemes to market the metropolis, which ranged from lobbying diplomats to dispatching lecturers across the Atlantic.[56]

Boosters needed evidence to make their claims credible. "The friends of Philadelphia," one writer complained in the late 1850s, "have not been furnished with facts" to counteract the "prejudicial statements" of rival cities. In an Atlantic World shaped by Enlightenment rationalism, ostensibly objective data offered a firmer foundation for decision-making than mere opinion, and numbers had the power to sway. To McMichael's *North American*, indeed, statistics offered "the basis of various useful speculations regarding the influences that affect the material and moral fortunes of society."[57] Bitter experience strengthened the statistician's hand. The boom and bust in the mid-1830s, when speculators poured paper money into imaginary cities, left investors in Europe and the United States wary of acting without credible information. To take on New York, Philadelphians needed to arm themselves with abstractions of metropolitan might. They therefore set out to map urban manufacturing.

In doing so, boosters ran into many of the same obstacles that obstructed a wider "great study" of Philadelphia. Production proved much harder to measure than commerce: goods were often consumed before they could be counted, and factories were dispersed across the city. Manufacturers, moreover, rarely wanted to open their books to rivals, workers, and tax assessors. A Statistical Society, formed in 1846 to investigate the city's industry, "suddenly evaporated" a year later when workshop owners ignored its request for information. But the Board of Trade, Franklin Institute, and leading newspapers took up the baton, calling on the municipal authorities to follow New York's lead and conduct a census that would measure the "social civilization of a community." Following the union of city and districts in 1854, however, the *North American* was still having to urge Philadelphians to "consolidate our statistics."[58]

The refusal of the new city government to act led to a renewal of associational efforts. With support from the Board of Trade, the Corn Exchange, and a handful of businessmen, boosters hired Edwin T. Freedley to write a lengthy book on the city's manufactures, which they distributed to western markets. Freedley had published a self-help manual for aspiring capitalists, explaining "How to Become Millionaires," and the book's popularity either side of the Atlantic probably convinced his backers in Philadelphia that he was the man to popularize their cause. Learning from the "numerous attempts" over the preceding decade to undertake an industrial census, Freedley shunned statistics and relied instead on his conversations with experts in the trades he encountered as he surveyed suburban districts. Much of his lengthy compendium therefore offered overviews of the city's various industries, and the final product, as he put it, provided "a *readable* exhibit" rather than a definitive statement of the city's productive might. Its utility to boosters, though, was clear enough: the first third of the manuscript used general principles and particular examples to demonstrate Philadelphia's destiny as the first manufacturing city of the continent. Like so much city knowledge, the book was as much about foreseeing the future as mapping the present.[59]

Freedley's amalgam of company biographies and booster prophecy ran counter to the tale of decay and disorder that came out of the depression. *Philadelphia and Its Manufactures* passed over the riots in a couple of sentences, and rather than linger on the violence, it enlisted producerism and patriotism in the service of the economic elite. Borrowing from the rhetorical arsenal of Jacksonian Democracy, which just a few years earlier had been aimed at Chestnut Street's Second Bank, it claimed that Penn's metropolis rested on productive labor, the true foundation of wealth. The implied contrast between manufacturing Philadelphia and commercial New York may have been overdrawn, but it fulfilled a valuable purpose: again and again after 1844, boosters pointed to historical precedent to show that trading marts never dominated for long, and that, as Freedley argued, industry was "more important in every truly national point of view than Foreign Trade." By placing their metropolis ahead of its great rival in terms of historical progress, boosters reframed Philadelphia's space and society, as riotous suburbs became heralds of an industrial future rather than vestiges of a barbarous past.[60]

Marketing the metropolis fostered institutional integration too among the economic elite. The short-lived Statistical Society brought successful manufacturers like Matthias W. Baldwin into contact with leading merchants. Industrialists, though, remained outside the mercantile Board of Trade. By 1854, after the *North American* demanded "a practical social union" of merchants and manufacturers, the organization discussed opening its doors to factory owners, which it did three years later. For McMichael, this corrected a grave error. The Board, his paper charged, had failed to represent "the diversified business interests of the community," and as a result, myopic individualism inhibited "combination." Given that "every man takes pleasure in the elevation of the social class to which he belongs," it argued, businessmen needed a "habitual resort." The revamped organization would open a reading room, collect statistics, and "disseminate useful knowledge," enabling bourgeois Philadelphians to act in association.[61]

Despite the difficulties they faced, antebellum boosters enjoyed some success in measuring Philadelphia's economic might and bringing merchants and manufacturers together. They did not deny the differences between the city proper and outlying suburbs, but rather implied that both had their place in a metropolitan division of labor with the interests of capital in each mediated through associated bodies: the Statistical Society, the Board of Trade, and—in the ambitions of Consolidators—a government with greater reach. As a way of selling the city and promoting social intercourse among the economic elite, their methods were fit for purpose.

On the pressing matter of disorder, though, they had understandably little to say. Boosters' portrait of prosperous manufacturing suburbs offered a welcome antidote to depictions of a violent suburban frontier. But the two could not be separated so easily. Kensington and Southwark's rioters in 1844 had not taken to the streets as a working-class, but they came from heavily working-class districts, and if Philadelphia's destiny lay in industry, then the men and women who made up mobs would surely multiply in number. Promoters would need to find a way to consolidate suburban labor as well as capital into the urban community.

Surveying the Suburban Frontier

In the immediate aftermath of 1844, though, only a few radical reformers read the riots as a symptom of a coming conflict between labor and capital. As we will see, Philadelphia's radicals blamed the violence on a corrupt social system, and accused an idle aristocracy of stirring up sectarian strife. Though bourgeois citizens sometimes compared the street battles to the French Revolution, few believed that the city's industrial transformation led directly to the trouble, and even the pessimistic Fisher doubted whether the upheavals he witnessed really mirrored European experience. Why, he wondered, had trouble broken out "in a country where the usual causes of popular tumult do not exist"? Forgetting his usual fine gradations of rank, Fisher fell back here on the most common explanation from the time, dividing citizens into friends or foes of order. Attacks on Catholics, blacks, and employers, he argued, were merely the manifestations of "the growing spirit of misrule."[62] Disorder for him sprang from the disintegrative influence of democracy rather than of capitalism. It would take another wave of European revolutions in 1848 for the two to conjoin in studies of the city.

Yet bourgeois observers did see suburban disorder as part of a wider crisis of social discipline. While that crisis extended into the workplace, its roots lay elsewhere. Philadelphia's manufacturers, like their counterparts across the industrializing world, struggled to impose time and work discipline on laborers accustomed to the rhythms of preindustrial life.[63] To maximize returns, they experimented with the likes of wage labor, piece rates, and new managerial structures.[64] But the challenge of controlling labor within workshops was made harder by the changes that had taken place outside them. The problem seemed to spring from the prizing apart of work and home. As factories slowly superseded household production, masters' power over apprentices waned, freeing young men to enjoy the city's taverns, fire companies, and street gangs. Here, rioting could seem like a generational revolt, albeit one made possible by the new social geography of the industrial city. Commentators who noted mobs' youthful character blamed a want of discipline at home and work. Trouble sprang from "the lamentable neglect of domestic training of the young," one citizen wrote, for "neglected youths" formed the "nucleus around which mobs gather." Cities, as an evangelical put it in 1841, allowed the nation's young *"to throw off parental restraints."*[65]

Reformers looked to refasten the shackles. In the Southwark riot, wealthy citizens urged "heads of families and masters" to "keep their young men and boys at home during the prevailing excitement." Baldwin banned young men in his factory from joining fire companies. Others suggested that restoring apprenticeship offered a better solution to disorder than centralizing projects like a citywide police or government. Incapable of intervening in disorderly suburbs themselves, they imagined devolving power to respectable heads of household, rather than consolidating control in a strengthened bureaucracy.[66]

More often, though, the city's economic elite attempted to establish vantage points to survey and reform the suburban poor. Manufacturers, who had played a supporting role when "respectable" citizens rallied against the rioters, came to the fore, creating a network of institutions that aimed to impose moral order on the districts. These associations—part of antebellum reformers' "benevolent empire"—were often led by evangelical and Quaker industrialists. They proved particularly influential in the Philadelphia Society for the Employment and Instruction of the Poor (PSEIP). William J. Mullen—an erstwhile radical who, like many of his comrades in the General Trades' Union, had embraced evangelical Protestantism after the Panic of 1837—formed the society with the suburban iron founder Merrick just two years after the riots. They set themselves up in Moyamensing, the poorest and most violent of Philadelphia's satellites and one that lacked the industrial base of neighboring Southwark. Donors and managers included several of the wealthiest manufacturers below the city proper. But in contrast to New York, where a similar institution was an industrialist stronghold, the mercantile and professional elite were well represented too.

Supporters and managers included several Proper Philadelphian names, the Board of Trade president Cope, and the attorney and Consolidation leader Eli Kirk Price. Like the Statistical Society, then, the organization brought different branches of the economic elite into closer communion, though this time with the object of saving rather than selling the city.[67]

Mullen and Merrick's society prescribed manufacturing as a medicine for Moyamensing's ills in much the same way as boosters recommended it as tonic for the whole city. Following a transatlantic trend that stretched back to the 1820s, the association argued "indiscriminate almsgiving" encouraged dependence and burdened taxpayers, not least as the cost of poor relief fell on the whole county. The idle needed to be put to work and that required distinguishing between the worthy and unworthy pauper; a later proposal even suggested that employers furnish a central committee with a list of the laborers they had laid off in hard times to sort the unlucky from the work-shy. Here was benevolence with a hard edge.[68]

The Society's "general plan" in Moyamensing suggests how bourgeois citizens envisaged incorporating a supposedly wild and worthless frontier as a productive part of a manufacturing metropolis. Aiming to get near to the "very centre of destitution," the managers began work in 1848 on a House of Industry, just below the notorious Bedford Street (see Figure 5), and opposite a market house said to double as the den of a riotous gang, the Killers. In the new building, designed by the architect of the Capitol, Thomas U. Walter, able-bodied paupers sewed rags and crushed bones. Reformers linked such "employment" to the "moral and intellectual improvement" of their inmates. On the shop floor, managers believed, "vicious and squalid vagrants will be lured to lives of industry and virtue," while the children who "ran wild" despite living in a "civilized city" would be reformed. Such a systematic approach to poverty sought to reconstruct character as much as to provide relief.[69]

In the years after the riots, new philanthropic institutions colonized the suburbs. Soup kitchens, workhouses, and domestic missions sprang up over the following decade. During the hard winter of 1855, a sharp economic downturn, which all but emptied the treasury of the Union Benevolent Association, led Horace Binney, McMichael, Merrick, and several other veterans of efforts to suppress rioters and reform paupers to propose bringing public and private relief under one organization. The report they commissioned calling for a "consolidation of charities"—a measure that would have predated London's influential Charity Organization Society by fourteen years—was coauthored by the future financier of the Union war effort and devout Presbyterian Jay Cooke. Though the plan secured support from the *North American*, amalgamating state, secular, sectarian, and ecumenical institutions proved impossible. It nevertheless represented an extraordinary proposal for a bourgeois seizure of the city's entire welfare apparatus.[70]

Legibility mattered as much for the economic elite in their philanthropic interventions as it did for their business investments. The want of "accurate statistics" of "missionary labor," McMichael's paper complained, impeded "a rightly ordered and organized system of charitable effort." Reformers sought to see troublesome neighborhoods from the street and the sky. Charity consolidators, for instance, planned to set aside "centres of wretchedness and depravity" as "Special Districts," for an Executive Committee to investigate "the causes of pauperism and want." Ward organizations would assess applicants for aid in person, then forward their reports to metropolitan-wide overseers, who would use their synoptic overview to make strategic decisions. By encouraging closer contact between the benevolent rich and the supplicant poor, the plan built on long-established patterns of paternalistic almsgiving, but married traditional practice to a scientific, centralizing ethos.[71]

Institutions that managed to penetrate suburban "purlieus" awakened residents of the historic center to what lay beyond their boundaries. "The public looked with but little faith upon the facts which it became its province to lay bare," Mullen's society said of its early career in 1851, for while the beggars of Philadelphia proper could be ignored as "social outcasts," it was harder to accept "that within a few minutes walk of the courts of justice there dwelt a community of such." The *North American* agreed. When the poor hid in "obscure alleys, courts, lanes, and by-ways," they were hard to know.[72]

Juxtapositions of visible wealth and veiled poverty—so common in midcentury writing on "great cities"—stressed social distance and spatial proximity in a manner that blurred metropolitan borders. Sensational journalists and evangelical reformers drew on jarring contrasts to good effect. The *Inquirer* guided its readers from the "crowds of elegantly dressed people" on Chestnut Street to the "small streets" a few blocks south, where humanity appeared "in forms so degraded that it can hardly be recognized as part of that which proudly displays itself on the fashionable promenade." Similarly, a postbellum writer, horrified by a "plague-spot in the very heart of our civilization," pictured "Wealth and Poverty" sitting "down side by side," staring "one another in the face," and "each asking his neighbor, What right do you have to be here?"[73]

When searching for metaphors to make sense of such stark differences, Philadelphians turned to empire. Domestic missionaries compared their work with the "*HOME HEATHEN*" of the city's "dark regions" to that of their counterparts among the Hottentots; Bedford Street became a "Citadel" awaiting capture. Others invoked the West to justify their civilizing mission. In gangs of young men, newspapers saw "mighty tribes of Philadelphia Indians." In riotous Southwark, they mapped "the Coast of California." Even Mullen's society, which preferred sentimentalism to sensationalism, depicted Moyamensing as a wilderness.[74]

Reformers encountered forms of resistance that resembled anticolonial politics. Among the officers of the PSEIP, only the old radical Mullen lived in the southern districts, with the remaining merchants, manufacturers, and professionals residing in the city proper. Their attempts to enclose the suburban frontier rarely went down well. Moyamensing's Board of Commissioners looked to protect their Catholic constituents from meddling Protestants by trying to block construction of the House of Industry, but if local government could not protect them, citizens took matters into their own hands. Residents overlooking the Bedford Street mission, for instance, reportedly pelted evangelical preachers with "a shower of dead cats and rats," stones, and brickbats: a replay on a smaller scale of the troubles that had started the Kensington riots in 1844. Such stories should be read with a skeptical eye, but they hint at the limits on consolidators' power. One newspaper sympathetic to calls for a door-to-door sanitary census in Moyamensing even warned that "such a system of espionage" would probably "excite a violent resistance."[75]

Ironically, though, the same imperial metaphors that made the suburbs seem so different could serve as a justification for extending the power of the center outward. Journalists, missionaries, and reformers who ventured off-grid did portray an upside-down world that turned the bourgeois order of the city proper on its head. Almost every report raises the specter of racial amalgamation by showing white women and black men mingling promiscuously. There is no doubt here that the lives of the suburban poor became a prized commodity in the literary marketplace.[76] But readers could be titillated and terrified at the same time, as the popularity of works on the French Revolution attests, and accounts of the city's "plague spots" urged citizens to act before the epidemics that ravaged them consumed the whole city. And if comparisons to Paris and London legitimized an authoritarian response to disorder, frontier metaphors in the heyday of Manifest Destiny held out the possibility of domesticating the foreign. To speak of Philadelphia harboring "savages in civilization," as the *North American* did as war raged in Mexico, implied an intolerable contradiction. Subduing the suburbs here mirrored the work of nation-building. "The instinct of self-preservation ought to nerve every muscle of philanthropy to the work of regeneration," the *Evening Bulletin* had argued of Henry Mayhew's London, or else "the Metropolis, and with it the nation, will sink eventually into the vast, yet extending abyss." That lesson in interdependence applied to Philadelphia too where "portions of Southwark and Moyamensing" harbored "a population so morally and physically diseased," it was "a miracle the whole county is not infected."[77]

Here Fisher's 1844 prophecy of an insurgent underclass threatened to come true in Philadelphia's riot districts. All "great cities" were "infested" by revolutionary "barbarians" and "*canaille*," the *North American* declared, and home missionaries and houses of industry could only ameliorate their condition. Until "a combined and powerful effort" incorporated the suburbs, such outcasts "must make the orderly portion of society their prey."[78] But where did the roots of those evils lie? Cartographies of the city proved insufficient as an answer; the rules of the metropolis needed to be explained instead.

Explaining the City

Beyond mapping the suburbs, reformers sought to understand the workings of the "great city." They strove to comprehend the causes of the epidemics of riot and disease that visited Philadelphia in order for their metropolis to heal and grow. Strikes troubled them, but prior to 1848, wage labor—in combating idleness—appeared more often as a solution than a problem. It was not so much relations within workshops, then, but the relation between people and places that came to characterize midcentury bourgeois thinking on the city.

For many critics, the root of the city's problems lay in rum. The miseries of one Moyamensing alley, a paper wrote in 1845, were simply "the offspring of the countless groggeries that abound in that purlieu." Campaigners insisted that the drinker's lack of self-restraint brought disorder to the streets and disease into the home. Across the nation, the ranks of temperance advocates swelled in the 1840s, and while the movement drew workers as well as bosses, bourgeois Philadelphians broadly agreed on the need for some kind of action against the city's rum shops. In Irish and German neighborhoods, however, it struggled to win converts. Where persuasion failed, reformers looked for legal remedies, albeit with mixed results. Mullen alone brought sixty private prosecutions against Moyamensing's unlicensed innkeepers. Consolidators hoped that a stronger municipal government would prove more effective than individual efforts in turning the city dry.[79]

But grog could be the consequence as well as the cause of disorder. Links between drink, disorder, and disease seemed perfectly clear to the midcentury bourgeoisie. When respectable Philadelphians talked about the "infected districts," the symptoms they had in mind were often rum, riot, and the cholera, and not infrequently all three. From what though did each spring? Midcentury medical knowledge held that epidemics emanated miasmically from rotting matter. Sanitary reports and mortality statistics seemed to support the hypothesis that foul vapors arose in warrens of courts and alleys. Historians have sometimes seen miasmatic theory as convenient for merchants, for whom the rival, contagionist epidemiology threatened maritime trade.[80] But citizens' readiness to apply it as a way of explaining moral as well as physical well-being indicates its deep roots. The sense that environment molded character had a long history in American thought. Thomas Jefferson justified the Louisiana Purchase by arguing new land would alleviate overcrowding, while the urbanists of the Early Republic equated orderly space with orderly citizens. The conviction that corrupt institutions would eat away at the health of the republic, indeed, transposed easily onto urban space, where physical decay threatened a similar malaise. Even evangelicals eager to close down taverns conceded that sound family life was all but impossible in "pent-up courts and alleys." Filth caused more than fever: it corroded the moral fiber of the metropolis.[81]

The link between urban disorder, disease, and degradation made the physical condition of Philadelphia's suburbs a matter of concern for prosperous residents of the city proper. Some went so far as to embrace a rigid environmental determinism. A prize-winning essay submitted to the House of Refuge in 1855 argued that a child "from the most luxurious palace and most refined family," if forced to work in a filthy factory and "retire to a dirty, offensive court," would struggle to "resist the demoralizing influences" surrounding him. "All these abide together," the author said of poverty, intemperance, brutality, and crime, and "vice is produced, directly, by impure air." Those who wanted to purge the city of sin would have to reconstruct space as well as save souls.[82]

Such moral environmentalism focused minds on metropolitan interdependence. Neighborhoods were harder to quarantine than ships. Pestilence spawned in filthy "cellars and garrets," one paper warned in the 1850s, threatened to "decimate alike the high and low." With city life "a singular sodality," a reformer had observed a few years earlier, the citizen should not "flatter himself that he is segregated" from evil influences "in person or property." Moral and physical epidemics paid no more heed than rioters to district boundaries.[83]

Institutions that mapped the suburban frontier helped to popularize these ideas about environment, health, and moral order. Mullen's society saw its workhouse as a refuge from the street. "The comparative comfort which its inmates found themselves to enjoy while leading lives of order, cleanliness and temperance," the managers argued in their 1848 report, disposed "their minds to receive moral instruction." The practice of isolating people from corrupting influences had a long history in Philadelphia. Eastern State Penitentiary, which received its first inmate in 1829, cut convicts off from the world beyond their cells, and calls for returning apprentices to the homes of master craftsmen in the aftermath of the riots amounted to a milder dose of the same medicine. Even the humane judge and future Radical Republican William D. Kelley admitted in 1849 that the city's House of Refuge shared with prisons the ethos of secluding "inmates from society." Philadelphia's institutional landscape at midcentury reflected assumptions about the corrupting nature of the urban environment. Penitentiaries, schools, and workhouses each removed citizens from the immoral streets beyond.[84]

The limitations of this policy, though, were self-evident: to quarantine the entire population would bring the city to a standstill, halting the flow of people and goods through the streets. By the early 1850s, new plans circulated, championed first and foremost by McMichael's *North American*, and closely tied to the project of Consolidation. These envisaged reconstructing Philadelphia's savage suburbs as cathartic spaces, capable of nurturing peaceful, productive, and healthy citizens, rather than riotous, idle, and sickly ones.

The Limits of Consolidation

Either side of midcentury, bourgeois citizens sought to understand how their city worked and where they belonged within it. Through statistics, social surveys, maps, and comparisons, they explored Philadelphia's present conditions and future prospects. In counting the cost of riots and the potential of manufacturing, they began to incorporate a suburban frontier into their imagined community. Their efforts brought together branches of the economic elite and forged alliances with evangelicals and news-papermen.

Though shaken by the experience of disorder and decline, few were as pessimistic about democracy's place in the city as Fisher, yet plenty doubted whether Jacksonian politics were thrusting the right men to the fore. Many of those who came of age in the troubles of the 1840s led a series of bourgeois-dominated reform movements over the following decades that attacked corruption, pushed for Consolidation, and eventually invoked the professional authority of "social science" against the might of the city's postbellum Republican machine.

Yet the terms of the suburbs' consolidation with the city remained con-tested. With only a few exceptions, bourgeois Philadelphians backed the militia's assault on the crowd in Southwark, but they were well aware that relying on citizen soldiers to police the streets proved neither practical nor popular. In an 1838 riot, for instance, men in a militia company, fearing they were about to be ordered to fire on the crowd, had requested leave to bake bread. General George Cadwalader received threats after his men did train cannon on a mob in 1844. With only a few watchmen and constables scattered through the districts, though, a civilian police force barely existed. Fugitives could flee the law by crossing municipal borders. The months that followed the riots saw intense debate over how to impose order. Some advocated a permanent armed force; others warned of aping the "martial despotism" of the Old World.[85]

Enlarging the terrain of the civil authorities, though, offered a plausible republican alternative. On November 11, 1844, just months after the sum-mer's violence, a group of Philadelphians assembled at the county court-house to plea for a union of the city and its outlying districts. The chair of the meeting, Samuel Webb, had counted the cost of riots before. An anti-slavery Quaker, he helped organize the construction of Pennsylvania Hall, which a proslavery mob torched within days of its opening in 1838. Worried that a "scattered, sub-divided and sectioned" system of metropolitan government could not protect public order, these pioneering Consolidators called for political boundaries to correspond to what was "in reality but one city and one community." The meeting marked the first stirrings of a decade-long campaign.[86]

That it took ten years to consolidate the city appears surprising. A measure promising to extend the city's authority over turbulent suburbs seemed likely to win considerable support from an economic elite horrified by the summer's riots, and several merchants and attorneys attended the November meeting. Much as Baron Haussmann would do in 1860, when he extended Paris's police control outward "to gain mastery over a *ceinture sauvage,*" advocates of Consolidation focused on the problem of public order. They did not blame religion, democracy, parenting, rum, or environment for the violence, but the city's political geography. To the *Ledger,* the "egregious error of dividing and subdividing" had cost the population its "homogenous character." From this initial mistake, the city's "unseen divisions" had become the "real divisions of sentiment and action." Consolidating a new metropolis across those arbitrary lines would nourish the "alliances," "common interests," and "common feelings" on which any republic had to rest. This was the nineteenth-century language of nationalism applied to the metropolis.[87]

Soon, however, a powerful anti-Federalist movement coalesced. Within a few days of the courthouse gathering, many of the city proper's prominent citizens organized against Consolidation. At their head stood the attorney Horace Binney, who had led the meeting of gentleman in the Southwark riots, but feared the costs of civic union. Others worried about absorbing district debts and having to bankroll their improvements. Even Thomas Pym Cope, who supported Consolidation in principle, feared that the city "will not be met on fair & liberal terms." When Pennsylvania defaulted on its debt in 1842, Philadelphia had suffered for being part of a larger whole, and the economic elite were reluctant to risk further financial chaos.[88]

But critics of Consolidation cared about more than dollars and cents. They also feared that a hastily arranged marriage between the Whig center and Democratic suburbs would bring little domestic harmony. The Court

House meeting drew natives, Whigs, and abolitionists, but leaned Democratic, with suburban party leaders and wealthy supporters from the city in the audience. To Fisher, who equated the Democrats' rank and file with Jacobins, political concerns explained bourgeois opposition. "The chief objection to the proposed plan is one which cannot be insisted on publicly," he confided in his diary. While "the city is conservative, the districts are radical."[89] Couched in more euphemistic tones, his argument would become a central tenet of opposition to Consolidation. It signaled a drawing of the battle lines between two segments of the economic elite: those who favored strong, active local government, and those who believed such a centralization of power would threaten their property and political authority.

Opponents questioned the unionist claims of the urban expansionists. Where Consolidators, echoing nineteenth-century nationalism, stressed the need to overcome sectional interests for the good of the metropolitan whole, their critics embraced subdivision as a natural byproduct of republican rule. "The districts are distinct from the city and from one another, in the character, pursuits and interests of the people who compose them," argued one correspondent to the *Pennsylvanian*, "and government ought in all cases, to grow out of natural combination, and be the expression of actual, social distinctions." "It is not democracy; it is not federalism; it is centralization," the writer insisted. These themes recurred in the anti-Consolidation movement's memorial to the legislature. The remonstrance pointed to the advantages of fragmentation, "where the interest of a part was different from the whole." The wisdom of past precedent stood in stark contrast to proposals for an enlarged city. "There never was embraced within the same limits a greater conflict and opposition of interests," the memorialists protested. One opponent of annexation a few years later even warned of amalgamation, evoking the fear of racial mixing that fueled rioters' rage at Pennsylvania Hall.[90]

For all the evidence of interdependence the riots had offered, the union of city and suburbs still seemed unnatural. When the state legislature met in Harrisburg in January 1845, it rejected the Consolidation bill in favor of a proposal to improve the county police. Even that act, however, did not tinker with the city's political boundaries. Ordering each district to maintain one policeman for every one hundred and fifty taxables, the new law sought to nip riots in the bud, without providing for cooperation across municipal boundaries.[91] For Consolidators, such a limited measure was never likely to be enough, but in 1845, the reform's wealthier backers found themselves in a minority even among their own class. To unite Philadelphia, they would have to heal their rift with prominent citizens, and persuade them that an interdependent metropolis needed one government.

*   *   *

As Consolidation's opponents in Philadelphia were winning the battle to prevent the enlargement of their city in February 1845, Congress approved the annexation of Texas. Fisher, who wrote to the *United States Gazette* against a scheme he believed would end the "separate existence"[92] of the city proper, had pondered the previous year the prospect of national dissolution: "A Union between two people who, in fact, in all important characteristics are broadly contrasted, must be a weak one. . . . In such a country there can be no strong national feeling, no sentiment of identity, none of the thousand ties formed by a community of origin, recollections, hopes, objects, interests & manners, which make the idea of country sacred & dear. Such a Union is one of interest merely, a paper bond, to be torn asunder by a burst of passion or to be deliberately undone whenever interest demands it."[93]

Fisher's prescient words closely resembled the case against Consolidation: they hint at how the political construction of city and nation stood on similar foundations. Indeed, over the next decade, sectional conflict often shaped debates over municipal union. Questions about the wisdom of incorporating a population that looked very different to the prosperous Protestants of the city proper would recur just as they did with the annexation of Mexico. So too would concerns over whether a union divided by party, class, and creed could ever hold together. This, then, was the question that the "great study" had to answer: How could a metropolis made up of such manifestly different parts ever associate as one?

CHAPTER 2

"The Guilty and Blood-Stained City"

Radicals and the Second American Republic

On the evening of November 11, 1844, Philadelphians on their way to the Consolidation meeting at the county courthouse might have hurried past a crowd outside Chestnut Street Theater. The people had gathered to protest the cancellation of the premiere of George Lippard's "The Monks of Monk Hall." Lippard had adapted the play from serialized extracts of his scandalous novel, *The Quaker City*, a thinly veiled attack on Philadelphia's bourgeoisie. Its main target was the merchant Singleton Mercer—a relative and namesake of a wealthy supporter of the Philadelphia Society for the Employment and Instruction of the Poor (PSEIP)—whom a jury had recently acquitted of murdering his sister's seducer. The prospect of the affair being played out on the stage so troubled Mercer that he reputedly purchased three hundred tickets with the intention of distributing them to arson-happy Southwark "rowdies." In a city the mob had torched twice during the preceding months, the rumor sufficiently unnerved the mayor for him to bar the performance from proceeding. This brought Lippard's admirers out in force, and "for hours," a newspaper reported, "there was every appearance of a destructive outbreak." The "emeute," as one journal (borrowing a term that evoked revolutionary violence in France) called the incident, no doubt focused Consolidators' minds as they met a few hundred yards down the street.[1]

Chestnut Street Theater that night avoided the fate meted out a few months before to Catholic churches. For Lippard, though, the affair provided another example of wealth arraying itself against the people. Critics might have dismissed the twenty-two-year-old as "a mere boy" with an

effervescent "spleen," but the author defended his writing as a way to "deli-
mate *principles*."[2] *The Quaker City* in this regard provided a cartography of
Philadelphia's present and a prophecy of its future that traced the terrain
of a corrupt elite. Where bourgeois citizens saw danger in the miasmas
emanating from the courts and alleys of working-class suburbs, then, Lippard argued the real "mysteries" of Philadelphia lay behind the facades of
the mansions that lined the main streets. Conspiracies hatched in the drawing rooms and clubhouses of the rich impoverished the real producers of
the city's wealth.

Throughout the Atlantic World in the mid-nineteenth-century, radicals
joined businessmen, reformers, and governments in trying to comprehend
the workings of the new metropolis. Radicals like Lippard shared boosters'
conviction that the age of the "great city" had arrived, and that Philadelphia
had more in common with a London, Paris, or Manchester, than with
provincial American towns. But from this common point, the knowledge
they produced diverged. Bourgeois surveyors sought to mold the discordant
phenomena of urban life into a coherent whole with discernible rules and
manipulable parts. For Morton McMichael and his Old World counterparts, the "great city" might have been an ugly, violent, and even insurrectionary place, but it contained within it the potential for beauty, order, and
wealth. Radicals did not share their optimism. Take for instance Friedrich
Engels, who published *Condition of the Working Class in England* in 1845,
the same year *The Quaker City* appeared in full.[3] Engels's analysis of social
relations and the urban form mapped the city in a very different way to
Lippard's gothic mysteries, but both writers argued that capital produced
space in a manner that pressed down on the working class. Metropolitan
growth did not scatter its benefits evenly, but left a trail of misery in its
wake, as the labor that built up the city found itself banished to insalubrious
quarters for shelter.

Philadelphia's radicals found common ground in their reading of the
"great city." Heirs to a tradition of artisanal politics that went back to 1776,
they drew on classical republicanism, the labor theory of value, and Atlantic
revolutionary upheavals to critique the society and space of unreformed
capitalism. Lippard and his allies cast themselves as an intellectual vanguard: missionaries tasked with explaining the workings of the city to the
workers who built it. Their project of consolidating class involved imagining a different society in which producers, rather than capitalists, reaped
the rewards of what they had sown.[4] Radicals, then, differed from their

booster contemporaries. Bourgeois Philadelphians targeted manufacturing suburbs and riot districts for consolidation. Once they could dictate terms, they would incorporate the metropolitan frontier into the city, enclose the city's borderlands, and inoculate themselves against epidemics of disorder and disease. Lippard, in contrast, equated industry with exploitation, and believed moral miasmas festered in wealthy homes rather than rickety tenements. For him, the work of purification began in mansions, not hovels.

For Lippard, as for McMichael, reconstructing Philadelphia required association. The memory of worker fighting worker in 1844 haunted radicals. In the years that followed the riots, they tried to rebuild solidarities, and link the city's producers to national and international struggles for the rights of labor. Their own fragmentation, though sometimes overstated, worked against them.[5] Some were middle-class reformers swayed by the appeal of utopian socialism; others, working-class journeymen with long experience of the shop floor. Some rallied around party flags; others urged independent political organization. Some saw craft unionism as a panacea for workingmen; others believed strikes offered short-term gains at most, and envisaged a more lasting social reconstruction. But if factions argued over the best way to consolidate Philadelphia's producers, radicals agreed on the need for union—and especially in the wake of the 1848 European Revolutions—mounted a powerful attack on the bourgeois understanding of the city.

Even then, however, they found it hard to agree on the boundaries of the producers' community in a city divided by creed, color, and class. In the sectional crisis of 1850, the divided house of radicalism tumbled to the ground. Yet the challenge Lippard and his allies presented before midcentury left an imprint on metropolitan life up to the Civil War and beyond in an associational politics hostile to individualism.

The Labor Question in the Riot Era

Philadelphians confronted what would come to be called the "labor question" long before the Gilded Age. When masters and merchants began to reorganize production in the Early Republic, they faced resistance. "Traditionalists" fought attempts to impose time and work discipline; radical artisans channeled the rationalist spirit of Tom Paine to oppose the new order. By the Jacksonian era, indeed, the growing metropolis had become a frontline in a battle to define the terms of American capitalism. Workers, though, were not simply fighting a rearguard action; instead many imagined that the power of industrialization could be put to work in their interests. In this regard day-to-day struggles on the shop floor and ambitious designs for social reconstruction each informed the way citizens thought about the relations between labor and capital.[6]

By the time Lippard published *The Quaker City,* Philadelphia had been a center of labor organizing for more than two decades. In 1827, journeymen from across the city's trades came together in the Mechanics' Union of Trade Associations, the nation's first metropolitan-wide labor federation.[7] A few years later, at the height of the Jacksonian boom, coal heavers walked off the wharves on the Schuylkill River, beginning a strike that drew twenty thousand workers together across lines of craft and culture: "an awakening of class solidarity," David Montgomery argued, "as significant as any in American history." Under the leadership of the General Trades' Union (GTU), Philadelphia's workers brought the city to a halt, and despite the best efforts of the municipal authorities, businessmen struggled to fight back. The Panic of 1837 succeeded where others had failed in destroying the GTU, and in the dog days of the depression, its leaders either decamped to the antimonopoly wing of the Democratic Party or were swept up in the Protestant revivals that burnt over the city. Workingmen who had marched under the banner, "We are all day laborers," found new solidarities in political parties and confessional culture—a path that led to the atavism of the 1844 riots.[8]

Yet simmering unrest in the hard times that followed the Panic reminded employers that the labor question had not gone away. Ethnic affinities, which the GTU had worked hard to overcome, now became a basis for solidarity, especially among Irish coal heavers and handloom weavers. The former torched a Reading Railroad bridge in 1842; the latter chased off the sheriff and his posse during a dispute in Kensington a few months later. But strikers, like most Jacksonian Americans with a grievance, tended to use violence discriminately, targeting bosses and journeymen who ignored union scales. Another coal heavers' strike, this one on the Richmond wharves of the Reading just a few weeks before the first 1844 riot, provides a telling illustration. Demanding an increase in pay, the men forced "all the different laborers in the vicinity to join them," and by the time Sheriff Morton McMichael turned up with his posse, the employer had evidently caved in.[9]

For bourgeois Philadelphians, the "labor question" in the early 1840s could seem like just another manifestation of suburban disorder in a city that had become a "war-field for every faction and party." Thomas Pym Cope read the May 1844 riot in this vein as one more episode in a district characterized by "the frequent demolition of private property."[10] Strikers, who tended to coalesce around a trade, neighborhood, or culture, lacked the metropolitan-wide reach of the GTU, and their militancy proved easy to subsume into a broader pattern of suburban violence. Few assumed their disturbances had roots in the relationship between labor and capital.

Wealthy residents of Philadelphia, however, could not afford to ignore militancy even where it was geographically contained. The city proper's economic elite may have had few reasons to follow the battle between hand-loom operatives and master weavers in Kensington—a struggle in a dying craft that pitted impoverished workers against petty entrepreneurs—but plenty paid taxes to support the sheriff's posse or owned stock in the strike-plagued Reading Railroad. Moreover, frequent strikes risked further damage to the city's reputation. By 1845, then, even Cope's merchant-dominated Board of Trade had identified fraught industrial relations as a threat to the "prosperity of Philadelphia," as it attacked the "mad attempts" to "resist by combination and by open violence, the law of demand and supply."[11]

Lippard and his allies saw virtues where the board saw vices. For them, combination offered the best form of resistance to the commodification of labor, which for all the elegance of liberal theory reduced free men to what they termed wage slaves. In the years after the riots, they launched an attack on the "law of demand and supply" that led them to explore how the city worked. If citizens wanted to understand the earthquakes that shook Phila-delphia, radicals insisted, they needed to look beneath the surface and map its social fault lines.

The Social Cartography of Radical Philadelphia

The man who caused such a stir at the Chestnut Street Theater, George Lippard, shared McMichael's sense of the city as an interdependent but illegible whole, yet saw the metropolis very differently than the *North American* publisher. Born in 1822, he grew up in Germantown, a rural borough annexed to the city in 1854, and after turning his back on careers in the church and law, began writing in the shadow of the Panic of 1837. Lippard

spent the hard times as a jobbing journalist and romance author, and having slept rough in the city's streets and cellars, started work on his first
political novel, *The Quaker City*, which appeared in serial form in the
months that followed the 1844 riots. He was working on the book when the
mayor halted the stage adaptation—Lippard alluded to the censorship in
subsequent chapters—but the controversy heightened public interest and
secured him a salary. When it appeared in 1845, it sold 60,000 copies, making it the most popular American novel prior to *Uncle Tom's Cabin*. Before
his death at 31—just a decade after his literary breakthrough—he wrote
over twenty books and countless newspaper articles. He became best known
for his "city mysteries" fiction: novels that lifted the veil on metropolitan
life.[12] Through his writing and politics, he played a leading role in a radical
subculture that challenged bourgeois citizens' reading of the city.

Lippard was both a product and a critic of Philadelphia's capitalist
transformation. New printing technology and rising literacy created a mass
market for cheap fiction, and mysteries novelists' audience crossed social
boundaries.[13] But if genteel Philadelphians sometimes enjoyed a snigger at
Lippard's tales, the author saw himself, in the words of a radical cleric, as
"the age's leading spokesman for the common man." He found his calling
in the task of consolidating the toiling but ignorant masses around a project
of social reconstruction. Lippard wielded his pen as a weapon in a class
war, which a recent critic sees as the "literary equivalent" of the riots.[14]

Lippard's task, as he stated in an 1849 preface to his best-known book,
lay in explaining "all the phases of a corrupt social system, as manifested in
the city of Philadelphia." His mysteries fiction did so in ways that would
have resonated with veterans of the GTU and generations of American
populists. Like them, he divided the world into producers and idlers, lauding the former for creating value through their labor, and lambasting the
latter for living off the work of others. Lippard hurled invective here not
just at bankers, merchants, and lawyers, but also at politicians, publishers,
priests, and the manufacturers he called "white slaveholders."[15] Ignoring
divisions among Philadelphia's economic elite, he portrayed such figures as
a conspiring cabal. In trying to unite producers, Lippard consolidated a
bourgeoisie.

His writing guided readers through a metropolis that class had cor-
rupted. Mysteries novels crossed the Atlantic from France, where Eugène
Sue's *Mysteries of Paris*—published just a few months before Lippard began
The Quaker City—captured the attention of writers ranging from Edgar

Allen Poe to Karl Marx. The magnitude of fast-growing American metropolises gave works that purported to reveal their secrets wide appeal and inspired authors in Philadelphia and elsewhere to mimic Lippard's method. Only some of these imitators shared his radical politics, and few embraced the gothic elements that owed more to Poe than Sue, but nearly all of them blurred the boundary between fact and fiction in their depiction of the city.[16] Indeed, novelists frequently insisted on the veracity of their findings and emphasized the labor that had gone into their research. "He who would learn the mysteries and miseries" of New York and Philadelphia, wrote one, "must, as we have done, make it" his "sole occupation." To "penetrate all the haunts of dissipation and crime," he claimed to have divided the city into eight districts, which he systematically explored over the course of six months. Lippard made no pretense of social scientific rigor but still promised to bring to the surface "the strange and thrilling scenes that lie buried beneath" the "exterior of society."[17]

In doing so, he demystified the shadowy spaces of urban capitalism. Like Marx, Lippard asks his audience to see beyond labor's objectification in the commodity, and gaze instead on the hidden process of production. As he walks his readers through the riot district of Kensington in *The Nazarene* (1846), for instance, he points to the windows of an immense factory, behind which "miserable forms, swarming to their labour," work from before dawn to after dusk.[18]

But Lippard's cartography also mapped the inequality woven into the urban form and plotted how a morally bankrupt capitalism reproduced it. Like lithographers, Lippard sometimes saw Philadelphia synoptically, rising above its rooftops to look down on the metropolis below. Where the bird's eye view gave boosters a sanitized snapshot of urban greatness, Lippard used the panorama to show the city's social depravity, bringing into view chains of interdependence and exploitation. From a pulpit on the dome of the new Girard College, for instance, "a writer of immoral books" surveys the "great city." The vantage point allows the preacher—a thinly disguised version of the author himself—to see the metropolis as a whole. "Sweep the roofs from this large City at midnight," he tells his congregation, and the "anatomy of civilization lies open to your gaze." Lippard's perspective soon shifts from sky to street, as he peers into the homes of wealthy judges and starving widows, juxtaposing "dens of want, in the narrow alleys" and "the great mansion, where the revel, bought with the poor man's labor, roars on from midnight until break of day." As he stresses the gulf between

what he called the "upper tenth" and "lower million," he also suggests how
the two classes are bound together, with one's wealth the fruits of the other's toil.[19]

When he wanted to show the power wielded by a consolidated class,
though, Lippard distilled Philadelphia to a single setting. Monk Hall, a
mansion that connects his novel's subplots, compresses the "social and sex-
ual relations" of the city. That is not to say it is easy to navigate. The
structure, "lonely even amid tenements and houses," lies hidden amid a
"tangled labyrinth of avenues," defying the legible grid. Within its walls, a
young man warns his companion, "it is easy enough for a stranger . . . to
find his way *in*, but it would puzzle him like the devil to find his way
out."[20] Riddled with secret passages and subterranean lairs, the building sets
Philadelphia's mystique in stone.

Yet when Lippard resumes his role as guide, it becomes evident that the
disorienting space disguises clear social divisions. The powerful people who
plot urban fortunes in its rooms are easy enough to identify. Monk Hall's
"monks" are not the despised papists targeted by the church burners of 1844,
but a canting, conniving bourgeoisie. "Here were lawyers from the court,
doctors from the school, and judges from the bench," Lippard writes, as
parsons, publishers, and politicians scheme frauds and seductions. If the conspiracies are hard to decode, the class that hatches them is perfectly readable.[21]

By vesting metropolitan power in a powerful and corrupted class, Lippard and his allies challenged bourgeois readings of the riots. Monk Hall's
Southwark setting might be telling here. After the July clash between the
militia and the mob, wealthy Philadelphians blamed the district's turbulent
population for civil war on the streets; *The Quaker City*, in contrast, identi-
fies "respectable citizens" as the real dangerous classes. "The poor man toils
in want," its author insists, "and the rich man riots in his sweat and blood."
As another radical put it, the "authorized fraud and force of orderly society"
lay behind the "spontaneous outbursts" of mobs.[22] To them, the 1844 violence sprang more from a dissolute rich than a disorderly poor.

Lippard and other radicals thus linked a corrupt environment and civic
ruin.[23] But their environmental determinism differed from that of their
bourgeois contemporaries. Where elements of the economic elite worried
about the moral miasmas emanating from suburban courts and alleys, Lippard labeled luxury as corrosive. In his account of an 1849 race riot, for
instance, a fictionalized leader of the real street gang that provoked the
outrage was ruined by a childhood that tended "to pamper the appetite and

deprave the passions." Elsewhere Lippard chastised newspapers for failing to pay more attention to "Respectable Killers": not the boys who "get up riots, hunt negroes and burn houses," but rapacious manufacturers, land-lords, and bank presidents.[24]

When he did portray a dissolute poor, they were brutalized by avarice. Devil-Bug, more monster than man, was described by a contemporary of his creator as "the product of a rotten civilisation," while *The Quaker City* has him raised "in full and continual sight of scenes of vice, wretchedness and squalor." Philadelphia's "outcasts"—"vagabond tribes" who speak "a language of their own"—are kept "in the underground recesses of Monk Hall by day before being set loose "to beg, to rob, or . . . to murder" at night.[25] In Lippard's city, producers confronted the conspiracies of capital and the savagery of its slavish victims.

No republic, Lippard believed, could long endure in such a state. Allud-ing, perhaps, to a year of apocalyptic fervor—a few weeks before the Ken-sington riot, a millenarian sect, the Millerites, had loudly proclaimed the End Times were at hand—he foretold the "Last Day of the Quaker City" in a reverie, which carried the keeper of Monk Hall, Devil-Bug, forward to 1950. Lippard's futuristic Philadelphia had degenerated almost beyond rec-ognition from its egalitarian roots. The ruins of Independence Hall provide stone for a royal palace; Washington Square had given way to a penitentiary and gallows. Carriages of a "proud and insolent nobility," who had "wrung the sweat from the brow of the mechanic," ride past beggars on wide boule-vards. As "slaves of the cotton Lord and the factory Prince" prepare to crown their king, the dead rise from the grave, chanting "Wo Unto Sodom." Judgment day arrives as lightning rains down from the sky and houses fall into the ground. For Lippard, the fate of the "guilty and blood-stained City" is retribution for its moral rot.[26]

His radical cartography mapped the city in a very different way than the bourgeoisie. The sermon from Girard College used the form of evangel-ical piety in pursuit of radical ends; the prophesy of Philadelphia's destruc-tion turned booster dreams of what the metropolis might become into a nightmare that multiplied the horrors of the riots. Outward signs of wealth—"temples of marble," "glittering domes," "the grandeur and mag-nificence of the streets"—fail to cover the corruption within.[27] The path to peace and prosperity did not run through industry and commerce. As long as the social system remained unreformed, urban growth would multiply misery within, hastening the city's doom.

Lippard therefore joined boosters in employing Philadelphia's past, present, and future as political weapons. McMichael and his allies used visions of civic greatness to bring together a bourgeoisie, but the radical novelist warned that unless citizens awoke to the danger, the metropolis would decay into an imperial oligarchy. Seeing glaring inequality all around them, he and his allies aimed to demystify the process of expropriation that enriched the few at the expense of the many, and consolidate producers around a project of social reconstruction to redeem the Quaker City.[28]

The blood spilled in 1844 made association imperative. After the riots, the lyceums and halls that had flourished before the Panic of 1837 provided meeting places for rebuilding, as radicals tried to turn theory into practice. Working people and their allies formed fraternal clubs, Fourierist sects, cooperative stores, craft unions, Chartist sympathy leagues, and social improvement societies. Historians have sometimes seen the rush to associate in Jacksonian America as part of a search for belonging, as the intimacy of the "walking city" gave way to the anonymity of the industrial metropolis.[29] But the community envisaged by radicals pursued social ends as much as it met psychic needs. Organizations varied, with some inviting African Americans, abolitionists, and women to their meetings, and others limiting themselves to white, male producers. They ran the gamut ideologically too from utopian socialism to a brand of producerism that would not have looked out of place in the two major parties. Democrat, Whig, Liberty, and Free Soil partisans all participated. But their fragmentation is easy to overstate. Radicals often moved from one organization to another and shared basic principles: capital, at least in the form it had assumed in industrializing Philadelphia, exploited labor, and the consequences of that process were engrafted into the urban form. Only through union could producers emancipate themselves. "COMBINATION! ASSOCIATION! These are the words of the last Gospel which God has uttered to man," Lippard declared in 1849.[30] By then he had found a model abroad.

The Second American Republic

Radicals' inspiration in the 1840s came not only in the inheritance from the Jacksonian labor movement, but also along the revolutionary currents of the Atlantic. The tide of immigration from the British Isles and Germany brought an infusion of militancy. From Yorkshire came John Shedden, a radical tailor who later joined the First International, Knights of Labor, and Sovereigns of Industry. The Irish-born handloom weaver John Campbell fought for working-class suffrage in the factory districts of northern England as a leader in the Chartist movement before fleeing to the United States after a failed general strike in 1842. Such figures, having seen firsthand the industrial transformation of the Old World and the New, understood Philadelphia's development in world historical perspective.[31]

The European Revolutions of 1848 gave them hope. Initially, Philadelphians, like most Americans, welcomed the fall of France's July Monarchy as a vindication of the principles of 1776. That consensus was supposed to have found expression at a vast public meeting on Independence Square in late April. Citizens from across the city's partisan and ethnic divisions gathered to the strains of the Marseillaise to hear eminent speakers proclaim the rights of man. Among them was McMichael, who admired how dynasties that "seemed indestructible" had "melted away or, thrown into the crucible of reform," had "assumed new forms and new existence."[32]

Radicals sang from the same hymn sheet but added an extra verse. For them, the Second French Republic—and especially the National Workshops, which guaranteed employment to the poor—could inspire a Second American Republic. When Francis J. Grund took to the stand, he surveyed the history of Europe from 1789. The revolutionaries who uprooted the Ancien Régime, Grund argued, "had to pull down the *social* culture of Europe as well as the political one," but once they had done so, "the *Bourgeoisie*" rose on the ruins of the nobility, and "the struggle between capital and labor commenced." Assailing classical political economy, he warned that the law of supply and demand degraded man "to a marketable commodity," and praised the French government for embracing "associated labor."[33]

Grund's dialectical materialism echoed radical readings of the European Revolutions. Lippard, who devoted column after column of his weekly paper the *Quaker City* to making sense of 1848 and its aftermath, described the events in France as a reaction to "social" more than "constitutional" evils. The journalist and reformer George G. Foster, who also spoke at Independence Square, coauthored a hastily written account of affairs in Paris with Thomas Dunn English. Foster and English rejected the common assumption that the French had merely emulated the American example. Instead, Parisians had embarked on a glorious new course, for their revolution had social consequences as well as origins. "Capital arrayed itself

against labor; and the latter only awaited the proper moment for its emancipation," they argued, but the Second Republic's pledge "to guarantee
work and existence to the laborer" had addressed "the problem of the Nineteenth Century!"[34]

The authors joined Grund in blaming the "bourgeoisie" for France's
woes. Bourgeois citizens became a kind of Monk Hall International, who,
they hinted, threatened American liberty too. The class's corrupting influence extended from the throne to the factory. An "oligarchy of the bourgeoisie" made King Louis Philippe its head; their "sordid desires" and
"thirst for accumulation" led them to "acquiesce in any state of affairs
which gratifies their avarice." Encompassing all the "capitalists," "trades-
men," "bankers," "monopolists," "venders," and "men reposing on their
cotton bales," the bourgeoisie marked a new name for the corrupt elite
that Lippard portrayed lording over Philadelphia. But above all Foster and
English defined them by their antithesis: productive citizens. Out of this
dialectic came the 1848 Revolution: "the working class" in its "final struggle"
had "emancipated itself from the chains of the bourgeoisie."[35] They did not
just describe a class, but a class struggle.

Class struggle stalked Philadelphia too, for radicals rejected any idea
that the United States enjoyed immunity from the social processes ravaging
Europe's great cities: "Labor itself, under the influence of unlimited competition, is forced down and down, until it is compelled to accept gladly of
the merest and least possible amount of wages that will prevent absolute
starvation. Under this state of things, the laboring classes, forced to pack
themselves into filthy garrets and noisome cellars . . . either become beasts,
or learn to pray for death. Such is the condition of the great mass of laborers throughout the world."[36]

When he introduced Philadelphia's "bourgeoisie" to a domestic audience, Foster became more circumspect, but he still mapped French social
relations onto an American urban form. In late 1848, he wrote a series on
Philadelphia for Horace Greeley's New York Tribune, the radical Whig
paper, which would soon hire Karl Marx as its European correspondent.
Events in Europe, Foster noted, had familiarized citizens with the "bourgeoisie," though he doubted that many of the writers who used it "know
what it means." Despite the problems of determining the word's "true sig-
nification," Foster claimed that "the most distinguishing characteristic of
Philadelphia is its Bourgeoisie," for it had "reached a higher state of development" in the city than anywhere else in the Union. The first of his "slices"

of Philadelphia life therefore dissected the class, and while he stressed its mercantile character, he did not leave out manufacturers: a bourgeois was "a man who keeps a shop or lives by making a profit from the product of the labor of others." His sketch of staid respectability in the city proper, though, provided a foil for subsequent forays into turbulent suburbs. Here his interest in social taxonomy faded as he turned to recounting salacious stories of street gangs and dance halls.[37]

Hints of Foster's radicalism nevertheless crept in as he mapped Philadelphia's people and progress. In taking a similar path to Southwark as Lippard's "monks of Monk Hall," he pointed out "the immense army of *proletaires* which exist in every city, who live hardby in poor cabins and shanties, and whose labour supplies the profits upon which the merchant-princes and their aristocratic families subsist in luxury." Here, he made the city look rather like Paris, with its prosperous center surrounded by an oppressed suburban poor. Later, in visiting Independence Hall, Foster asked whether Americans had "suffered Europe to overtake and pass us." Had citizens, he wondered, "secured to Strength Employment" and "to Employment Reward" by "developing all the benignant powers of the elements for the benefit of the whole people"? Or were Americans now "enviers of the progress of others"? He left readers to ponder the matter themselves.[38]

Among Philadelphia's radicals, affinity for European revolutions ran deep. The year before the 1848 Revolutions, an anonymous novel, *The Almighty Dollar*, portrayed Moyamensing's Killers as primitive rebels who promise to liberate the land "from the iron sway of the rich." Although the gang take the Jacobin club as their model, it soon becomes clear that they owe as much to George Washington as to the Committee of Public Safety, but the links the novel draws between the American Revolution, the French Revolution, and antebellum urban violence are striking. In reality, an Irish American gang made up mostly of apprentices and laborers hardly amounted to "proletarian heroes," but its reinvention in the hands of an anonymous author hints at the way radicals challenged the widespread anti-Jacobinism of the antebellum republic. Campbell and one of his collaborators, indeed, heaped praise on Robespierre, Marat, and St. Just for attempting "to secure to the producers all that they produced."[39]

But it was 1848 rather than 1789 (or 1793, for that matter) that focused minds in Philadelphia by raising the possibility of millennial social transformation. Campbell, who had been putting the finishing touches to his

Theory of Equality—a pamphlet that ranged across continents and centuries by weaving Rousseauian inequality, Paineite republicanism, and Democratic antimonopoly into a project for social reconstruction—hastily added a fawning dedication to the new French government, lauding its efforts to "elevate the proletarians." And Lippard hoped the 1848 Revolutions would reverberate in the United States. "Shall the world look for the redemption of the workers from the chains of social wrong," he asked, "and our Union be left hopeless and desolate?" The land reformer William Elder, who had shared the stage with McMichael and Foster at the Independence Square meeting, renounced the cry of "bread or blood," but warned that conservative wealth "must expect at last to meet its victims at the barricades." "Gradual reform or violent revolution," he counseled, "is the necessity of our condition."[40]

Rival interpretations of what the 1848 Revolutions were—and what they might mean for Philadelphia—shattered the consensus of the Independence Square meeting. In one corner, free blacks had assembled to welcome the abolition of slavery in French colonies, and when a policeman tried to end the gathering by stopping one of the speakers, whites intervened and "bade him go on." African Americans' readiness to claim 1848 as their own illustrated that the economic elite enjoyed no monopoly in making sense of the upheaval. Yet when Elder, in words dripping with socialist and abolitionist sentiment, persuaded the main meeting to resolve that the Second Republic's destruction of slavery; its organization of industry; and its proclamation of liberty, equality, and fraternity revealed the principles "of our own Revolution," the resolutions were left off the published proceedings. A few weeks later, radicals and abolitionists returned to the spot to protest the "mutilation" of the record.[41]

The 1848 Revolutions divided the meeting but bound radicals together. European turmoil gave them a vocabulary to name what was happening in Philadelphia, an understanding of how their republican ideal differed from that of the bourgeoisie, and a spirit of solidarity that brought rival factions together. By the summer, the elation that had greeted the revolutions had given way in much of the Union to skepticism about their permanence and doubts about their character, especially among conservatives in the North and South. But when the *North American* backed the Second Republic's bloody suppression of labor unrest in the June Days, and began to worry about "red republicanism" in American cities, radicals continued to praise Parisian workers.[42] In Philadelphia, the three years that followed 1848 witnessed an upsurge in radical association. The likes of Lippard and Campbell set about the task of consolidating producers around the project of building their own second republic.

Consolidating Producers

The 1848 Revolutions lifted radical morale. Over the preceding years, they had built an institutional base from which to challenge bourgeois ideology. A stronger economy after 1844 gave craft unions the chance to flourish alongside the Chartist leagues and Fourierist associations. By 1847, trade unionists who hoped to revive the spirit of the General Trades' Union were discussing plans for some form of citywide organization.[43]

Radicals' designs for consolidating producers extended beyond workplace bargaining into organization and education. Lippard, convinced that secret fraternal orders had prepared the way for the French Revolutions in 1789 and 1848, tried to "bind the masses together" in a "one-minded body." In 1849, he founded the Brotherhood of the Union, which soon spread across the republic. Lippard's Brotherhood looked to the bloodless overthrow of capital and the union of the "Workers of the World" (unlike Marx and Engels he actually used the term). But it embraced reform as well as revolution. Like Campbell, Lippard advocated cooperative enterprise, factory regulation, and free homesteads in the West. Indeed, both radicals joined George Henry Evans's national land reform movement.[44]

Institutional consolidation—whether via national organizations like Lippard's Brotherhood of the Union and Evans's National Industrial Congress (NIC), or local ones, like trade assemblies—mattered to radicals who saw "association" as a path to power. Most often, association referred to the principle of workers pooling capital and sharing profits, effectively cutting out the merchant or manufacturer who claimed a portion of their labor. Schemes for producer and consumer cooperatives abounded around midcentury. But association, as the call for "fraternity" in 1848 and "brotherhood" in Lippard's secret society implied, had other meanings too. Perhaps most importantly, it marked a cry for producer solidarity in the wake of the riots. Association meant here the "Union of the Workers against the Idlers who do not work."[45]

Radicals crafted a role for themselves that today we might call that of the "organic intellectual." To raise the consciousness of the city's producers and awaken them to their common interests, however, required challenging the economic elite in civil society. Radicals attacked the American bourgeois press for its hostility to European revolutions, for instance, while Lippard decried Philadelphia's "Anti-Socialist" papers. In *The Quaker City*, the author portrays a newspaper editor, the risible Buzby Poodle, as one of the "monks" lording it over Philadelphia.[46] Class consolidation required continually challenging such voices.

The years leading up to midcentury saw a host of efforts to ensure a counterhegemonic voice could be heard in the city. Philadelphia's district halls, mechanics' institutes, and open lots offered a promising terrain for association. Campbell, who believed "the monopoly of education" left producers ignorant of the processes that reduced them to penury drew on his experience as an itinerant lecturer for British Chartists in tramping from meeting to meeting to rally support. Lippard's Brotherhood, meanwhile, urged members to "open your halls to the public of both sexes" to discuss "Land, Labor, and Social Reform."[47] Radicals also sought to establish a rival to the bourgeois-dominated press. Impressed by Greeley's *Tribune*, for which he occasionally wrote, Campbell toyed with the idea of starting a reform paper of his own, as did several craft unions. Instead, though, he entered the publishing trade with a fellow Chartist exile, Edward P. Powers. Their first pamphlet, by the judge and former factory reformer William D. Kelley, decried the "heartless theory" that "points to the labouring population reduced to want and pauperism." Lippard, just as convinced of his vanguard role, did set himself up as an editor. The *Quaker City*, a weekly, which made its bow in 1848, serialized his fiction, served as a mouthpiece for the Brotherhood of the Union, and cheered on revolution and reform.[48]

Radicalism in the late 1840s may have lacked the impact of the GTU, but its institutional piquancy and ideological thrust troubled the economic elite. The sense that Lippard, Campbell, and their allies were (as one historian has said, in a related context) "domesticating foreign struggles" proved particularly alarming.[49] Bourgeois consolidators began to respond. McMichael's *North American*—the paper that fought harder than any other for the economic elite to speak with one voice—attacked the "radical, fiery, Fourierish" tone of Foster's *French Revolution of 1848,* and its singling out of the "bourgeoisie" for criticism especially. The daily found the definition of the term Foster arrived at "tolerably just," but rejected his take on the class's boundaries and politics, arguing that the word was simply a synonym for what the English called "the middle classes" and Americans called "the *business men* of our towns and cities—merchants, manufacturers, master mechanics, employers of all kind, but including capitalists, house owners and house holders." "In America in fact," it argued, "we all belong to the bourgeoisie," for "every head of a family, is a bourgeois—a free citizen." Rather than finding solace in the republic's exceptionalism, though, the paper cast the class in international terms. "The bourgeoisies of all countries have great respect for the rights of property," it declared, and "desire and require peace and quiet, and order, for the successful prosecution of trade." Thus "a civil tumult of any kind" could "offer nothing but severe loss and suffering." Bourgeois Frenchmen had joined the 1848 Revolution then only at great sacrifice.[50]

The *North American* simultaneously defined the bourgeoisie as an international class while denying the existence of class distinctions: a rhetorical strategy it would employ frequently over the following decades in seeking to harmonize social interests across the city. McMichael did all he could to break down barriers between propertied citizens, yet here his paper claimed that class had no meaning. To admit Foster's point, however, risked legitimizing labor conflict. McMichael saw such battles at firsthand as county sheriff in the 1840s and in his own office in the 1850s, when he confronted (usually without success) well-organized printers. Newspaper publishers, indeed, continually found themselves negotiating with staff, which may help account for their hostility to craft unions more generally: even the *Public Ledger*—a paper more sympathetic than most to journeymen—dismissed Campbell's design for "equal exchanges" and toed the liberal line that laws of supply and demand properly regulated the price of labor.[51]

Workplace militancy, revolutionary turmoil, and radicals' determination to plot the present and future course of the city drew Philadelphia's economic elite into confronting the labor question well before the Civil War. Richard Rush, who as U.S. minister to France had recognized the Second Republic in 1848, returned to his home city around midcentury, concerned that North might prove fertile ground for "Communism." About the same time, the iron manufacturer Stephen Colwell called socialism "one of the greatest events of this age," and warned that "no man can understand the progress of humanity or its present tendencies who does not . . . watch its movements." Rush and Colwell played prominent roles in the battle for metropolitan Consolidation over the following years, but even Sidney George Fisher, who remained aloof from upstart manufacturers and reform politics, exchanged ideas about labor and capital in the mid-1850s with a British factory owner who had written one of the first treatises on industrial relations. Fisher probably never set foot on a factory floor, but he acted as the attorney for the strike-plagued Reading Railroad, and by the postbellum era, read his running battles with household servants as a miniature of the wider struggle between employer and employee: one fought in homes, streets, and polling booths as well as suburban workshops and southern plantations.[52]

Here, at least, radicals and workers had succeeded in unsettling propertied citizens, as a joke insert in an April 1851 issue of the *Ledger*—which none too subtly name-checked various radicals—indicated. "*Let the mechanics and Workingmen Beware*," it began, "of the POWERS of the DEVIL and the CAMP-BELLS of HELL" that "would make *America* another *Atheistical France*" and "under the garb of '*Reformers*,' establish *Brutalism!*" Either side in the newspaper stood notices for meetings of a trades' assembly, two craft unions, and a cooperative store.[53] But the vigor of midcentury radicalism, so evident in the advertising columns of the *Ledger*, masked inner divisions. Those fractures would soon be exposed.

The Midcentury Crisis of Union

The project of consolidating producers ran into many of the same problems as projects for consolidating the economic elite or the city and districts. In each case, the difficulty lay in drawing boundaries, and determining who belonged in or out of the community. For radicals, the civil wars that raged on the city's streets—Protestants fighting Catholics, whites fighting blacks—made this question unavoidable. Designs for working-class association ultimately foundered on the conundrum, but midcentury radicalism left a critique of urban capitalism that shaped growth politics and its critics.

Radicals, surveying the wreckage of the riots, realized the biggest obstacle they confronted lay in working-class fragmentation. The main beneficiaries of the riots had been the nativist American Republicans, whose candidates swept Democrats from office in most of the suburban districts, including Kensington and Southwark. Their ascendancy did not last long, but like radicals, they established a foothold in working-class neighborhoods. The Order of United American Mechanics, a fraternal association of Protestant masters and journeymen, welcomed employers into the producers' community but excluded the fast-growing Catholic working class.[54]

In their religion, radicals ran the gamut from atheist infidelity to evangelical Protestantism, but they agreed that sectarianism threatened association. Lippard provides an instructive example. Critics have picked up on the anti-Catholic tropes in his work: the "monks" who make up *The Quaker City*'s bourgeoisie meet in a former monastery, after all.[55] Yet the novelist who conjured up images of conspiring priests loathed militant Protestantism. In 1846, he began a novel, *The Nazarene*, that blamed the nativist riots on religious intolerance; when a home missionary tells his audience he had seen Catholic bishops doing good work in the "alleys of Southwark and Moyamensing," his hateful audience accuse him of blasphemy. A few years earlier, in *The Quaker City*, he had satirized nativist Pope-baiting with the "Universal Patent Gospel Missionary Society," who combine "violent appeals to excited mobs" with "insidious endeavours to create those very mobs." Even in 1849, when in response to the Catholic archbishop of New York's support for the Pope in his struggle with the Roman Republic, Lippard asked if "*the Assassins of the Roman people*" have "*their paid minions on American soil,*" he admitted to speaking "of this subject with great reluctance," and prefaced the article with a lengthy recapitulation of his hostility to "No-Popery bigots." The Irish-born Campbell also disdained nativism. In 1850, he asked readers of the *Tribune* whether "American citizens" could really say to "the flying refugee from the despotism of Europe 'Back, back again to your stripes and chains, killed dungeons and scaffolds!' "[56]

Campbell invoked the spirit of solidarity that followed the 1848 Revolutions here to unite producers regardless of creed. Among radicals he was not alone. Within a few days of the Independence Square meeting, German workers raised the cry to "operate in concert with the American Laboring Classes in this city." The Social Improvement Society (SIS), which drew a mixture of active trade unionists and middle-class reformers, often debated immigration, and while there is no record of their meetings, we can assume from the figures involved that an unreformed social system rather than an influx of foreign labor was said to present a greater danger to native-born workers. "Humanity is of no caste, country, or clime," began *The Almighty Dollar*, which has the Killers street gang welcoming natives and naturalized alike. One of the leaders encapsulated the gang's ecumenical approach: "*We're all brothers when oppressed.*"[57]

In practice, though, the Killers proved rather less tolerant. After a summer of endemic fighting among Moyamensing firemen and street gangs in 1849, members of the gang crossed fifty yards into the city proper, where they torched a tavern run by a mixed-race couple. The race riot that ensued pitted Irish Catholics from the southern suburbs against the free black community that straddled the city boundary. Lippard quickly penned a short story on the riot, which he worked into a lengthier novel, and while rejecting the romantic version of the Killers as advocates of the rights of labor, he refused to see the conflict purely in terms of internecine strife. For him, apprentices, bored young men, and a handful of the "very worst specimens of the savage of this large city" made up the gang, but at their head stood the son of a millionaire: as usual, then, Philadelphia's moneyed elite orchestrated the mayhem.[58]

Beyond Lippard's novella, little trace of the radical response to the riot remains, but in laying bare the racial as well as religious hatreds that divided the working class, the fighting presented them with another problem. In the giddy aftermath of 1848, African Americans had publicly linked the European revolutions to their own struggle for liberation, and had won praise for doing so. The California House Riot (so-called for the tavern that burnt to the ground), though, marked a return to the old pattern of race riots, where blacks who became too visible in public or crossed racial boundaries faced violent reprisals.[59] Radical reformers did not know how to respond. Many, including William Elder, already had close ties to abolitionists. Antislavery activists like the feminist Lucretia Mott and African Americans Samuel Ringgold Ward and Robert Purvis spoke at Social Improvement Society meetings. Elder's land reform club sent the black abolitionist John C. Bowers—another SIS debater—as a delegate to the National Industrial Congress in 1851.[60] While Lippard and Campbell sometimes argued southern slaves were better off than northern workers, they did not mean to trivialize the sufferings of the former. Campbell's *Theory of Equality*, indeed, denounced slavery in all its forms, and attacked his own Democratic Party for failing to abolish it. Lippard, like Campbell, held British abolitionists in contempt for their blindness to the evils of capitalism, but wondered how any radical could "attack Wages Slavery and be silent about Chattel Slavery." He proudly printed mail from southern whites who accused him of belonging to the "school of Robespierre and Fourier."[61]

The coincidence of sectional and social conflict forced radicals to confront slavery. In 1848, with Pennsylvania congressman David Wilmot's proposal on the table to keep slaveholders out of any land acquired from Mexico, antislavery Democrats—Kelley among them—supported the measure. Elder, a veteran Liberty Party organizer, backed the Free Soil movement, while Lippard and Campbell stumped for the Whig and Democratic nominees, respectively.[62] Such political fragmentation was nothing new, but with the future of the nation at stake, radicals began to think more often about the relationship of black and white labor. Toward the end of 1850, the SIS regularly discussed the Fugitive Slave Law, and soon moved onto a series of debates—reportedly drawing large audiences—which considered whether the African race was capable of civilization. Most radicals answered in the affirmative, and over the following years, they provided a phalanx of opposition to the act: the operation of which in Philadelphia formed the backdrop to Lippard's final, unfinished novel. Such a course ought to warn us off schematic outlines of the making of a working class committed to white supremacy, but as the California House Riot showed, radical reformers could not debate racial conflict away.[63]

Nativism and slavery combined to sink one of the most ambitious projects for class consolidation. In October 1850, representatives of the various trades gathered at the county courthouse to consider a plan to "free each individual from the arbitrary and oppressive rule of capital." Though Lippard and Campbell were absent—only journeymen were allowed to participate—many of their radical associates attended, including land reformers like William J. Mullen and John Shedden. Out of the meeting emerged the trades' assembly first mooted in 1847. Unlike its predecessor in the 1830s—the GTU—the citywide body only included skilled male workers, which left out the Irish, black, and female laboring poor. Still, its organizers aimed to build a movement culture based around cooperative enterprise, a regular paper, and a political party. By early 1851, it represented more than thirty trades.[64]

Cracks soon began to show. In mid-1851, when Elder's land reform club sent the African American abolitionist Bowers to the National Industrial Congress, he had secured his seat over the protests of some members. The trades' assembly, acting in the name of Philadelphia's "Industrial Classes," disclaimed any connection with Evans's organization in disgust. Soon after, the new Workingmen's Party nominated Kelley, a longstanding "advocate of the Rights of Labor," as its candidate for the Court of Common Pleas. Kelley, who had just lost the Democratic nomination for his apostasy in a contested election case, had strong radical credentials—as a young man he had struck for the ten-hour workday, and Louis Kossuth later singled him out for thanks for his support of Hungarian liberty—but he was also a known abolitionist sympathizer. This troubled some workingmen less, however, than his hostility to nativism. Despite his Presbyterian roots, he held "church-burners" in contempt, and had pursued rioters in court after 1844. In the second half of 1851, his ardent internationalism still had its adherents. That summer, radicals fighting for land reform, laborers' rights, and equal exchanges declared that with the "world being our country, it is hoped that all nations will flock around our standard." A few months later, the rump of the trades' assembly expelled a group of nativists who had come to the meeting to solicit support for their ticket. But Kelley's candidacy still split the party.[65]

In the thick of the debate over immigration and slavery, Campbell, who had recently been described as a "brawling abolitionist," redrew the boundaries of the producing class to exclude African Americans. Barred (to his evident displeasure) from the assembly, and finding diminishing returns from his attempts to rally workers to his banner with *Theory of Equality*, he changed tack. His allies at the NIC had walked out after the admission of the black delegate Bowers, and in a letter copied to the negrophobic *New York Herald*, he explained to the congress why he backed them. His objections partly derived from racist pseudoscience. "The negro is inferior to the white," he argued, and any association between the two would act to the detriment of the latter. But he also pointed to tactical considerations. Admitting an African American would "array all the prejudices of ninety-nine hundredths of the whites against the cause of land reform," he insisted; and after twenty years of working to "emancipate labor," he refused to sacrifice his cause on the altar of racial equality when it had finally acquired "national importance." "It behooves us to act wisely," he concluded, "and not permit any element introduced among us which may either distract or divide us."[66]

Campbell was being disingenuous, for with nativism on the rise and his own Irish roots leaving him vulnerable, race was no longer a distraction for him but rather the foundation of his project for white working-class consolidation. He accused British abolitionists of trying to destroy the Union and argued their wealthy American allies turned a blind eye to wage slavery.[67] When the Philadelphia trades' assembly endorsed his stand against integration at the NIC, he must have taken heart, and over the summer of 1851, he cribbed together *Negro-mania*, a hastily edited compendium of ethnology inspired by the SIS debates on race. While the book veered wildly, Campbell tried to show that the only racial boundary that mattered lay between black and white. Chillingly, he concluded, Pennsylvania had to rid itself of its free people of color by "colonization or otherwise." Campbell, though, built his white supremacist ideology on the foundations of antebellum radicalism. For radicals like Lippard, the conviction that nonproducers lived off the fruits of others' labor had provided a bedrock for an emancipatory politics, but when Campbell made it bear the sophistry of racial science, he claimed that idle freedpeople would impose an impossible burden on white workers. He therefore exiled blacks beyond the borders of his producers' republic.[68]

But Campbell's project of class consolidation, which aimed to overcome the divide between Protestant and Catholic and unite white producers around threats from below as well as above, did not work.[69] The Trades' Assembly could not overcome the divisions between nativists and their critics, while Campbell's about-turn fractured radical unity. Surveying the wreckage, Elder (who Campbell had confronted at an abolitionist meeting) complained of the "frequent and flagrant apostacies from principle in the ranks of allies which the friends of Liberty relied upon with the greatest assurance." "In truth," he said of the immigrant working class, "it is the great problem of labor, its relations to capital, or the system of property, that occupies these people. Bring them a system of rights and remedies in this interest, and they will listen." For him, only a political movement that could unite the interests of black and white workers would win support, and three years later, he joined the new Republican Party, in which he became one of the strongest advocates of the "harmony of interests" doctrine in Philadelphia.[70] Over the course of the 1850s, indeed, figures like Elder came to embrace a different kind of class consolidation: not one that united a bourgeoisie or proletariat, but one that associated labor and capital.

*   *   *

Lippard did not join this movement himself. When radicalism splintered, he continued to build his Brotherhood and remained active in the national struggle for land reform, even as he lamented the "want of unity and organization" in the movement.[71] His consolidationist convictions had not faded. When the storm of counterrevolution and sectional strife rained down on Europe and America after 1848, Lippard sought shelter in association. Assailing the agitators who were trying to prize the republic apart, he praised the "Thirty United Nations" that made up his country as "a type of perfect Brotherhood," which would eventually embrace "not only the inhabitants of the American continent, but the vast Family of Man." "We love the Union," he proclaimed, and "there is not an evil now in existence, that cannot better be reformed *with* the Union, than *without* the Union." Lippard had no intention of compromising with slaveholders—"we abhor with the same hatred the White Slavery of the North, and the Black Slavery of the South," he declared—but for all its faults, his nation remained the last, best hope on Earth.[72]

Lippard's unionism transposed easily to the urban form. His writing on the metropolis may have emphasized its divisions—"Philadelphia is manifold," he once wrote—but he saw bonds of interdependence holding it together. Following the lead of the Consolidators who had demanded a union of the city and districts on the same night as the theater émeute, he too called for overriding the lines on the municipal map. Philadelphia needed "ONE City, under ONE government, and under ONE code of municipal laws," proclaimed *the Quaker City* in 1849. But it was not enough to redraw political boundaries. The metropolis required a thorough social reconstruction: it had to house its apprentices, reform its theaters, and purge sin from the "purlieus of the city." Moreover, voters must overthrow the "petty Oligarchy" of twenty or thirty families who held the reins of power, and restore control to good citizens.[73] To consolidate Philadelphia, then, Monk Hall had to be torn down, and a model republic erected on its ruins. His city, Union, and world awaited the redemptive labor of social reconstruction.

Lippard's call for metropolitan Consolidation appeared soon after the California House race riot of October 1849. A few weeks later, bourgeois Philadelphians—the only radical of note in attendance was Elder—met at the county courthouse to renew the cry for annexation.[74] Like Lippard, they had higher hopes for what Consolidation might achieve than their predecessors, who in meeting at the same spot in 1844 had made the restoration of order their goal. If they shared Lippard's concerns about unsupervised apprentices and corrupt politicians, though, they had a very different vision of what the city might become under a united government. Speakers at the meeting looked forward to rising rents and flourishing factories. Over the following years, as their cry for a new charter struggled to win support in Harrisburg, they embraced the growth politics Lippard despised, and promised that the union of city and districts would benefit worker as well as capitalist. In 1851, this would win them the backing of the short-lived Workingmen's Party, as their vision of association united Philadelphia across social as well as municipal borders.[75]

"Some day or other," Lippard had mused in 1849, "the people of Philadelphia, may wake up, and protect their throats and homes, by the passage and enforcement of wholesome laws. When that day arrives, we will duly notify our readers." He never got the chance. In 1851, he lost his daughter and wife in rapid succession, and haunted by his loss, he died on February 9, 1854. It turned out to be the last day of the old Quaker City, for the following morning, the governor signed into law a new charter that extended two-square–mile Philadelphia proper to the county line. As Philadelphians celebrated passage of the act, thousands came onto the streets to see Lippard interred at Odd Fellow's Cemetery.[76]

Lippard did not live to witness it, but he played a part in the city's Consolidation, for he provided Philadelphians with a lens to see their metropolis as a whole, which refracted urban experience in a very different way than that of bourgeois boosters. And his critique of the city survived him. While Kelley and Elder tried to build a more humane capitalism, others—like the printers—turned to pure and simple unionism, forming journeymen combinations that weathered the Panic of 1857. Some radicals continued to oppose the social order. Lippard's Yorkshire-born ally Shedden migrated via Marx's International Workingmen's Association to the Knights of Labor: a postbellum secret society, which took root in a Philadelphia soil fertilized by the Brotherhood of the Union. The principle of association Lippard and his friends extolled, meanwhile, found enduring expression in the land and building societies of the Civil War era, which promised to transform tenants into owners.

The radicals of the 1840s did not leave just an institutional legacy. Their cartography of the city and their warning of where it was tending compelled bourgeois Philadelphians to organize and respond. Lippard and his allies gave form to inchoate resistance against the emerging urban order, finding a way to link the experience of weavers in Kensington, coal-heavers on the Schuylkill, tenants in Moyamensing alleys, and mechanics in Spring Garden's factories. In their critique of the space and society of the new city, radicals lay the foundations for future battles over the course of metropolitan development. Debates over how the city should grow, look, and function could no longer leave out labor. Indeed, even by the mid-1840s, boosters in two of the city's most important sectors—railroads and real estate—were already striving to show that their manifestos for growth would scatter benefits across the whole metropolis. Metropolitan expansion, they argued, led to peace and prosperity for all, and not the urban apocalypse Lippard had foretold.

CHAPTER 3

"The Manifest Destiny of Philadelphia"

Making Antebellum Growth Politics

In December 1853, the *Commercial List* peered into the metropolitan future and foresaw a reorientation of the city's economy from east to west. The paper showed less interest than usual in the transatlantic commerce that had made the fortunes of early national merchants. Instead, it argued, a "great evolution" in the business of the city was underway, as "railroad arteries," extending "to all the extremities" of the Union, opened new markets for the city's manufacturers. "Over the continent westward, as well as the ocean eastward, trade finds abundant food for its most active and profitable life," the journal declared, and before long, millions in the Great West would turn to Philadelphia for their wants. "This," the *List* concluded, "is the manifest destiny of Philadelphia."[1]

Around midcentury, metaphors of empire migrated easily between nation and metropolis. As railroads annexed new markets for Philadelphia, the city prepared to annex new land. A few weeks after the *List*'s article appeared, the governor approved the act to consolidate the two-square-mile city proper with the outlying county, creating the biggest city in territorial terms in the nation. Within days of the charter's passage, the first locomotive crossed the Mountain Division of the Pennsylvania Railroad, binding Philadelphia to the Ohio Valley. By the end of the decade, the Pennsylvania Railroad had risen to the rank of the world's largest corporation. The associated power of city and railroad, boosters believed, would make their metropolis the beating heart of an imperial republic.[2]

Like other forms of empire-building around midcentury, though, the urban imperialism of railroad- and city-building reveals as much about their advocates' anxieties as their ambitions. Prophets of Manifest Destiny saw the West as a sanctuary for surplus labor, a safety valve for nervous slaveholders, and a citadel whose conquest would strengthen solidarities between whites in the North and South.[3] Similar consolidationist designs inspired local boosters. The urban crisis of the 1840s revealed a metropolis almost as divided as the nation. Economic malaise, recurrent rioting, and resurgent radicalism threatened to bring the bourgeois city to its knees. Seizing remote markets and incorporating the metropolitan frontier offered a fix.

This chapter explores the twisting route to social and spatial consolidation in the antebellum city by focusing on three agents of that process: the Pennsylvania Railroad, the municipal government, and the real estate market. Growth politics, I argue, was a public project in which antebellum boosters put in place the institutional and ideological props for rapid economic expansion.[4] Philadelphia's promoters equated stagnation with decay, and argued that rising population, production, and property values were the objects of wise municipal administration. This drew them into fierce debates as they sought to build corporate monopolies to advance metropolitan interests; extend, regulate, and sometimes unshackle markets; and ensure the security, improvement, and alienability of urban property. Their economic vision rested on recalibrating public power.

Realizing that vision required coalition-building. Many of Philadelphia's wealthiest merchants, manufacturers, and property owners worked together to a degree that surpassed anything that had occurred after the 1844 riots. For them growth politics offered the promise of ready markets for goods and rich returns from rental income and real estate. But growth eventually won over some radical critics of capitalism too, who came to believe that the association of capital and labor could obliterate inequality across the city. Such ambitions hinged on securing remote markets and nearby meadows: the terrain of urban empire builders.

Empire gave the growth coalition a language of legitimation, which obscured real conflict over political economy. Citizens speculated—with minds and money—on the city to come. But making that metropolis required borrowing on a scale that some Philadelphians baulked at. A city burdened with such a vast debt, they warned, was heading for ruin rather than riches. The advocates of debt-financed growth politics eventually defeated the doubters, built the Pennsylvania Railroad, and consolidated the city and county: a record of success that informed their approach to nation-building over the following years. Yet urban imperialism, like its national equivalent, also exposed fractures. With growth came growing pains that would require further innovations in city planning and political reform—the subject of the next two chapters—to resolve.

Railroads, Debt, and Destiny

As U.S. troops advanced into Mexico in 1846, Philadelphians planned their own conquest of the West, albeit using steam rather than arms. The iron bonds of the booster-backed Pennsylvania Railroad promised to bring the bounty of a vast national domain to Philadelphia's riot-torn streets. Capturing the continent would guarantee the peace and prosperity that had proven so elusive over the preceding years. But that prize, purchased by public debt, proved too costly for some.

Philadelphia may have stood on the Atlantic edge of an empire reaching toward the Pacific, but its citizens felt the force of "manifest destiny." The land grabs of the mid-1840s had divided the city. Wealthy citizens, mirroring their opposition to annexing the suburbs after the 1844 riots, questioned the wisdom of incorporating Catholics into a predominantly Protestant political community. In a republic, one journal argued in 1846, imperial expansion multiplied "masters" at the ballot-box, allowing men "unfit for self-government" to "control their conquerors." Yet even expansion's opponents believed the course of empire could not go backward. A good Quaker and Whig like Thomas Pym Cope, for instance, loathed military conquest, but assumed that "the Saxon race is destined at some period to spread all over North America." As president of both the Board of Trade and the Pennsylvania Railroad, Cope wanted to ensure Philadelphia reaped the commercial fruits of empire.[5]

Peering far into the future, boosters like Cope imagined the trade of a continent coursing through Philadelphia's streets. The dream was an old one, and attempts to improve communications with the West stretched back to the Early Republic, when Philadelphia had led the way in early improvements like turnpike roads. After the Erie Canal redirected trade to New York in the 1820s, wealthy members of the Pennsylvania Society for the Promotion of Internal Improvements lobbied legislators to build a network of canals and railroads to link Philadelphia to the Ohio Valley. But sectional compromises, political patronage, and transshipment costs made the Main Line, as it was known, an expensive error, and the state defaulted on its vast debt in 1842.[6] The fate of the State Works cast a long shadow over growth politics in the 1840s. Yet by the middle of the decade, the power of steam and the force of American arms reinvigorated boosters, as these tools of empire opened a continent to the possibility of easy communication. Years before Karl Marx used similar language, Philadelphians were talking about the railroad's "absolute annihilation of time and space."[7] Iron tracks blazed the trail for metropolitan empire.

Initially, though, the impetus for the Pennsylvania Railroad came less from the imperial designs of empire builders and more from the exertions of rival cities. In 1845, the directors of the Baltimore and Ohio Railroad applied for a right of way to Pittsburgh, where they would compete directly with the Main Line. Worried Philadelphian merchants urged representatives to reject the overtures of a "foreign" corporation in favor of their own route. After a series of meetings in the city between the fall and spring, state legislators reluctantly chartered the Pennsylvania Railroad, with the proviso that if its progress proved too slow, the right of way would revert to the Baltimore road.[8]

Even at this stage, boosters' ambitions extended beyond Pittsburgh. Promoters implied that their line was the natural channel down which the riches of the Great West would course. Like great rivers, the merchants claimed, the Pennsylvania would be nourished by "the wealth of a thousand tributaries," each carrying a "torrent" of trade toward Philadelphia. But despite an outpouring of maps and mileage charts to prove the contrary, there was nothing inevitable about Philadelphia's coming dominion. Rather, boosters' riparian metaphors marked attempts to naturalize what equated to a vast hydraulic project to engineer the flow of goods toward Philadelphia. Merchandise that might otherwise have gone to the Gulf, Chesapeake, or New York would instead cross the Appalachian ridge and enrich the Quaker City. The Pennsylvania, one paper declared in 1846, would be "the iron Mississippi of the unbounded commerce of the West."[9]

Boosters foresaw their artificial drainage basin eventually extending across the Pacific where the First Opium War (1839–1842) had opened China to western traders. Soon after the start of that conflict, Morton McMichael pictured a time when "the Pacific acknowledges our dominion," and the "national standard" stood "in the capital of the celestial empire." The Pennsylvania, one paper argued in 1846, would carry those imperial ambitions westward, helping the metropolis capture an Asian hinterland that stood as the "foundation of all empires." Boosters joined the national campaign for a transcontinental line well before their route to Pittsburgh was complete.[10]

The acquisition of new land, the opening of new markets, and the promise of new technology in the form of the iron horse therefore energized Philadelphia's promoters in the mid-1840s as they sought to turn their city into the central place between the Atlantic and Pacific. Supporters of the Pennsylvania promised citizens it would make the metropolis the "London of America."[11] But imperial reveries—spurred by civic rivalries, stoked by war in China and Mexico, and seemingly made possible by steam's annihilation of space—came at a cost. Just building a railroad to Pittsburgh required vast political and financial capital.

And it was capital that Philadelphians lacked. Chestnut Street's decline following the Panic of 1837 and the low esteem of state credit overseas after the Commonwealth defaulted on its Main Line debt made domestic and foreign investment hard to obtain. Merchants and manufacturers, moreover, had money tied up elsewhere. The spectacular failures of the depression years encouraged investors to pursue slow but steady returns over risky railroad stock, and when the books opened in June 1846, potential buyers stayed away. On just the second day of subscriptions, Cope confided that sales were proceeding too slowly. He struggled to persuade the directors of one of the city's biggest insurance companies to buy just a hundred shares in the venture.[12]

Though Cope's travails owed to what one historian calls "excruciatingly poor timing"—war with Mexico and the high price of iron discouraged investment—some observers blamed miserly behavior for Philadelphia's decline. Radicals could be especially damning. To George G. Foster, the "penny-wise and pound foolish" inaction of the "bourgeoisie" had cost Philadelphia trade with the South, the West, and Europe. But boosters too accused the economic elite of lacking "enterprise, industry, or activity." Railroad backers even questioned wealthy citizens' manliness when they asked whether they would allow the state to be "pinioned by the iron grip of her sisters." Neither the promise of western riches nor the slur to male honor, though, could raise the $2.5 million need to secure the right of way.[13]

Boosters were not just encountering another expression of a persistent privatist ethic. Instead, they ran into a recurrent problem of underinvestment in infrastructure that, while not necessarily remunerative in itself, provided a foundation for subsequent accumulation. The Pennsylvania did promise its stockholders a return, but after the Main Line debacle, plenty of wealthy Philadelphians doubted its capacity to deliver. One newspaper summed up the dilemma: "railroad, canals, and other avenues of trade" might not be "directly profitable" in every instance, it conceded, but "like the pavements before shop doors," they could turn a 1 percent return on capital into a 20 percent growth in business. That was all very well, but Philadelphia's business community had better places to invest than enterprises offering indirect rewards at some distant point in the future. David Harvey has argued that underinvestment can be overcome by a "functioning capital market" or strong state. But since the 1830s, Philadelphia could barely boast of the former, while the Commonwealth had been trying to get out of the transportation business after the Main Line default. The duty of financing a private corporation therefore fell on a public one: the city proper.[14]

When boosters called for a $2 million municipal investment at one of the first public meetings in favor of the road, they were following in the footsteps of mercantilist monarchies and republics. This they well understood: one supporter of the subscription compared Philadelphia proper's policy to the towns of medieval Italy and the ports of the Hanseatic League, where municipal governments primarily concerned themselves "with the security of *trade*" beyond "the limits of their communities." Though the American revolutionaries set themselves against chartered monopolies, the states of the new republic localized mercantilism, vying with neighbors to improve their balance of trade. State-owned works like the Erie Canal and Main Line were well-established weapons in the mercantilist armory. The Pennsylvania, though, was a private corporation with the power to ask for public funds. For railroad boosters, this "mixed enterprise" offered the appealing combination of government funding without democratic oversight; in contemporary terms, the incorporators privatized profit and socialized risk.[15]

In urging the city government to commit wholeheartedly to urban imperialism, railroad boosters equated Philadelphia's growth with the common good. But the debate over municipal funding revealed similar divisions in the bourgeoisie to the struggle over municipal union in the period from 1844 to 1845. Indeed, no issue in the era, including the Consolidation of the city and county itself, provoked such a flurry of activity among Philadelphia's bourgeoisie than the "railroad subscription." Those for and against the purchase agreed no more important matter had ever come before the municipal government. On its resolution, a citizen wrote, hinged nothing less than the "fate of our beloved city."[16]

The threat from the Baltimore and Ohio had initially drawn the economic elite closer together. Board of Trade merchants, led by Cope, headed the movement to stave off the right of way. Joining them were lawyers, among them the future architect of Consolidation Eli Kirk Price and the nationally renowned Horace Binney, and a smaller number of manufacturers, including the locomotive builder Matthias W. Baldwin. Despite the febrile atmosphere of the Second Party System, partisan divisions mattered little. Whig backers included a vice-presidential nominee, a sitting congressman, and a future secretary of the treasury; Democrats could count a veteran of Jackson's cabinet, Martin Van Buren's attorney general, and a post-Consolidation mayor.[17]

The subscription question, though, soon divided them. Few questioned the railroad's value to the city, but many doubted the wisdom of risking public credit on the venture. Commercial interests embraced the mercantilist logic of urban imperialism; it behooved the city, they argued, to improve its balance of trade by annexing a larger hinterland. Industrialists, who were outnumbered by merchants by about three to one in the campaign to build the road, were less convinced. Textile bosses placed coastwise trade with the South ahead of overland connections to the West. Factory owners already had the Schuylkill Navigation and Reading Railroad to ship coal. The strongest support for the subscription among manufacturers came from engine builders and iron manufacturers who were on good terms with wealthy merchants and eager to benefit from the business the enterprise would bring.[18] Samuel Vaughan Merrick, a well-connected Southwark foundry owner and benevolent reformer, served as the Pennsylvania's first president; while another iron founder, Stephen Colwell, sat on the board. The divide over the subscription, though, owed less to tensions between merchant and industrial capital, and more to concern over two bourgeois preoccupations: property and debt.

The struggle over capitalizing the Pennsylvania in 1846 pitted rival ideas of how cities grew against one another. Critics of municipal funding argued it would destroy Philadelphia proper's prosperity and redistribute power and wealth to the suburbs. In a realigned political and economic geography, a ravaged center would be left at the mercy of its colonies. Boosters, in contrast, portrayed trade as a Nile flood inundating the whole metropolis and nourishing urban growth.[19]

Opponents of the subscription, pointing to the cautionary tale of the state's default on its Main Line debt, argued only sound public credit could stimulate Philadelphia's development. Over the past two decades, the city government had steered away from the spendthrift ways of the state. The total funded debt of the city stood at roughly $1.7 million—$300,000 less than the proposed subscription—which had gone toward extending the waterworks, improving the port, and meeting everyday obligations. Since 1839, though, parsimonious councilmen had barely borrowed a dime, and in uncertain times, the "precious jewels" of city loans proved a secure investment for citizens like Binney. Unlike heavily discounted state debt, these traded at par or above at the Philadelphia Exchange. Fears that civic unrest would lower their price almost certainly emboldened the wealthy citizens in the 1844 riots, who, with Binney at the forefront, vindicated the use of troops. But two years later, growth politics threatened to finish off what the mob had begun, for if the Pennsylvania struggled like the Main Line, the city's paper would be as devalued as the state's.[20]

Damage to the public credit, moreover, threatened property—another favorite bourgeois investment. Even if the municipal authorities honored their obligations, doubters warned, they could only do so through increasing tax on real estate. This prospect terrified landholders, who already blamed "oppressive taxation" for depressed prices in the districts. If the city proper needed to raise revenue to pay its railroad debt, opponents of the subscription argued, then values would collapse as capital fled.[21]

Spiraling debt and taxes threatened to bring about what so many bourgeois citizens had feared in 1844 to 1845: a union of the city and districts. The city, lacking the capacity of a national state to inflate its way out of trouble through increasing the money supply, would be forced instead to extend its revenue base by annexing territory. When riots sparked calls for metropolitan Consolidation in 1844, opponents warned of amalgamating indebted suburbs with the prudent center. But the railroad loan threatened to invert the debt ratio, so that if Consolidators tried again, it would not be "possible that a defence can be made successfully against them." Enemies of the subscription therefore tied their rejection of public funding to the ongoing fight against municipal annexation. If the city borrowed the money, a writer (probably Binney) argued, the "only obstacle" to the "extinction of our corporate existence" would be the "unwillingness of the districts or the county to receive us into a connexion with them."[22] Public funding for the Pennsylvania would not build up an imperial metropolis; rather, it would prostrate the civilized center before its barbarous frontier.

Even without Consolidation, though, the municipal subscription threatened to redistribute economic power from core to periphery. Building the
railroad with city money, critics charged, would drain wealth from the center. Opponents of the subscription pointed out that Pennsylvania trains
would terminate outside the city proper. A few years earlier, the completion
of the Reading Railroad's depot in the independent suburb of Richmond
siphoned the coal trade away from the Schuylkill wharves, where property
quickly depreciated. Despite Philadelphia capital bankrolling the venture,
the Reading left one part of the city proper in a "deserted condition," while
turning a distant district into a hive of "bustling activity." The Pennsylvania
threatened a more radical redistribution of metropolitan wealth. "Who can
tell," asked one citizen, "where this new and immense Corporation will
carry the business which it is to create?" Skeptics accused boosters of calling
Philadelphia by an "ambiguous name," and blithely ignoring that "future
growth" would take place beyond its two-square–mile limits. Before long,
the citizen predicted, a neighboring suburb would boast "the great mass"
of the merchant community. Imprudent investment would enable the city's
colonies to lord it over the once great center.[23]

To allay fears of political and economic ruin, boosters began to codify a
cluster of ideas about growth and government, which would shape the city's
development for the next decade. At the heart of their case lay the alchemical
power of debt. The Pennsylvania, they reasoned, could not be built with the
capital of Philadelphians alone, but needed conjuring into being with municipal credit. At a cost of 6 percent annual interest, the city could create a
corporation to scatter wealth across the metropolis. As real estate rose subse-
quently, tax revenue would increase with it, leaving the city well-placed to
pay creditors without financial embarrassment. Proponents of debt-financing
preferred to look far into the future, for what seemed like a vast burden in
1846 would be reduced to miniscule proportions if urban growth continued
its frenetic pace. Yet that growth was contingent on securing western riches:
without that trade, ruination would soon follow. "Philadelphia has not only
much to hope from this improvement," Cope wrote on behalf of the Pennsylvania, "but more to fear from its abandonment." Boosters therefore drew
very different lessons from the lean years that followed the Panic of 1837.
Rather than reading recent history as a warning of the consequences of
extravagance, they saw it as evidence of the dangers of standing still.[24]

Like opponents of the subscription, boosters were probing here the relationship between debt and property, but they arrived at very different

conclusions. As the Pennsylvania annihilated distance between the city and its markets, they argued, it would spread metropolitan development ever further outward. The subscription's supporters stressed that such growth stood to benefit property as well as commerce. From the first meeting in late 1845, indeed, the case for Philadelphia's route to the West rested in part on the nourishing impact an imperial torrent of trade would have on real estate values. As people and commodities coursed through streets fertilized by the railroad, property would shoot upward at a miraculous pace, with boosters commonly predicting a doubling of assessments in a decade.[25] Rich harvests of rent and taxes would soon dwarf the enlarged debt. Even the "most indifferent" observer, the *North American* argued, had to be aware of the "rise which must take place in the value of Philadelphia property when this great artery leads the wealth of the West to our doors."[26] If the railroad was cast as a river, the city's streets became its irrigation canals.

Failure to subscribe, on the other hand, would leave the city barren as its rivals reaped the harvest of manifest destiny. The danger of growth going into reverse played as much a role in arguments for the subscription, as it did in the case against it. Picturing a metropolis without the railroad, boosters foresaw streets lined with empty lots, warehouses, and factories: Philadelphia as a "Lilliputian village" rather than the "London of America." Denying the city the life blood of trade would arrest the circulation of capital in the real estate market. Without the Pennsylvania, the merchant and manufacturer David S. Brown counseled, property would fall "to an extent which the boldest among us would hesitate to predict." As "the comparative depopulation" of the city reduced Philadelphia to "utter ruin," real estate owners would be left behind to mourn a metropolis laid waste as much by the lethargy of its own citizens as the enterprise of its rivals. "Empty houses," "vacant stores," and "grass-grown wharves" would be all that remained as a proud mart sank "to the sad state of a decaying provincial town." "The declension and ruin of cities is nothing new in the history of the world," the *North American* reminded "owners of Real Estate." Boosters' prophecy of civic decline may have been less spectacular than the urban apocalypse in George Lippard's 1844 radical novel *The Quaker City*, but they too warned of a city sinking into the ground without urgent action.[27]

By doing so, railroad promoters turned the question of the municipal subscription into a referendum on the city's future. They narrowly won: enough citizens were persuaded by portentous talk of greatness and ruin to push funding for the Pennsylvania through. After the city proper's councils failed to act, boosters broke free from the Whigs and Democrats to nominate their own ticket in the 1846 municipal elections, while Binney organized an antisubscription slate. The Pennsylvania's backers failed to secure an outright victory, but after several months of legal and political wrangling, the city proper purchased the stock. Over the next few years, the municipal investment grew to $5 million, which by 1851, amounted to nearly two-thirds of Philadelphia's debt. The subscription made the city proper the biggest shareholder in what would quickly become the world's largest private corporation. And in the eyes of many citizens, at least, it made the Pennsylvania Railroad a public servant.[28]

Selling Philadelphia

Railroad boosters promised the Pennsylvania would be the "making of Philadelphia." Just as the Declaration of Independence had "emancipated" the colonies from economic fetters, the corporation would free the city to grow.[29] Prosperity would soon take physical form in mansions, stores, and warehouses. But the fierce debates over the subscription's impact on land and debt revealed that such confidence was by no means universal. Bourgeois citizens, scarred by the long depression, tended to see real estate in a similar vein to municipal bonds, casting it as a prudent place to secure their wealth, and not the dynamic route to riches promised by so many railroad backers. Binney's conservative course made sense to them.

Critics often blamed the hoarding tendencies of Philadelphia's large property owners for impeding the flow of investment. Wealthy landowners, radicals complained, were "too fond of investing in suburban farms, and leaving them to descendants as city property," which tended to lock capital up in "unproductive darkness." But boosters also blamed property for stagnation. The *Commercial List* compared the city's real estate owners to the French Bourbons swept away by the revolution. Even Cope's son-in-law Job R. Tyson bemoaned the "immobility" of landed wealth; by giving "stability to fortunes," he argued, "it stops the currency of capital."[30]

Yet to exclude hoarding landowners from a dynamic bourgeoisie, as the likes of Tyson were wont to do, is not altogether fair. Admittedly, many of the great colonial estates on the outskirts of Philadelphia persisted well into the nineteenth century, and a list of the city's wealthiest residents compiled in 1846 contained plenty of heirs enjoying "horses, dogs and hunting" on the property that had fallen into their laps. But many of the city's businessmen invested heavily in real estate too. Take for example, Richard D. Wood, a dry goods merchant, Pennsylvania Railroad director, and investor in coal and iron. In the years before the Civil War, Wood bought city lots and suburban property, until his portfolio extended from the downtown to the distant suburb of Germantown. By 1868, George Cadwalader—commander of the state militia in the 1844 riots—owned property in thirteen wards across the county. Supporters of railroad-building, among them the Consolidator Eli Kirk Price and druggist George Carpenter, poured money into suburban tracts, while others, including another druggist David Jayne, bought in the city proper. Industrialists, when they had the cash to do so, also purchased real estate.[31]

Boosters did not condemn such investors but celebrated their heroism. Carpenter, with four hundred houses and a seat on the Pennsylvania's board to his name, was eulogized for giving "impetus" to Germantown's development, while a biographer insisted "no man of the present generation" rivaled Jayne—who developed several lots on fashionable Chestnut Street—as "an improver of the city." Both appeared among a list of Philadelphia's twenty-five millionaires in 1857; less prosperous peers mimicked their strategy on a smaller scale. Merchants, manufacturers, and professionals therefore found they had overlapping interests as owners and rentiers. It drew them to public and private schemes to raise real estate values.[32]

Investors' tendency to spread their assets over the county lessened the force of the antisubscription argument in 1846 that free rider suburbs stood to gain most from the city proper's railroad-building. The burden of additional taxation in the center, owners reasoned, would have been more than offset by rising property in outlying areas. Thus, just as riot, disease, and industry brought the suburbs into the metropolitan community, so too did real estate speculation. Like factory owners, the interests of real estate owners often crossed district boundaries.

Around the time of the subscription debate, then, real estate had begun to shake off its conservative reputation. As property began to augment appreciably over the following years, that process continued. By Consolidation, McMichael's *North American* could plausibly argue, construction had become the "most extensive and important" enterprise in the city. Boosters attributed the turnaround to the building of the Pennsylvania Railroad. The "empty houses" of 1846, they claimed, were now occupied thanks to the bounty of western commerce; only new facilities for "trade and travel" that poured "into our limits the profusion of the earth and the workshop" could explain the boom.[33] But Philadelphia's demographic growth, and an economic boom driven by California gold, had much to do with the resurgence in property too. Whatever the causes, the period of sustained expansion from the mid to late 1840s until 1854 left its mark on urban politics and space.

Bourgeois Philadelphians marveled at the creative destruction of the built environment. "Old edifices are in process of demolition in every direction," reported the *Commercial List* in 1854, giving way to "stores and dwellings of the most elegant manner." As spiraling land values uprooted residents from the commercial downtown, commentators wondered whether the entire city east of Broad might be given over to business. Commercial papers frowned on the unproductive use of real estate. Boosters, for all their hymning of nature's virtues, celebrated the conversion of meadows into lots. The "march of improvement" sweeping across the city proper led McMichael's daily to foresee a time a "few years hence" when the "landmarks of our fathers will be entirely obliterated," but even new buildings were sometimes swept away as investors sought to maximize returns. To the *North American*, all this revealed how the "rebuilding of a great city is a never ceasing work," one that in the paper's own metropolis meant "we tear away ruthlessly, and we build up desperately." By the end of the antebellum era, then, real estate no longer seemed so reactionary. Instead, it came to be celebrated as a symbol of capitalist dynamism. "Society is inevitably, irreversibly democratic and revolutionary," Philadelphia's most haughtily conservative journal concluded. "It must demolish something. If it be not a dynasty, or a corrupt institution, it will be a house."[34]

Though such pronouncements cloaked the real estate market with almost supernatural powers, boosters encouraged bourgeois Philadelphians to adopt a calculating attitude to property, urging them to discern the patterns that lurked behind the drama of knocking down and building up. Investors believed sorting and sifting would turn land to its highest and best use, and the beginnings of the functional specialization Samuel Bass Warner Jr. noticed in the midcentury metropolis seem to bear out the claim that the market was doing its work. Here, the city became the product of thousands of decisions: a landscape molded by market logic rather than conscious manipulation.[35]

That market was no metaphysical force, however, but a product of human hands. Reading its rules and reforming its operations became an

obsession in the antebellum city. To fuel reconstruction, boosters looked to
make the city easier to buy and sell. Mapmakers like J. C. Sydney helped
speculators and builders locate suitable tracts. Newspapers reported on new
structures, estate sales, and suburban developments. The press too strove
to trace the patterns that underlay property transactions in detailed taxo-
nomies of the real estate economy. Access to information—so important to
merchant capitalists—also mattered to landowners in a metropolis too big
to know informally.[36]

Where private initiative struggled to provide market knowledge,
though, boosters turned to government. Philadelphia's grid seemingly
made property easy to parcel out. Like the Northwest Ordinance, which
flattened the West into square blocks, or the New York Commissioner's
Plan, which did the same for uptown Manhattan, the street plan reduced
nature to a series of uniform rectangles. Space here became easier to con-
ceive as an abstract commodity. Armed with a map and a newspaper, a
speculator could buy up lots he had never seen. But closer up, Philadelphia's grid was less transparent than it appeared on paper. The numbering and naming of streets particularly irritated boosters. A lack of
coordination among public authorities and private developers meant that
by 1850 George Washington had given his name to eleven different streets
and almost fifty courts and alleys. House numbering too lacked all
the sense of system the grid implied. Identical addresses stood hundreds
of yards apart; one block ran inward from either end with duplicate
numbers.[37]

Inscrutability threatened growth. "All classes of citizens engaged in
business," McMichael's paper declared in 1853, "must experience the absolute need of a remedy." Reformers therefore sought to make the city into a
more legible marketplace: one in which people, goods, and property could
circulate without intimate local knowledge. Some of their recommenda-
tions, like renaming north to south streets in the western half of the city
proper, were implemented by the local authorities before 1854. Others,
including the eradication of duplicate street names (the ordinance specified
960 changes) and the systematic renumbering of properties, became part of
the program of "practical consolidation" afterward. A few—notably designs
to rename streets running between the rivers as numbered or lettered
avenues—were never adopted, despite support from booster papers. Such
proposals, which rested on the regulatory power of the local state, promised
to realize the commercial potential of the grid.[38]

Real estate reformers looked for ways to level other obstacles to the
circulation of capital in the built environment. Changes to institutional
practice brought land into line with different securities and made it easier
to buy and sell. Evening sales at one of the big auction houses shifted in
1859 to working hours. The new time, McMichael's paper argued, would
help those who "feel disposed to speculate," with real estate, after all, "being
an investment, like stocks or bonds." Daytime sales at the Merchants'
Exchange also put buyers in contact with the mortgagees who financed
their investments, the architects who designed them, and the builders who
procured them labor. The measure promised to "concentrate the real estate
business" and "control and direct its tendencies." Most investment
remained small-scale, as buyers picked up a house here or a lot there, but
property—like transportation—was becoming a sphere of the economy
that needed institutions capable of consolidating capital and labor.[39]

Meanwhile, boosters looked to shake off legal shackles on property, emancipating market forces to do their work. The most important
real estate reformer of his day—and not coincidentally the "father of
Consolidation"—was Eli Kirk Price. Born in 1798 to a Quaker family in
nearby Chester, Price came to Philadelphia as a young man to work for
Cope's merchant house. With foreign trade waning, however, he moved
into law, where he studied under John Sergeant, the Whig vice-presidential
candidate in 1832. His ties to two of the city's leading boosters probably
drew him to growth politics, and either side of midcentury, he and his
brother backed railroad-building. Price opposed the expansion of the
American empire in the 1840s, yet talked up the city's imperial prospects.
But it was his skill in navigating the terrain of real estate law that brought
him into regular contact with the economic elite. Heirs of colonial estates,
Board of Trade boosters, and upstart manufacturers all trusted Price to
handle their transactions. With thousands of titles passing through his
hands, he could cast his eye over the metropolitan real estate in its entirety,
and he put his knowledge to good use as an investor. Along with his
brother—the surveyor in the flourishing district of Spring Garden—Price
purchased city lots, developed suburban property, and established the
romantic Woodlands Cemetery near his land on the far side of the Schuylkill. By 1870, he owned real estate to the present-day value of about $7.25
million, placing him among the largest speculators in the city.[40]

His private interests, though, are hard to disentangle from his public
commitment to modernization. "The law must be progressive," Price

wrote, "as the world is progressive." He shared with his friend McMichael a belief in the interdependence of the big city and used public and private power to push for reform. To call him a classical liberal would be misleading—he had few problems defending mercantilist urban imperialism and supported a strong local state—but his admiration for another Quaker, the English Corn Law repealer John Bright, is telling. For what a free market in corn was to Bright, a free market in land was to Price, and he aimed to bring real estate law up to speed in an era "driven forward by the impulses of steam and the electric telegraph."[41]

Price saw property rights as the foundation of a humane republic. His reform agenda here took him from feminist politics to the frontier. As a legislator, he strengthened Pennsylvania's married women's property laws, granting wives a measure of economic autonomy from alcoholic husbands. Horrified meanwhile by the "heavy and grievous national sin" perpetrated on Native Americans, he helped to establish the Philadelphia Indian Aid Society, through which he aimed to prepare them "for the individual ownership of their lands" and secure their "legal title to the soil." Once they were "secure proprietors," Price argued, "they will become part and parcel of the American people."[42]

But Price believed that even everyday real estate law needed Americanizing. At midcentury, Pennsylvania's property laws still bore what one journal called "some tincture of the feudal system." Tracts encumbered by entailments and trusts proved hard to break up without special legislation. On the outskirts of Philadelphia, where the large estates of William Penn's original colonists often remained intact, this blocked development. Property, Price remembered years later, "remained long unimproved;" "vacant ground and dilapidated buildings," as a friend put it, were often "out of the market and unproductive." Real estate in American society, Price protested, could not tolerate such "obstruction and stagnation." It had to be easily convertible into money. Charged by the governor to seek a remedy, he drafted a new law, which came into effect in 1853 and granted courts power to dissolve entails.[43]

In his own estimation, Price transformed real estate from a remnant of the "feudal system" into an asset entirely in keeping with the "policy of a Republic." His commentary on the bill, written in the early 1870s, began with the Norman Conquest of England, and ended with an attack on Paris's Communards as "enemies of mankind." Somewhere between feudalism and communism, though, stood a policy fit for the commercial United

States. The *Public Ledger* later claimed the measure had transformed "dead capital . . . into living, growing, interest-bearing fortune," while Price's student, the future U.S. Attorney General Benjamin Harris Brewster, argued the reform had "unfettered" the money locked up in land to beautify cities, raise revenue, and circulate "into the world's commerce." Like the renaming of streets and the changes to auctioneering, his act cleared the way for Philadelphia's creative destruction, ensuring that the tribute coursing its way into the city along the lines of the Pennsylvania Railroad would flow—as boosters in 1846 had promised—through the property market.[44]

Radical Growth Politics

Price may have believed his act brought real estate into line with the principles of 1776, but he was not alone in claiming a revolutionary lineage for property reforms. Radical critics of the city's economic order also saw feudalism at work in the metropolis. For them, though, growth was not a panacea, but a process in which aristocratic speculators like Price strengthened their grip on the fruits of producers' labor. Boosters countered by claiming that rapid economic development would enrich the community as a whole rather than concentrating wealth in the "upper tenth." Philadelphia, they argued, was not veering in the direction of Lippard's dystopian *The Quaker City*, but marching toward a future in which capital and labor associated for the good of both.

Selling growth politics to working-class citizens hostile to concentrations of wealth and power was not easy around midcentury. During the Bank War, the city's journeymen and laborers had often sided with President Andrew Jackson against the "monster" of Chestnut Street. The bankruptcies and hardship that followed the Panic of 1837 hardened anti-corporate ideology. Monopolies, critics charged, were conspiracies for redistributing wealth and power upward, not associations that worked to the good of all. Booster pleas for cooperation here ran into a radical interpretation of the labor theory of value. In "an age of capital," a craft union supporter had argued in the 1830s, "no man can become rich, without making another one poor." Lippard revealed his disdain for growth politics the following decade. For him, the "trophies of enterprise" and "telegraphs that annihilate space" did nothing to elevate "the little children, in rags and naked feet, sweeping the crossings of the street." When, in Lippard's *Quaker City*, Devil Bug's dream carries him forward to 1950, Philadelphia's "liberal mob" praises the "monopolist" for giving "labor to the poor," before meeting its fate in the fires of an urban apocalypse.[45]

Railroads' enormous size made them particularly dangerous. In the battle over the municipal subscription, even a Whig state senator tried to rouse opposition to city funding of the road by comparing the corporation to the Second National Bank. A few years later, politicians rallied voters to the polls to fight the "CENTRAL RAILROAD CLIQUE" in its attempt to "RULE THE CITY!" Lippard satirized plans for a route to the Pacific in the late 1840s by imagining an everyman offering to build the line in exchange for tens of thousands of square miles of the public domain: a way of funding the project that many bourgeois Philadelphians supported. He joined the future First Internationalist John Shedden in opposing a scheme that threatened to "plant the germ of tyranny" on American shores. Such concerns were not without reason: corporations, after all, deliberately shielded economic power from democratic control.[46]

Perhaps the biggest monster for radicals lay in land monopoly. All wealth, radicals agreed, came originally from labor and land. The capacity of capital to dominate one or the other therefore presented a political as well as an economic problem. As William Elder put it, "landlordism and monopoly of wealth" in a free labor society "converts those who were once serfs, through the process of emancipation and wages slavery, into public paupers." After "free toilers" had "converted the wilderness into a garden" and "covered the land with palaces," they were left to "perish in their poverty." Frontier land might for a time elevate the American worker above his European counterpart, but once the national domain had been parceled out, the United States could expect a repeat of the revolutionary violence that plagued the Old World.[47]

Elder, like other radicals, saw the solution in land reform rather than in liberalizing markets. By midcentury, the cry for free homesteads in the West had become a mass movement. The National Reform Association (NRA), which organized petition drives and industrial congresses, enjoyed wide support among Philadelphia's radicals. Alongside the local branch of the NRA, several organizations embraced the cause, including John Campbell's Social Improvement Society, Elder's Union of Associationists, the German Union of Working Men, the Ten Hour Association, the Real Estate Association, and the midcentury trades' assembly of thirty craft unions. Lippard's

Brotherhood of the Union declared the universal right to "Life, Liberty, Land and Home."[48]

Land reform ran through radicals' designs for a social republic. Real estate's upward trajectory around midcentury may have benefited speculators and rentiers, but it did little for working-class tenants. Rising rents may help to explain a rise in internal migration from richer to poorer neighborhoods in the 1850s. This was something radicals sometimes seized on when depicting a city divided spatially as well as socially into an "upper tenth" and "lower million." Capitalists' monopoly on the best land, they argued, drove labor to seek shelter in the warren of lanes that ran off the grid. "All the dwellings in our country are erected by stone masons, bricklayers, carpenters" and other laborers, wrote a mechanic in 1849, but "the capitalists say, in practice, they themselves only shall have good houses" on "wide streets."[49]

By juxtaposing the "dirty, narrow court" of the "working man" with the "beautiful, airy building" of the capitalist, radicals warned that urban growth without social reconstruction would only increase inequality. Land reform offered respite from the upward pressure on rent in the same way that craft unions offered relief from downward pressure on wages. Where boosters imagined the city as the heart of an empire, indeed, land reformers imagined the empire as an escape from the city. When Lippard founded his revolutionary Brotherhood of the Union in 1849, he barred new circles from forming in large towns on account of their *corrupting influence.* Arcadian dreams of enjoying the "free air of heaven" and "the well stocked barn" seemed more likely to come true as the NRA's support expanded with the national domain. On far-off homesteads, no "factory tyrant" or "landed aristocrat" could deprive the producer of "the fruits of his industry." Property was not something to be traded for profit, land reformers claimed, but the foundation of a republic of small proprietors. Their West of yeoman farmers stood starkly opposed to the city of wealthy speculators.[50]

Like Price, then, radicals cast themselves as modern crusaders against feudalism, though for them the shackles that needed loosening fastened on producers rather than the market. Turning to the city, Lippard called the relationship "of the Tenant to the Landlord" a "ragged patch of the Dark Ages," for "the man who rents a house," he argued, "is still the vassal of the Man who owns it." He urged citizens to combine "in a form that will tell upon the Land Lord's pocket" and fight the law that gave owners a lien over their renters' belongings. "By one unanimous impulse," Lippard hoped his proposed reform would become "*the* popular question of the day." There is little indication in the papers as to whether his call for mass meetings came to anything, but a few weeks later, state legislators passed a new tenant law, which exempted $300 of personal property from seizure for rent arrears. The battle was a minor skirmish in a series of struggles for tenants' rights across the antebellum North, and the critique of the real estate market's tendency to monopoly outlived the fracturing of radicalism after 1850. In the Panic of 1857 and the Civil War, unemployed laborers and craft unionists found common cause as renters. Philadelphia's workers' shared experience as tenants had the potential to overcome divisions.[51]

Advocates of growth politics therefore needed to convince working-class Philadelphians that new concentrations of economic power could work for them. While the debate over the municipal subscription to the Pennsylvania Railroad in 1846 hinged on bourgeois preoccupations over property, debt, and tax, boosters also stressed the work that would come to the "laboring man." They could hardly have said otherwise. The Pennsylvania, after all, was a private corporation chartered to pursue a public good, and councils elected on the basis of white male suffrage would judge its plea for municipal funding. But in the troubled times of the 1840s, the promise that growth would bring peace and prosperity to the city was more than a rhetorical obligation. Advocates of growth politics linked surplus labor and social order. "We shall not be troubled by riots," one Pennsylvania backer wrote in 1846, "if our young men are profitably employed."[52]

That employment would come in part through an invigorated property market. The Pennsylvania, one booster wrote, would "enable the builder to take up lots and build houses." This was no small consideration, given about a fifth of the city's craftsmen were tied to the building trades. Boosters who recognized the danger of unemployed or underemployed labor called for public stimulus of construction before the building of the Pennsylvania. In 1838, Price helped lead an unsuccessful campaign to turn the "barren wastes" around Broad and Market into the site of a new city hall, in a project supporters claimed would preserve "mechanics and laborers from want." Before long, the plans had won the backing of unemployed workingmen, who, in an astute appropriation of booster rhetoric, talked of the land soon holding "the boundless resources of the expanding west." Capital could occupy labor and build up the city.[53]

Such growth, boosters insisted, harmonized the interests of labor and capital. Rather than multiplying inequality, as radicals often charged, economic expansion would scatter benefits liberally across the city. By 1853, boosters could even tie municipal subscriptions to access to housing: more railroads would mean more homes for working-class Philadelphians. Some workingmen appear to have responded to the message. Nearly 10 percent of the citizens appointed in late 1846 to solicit subscriptions for the Pennsylvania worked in manual trades. The purchase of a few shares by a handful of mechanics, meanwhile, showed one newspaper how all the laborers "engaged in the industrial pursuits" identified the cause of the railroad "as their own." A General Trades' Union (GTU) veteran later said the city's workingmen had come forward first to support the road while the propertied held back.[54]

When it came to building railroads, such investment mattered most for its symbolic value, but in the metropolitan property market, the mobilization of small capital counted a great deal. State law allowed owners to convey land in fee simple subject to an annual ground rent. The system at first glance looks like another feudal remnant. Even a booster newspaper called ground rent "an ancient seigniorial interest," and legislators prohibited the creation of perpetual entailments in 1850. Yet as historians have shown, rent charges were bought and sold like other securities, and by reducing the price of land to an annual charge (typically 6 percent of the principal), it lowered capital costs for craftsmen while freeing money that might have gone into mortgages to circulate elsewhere. Builders would then reap the rewards of what one paper called the "*living* value" of improvements erected on the property, while the ground rent–lord received an annuity for the "dead value" of the tract. Moreover, ground rent kept the cost of housing down, giving a necessary boost to Philadelphia's reputation as a "city of homes." Radicals accused the speculative land market of stirring social conflict, but for the *North American*, real estate provided a recipe for consensus. "On this ground," it wrote of urban property in 1858, "the extremes of society meet, for while it is occupied by the humblest, it is the peculiar safety of persons of large fortunes."[55]

By the 1850s, boosters were trying to draw working-class Philadelphians into a speculative real estate market through suburban land associations, which distributed small plots of land in far-flung corners of the outlying districts and townships to shareholders. The ventures broadened the base of growth politics by bringing together "men of means" with journeymen investors. About half the stockholders in the Walnut Street Land Company appear to have come from manual trades. Indeed, the companies, one observer noted, were "extensively patronized by the working classes."[56]

In the boom times of the early 1850s, the associations taught these expectant entrepreneurs how to profit from property. Promotional literature cultivated a calculating capitalist ethic; one pamphlet even cast Benjamin Franklin's petty bourgeois hero Poor Richard as the stockholder's spiritual ancestor.[57] Companies talked up the prospects of getting rich quick and promised three- or fourfold returns in a matter of years. By the mid-1850s, land association shares traded alongside other forms of equity at the Philadelphia Exchange.[58]

Yet the companies borrowed from the rhetoric of land reform as well as property speculation. Beneath their boosterish pronouncements lay the same producerist principles that animated the likes of Lippard and Campbell. The associations, a radical paper insisted, gave the "laboring portion of the community" a chance to rival the "knaves 'who neither work nor spin.'" Here, the fruits of suburban expansion would not simply accrue to large landowners like Price, but would be shared among investors of moderate means. One of the most active figures in the organizations was the young Ignatius Donnelly, who would take his experience in the companies with him to the West, where he became a prominent Populist, a leader of the last great republican movement of the nineteenth century. The producerism that later animated the Populist insurgency tempered land association's speculative ethos. "Every man," one association contended, is "entitled to the exclusive property on which he expends his own labor."[59]

But if each land company lot served as a saving fund for dead labor, it also offered the foundation for a future home. Indeed, the associations offered a path to homeownership in a city that many feared stood on the verge of a housing crisis. Companies promised to speed a suburban exodus; one boasted that it sought "the extension of homesteads to all classes." Through association, then, they offered to free the "inmates" of rented properties to enjoy "the fresh and invigorating air of heaven." Like Lippard's Brotherhood of the Union they sought to replace the "pestilential nooks of great cities" with "the Homesteads of a Free People." Their remedy to the radical critique of the "crowded court" and "unwholesome alley," though, rested on associated enterprise rather than on land reform.[60]

Although few of them offered anything approaching the promised returns, and most proved too far from the built-up city for working-class suburbs to develop, their success in attracting investors suggests just how widespread ideas about the dynamism of Philadelphia's real estate market had become. Over the following years opening working-class opportunities for property ownership would become an object of public policy for both municipal and federal governments.[61]

The support radical journals offered speculative real estate companies hints at the appeal of growth politics. When radicals split around 1850, some influential critics of capitalism came to see the association of capital and labor, rather than the struggle of one against the other, as the best path to social progress. Their vision of full employment, high wages, and widely diffused property ownership mirrored on a metropolitan scale the Republican Party's national political economy.

Growth politics did offer working people real economic opportunities. One of Campbell's last attempts to rally striking workers in 1851 came to naught when William J. Mullen—the founder of the Moyamensing Workhouse—promised to help the audience find work on the Pennsylvania Railroad or State Works. Mullen, a former craft unionist and leader of the Workingmen's Party, had few political connections to secure patronage, but knew the first president of the Pennsylvania well through his social reform. Edward A. Penniman—a General Trades' Union veteran turned radical Democrat—was not only a staunch supporter of municipal funding for the Pennsylvania, but also joined Price's three-man commission to liberalize the real estate market. His journal lambasted "land monopoly" but argued the soil should be bought and sold like any other form of property. Unsurprisingly, then, it backed land associations, which it praised for serving the interests of the "laboring classes."[62]

Radical migrants to growth politics carried with them the conviction that capitalism had to spread its bounty in a way that benefited working people. William D. Kelley, for instance, mixed with radicals and shared their unease at growth. "Wealth increases," he wrote of London's expansion, "but its aggregation into few hands takes place with ever-growing rapidity." Yet only McMichael, perhaps, surpassed in eloquence Kelley's booster prophecies of the empire city to come. He therefore urged citizens "to penetrate every section of the State with railroads and canals" and make Philadelphia the "London of the Western world."[63]

In a Saint-Simonian vein, though, Kelley continually tied economic expansion to social reconstruction. Seeing the Pennsylvania as the first chain in a link between Europe and Asia, he had knocked on the doors of wealthy citizens in 1846 to convince them to come along to a meeting in support of Asa Whitney's design for a Pacific Railroad. But Kelley was less interested than the city's bourgeoisie in accruing profits from the grain trade or augmenting the value of metropolitan real estate; instead he saw the road as a revolutionary force. He expected the line to "organize a vast system of immigration" from Eastern cities and the European countryside. Workmen on the railroad would be paid in land; a labor corps would follow behind to prepare the soil for cultivation. In this manner, the transcontinental route would clear a path for the elevation of "many millions of poor and oppressed people" to the rank of "free-holding American citizens," while opening "the great route for the commerce of the world." For Kelley, the project offered a way to reform the city, the nation, and the globe: it used state power and associated capital to defuse the nativist tensions of 1844, energize dormant labor on a scale the Second Republic's National Workshops would barely emulate, and turn the wilderness into a producers' republic. Kelley's growth politics—which did for the Far West what the land associations promised to do for the metropolitan frontier—could humanize capitalism.[64]

Kelley, like the radical land reformer William Elder, would migrate toward the "harmony of interests" doctrine of Philadelphia protectionist Henry C. Carey over the following years. They had come to the conclusion that state intervention could harmonize the relations between labor and capital. Their capitalism did not lionize the entrepreneur fighting for survival in the marketplace—free markets, they believed, led to chaos and conflict—but rather valorized an economic system based around the power of associated enterprise. They carried through the Civil War years a belief that any settlement that failed to materially benefit working people would lead to the anarchy Philadelphians had glimpsed in 1844. Infused by radicals' faith in association and interdependence, boosters' growth politics offered a blueprint for national consolidation and social reconciliation, which would shape the Republican Party for a generation. More immediately for Philadelphia, though, it provided a model for metropolitan union.

Building the Growth Polity

The new city charter of 1854 became an engine of growth politics. By then civic union had become to the *North American* "the one wish of Philadelphia." Beneath the rhetoric of metropolitan unity, though, lay a coalition of interests eager to benefit from the annexation of urban borderlands.

Radicals like Kelley and Elder backed the cause, while the short-lived Workingmen's Party of 1851, led by craft unionists and middle-class reformers, put municipal expansion in their platform. Consolidation, a correspondent to the *Ledger* insisted, "belongs particularly to the interests of the laboring classes." Boosters promised it would "furnish unfailing opportunity of LABOR and full wages." Yet only a small handful of manual workers appear to have campaigned actively for it. Even the writer in the *Ledger* acknowledged that the leaders counted men "who occupy the front rank of our most respectable and influential citizens."[65]

Consolidation certainly brought together Philadelphia's white male bourgeoisie. The movement built on efforts to unite merchant and manufacturing capital evident in the struggle over the Pennsylvania Railroad. Wealthy merchants, including Cope, made up 13.5 percent of the activist base, but their numbers were almost equaled by manufacturers. The Spring Garden factory owner Matthias W. Baldwin won election on an independent ticket to push Consolidation through, and several other locomotive, iron, and steel manufacturers—the strongest supporters among industrialists of railroad-building—also backed annexation. These men often lived in the city proper but owned capital and hired labor in the suburbs. Making up almost a quarter of Consolidation's supporters, meanwhile, were lawyers, many of whom, like Price, had professional familiarity with the urban property market. Auctioneers, real estate agents, and master craftsmen in the building trades comprised a further 9 percent of the growth coalition, while boosterish newspaper publishers played a significant supporting role. The *North American*'s McMichael was a fitting choice to chair the committee commissioned to draw up the new charter.

Under McMichael's direction, Consolidators pushed for a metropolitan land grab that mirrored the nation's territorial conquests of the 1840s. In 1844 to 1845, then again in 1849 to 1850, reformers had drafted charters to unite the city with its built-up suburbs, leaving sparsely populated outlying townships intact. In October 1853, however, the first meeting of McMichael's Executive Consolidation Committee gave attorney Henry M. Watts the chance to propose annexing all 125 miles or so of the county, most of which was farmland. The measure split the committee, but McMichael immediately offered his support. When another lawyer, William L. Hirst, drafted an outline of the charter a few days later, he included the whole county; McMichael used his columns to urge the rural districts to "embrace consolidation." Philadelphia, the *North American* argued, needed a "single strong, simple and cheap supreme government for the entire people and territory." The move to annex the entire county changed the temporal framing of the debate. Before, advocates of civic union could argue that annexation was simply the present catching up with the past, as the city extended to embrace the metropolis that had grown up around it. In laying claim to thousands of acres of meadows, though, Consolidators looked to the future. As in the subscription debate, then, talk shifted from rectifying previous mistakes to realizing coming prospects.[66]

The similarity to booster rhetoric in 1846 indicates how Consolidation came out of the railroad-building as well as the riots of the 1840s. Ten directors of the Pennsylvania—including the first two presidents of the road—campaigned for annexation. The program of urban imperialism inaugurated by the municipal subscription made the measure attractive to opponents and supporters of the city's investment. Those who had argued against the purchase, having warned a burgeoning city debt would compel civic union, now saw the benefit of extending the city's tax base and ending the free rider problem in the immediate suburbs. Binney was one of many anti-Consolidators who switched sides. By 1853, concluding the "grounds of my opposition have become obsolete," he wrote via his son to Price, urging him to join a pro-Consolidation ticket.[67]

With the cost of the still incomplete Pennsylvania rising and the municipal corporation pouring in more money, it was now the districts that feared the financial consequences of amalgamation. In a memorial against Consolidation in 1851, the state senator Thomas S. Fernon argued annexation would unjustly burden his suburban constituents with city debt. Suburbanites made the same case in meetings to draft a new charter in 1853 and 1854, as rural taxpayers decried an "anti-republican scheme," but Consolidators retorted that future borrowing would benefit the county especially, and (drawing perhaps on Hamiltonian precedent) that "a union of debt was a necessity of a consolidated government." The battle over debt and taxes echoed the struggle over Consolidation and the railroad subscription between 1844 and 1846. Then, however, citizens of the frugal city proper feared mingling their finances with the poor suburbs'. By 1853, the roles had been reversed, and growing districts now needed annexing to protect city property.[68]

For supporters of the subscription, though, Consolidation—by increasing the capacity to tax, borrow, and spend—promised to advance the city on its imperial course. The economies of scale that would come with amalgamation, "Franklin" argued in the Ledger, might have already allowed the city to "spare half a million annually" to aid in capturing the trade of the Mississippi Valley. It was a point reiterated by Henry M. Watts at a meeting calling for Consolidation in 1852. With Cope looking on, he argued that to promote "the foreign commerce and internal improvements" of the city required "a union of all in one solid body, with one heart imparting life and strength to the whole." One municipal reformer even warned that New York would monopolize the benefits of the opening of Japan and China without a new charter.[69]

The ties between annexation and debt-financed internal improvements tightened in 1853 and 1854, as the final push for the new charter began. Consolidators' efforts coincided with a renewed spate of railroad-building. Boosters revived calls to build the Sunbury and Erie—a route to the Great Lakes that had languished through the late 1840s—and by 1852, were lobbying for municipal funding. The North Pennsylvania and a series of smaller lines soon asked for aid too. Boosters faced less opposition than before in pushing for state help. Thus, while the *Sunday Dispatch* mocked promoters' rhetoric (one imaginary line just a mile in length, it told its readers, needed a loan of $1 million from councils or "every man in the city will be insolvent, and the *North American* and *Bulletin* . . . will be consumed by the fire of their own indignation"), and a few stalwarts continued to fight public investment, the stage was set for a new round of subscriptions.[70]

Consolidation proved the catalyst. Once it became clear that a bill for the union of the city and county would pass in January 1854, several suburbs— aware their debts would be absorbed by an enlarged metropolis— subscribed to the North Pennsylvania and Sunbury and Erie. Though some opposed what was seen as a move endangering the passage of the Consolidation Act, others welcomed a harbinger of what greater Philadelphia might achieve. One legislator even joked that all it would take was another bill for annexation to complete the road to the northern portion of the state in three months.[71] Any notion that the new charter would bring the spending spree to a stop disappeared when councils subscribed to several roads, raising the city's total railroad debt to almost $8 million. If the likes of Binney had hoped a union of the city and districts would check expenditure, they had been mistaken. Flush with the apparent success of the Pennsylvania, boosters drew on the strength of associated Philadelphia to compete for far-flung markets.

That Consolidation was "also to the interests of our men of property," one writer sagely noted, was "too apparent for comment." A few years later, the *North American* divided real estate owners into "two principal classes." The first, "composed of many thousands, owning one or two houses each," provided strong support for annexation outside the city proper. But the second, "limited in number," yet embracing "vast amounts of property," took the lead in the campaign for civic union. Several of the city's largest landlords, including Carpenter, Cadwalader, and Price had enlisted in the struggle to enlarge the city by 1853. Two hundred and seventy-one Consolidators traceable in the 1850 census held nearly $8 million of real property: an average of $33,464 per person. The hundred or so most committed reformers were even wealthier, owning a mean estate of $39,568 in 1850, and $81,353 a decade later (see Table 1). Critics certainly accused Consolidators of seeking to drive up the value of their "property outside the city." Annexation, a political advert warned producers," would make a speculator like Price "a *millionaire!*"[72]

Such claims were not far off, for like railroad boosters, Consolidators had every intention of using public credit to raise the value of private land. Replacing forty overlapping jurisdictions with one government did promise economies of scale. But the potential of the enlarged government lay less in its efficiency and more in its capacity to increase the value of property across the metropolis. Consolidators understood that though the price of suburban land depended on its proximity to the city, distance was manipulable, for just as the Pennsylvania Railroad had brought the West closer to Philadelphia, local internal improvements could draw remote tracts into the metropolitan marketplace. Left alone, though, "weak and neglected" suburban districts lacked the resources to bind themselves to the city. "Lands lying beyond metropolitan bounds, the *North American* claimed in making the case for annexing the county, "are prevented from becoming attractive to capitalists speculating upon probably future advance in real estate." Only a united metropolis, a speculator who ran on the Consolidation ticket argued, had the power to build a sewerage system to "rival the works of ancient Rome." Price himself saw annexation as an investment in which the "future availability" of "young and thrifty" suburbs would be well worth the cost of bringing them up to scratch. Like the railroad loans, then, borrowing now promised riches later. "We should look . . . to the future," the ex-Pennsylvania Railroad president Merrick told members of the committee tasked with drafting the new city charter when they discussed apportioning debt, "as well as the past."[73]

Table 1. Profile of leading municipal Consolidators.

	Number	Total Real Estate	Total Personal Estate	Total Servants	Percent (%)
Agriculture	1	$20,000	$5,000	1	1.43
Commerce	9	$527,500	$160,500	24	12.86
Finance	3	$335,000	$150,000	10	4.29
Law	24	$870,500	$827,000	68	34.29
Medicine	3	$61,000	$3,000	6	4.29
Mining and Industry	11	$762,200	$497,900	29	15.71
Property	7	$189,500	$25,970	7	10.00
Publishing	2	$20,000	$5,000	4	2.86
Retail	6	$2,843,500	$250,450	20	8.57
Retired	2	$310,000	$2,000	3	2.86
Other	2	$5,500	$400	0	2.86

Source: 1860 Federal Census.

Prophecies that Consolidation would raise the value of rural real estate by fifty or a hundred times inside a generation helped secure support for annexation among property owners in the county. As land associations rushed to incorporate after the passage of Consolidation, they portrayed their tracts at the center of a web of projected improvements, and lobbied the new government to build roads and bridges. The *Germantown Telegraph* urged its rural readership to back the new charter to raise property values, while in Penn District—not too far from the metropolitan frontier—three of the seven residents to join the campaign for municipal union owned more than $100,000 of real estate in the 1850 census. When limited to landowners, at least, Merrick's claim that "the outer districts" were "all crying out for improvement" was not misplaced.[74]

The alliance between speculators in the city and districts, though, was perhaps most evident in the built-up district of Moyamensing. Over the preceding years, the suburb's Board of Commissioners proved either incapable or unwilling to deal with the frequent outbreaks of violence, and a race riot blamed on Moyamensing roughs in 1849 had spurred the last major bid for municipal union. As they had done after the violence of 1844, bourgeois citizens counted the economic cost of disorder. "Property is rendered valueless by popular outbreaks and riots," the Whig mayor John Swift remarked, so though Moyamensing had "every natural advantage," many owners struggled to "yield two per cent per annum." Even the radical

Lippard portrayed Moyamensing as a microcosm of the South: a decadent, impoverished, and turbulent colony in need of reconstruction.[75]

Consolidators understood that only credit could make Moyamensing a credible place to invest. The district was the poorest in the built-up portion of the metropolis, and improvements were few and far between. In contrast to McMichael and Price's old suburb of Spring Garden, which had borrowed to the tune of about $1.75 million to fund development, Moyamensing's debt stood at just over $100,000 on the eve of annexation. This "penny wise and pound foolish" system of administration, critics charged, was more fitting for a "sequestered rural village" than the southern extension of a major metropolis. One attempt to establish a municipal gas works had sparked protest meetings when the district proposed to borrow $30,000.[76] The scheme's failure indicated a wider problem of underinvestment in poorer suburbs. Most districts, for instance, funded improvements out of special assessments on affected property owners rather than using the city proper's preferred method of general taxation. In Moyamensing, like elsewhere in the built-up districts, support for Consolidation came mostly from native-born real estate owners, especially in the building trades. But boosters in the city proper, eager to see property there "pay a fair portion of interest," hoped annexation would redeem the suburb too. Consolidation, the *North American* argued, promised to wipe the stigmatized name of Moyamensing from the map, and give its citizens access to "the benefits of a powerful metropolitan organization." If, as one meeting put it, civic union "will unlock and distribute capital," then it was the "only remedy" to the disease of underdevelopment.[77]

Advocates of Consolidation looked beyond the boundaries of the city proper and saw the promise of rich yields of rent and tax. When talk turned to real estate, indeed, land lost any affective meaning and became a priceable asset. The empty gridironed squares that atlases showed crisscrossing the 127 square miles of the new city turned that asset into an abstraction. The potential of a district, one citizen argued, could simply be determined "by the number of acres" it contained. All that was needed to magic wealth into being was a municipal regime capable of extending improvements outward. The language here was just as imperial as that of railroad boosters. For McMichael's *North American*, imaginary streets ploughing their way through "fields and commons" marked the "destined course of metropolitan progress." Westward from the Delaware, the course of empire would take its path. In an age marked by such rapid imperial, economic, and urban growth, such prophecies inspired working-class subscriptions to ill-fated land companies and bourgeois speculation in suburban real estate. Like the national domain, land would be parceled up, titles secured, property protected, and profits reaped.[78]

*   *   *

In March 1854, Philadelphians gathered to celebrate passage of the Consolidation Act. On Independence Hall's columns, the names of the annexed districts hung on draperies alongside portraits of William Penn, George Washington, and Eli Kirk Price. The banquet that evening assembled a microcosm of the bourgeois growth coalition. McMichael gave the opening address, before representatives of Philadelphia's merchants, manufacturers, lawyers, and railroads spoke on behalf of their respective interests. Murmurs of criticism at the absence of artisans ("the great mass of the community," one critic wrote, "are as deeply interested as the capitalists" in celebrating) pushed the *North American* to propose holding a trades' procession to mark the new charter, but the dinner itself was reserved for the city's economic and political elite.[79]

The orators included the Philadelphia lawyer George Mifflin Dallas. At the time of the Mexican War, Dallas had been James K. Polk's vice president, and he applied the lessons of that conflict to the city's land grab. Americans had refuted Samuel Johnson's aphorism that "extended empire" exchanges "solid strength for feeble splendey," he argued, for as a people, they had "never yet been debilitated by enlargement, whether of City, State, or Nation." Others at the festivities likewise linked local and national growth. "Manifest destiny" had forced the "unwilling denizens of the city" westward to the Schuylkill, the governor declared, until the "old city . . . has swallowed up all the other districts and the surrounding country." In an age of continental conquest, imperial metaphors naturalized Consolidation, but for the railroad builders and urban annexationists of midcentury, empire was not just a rhetorical veneer. On the contrary, it lay at the basis of their calculations, as they wagered that growth would drive values upward.[80]

By the 1850s, growth politics advocated consolidation in its manifold meanings. Railroad-building, real estate reform, and municipal union would bind the city to far-flung corners of the continent, unite the metropolis across its social and spatial fault lines, and bring merchants, manufacturers, and men of property together. Consolidators' vision of urban capitalism hinged on state power. Government had to offer finance for big corporations, security to property, and lubrication for market forces. This booster political economy did not go unchallenged. From within bourgeois ranks, critics of public borrowing foretold financial ruin. From radicals came the claim that growth would enrich the propertied at the expense of the poor. Yet after midcentury, representatives from both groups were reconciling themselves to a growth regime that conceived of economic life as cooperative as well as competitive, and as associational rather than atomistic. The idea of labor and capital working harmoniously toward realizing the city's imperial prospects legitimized transportation monopolies, land associations, and Consolidation itself. Such a seductive vision drew radicals like Kelley and Elder and boosters like McMichael and Colwell into an alliance that through the Republican Party would eventually reshape the nation as well as the city.

Yet torrents of trade and the unshackling of real estate did not always build up the city as boosters wanted. Instead, they threatened to bring about the kind of social and spatial problems that reformers sometimes blamed for the disorders of the riot era. A consolidated city government, some reasoned, might need to restrain rather than liberate market forces if Philadelphia was to grow harmoniously. But this would place reformers at odds with the lynchpins of growth politics: the Pennsylvania Railroad and property owners. It required the apparatus of the state to be turned toward disciplining a bourgeoisie as well as a working class. And it led some to embrace city planning.

CHAPTER 4

"To Give Shape to the Destinies of Our City"

Molding the Metropolis

On the night of July 5, 1854, a careless stagehand set fire to the National Theater on fashionable Chestnut Street. The blaze tore through the structure and soon spread to the Chinese Museum, where, just four months earlier, thousands of Philadelphians had congregated to celebrate passage of the Consolidation Act. Before long the inferno had consumed a block of stores that were "once the residence of the first families" and threatened the Girard House hotel. "A lurid glare was cast over the sky," the *North American* reported, as "the flames spread with a rapidity that defied all the efforts of the firemen."[1]

Fire, a constant hazard in a city part-built with timber, nevertheless had merits. Within weeks, indeed, Morton McMichael's paper noted how the disaster had made space for widening the pavement on narrow Chestnut Street. Like some Chicagoans after the calamitous blaze of 1871, boosters believed the flames purified as they destroyed, accomplishing in a few hours "what the slow hand of improvement would have taken years to perfect." "Philadelphia is more largely indebted for its progress to the calamitous but useful desolations of great conflagrations," the *North American* would write in 1858, "than many are apt to imagine." The elemental forces that leveled "private fortunes" were "great improvers of cities."[2]

In fire, civic boosters found an unlikely friend. They needed its help. Those who saw Philadelphia as "one of the very few imperial cities of the New World" had hoped that the trade of an empire would build up the metropolis. As profits from commerce poured into the property market, dull streets would be transformed into elegant avenues. The city, they believed, might then become what one citizen called the "Paris of America," with parks, fountains, and columns drawing strangers to its thoroughfares. On its promenades, bourgeois Philadelphians would strengthen social solidarities while an urban poor learned from the example of their betters. The cityscape could elevate citizens and stand as a fitting symbol of urban greatness.[3]

Such demands overburdened the urban form with expectation. Streets would have to serve simultaneously as conduits for trade, markers of distinction, and sites of integration. In practice, as this chapter shows, matters rarely unfolded as planned. Attempts to prepare the grid for the rush of railroad trade ran into local opposition. Boosters frequently found that the capitalism they championed could unleash chaos of its own in the built environment. And even Consolidation, in creating a strong state with the capacity to borrow, spend, and plan, came with risks, especially in the Panic of 1857, when unemployed workingmen turned to local government for employment. In searching for a method to make the urban form conform to their wishes, bourgeois Philadelphians even proved willing to look beyond their borders, following with interest developments in Second Empire Paris, where Napoleon III's debt-financed works illustrated how a city might be shaped. Ultimately, though, the power to command space seemed to elude boosters. Those who did not dream of fire's purifying work began to question the nature of urban democracy instead.[4]

Designing the Bourgeois City

In 1853, a correspondent of the *Evening Bulletin* called for the construction of drives, parks, and fountains, for without them, he feared, people would pass through Philadelphia without having any reason to stop. "Railroads," he argued, had "changed the nature of things." He was not alone in pondering what new routes to the West would mean for the urban form. Booming real estate values after midcentury appeared to fulfill the booster prophecy that the Pennsylvania would invigorate the property market. But a road that promised to be the "*making* of Philadelphia" required Philadelphia to be remade. When William Penn's surveyor Thomas Holme had sketched out his gridiron plan in the late seventeenth century, the straight lines and broad streets were a marked improvement on the cramped confines of a London ravaged by plague and fire. Philadelphia may not have grown into the green country town Penn had envisaged, but a century and a half after the city's founding, the rectilinear design endured. What was roomy in the days of Penn, though, had grown claustrophobic by the middle decades of the nineteenth century. The city had been laid out, McMichael's paper noted, by men "whose ideas of progress were formed in view of no such example of social advancement as ocean steamers, railroads, telegraphs, free institutions and a new world." They had failed to foresee what the *Public Ledger* called an "entire revolution in the width of streets."[5]

The metropolis here had much in common with Old World cities. Western boosters could build their towns around the needs of trade. In Europe, though, vast programs of reconstruction were often required to retrofit the built environment. Old lines of fortification gave way to boulevards; housing was swept away to make room for railroad termini.[6] Philadelphia would not witness anything as wrenching as the clearances that paved the way for streets and stations in London and Paris, but its boosters, like their counterparts across the Atlantic, strove to adapt an outmoded urban form to the demands of capital.

Railroad advocates, predicting as much as a six- or seven- fold rise in business, urged citizens to ready the city for the deluge to come. With business "extending its operations to the farthest limits of civilization in the West," the *Ledger* conceded in 1855, "it is scarcely to be expected that we can keep our main business streets as free from boxes and bales as a promenade on a Sunday." But even before the completion of the Pennsylvania, complaints about dusty thoroughfares, highways encrusted in horse manure, and obstacle-strewn sidewalks filled newspaper columns.[7] Boosters then had good reason to fear that the wealth of the West would ooze down streets like a sluggish stream. When the riches of Oregon, California, and the "great portion of the intervening wilderness" coursed down the Pennsylvania's tracks into Philadelphia, the demands on the urban form would be extraordinary.[8] With commerce "soon to be increased to a degree which many grave people cannot even now be persuaded to comprehend," the *North American* warned, the metropolis required "vastly augmented facilities for its transaction." Impediments "in the channels of trade" could not be tolerated.[9]

Calls for the "enlargement of local business facilities" reached a crescendo in the early 1850s. The impending completion of the Pennsylvania Railroad's route to the West provided a motive; the Consolidation of the city and county presented the means. Boosters eager to recapture foreign commerce from New York sought to build on the bequest of the merchant prince Stephen Girard, who left money in his will for the improvement of the port. The Board of Trade now demanded that Delaware Avenue must be "widened to an extent necessary to meet the prospective wants of the trade."[10]

Western ambitions shaped designs for other thoroughfares too. Market, which until 1858 was known officially as High, ran from the Delaware across the Schuylkill into West Philadelphia. At its eastern end, near the port, warehouses and commission merchants lined the sidewalks. It took its popular name, however, from provision sheds, which by the 1850s occupied the center of eleven blocks. A market had stood on the avenue from the founding of the city, and at midcentury, the "shanties"—with their master butchers, local farmers, and oyster vendors—were a place for ordinary Philadelphians to buy, sell, and socialize. But the occupation of a coveted commercial spot by men and women incapable of turning the land to its highest and best use irritated boosters.[11]

Such spaces, in serving the immediate needs of the community, seemed out of place in an imperial city. Market stood as the last chain in the link between Philadelphia and its empire. As a post-Consolidation mayor put it, the street was "the main artery of the trade from the sea . . . to the West," and as a result "should be free from obstruction as possible." For boosters, the "provincial" character of a provision market was "unworthy" of Philadelphia's "present position," and as commerce expanded, "local arrangements" would need to "accommodate the vast business which we have invited." Streets had to meet railroads' requirements. "The interests of trade," McMichael's paper asserted in 1853 in calling for the sheds' removal, "are paramount to any which relate merely to the domestic economy of a community."[12]

In expecting the urban form to correspond to the city's imperial future rather than its parochial past, boosters had architectural considerations in mind too. Not everywhere matched up to their ideal. The market sheds, renowned in the 1830s for their "convenient and modernized" design, seemed two decades later "symmetrical in nothing but ugliness and discomfort." For a correspondent of the *Evening Bulletin,* they were simply "repulsive to good taste"; others decried a "deformity," which mocked a city "with its half million of population and its untold millions of wealth."[13]

To realize Philadelphia's metropolitan destiny citizens had to retrofit the urban environment for cultural display as well as commercial convenience. Boosters often assumed that one would lead to the other. Trade would fertilize the city's soil and allow a beautiful built environment to bloom. Wealthy citizens certainly longed for embellishment. Before 1840, the genteel tastes of southern planters and northern merchants had spread to the broader middle class, who began to decorate their homes with fine carpets and furnishings. But the impulse for refinement did not stop at the front door. Beyond the domestic sphere, elegant promenades, verdant squares, and landscaped cemeteries served as sites for collective consumption. How citizens behaved on the urban stage distinguished the respectable from the rabble. The likes of McMichael juxtaposed the light, space, and air of the bourgeois city to the gloomy, fetid, and cramped lanes of disorderly suburbs. But the genteel metropolis proved easier to construct in the columns of the *North American* than on actual streets.[14]

Philadelphia stood as unprepared for the cultural demands bourgeois citizens made on the urban form as it was for the torrent of trade. The *Ledger*, for instance, conceded that the stores of a "rude an[d] uncouth" center "seldom united the qualities of beauty to the purposes of usefulness." Part of the problem lay in the grid as Philadelphia's seventeenth-century scale left little room for the perspectives of a monumental cityscape. The sheds and warehouses on Market had forced fashionable business one block south to narrower Chestnut Street. But there, the press complained, "the grandeur of architecture is of small effect," for "the passage way is too limited" to allow fine buildings to be "seen to proper advantage." David Jayne's eight-story skyscraper—built at the cost of $500,000 in 1850—provided a case in point. The edifice set in stone the ties between urban and manifest destiny: Jayne's pharmaceutical enterprise reached across the continent, and by 1860, Chinese translations of his almanac circulated in the Qing Empire. But the building struggled to attract attention commensurate to its scale. Philadelphia simply lacked the dimensions for imposing architecture. The New Yorker who found it "eminently inartistic, monotonous and uninspiring" was far from alone.[15]

Boosters reminded owners that riches lay in reconstruction. They argued that fine buildings and genteel streets, like western railroads, would bring business to Philadelphia.[16] Individuals therefore had an incentive to improve their tracts. But property, as David Scobey points out in New York, remained "almost completely relational"; its value, as another scholar writes, "held hostage by the vagaries of proximity and its relationship to other properties." A mansion in a fading neighborhood might be worth less than an unsightly lot in a fashionable spot. Real estate's peculiarity as a "spatially embedded commodity" had several consequences.[17] For owners, it could spur support for state intervention. Critics of growth politics sensed the presence of self-interested speculators in campaigns for removing market sheds, creating a park, and consolidating city and districts.[18] As well as shaping attitudes to government, however, real property also structured relations between individuals by introducing a measure of social obligation into the market. Owners often reaped returns through renting dilapidated buildings or holding onto unimproved ground. But their inaction irritated propertied neighbors as well as urban boosters.

Genteel city builders therefore set out to discipline their class in the use of urban space. Community pressure, arbiters of good taste hoped, could overcome individualistic privatism. Turning over a lot to a low land use invited censure. Assailing the owner of a plot on the site of the Chestnut Street fire, the *Evening Bulletin* claimed that though "a man surely has a right to do as he pleases with his own private property," he also has "certain duties toward the city where his property lies, and the community from whom he has long derived a handsome income."[19] Good urban development here rested on the interplay of private ambitions and public responsibilities. Bourgeois citizens were expected to prosper as investors while contributing to the collective ambitions of their class.

The proper use of property provided a path to social respectability. Real estate investment could secure status as well as store wealth. By 1850, William D. Kelley, making the transition from radical Locofoco to apostle of growth politics, won acclaim for his "handsome" Grecian residence in West Philadelphia. Matthias W. Baldwin poured profits from his locomotive works into suburban churches that graced fashionable neighborhoods like the West End.[20] But another locomotive manufacturer, Joseph Harrison (1810–1874), provides the best example of the link between building and becoming bourgeois. Harrison was born to humble circumstances in the Northern Liberties neighborhood, but after making his name as an engineer, left for Russia, where he built engines and railroads for the tsar. After spending the best part of a decade in St. Petersburg, London, and Paris, he returned to Philadelphia in 1852, a millionaire; a few years later, one Massachusetts paper erroneously called him the richest man in the Union. Harrison invested to make money—his inventory lists mortgages and lots alongside other forms of equity—and he backed booster schemes to increase the value of his land. But he tried to harmonize his pursuit of profit with (in his own words) the "adornment of his native city." Papers praised his fine buildings in the commercial center and the prosperous suburb of Spring Garden, while lauding his "palatial mansion" on Rittenhouse Square. In this regard he became the exemplary public-spirited capitalist: a man whose business success found fitting expression in the built environment. Harrison's improvements, the *North American* wrote, combined "taste and utility in the development of a great metropolis." The paper counted him among a "race of builders" who were turning Philadelphia into a "princely city."[21]

Such ambitions combined New World wealth with Old World culture. Modernizing the city, ironically, meant tying it closer to a Europe that Americans often consigned to the past. Bourgeois Philadelphians knew European cities through travel and reading and followed urban development there closely. For many, the continent remained a point of departure for a democratic republic, symbolizing despotism and decay. But where the Old World lagged behind in political development, its "great cities" served as prototypes, and Americans experiencing their own rapid urban growth admitted they had much to learn from their parks and public spaces.[22]

Of all European cities, Paris tended to leave the most marked impression, even before the reconstruction work of the Second Empire began in 1853. "Few Americans" visited the French capital, the *North American* wrote, "without returning full of its praises." It was not the Paris of the 1848 Revolutions, though, that dazzled them. Rather, they spent their time on the genteel promenades of its thoroughfares and gardens, where the "gay and busy multitude" thronged. The spectacle of Parisian street life helped make it "the finest city in the world" and offered a glimpse of what a Philadelphia shorn of its prosaic form might be. "We have heard it stated," reported the *Ledger* in 1853, that we are about to have Boulevards in Philadelphia." "Let us have the Boulevards by all means."[23]

Boosters believed that Philadelphia's wealth would find physical form in a Parisian promenade, the model to aspire to in the nineteenth-century city. The likeliest candidate was Broad Street. Broad's importance to mid-century urban design is hard to overstate: it was to the city's internal space what the Pennsylvania Railroad was to its external relations. At over one hundred feet wide, Broad formed the central north-south axis on Holme's original plan, intersecting Market at the Penn Squares. Maps in the 1850s showed it running in an arrow-straight line for nearly ten miles from the Delaware. Unlike Chestnut, then, it had the length and breadth to become "one of the most beautiful thoroughfares in the world." Prior to the 1830s, the avenue had stood some way beyond the urban frontier, but the westward drift of population, and the development of the Rittenhouse Square enclave nearby, soon spurred calls for improvement. In 1838 and 1839, a campaign to turn one segment of Broad into a street that would surpass the "far-famed Boulevards" of Paris brought more than sixty citizens to a public meeting. Over the following years, though, riots and railroad preoccupied the energies of city builders, while the divided system of municipal government discouraged collective action.[24]

By the early 1850s, however, Broad's improvement had become an obsession for boosters, who came to see the street as an index of metropolitan might. With Market, they argued, Broad could become one of the "two most celebrated avenues in the world," with each taking their place in a spatial division of labor. The former provided a channel for commerce; the latter, in contrast, would stand as a symbol for metropolitan might. McMichael's *North American*, reasoning that "the visitor is apt to judge of the city itself" by its principal avenue, became the most forceful advocate of Broad's improvement. With a boulevard, it argued, residents and strangers could gauge "at a glance the wealth, splendor and greatness of the city, which now permeate through numerous narrow channels." The paper sold the street over and over again as a representation of the city as a whole. Broad was "a mirror" in which "life in Philadelphia would be reflected in its true grandeur"; an "image" tracing "the lofty attributes, the proud consequence, the strength, the power, the magnificence, the wealth, and the resources" of a "mighty aggregation of people"; and a "metropolitan thoroughfare" with "sufficient capacity" to "reflect properly the character of the place." The *North American* strove to transform the profits of growth politics into the symbolic capital of a Parisian promenade. The avenue would "give shape to the destinies of our city."[25]

But the boulevard would be a real place as well as an urban metonym. Boosters imagined a reconstructed Broad at the center of a genteel cityscape. From the business houses of the downtown and the brownstone mansions of Rittenhouse Square, promenaders would spill on to sidewalks. Evenly spaced trees forming an "umbrageous arch" would shield them from the evening sun as they passed "fountains," "monuments," and "obelisks." At Broad's midpoint, where it intersected Market, they could linger amidst the "beauty and . . . bloom" of the Penn Squares: the green heart of Penn's original plan.[26] If such expectations corresponded to what David Schuyler has called the "new urban landscape"—a leafy ensemble of boulevards,

cemeteries, and parks—designs for Broad reveal more than a romantic ven-
eration of nature. Promoters pictured the blocks either side of the Penn
Squares as a fashionable resort full of "bustle and activity," which would
tempt the hotels, dry good stores, and civic institutions away from chaotic
Chestnut. Broad could concentrate the energies of an imperial metropolis
and display its dynamism in proper perspective.[27]

The genteel boulevard, in turn, would cultivate bonds of gentility. Broad
became vital to the seemingly contradictory projects of uniting an economic elite and bringing the city together across social divisions. The street
was not just a symbol of urban greatness, but also a space in which the
bourgeoisie would coalesce as a class. Wealthy equestrians, for whom riding
strengthened "social ties and matrimonial alliances," could take their horses
down the boulevard to a race track (opened 1855) that excluded the city's
riffraff; opera goers would find the avenue's Academy of Music (opened
1857) met "the wants and refinements of the time" better than the rowdy
theaters nearby. Boosters moreover talked up the coming avenue as a
"promenade," a stage for the elite ritual Scobey has described in New York,
in which genteel families forged fraternal bonds on evening strolls. Supporters of improvement on Broad predicted "the beauty and fashion of the
town will centre at certain hours of the day to take the fresh air." Boulevards, as the *Ledger* put it, were places for people to "see each other and
be seen." They would separate the bourgeoisie from the messy metropolis
beyond.[28]

Yet designs for Broad reflect a desire for association across the city's
spatial and social boundaries too. City builders claimed that like railroad
and real estate investments, the built environment could integrate a divided
metropolis. As so often here, they echoed the language of nationalism.
Unionists either side of midcentury took comfort in the power of internal
improvements to forge "iron bonds" of interdependence between North
and South. Boosters hoped Broad would bind the city in a like manner.
Philadelphia, the *North American* argued, "cannot rest content with a sectional avenue . . . as its central point." It needed a thoroughfare, "which is
convenient common ground to all the city" and "whose ample dimensions
may symbolize the new field upon which we are entering."[29]

But if Broad might consolidate Philadelphia as a single political community, its improvement could also bring cohesion across class lines. Advocates of boulevarding sometimes acknowledged the radical critique of a city
divided into an upper tenth and lower million. Americans, McMichael's

paper conceded, enjoy less "equality of social intercourse than people who live under monarchical government." Arguing that spatial segregation led to social ostracism, it called for the creation of sites, "which habitually associate the citizens of a community in their amusements and pleasures." Broad's development in this regard acquired "an interesting political and social aspect." The draw of light and air would ensure "all orders of our population may be constantly brought together," where they would grow "accustomed to mingle with feelings of mutual good-will and respect." When conceived as a democratic meeting ground, Broad had a didactic function, for like in New York, bourgeois city builders sought to forge citizens in their own image. In the boulevard's "close assembling of the cultivated with the less polished classes of the community," the *North American* concluded, "the rough bearing of a vulgar character" insensibly gives way "to the gentle and polished manners of the better bred people he sees around him." Here the bourgeois city served simultaneously as an index of progress and a force for progress in its own right.[30]

While boosters directed much of their energy in the early 1850s to a few discrete spots—Rittenhouse, Market, and Broad—their principles could be applied across the entire metropolis. Creating a park along the Schuylkill, where the city first purchased land for a pleasure ground in the riot year of 1844, became a priority. Supporters drew on the same arguments trotted out for boulevards: a park would draw wealthy residents, "keep pace with the progress and refinement of the age," and offer respite from crowded lanes and alleys. But the "close contact of classes" was intended to uplift public morals as well as public health. As the menacing-sounding "Anthrax" argued in the *Ledger*, the scheme, by transplanting laboring men from low taverns and ninepin-alleys to the benign influence of a romantic and respectable landscape, would do more "than all our public institutions" to "cultivate peace, harmony and the graces of polished life." Prior to 1850, reformers had sought to remove people from malignant influences in reformatory institutions like penitentiaries and workhouses, but after midcentury, a reconstructed built environment came to be seen as a schoolhouse of gentility.[31]

Planning principles applied to particular parts of the city had coalesced by Consolidation into what the *North American* called a "philosophy" of metropolitan interdependence. The architect of the 1854 annexation, Eli Kirk Price, perhaps influenced by Thomas Jefferson's design for checkerboard towns of built-up blocks interspersed with public squares, proposed laying out suburban extensions in the city's northern environs around evenly spaced patches of greenery. His "parks for the people" would "attach them to good order, enlist them on the side of government, and teach them to respect objects of ornaments and taste." McMichael's daily, meanwhile, codified the rules of urban design. "Give us wide streets and plenty of them," it declared in 1854, for therein lay the "city of all classes of our population." What brought business to the merchant would bring fresh air to the laborer. Both Price and McMichael, in common with their counterparts elsewhere in urban America, saw their labors as a hegemonic project—one that had the potential to consolidate a divided metropolis spatially and socially. Like growth politics, then, modernizing the built environment in the manner boosters intended would unite rather than divide. Somehow, city streets would satisfy the wants of every class, and lead Philadelphia on to greatness.[32]

The Limits of Capital

The boosters who pitted progress against backwardness in pushing for Philadelphia's reconstruction often ran into problems of their own making. Railroad tracks and real estate markets, it became clear over the course of the 1850s, did not necessarily lead to urban beautification. Modernization nevertheless proved a powerful ideological weapon in their push for reform. Stuck, one historian writes, in the "purgatory between the past and the future," midcentury boosters divided the metropolis into what once was and what might yet be. Remembering the rhetoric of railroad-building in the 1840s, they emphasized the obligations the present owed to posterity. Price, for example, urged citizens to contemplate the "future growth of Philadelphia" when weighing up the worth of improvements. Another called for rebuilding to "prepare the way for our future greatness."[33]

Boosters hid the politics of reconstruction behind this rhetoric of progress. Like free labor critics of slavery (with whom they often overlapped), they saw themselves as progressives sweeping away the detritus of the past. Philadelphia, one paper argued, "must respond to the spirit of the age." That meant anything "behind the times" had to go. The market sheds therefore became "*untimely*" relics of a "primitive" era—out of time as well as out of place. Citizens who stood in the way of inevitable

Figure 2. Bedford Street, Moyamensing. In this image from an antebellum missionary's memoir, Bedford Street is portrayed as the opposite of the orderly, bourgeois city: a moral wilderness in which "family government" and state power are sorely lacking. Source: Reprinted from Benjamin T. Sewell, *Sorrow's Circuit, or Five Years' Experience in the Bedford Street Mission* (Philadelphia: Philadelphia Conference Tract Depository, 1859). Courtesy of The Library Company of Philadelphia.

improvements were charged with "fogyism": a backward-looking mentality that in failing to appreciate the magnitude of Philadelphia's coming wants retarded its present advancement. Their minds, much like city streets, needed modernizing.[34]

Nowhere seemed more behind the times than the Bedford Street borderland that lay just below the southern edge of the city proper (see Figure 2). Providing shelter for the lower sort and salacious stories for the press, the Moyamensing district had acquired a reputation in the riots and epidemics of the Jacksonian era as Philadelphia's most notorious neighborhood. In an era of continental conquest, it came to be cast as an urban frontier populated by men and women akin to "savages." After a change of name to mark the purchase of "Seward's folly" from Russia in 1867, one newspaper even called the district "the near Alaska": a worthless wilderness tagged onto a civilized community. If Broad was Philadelphia's monumental future, then Bedford was its barbarous past. The former inspired Parisian dreams of elegant promenaders; the latter evoked Parisian nightmares of an idle and insurrectionary "canaille."[35]

Commentators after midcentury often blamed Bedford's woes on its outmoded form. Moral environmentalists saw the neighborhood, like the market sheds, as a relic. Where some parts of the city were "laid out and improved with regard for the health and morals of the residents," the *Pennsylvania Inquirer* argued, "original mistake and subsequent neglect" had made Bedford's courts and alleys "disgraceful to the city."[36] Their dated buildings and diminutive scale offended bourgeois taste. To McMichael's paper, "the houses are small, the windows are small, . . . and the minds of all who dwell there are of the smallest possible caliber."[37] Bedford's backwardness had no place in a modern metropolis. When one wit proposed the "philanthropic experiment" of bunking Bedford Street's poor in the market sheds, he left the reader in no illusion that neither belonged in the metropolis to come.[38]

Yet here boosters had a blind spot that also impeded their broader urban vision. If Bedford was so behind the times, then why had the "march of improvement" not swept it away? Creative destruction ought to have worked its magic on the street, yet at the height of the real estate boom in the early 1850s, Bedford's condition seemed to be worsening. A doctor at the nearby Moyamensing workhouse even wondered whether the poverty within sight of his building indicated that Philadelphia would "undergo all the social degradation we are accustomed to be horrified at in Europe."[39] The neighborhood here became the dark side of Philadelphia's modernity: a part of what Dell Upton has called a "morally and medically" subversive "shadow landscape." Bedford's own residents—a more resourceful bunch than observers implied—appear to have played along in constructing a "parallel society." They christened their taverns and tenements after the names of some of the finest buildings in Philadelphia and New York. Journalists meanwhile traced the circulation of "capital" through an informal economy of astrologers, dram sellers, and rag and bone men. The places and processes of the bourgeois city were mapped onto a street that inverted its values.[40]

Bedford mocked expectations that growth led to gentility. Where boosters like Harrison believed the pursuit of private profit encouraged urban embellishment, the very opposite seemed to be occurring in Moyamensing. The property market there encouraged overcrowding. A Bedford Street "*capitalist*," as a writer disparagingly called such investors, might engage in a petty "speculation" by taking a room at 12 cents a day, and then subletting it to lodgers at 2 cents. Others, with greater means, had tenements erected to rent out at a generous profit. One cluster of buildings, supposedly bought at a cost of $1,300, reputedly earned its owner $1,600 a year. They may have added nothing to the "beautifying of the city," but they were a rational response to demand for cheap shelter.[41]

Bourgeois Philadelphians recognized the economic opportunity. Tracing ownership in the "infected district" is not easy, but anecdotal evidence suggests that "wealthy and respectable men" leased property there through agents. By the postbellum era, papers widely reported that Bedford Street real estate paid "a larger per centage of profit than almost any other in the city." But getting up a cheap tenement, allowing it to decay, and renting its threadbare rooms to entire families was akin to class treason for genteel boosters. Cutting up the grid into narrow courts and alleys threatened "disastrous consequences" in a district renowned for riot and disease. One respectable paper even followed radicals in claiming it was "mainly the landlords who demoralize the people." The roots of Bedford's disorders here had gone from rum to the workings of the real estate market itself.[42]

By the Civil War, boosters were well aware that the path from growth politics to urban grandeur lay strewn with obstacles. Commerce's claims on space proved as big a block to advancement as an outmoded urban form. Repeated attempts by railroads to penetrate to the heart of the city proved especially contentious. In the early 1840s, residents of Kensington tore up the tracks of the Philadelphia and Trenton, burned a tavern owned by a railroad director, and forced the state legislature to revoke its grant of a right of way. The freight question in the suburbs, while never dividing neatly along class lines, pitted radicals against boosters. In Kensington, for example, craft union veterans attacked the railroad's actions; stalwarts of the merchant community, on the other hand, condemned the "evil example" of the crowd.[43]

Within the city proper, in contrast, opposition to commerce in the streets came from the "commercial classes" themselves. As the Main Line and Reading Railroad neared completion in the 1830s, the Board of Trade—eager for a route to the port—lobbied councils to lay tracks at street level along Broad, Market, Third, and Dock. But the City Railroad, as it became known, had unintended consequences. Horse-drawn cars maimed pedestrians, blocked the thoroughfares, and lowered the tone of the business district. The long-distance trade of the City Railroad could prove just as offensive to genteel tastes as local exchanges in the market sheds. When a train passed through, the *North American* complained, the neighborhood "resounds for twenty or thirty minutes together with a hideous din of whips and curses."[44] On Broad too, business held back beautification. For all the "profound schemes," and "grand visions," the boulevard stubbornly resisted improvement. Railroads took much of the blame. As many as eighty coal and lumber merchants, drawn by the tracks, lined the avenue in the late 1840s. A handful moved on over the following decade, but on the eve of the Civil War, four anthracite yards and a freight depot faced the new opera house. In discussing Broad's dilapidated state, boosters spoke in terms that sounded more appropriate for Bedford Street than a Parisian boulevard. "Business shuns it as though a pestilence afflicted the vicinity," the *North American* argued. The street was "a mere nuisance."[45]

Economic expansion here threatened to ruin bourgeois ambitions for the city. For if coal, lumber, and commerce drove Philadelphia forward— fueling industry, heating homes, and building the metropolis outward— they denied boosters the genteel city they craved. Advocates of growth politics wrestled with the contradiction. The statistician Cephas G. Childs, who claimed the only route to "public prosperity" lay in "an industrious developement [*sic*] of our unbounded mineral resources," counted the yards that disfigured Broad in his notebooks, while wondering at the marvels of Paris's boulevards.[46] The *North American* called for Market Street to be given over entirely to western trade, yet fought to remove the railroad that carried those goods. On their principal streets, bourgeois Philadelphians struggled to choose between private profit and class culture.

Tension between business needs and bourgeois ambitions pitted prosperous Philadelphians against the Pennsylvania Railroad in the 1850s. The corporation's demands on urban space grew with its business. As freight arrived on the far side of the Schuylkill, several miles from the Delaware front, managers of the line were keen to keep the publicly owned City Railroad—which by 1846, councils were already calling "a link in the great chain of Internal Improvements that unites us with the West"—running. Attempts to expel it from Broad and Market faced fierce opposition. Boosters warned that trade destined for Philadelphia would flow to New York and Baltimore if denied an outlet to market. J. Edgar Thomson, the Pennsylvania's new president, called attempts to remove the line "suicidal."[47]

In defending the City Railroad, boosters sometimes imagined an entire cityscape built around the needs of commerce. One citizen after the Civil War wondered why, when Philadelphia needed "to afford every facility to trade," a small cabal, "many of whom have been to Europe," were "clamorous for making Broad street a boulevard." The argument had been well-rehearsed over the previous decades. Bringing railroads "to the outer edges of outer districts," the *Commercial List* declared in 1854, "is not enough. Their freight must reach the heart of trade, circulating freely and rapidly back and forth, if we would insure growth and vigor." Philadelphia had to avoid what one New York historian has called "arterial sclerosis."[48]

Railroad boosters, though, had no monopoly on organic metaphors, as the battle over the "lungs of the city" showed. The lungs in question were the Penn Squares, which occupied the Broad-Market intersection (now the site of city hall), and which Penn had set aside for public use. Their historical significance and central location made them the most contested ground in the metropolis for a generation, as boulevarders, businessmen, and politicians fought over their fate. Yet at midcentury they mostly served as fodder ground. Thus, when the Pennsylvania Railroad asked its largest shareholder in 1851 to lease the land for a depot, its directors must have had high hopes of success. They would be sorely disappointed. The westward drift of wealthy citizens toward the nearby West End, plans for a promenade on Broad, and the cholera epidemic of 1849 placed the squares at the center of an imagined "geography of refinement," and inspired fierce resistance to their surrender.[49]

Soon after the Pennsylvania made its request, even its stockholders began drawing a line between private interests and public needs: a distinction largely absent outside of radical circles in the 1840s. Correspondents to booster papers refused to let a business corporation "disfigure a whole metropolis" or render it more vulnerable to disease. By labeling the squares the "lungs" of the city, critics of the Pennsylvania placed fresh air ahead of the free circulation of goods in importance. Thus, when councils, responding to immense public pressure, rejected the railroad's bid, one newspaper welcomed a decision that saved the space "from tuberculous disease." Inside five years, the Pennsylvania had gone from being a cure-all medicine for the city's ills to a malady that threatened metropolitan well-being.[50]

The depot debate demonstrated the difficulty of reconciling the wants of corporate capital with the cultural aspirations of the bourgeoisie. Few by the 1850s accepted the reasoning of a rare defender of the Penn Square scheme, who claimed " 'boulevards,' 'terraces' " and their ilk "would soon be the evidences of wealth produced by a flourishing commerce." Boosters still clung to the hope that private means might bring about public refinement, and plans occasionally circulated for railroads that skirted the city's built environs or soared above its main streets, but they never got far.[51] The Pennsylvania's search for a route to the waterfront, though, opened new opportunities. In 1859, directors commissioned Strickland Kneass, the city's chief surveyor, to investigate various alternatives to the City Railroad. The design of an obscure builder, Solomon K. Hoxie, caught the imagination.

Hoxie proposed an elegantly simple solution. If the city's streets could not simultaneously carry commerce and convey grandeur, then why not bury the goods underground? By burrowing under Callowhill Street—just a few blocks north of Market—the Pennsylvania could reach a new 1,300-foot-long depot on Delaware Avenue without offending the taste of its bourgeois stockholders. "Our beautiful city," Hoxie argued, "would be unincumbered by a traffic a hundred times its present extent." Hiding the unsightly roots of metropolitan greatness beneath the soil allowed a genteel cityscape to bloom on the surface, and boosters rallied round to offer their support. Backers even sold the tunnel as a kind of subterranean Broad Street. Hoxie's design, one newspaper stated, would "confer great credit on our city as the seat of such a noble work."[52]

For a moment on the eve of the Civil War, the tunnel plan enabled Philadelphians to glimpse a different city. Hoxie, fluent in the language of growth politics, foresaw a waterfront heaving with trade from the "teeming western States" and employing hundreds of workingmen. "Life and energy," he declared, would supplant "stagnation and decay." Meanwhile, the tunnel would reorient trade, driving bulky coal and lumber to underemployed Schuylkill wharves, and freeing Broad Street of encumbrances to improvement. Hoxie indeed made Broad's embellishment part of the plan by proposing a vast passenger depot on the avenue. Evidently taken with the scheme, Joseph Harrison proposed a variant, with a tunnel down Market and a *hauptbahnhof* in the vicinity of the Penn Squares, where he began to purchase property to prepare the way. Such designs, one citizen argued, would do more to build the city's reputation "than all the Opera Houses in Christendom."[53]

The tunnel resolved all the contradictions in bourgeois designs for the city bar one. Kneass had to recommend a depot in the interests of the

Pennsylvania's shareholders. As the corporation grew, the proportion of stock owned by the city dwindled, and much of the early mercantile leadership had been deposed in the early 1850s by expert engineers. The result was predictable. Kneass's report praised the practicality of Hoxie's plan but rejected it on grounds of cost. To boosters' disgust, directors opted instead to build a depot at Greenwich Point, some distance below the old city proper. Harrison was so disappointed by the failure of his attempt to redevelop Penn Squares that he left for Europe.[54]

"The Pennsylvania Railroad," a correspondent to the *Evening Bulletin* had written a few years earlier, "is so entirely a Philadelphia work, that the company ought to do nothing which can . . . disfigure any portion of the city."[55] By the end of the 1850s, though, the idea that growth would embellish as well as enrich the metropolis seemed hard to sustain. Capital might flow from commerce to property, but it did so in a manner that was as likely to build up a Bedford Street as a Broad. The voluntarism of Harrison's building work and McMichael's editorial bully pulpit struggled to make an imprint on the urban form. Citizens therefore faced a choice. As investors in railroads, mines, and tenements, they could (and often did) profit from chaotic growth. Yet their collective vision of class culture clashed with their private interests. It led them in some surprising directions.

Planning from Philadelphia to Paris

The struggle to improve the likes of Market, Broad, and Bedford by private means encouraged some citizens to look to public power. Where class duty and corporate responsibility had been found wanting, local government might step up. Like railroad boosters of the 1840s, city builders turned to debt-financing, as they argued the city had to provide for posterity. Even before Consolidation, Philadelphia's surveyor had urged spending millions on a sewerage system to meet the needs of a twentieth-century metropolis.[56] After 1854, citizens who pushed such schemes sometimes looked over the Atlantic for inspiration, where the fiscal might of France's Second Empire was being put to use in reconstructing Paris.

Designs for debt-financed improvements were more of a departure in scale than kind from previous city-building efforts. The antebellum American city was anything but stateless. Through the common law principles of eminent domain and police power, state governments could take property for public use and legislate for the public weal. When these rights were delegated to municipalities, they served as a pretext for everything from regulating markets to building railroads. Many corporate charters, moreover, placed no limit on borrowing before the Civil War.[57] For the *Ledger*, "good municipal government" involved punishing crime; securing property and people from "mobs, violence and outrage"; and watching, cleaning, and lighting the highways. But it required too ensuring "a healthy atmosphere," maintaining "public morals," and removing "all nuisances." The paper's list hints at the potential immanent in the local state. Contemporaries well understood the theoretical scope. William L. Hirst, a lawyer on the Consolidation Committee, noted "the powers of the city corporation are very extensive, and reach nearly every branch of municipal police."[58]

Theory, though, did not always translate into practice. Take, for instance, the *Ledger*'s insistence that nuisance removal was an object of city government. No attorney would have disputed the claim. But what was a nuisance? Few might object to the city authorities removing a rotting horse carcass from a public thoroughfare or compelling private owners to empty stinking cesspits. Yet Broad and Bedford had been declared nuisances. Did this bring them under the aegis of state power too? The *Ledger* certainly thought so. In advocating the demolition of Philadelphia's Five Points and the erection of city-owned dwellings on the tract, it acknowledged that such ends would better be achieved through private enterprise, but it had no doubt about the legal propriety of the measure. Yet to turn Bedford into a "paradise regained" required huge spending on property, demolition, and construction. The returns on the investment—a "general improvement in the condition and morals of the poor" and the "diminution of vice, crime and misery"—would be hard to measure directly and might have taken years to accrue. Similar concerns about cost led even the *North American*, which saw extensive urban planning as "part of the police system of every city," to shy away from designs to widen Chestnut Street.[59]

Consolidators attempted to overcome these limits by giving Philadelphia a government fit for the future. Annexation would unite the city under one set of laws and create the administrative machinery capable of funding reconstruction. It was no coincidence that calls for publicly financed improvement abounded as the campaign for civic union neared its endgame in the early 1850s. Members of the Consolidation Committee intended the new city to have wide planning powers. They made it a "duty" of the new city to provide parks and public spaces while creating a twelve-man Board of Surveyors to oversee "planning" across all 129 square miles. Subsequent legislation, pushed through by Price, established a building inspectorate. Unifying the metropolis under one government, meanwhile, overrode the check on municipal powers imposed by the old district boundaries.[60]

Developments abroad provided boosters with a glimpse of what such a government might achieve. As McMichael's Consolidation Committee met to draft the new city charter in late 1853, his paper reported for the first time on "magnificent works" underway in Paris. Earlier that year, the emperor Napoleon III—consolidating power after his coup brought down the Second Republic—gave his prefect of the Seine, Baron Haussmann, license to rebuild the capital. Already, the *North American* noted, $10 million had been set aside for encircling Paris with railroads; demolishing decrepit buildings; and erecting new markets, bridges, and boulevards. Despite McMichael's own connection to the Bonapartes—he had grown up on the New Jersey estate of the new emperor's exiled uncle—his paper initially denounced the imperial usurper. But the regime's public works led the *North American* to call for the "energetic spirit of enterprise and progress" evident in France to be "infused into our citizens and our municipal councils." Over the next decade, McMichael's paper sometimes saw Haussmann's designs for "monumental and architectural beauty" as a template for "how to make cities great," and by 1860, it had determined that Napoleon III's method was the "way to advance a town."[61]

Just as radicals had seen the Second Republic forging ahead of the United States in 1848, in addressing the labor question, boosters now wondered whether the Second Empire was surpassing them in city-building. "Foggy yet fashionable," Paris was "by far the most delightful city that I have ever seen," wrote a Philadelphian tourist in 1855. The improvements, another wrote from France, were "on a scale of unparalleled magnificence." But Paris's beauty had hitherto resided in the remnants of the past. Now the city was reimagined (in David Harvey's phrase) as a "capital of modernity." And here the French capital stood in chastening contrast to parts of Philadelphia that lagged behind the times. One critic of the market sheds, for instance, mocked the idea that Napoleon III would ever erect similar structures on his "far famed Boulevards."[62]

By 1869, a Philadelphian in France concluded that Haussmann had all but solved "the question of building the city of the nineteenth century."

Such observers saw a systematic plan behind the "elegance, gayety and fashion" that helped them think through the problems of their own metropolis. Like Hoxie's tunnel, here, Napoleon III's city-building promised to resolve the contradictions of urban growth. First and foremost, it seemed to safeguard the state and its supporters. The wave of reconstruction that swept over working-class neighborhoods gave employment to the poor, while creating broad boulevards better suited to massing artillery and circulating goods than spreading disease or raising barricades. Haussmann's admirers in Philadelphia knew full well that the prefect was dismantling the city of the *sans culottes* and replacing it with a metropolis of "order and beauty." Few were blind to the concentration of power and money required to bring about such designs, but they often admired the effects nonetheless. During the Civil War, for example, the *Press* noted how there had "not been one *émeute* in Paris" since the Second Empire commenced. Sidney George Fisher's cousin—part of a family preoccupied with the threat of revolutionary violence—concluded that the city "can never again be controlled by a mob." In a capital that, as another Philadelphian put it, had "made insurrection a science," this was no mean achievement.[63]

Bourgeois Philadelphians believed they had good reasons to find lessons in Paris. Riots in the 1840s had made their city look like the French capital. So too had immigration. First came Irish Catholics, who, ethnologists claimed, belonged to the same tempestuous branch of the Celtic race as the Parisians. These newcomers were closely followed by the "red republicanism" of 1848, which threatened to radicalize a foreign working class. Suspecting that Old World capitals provided a glimpse of their future, city builders had mapped the "canaille" of their suburban frontier, and dreamed of transforming Broad into a French boulevard. When private enterprise and public regulation failed to bring about the pacification of the one and the metamorphosis of the other, it was hardly surprising that McMichael and his allies would look to the Second Empire for guidance.

Take, for example, one citizen who wrote several letters to Philadelphia papers either side of the Civil War. Like many of his peers, he equated urban disorder in the Old World and the New, remarking after the bloody suppression of the June Days in 1848 that the "American and French people . . . are both armed, brave, impulsive, and disposed to offer forcible resistance to real or fancied wrongs." Around the same time—and still some years before the Second Empire's violent inauguration—he called for metropolitan Consolidation, debt-financed municipal improvements, and a professional police under one head. Unsurprisingly, then, Napoleon III's administration impressed him. When he found himself in Paris during the secession crisis, he was so gushing in his praise that he admitted readers in the United States might think he had "fallen in love with the man and his system." By 1868, he was arguing that Napoleon III was "bent on making [his] city a perfect one," and that if Haussmann were in Philadelphia, "five minutes' deliberation" would be enough to improve Broad Street.[64]

Few of his peers were anything like as enthusiastic. In the 1850s, at least, Bonapartist urbanism was an intriguing experiment. Philadelphians who admired it from afar warned it could only be adapted with caution. The apparent success of Haussmann's labors did provide a useful yardstick for boosters in the United States to measure their progress. But the political and financial risks were great. Even the *North American*, with its commitment to state-strengthening and public borrowing, conceded that the French empire's financial muscle enabled it to do things far beyond the power of Philadelphia's city government.[65] Consolidation would be the closest the metropolis got before the Civil War. When the paper praised Haussmann's work toward the end of 1853, the bill for municipal union had already been drafted, and the reconstruction in Paris, at most, would have strengthened Consolidators' conviction that they were part of a transatlantic trend in energetic urban administration. Still, with very different powers at their disposal, Haussmann and McMichael shared similar ideas about how to govern a city. Both recognized that metropolitan planning required commanding capital and coercing citizens. The question remained how to do so.

Growth Politics in Hard Times

Like Napoleon III, Philadelphia's Consolidators believed city-building required mobilizing money and power, yet after 1854, their commitment to reconstruction sometimes wavered. Soon after the new city charter came into force, the boom times gave way to a short but sharp financial downturn, which served as a prelude to a much greater crisis three years later. In the weeks leading up to the Consolidation Act taking effect, the old municipalities—aware their debts would be absorbed by the enlarged metropolis—had borrowed heavily to purchase local improvements and railroad stock. The new city then got in on the act too by investing $2

million in the Sunbury and Erie's route to the Great Lakes. Unlike the
Pennsylvania, though, these lines quickly faltered. The *North American*,
normally a staunch supporter of municipal subscriptions, suggested foul
means had been used to secure the Sunbury and Erie loan, and McMichael
was promptly challenged to a duel by the railroad's affronted president.
McMichael declined the invitation to defend his honor, but the spat suggests deeper concerns about debt-financed growth politics.[66]

Fear of financial over-extension after Consolidation hurt state-
supported city-building. Even Price counseled retrenchment. Echoing
opponents of the Pennsylvania subscription eight years earlier, he warned
that excessive spending would ruin public credit and "retard all progress."
Price was no more of an apostate from growth politics than McMichael.
Over the following decades, both men called for large-scale borrowing to
fund parks, boulevards, and bridges. But speaking for taxpayers, they were
suspicious of the municipal government's capacity to pay its way when
already heavily burdened. When growth was grinding to a halt, Haussmann's management of Paris appeared reckless. Even an admirer of Second
Empire urbanism admitted the municipal balance sheet was filled with
"apocalypses of modern finance."[67]

The Panic of 1857 increased bourgeois doubts about the wisdom of
Napoleon III's course. When working-class citizens became the strongest
advocates of public works in Philadelphia, the comparison that sprang to
mind was the Paris of the Second Republic. For a while, the financial crisis
was confined to New York, but on September 25, the Bank of Pennsylvania
closed its doors, and other institutions soon suspended specie payment.
Within weeks, thousands were out of work. In response to the hardship,
voluntary organizations—which had been strained to breaking point by the
1854 downturn—could not cope. Wealthy citizens, remembering the violence of the 1840s, feared the worst. "A nightmare broods over society,"
recorded the statistician Peter Lesley. "Bread riots are dreaded." Fisher
expected "popular tumult" and vigilance committees; another foresaw
"robberies, riots and crimes of all kinds."[68]

The Panic winter tested the consolidated city government. In early
November, a group calling itself the "Armed Champions of the Indigent"
paraded past the stricken banks of Chestnut Street bearing a banner that
read "We will protect the poor." One of their number told a reporter that
"being out of work," they "thought they had as good a right to create a
sensation as a bank president or a sugar speculator." The response to the

eccentric party hints at the nervousness of city authorities. Though the group mustered little support—journalists suspected the whole affair was a drunken prank—the police were concerned enough to arrest the ringleaders and accuse them of inciting riot.[69]

Though it came to nothing, the affair proved a foretaste of struggles to come. The previous years had seen a changing of the guard in radical leadership. Death and defection deprived labor reform of figures like George Lippard, John Campbell, and William Elder. Midcentury plans for consolidation in trades' assemblies and cooperative stores faltered in the face of sectarianism and slavery. But several craft unions prospered in the benign conditions of the early 1850s. At points during the decade, workers organized more than twenty trades though the Panic appears to have reduced the figure to around a dozen. Yet unlike previous downturns, the economic crisis did not lead to fragmentation. Journeymen and laborers instead found common cause as the unemployed.[70]

Mass meetings in 1857 brought Philadelphia's white working class together in large numbers. German immigrants organized in late October. In early November, the press reported five thousand predominantly Irish workers gathering in front of a "tenantless and deserted" Kensington cotton mill. The following day, another two thousand congregated at Spring Garden and Broad. On November 9, an estimated three thousand Philadelphians met at Washington and Jefferson, and finally, on the afternoon of November 12, Independence Square hosted what was said to have been the largest meeting in the city's history, with speeches in English and German. One speaker at an earlier meeting summed up the ecumenical sentiments of the organizers, when he claimed he did not care whether those in need of relief were "Methodist, Catholic, or Mormon."[71]

The unemployed movement followed in the footsteps of midcentury radicalism. Leaders included veteran craft unionists and echoed the late Lippard's division of the city into an upper tenth and lower million. A speaker claimed "every man who got along without" working for his daily bread "was a millionaire." Another called for workers "to overthrow the manufacturers and capitalists." At one meeting a citizen warned from the platform that workingmen must "steal, beg or starve," to which the crowd responded, "then we'll steal." Like their radical predecessors, moreover, organizers of the unemployed meetings sometimes challenged the "harmony of interests" doctrine that tied producers and employers together. A printer reminded the crowd, for instance, how easily the wealthy forgot the men who had built the "stately edifices" that "ornament and beautify our streets."[72]

Instead of pulling down Philadelphia, though, the unemployed offered to build it up. Rather than raise a riot, the leaders of the mass meetings—who formed the Unemployed Workingmen's Relief Association (UWMRA)—embraced elements of growth politics. By the time an estimated ten thousand citizens assembled on Independence Square, the UWMRA had assumed a loose control over affairs. The organization called for public works on an almost Haussmannesque scale. It was a common cry across the nation in 1857, but in big cities like Philadelphia and New York, the growing muscle of the municipal authorities enlarged workingmen's ambitions. Soon petitions to the mayor and councils calling for jobs on civic improvements circulated.[73]

The UWMRA's actual proposals indicated a willingness to experiment with new concentrations of political and financial power. They borrowed heavily from Mayor Fernando Wood's suggestion in New York of issuing city debt as a circulating medium: a scheme that, as one leader acknowledged, required citizens to lay aside longstanding "prejudices against paper currency," which went back to the Jacksonian era. Organizers of the Broad and Spring Garden meeting asked the municipality to issue $4 million in city warrants. These small notes would pay workers and settle debts with the city. The UWRMA went further in asking the city to contract an even larger debt to expend on urban improvement. Journalists quoted two figures here. The more plausible request was for $5 million, an amount close to the *Pennsylvanian*'s estimate of the amount needed to support the poor through the winter, but less than half the city's holdings in railroad stock. But the *North American* printed the extraordinary figure of $50 million. If spent as the UWMRA suggested on "improving property in the precincts of this great city," then such a sum would have gone some way to making Philadelphia the Paris of America.[74]

The unemployed movement welded the growth politics of debt-financed city-building to midcentury radicalism. Physical labor, its leaders argued, offered better collateral than a bank's meager gold reserves. One painter, in an echo of John Campbell's designs to peg currency to production, offered to "loan our labor—and our labor is capital," if the mayor could ensure the acceptance of city scrip for necessities like "bread and butter." Yet often the notes the UWMRA struck owed more to boosters than radicals. Reprising the argument of railroad promoters a decade earlier, the organization's supporters claimed that rising tax revenues—an offshoot of workingmen's embellishment of the built environment—would soon diminish the enlarged debt. Like the *North American*, then, it advocated borrowing to meet future wants as well as present needs. The UWMRA plan fused money, credit, and labor into a tantalizing program of urban growth and embellishment, which promised to stimulate demand as well as succor the poor.[75]

Yet in contrast to 1838, when Price had led a campaign for public works, and to 1846, when the bourgeois press had backed unprecedented borrowing to support growth, the UWRMA found few friends among the economic elite. Some boosters and politicians did support funding for parks, bridges, culverts, and reservoirs, and saw wages as better than charity. But a municipal committee that included a leading Pennsylvania booster rejected the plan for circulating $4 million in notes as potentially "disastrous to the city credit." Probably wary of extending the patronage powers of the Democratic mayor and councils, and afraid of spiraling debt, even McMichael's paper only offered lukewarm backing for improvements. Make-work schemes, it counseled, were "wholly opposed to the spirit of our institutions." "The idea of the Government being obligated to give employment to the working classes," a conservative Democratic daily concurred, "is of foreign origin."[76]

Indeed, bourgeois Philadelphians sometimes saw the shadow of the Parisian crowd of 1848 behind the unemployed movement of 1857. The resurgent radicalism reminded onlookers of France under republic and empire. The *New York Times* called the Germans' cry of "bread or battle" in Philadelphia "the communism . . . of the barricades of Paris." Others worried about the migration of "socialistic" doctrines to Philadelphia. While the UWMRA never made the link itself, its plan may have owed something to earlier radical support for the make-work schemes of the Second Republic. But "to open public workshops as in Paris," one paper insisted, "would only end as these have done, in universal anarchy, fraud, and the destruction of the public credit." Another wondered where it would all end: if the city could act as an employer, what was to stop it taking over factories or construction too? Rather than realizing dreams of the bourgeois city, critics argued, the demands of the unemployed would lead down the road to "red republicanism."[77]

Viewed in this light, Haussmann resembled a demagogue at the head of a mob rather than an enlightened expert. From the perspective of the Panic, the improvements to Paris, which employed tens of thousands, looked like a continuation of the National Workshops that had so impressed Philadelphia's midcentury radicals. Thus, when the Democratic mayor vetoed an austerity resolution passed by councils and cautiously endorsed debt-financed public works, he was condemned by a councilman of his own party as "acting Napoleon the III."[78] Once civic improvement became a concession to working-class demands rather than an expression of bourgeois authority, support for such measures waned. Here the Second Empire offered a cautionary warning. In absorbing surplus labor, the *Press* pointed out, the emperor had drawn ever-increasing numbers of the dangerous classes to the city. When the work stopped, they would revert to revolutionary type.

Though it failed in its bid for bourgeois support, the UWMRA demonstrated how the association of capital, labor, and state power—the three pillars of growth politics—might build up a metropolis. The organization's ambitions for urban embellishment proved so grand that the chairman resigned at the November 20 meeting after complaining that real estate speculators had infiltrated the movement. The collapse of the unemployed movement provoked much glee among bourgeois papers, which decried the "demagogues" at its head as idle drunkards. Yet those leaders had come as close as wealthy consolidators ever had to showing how the city might be reconstructed.[79]

The Panic of 1857 suggested that support for state-strengthening among Philadelphia's bourgeoisie was conditional on who controlled that state. When Napoleon III appeared to have pacified Paris, his achievement was lauded, but when he looked like a creature of the crowd, wealthy American observers recoiled. Debt had the alchemical power to transform the city—the railroad-building of the 1840s had demonstrated that well enough—but the capacity to borrow went hand in hand with the capacity to tax. Bourgeois citizens certainly feared the consequences of city-building slipping from their grasp. The harsh winter had briefly opened the possibility of an alliance between the economic elite and the working poor, but given the choice, boosters had mostly refused to lend their support to the UWRMA's program. After 1857, the leadership of growth politics would pass from the hands of both.

*   *   *

Bourgeois Philadelphians broadly agreed on what a modern city should be in the 1850s, and genteel designs for light, air, and space helped to define them as a class. Making the built environment behave in the manner they expected, though, proved far more vexing. The contradictions they confronted help account for the inconsistency of figures like Price and Mc-Michael. Capital, they found, both built up and blighted the city. Public visions of class culture ran into the private interests of profiteering individuals. And a newspaper that on one day might argue that a dose of Haussmannization would elevate Philadelphia to greatness, on another could claim that it would reduce the city to ruin. Every time boosters thought they had unlocked the secrets of metropolitan improvement, they found their way blocked. The 1850s therefore witnessed a cacophonous and often contradictory debate on the means of city-building, despite the near unanimity on the ends desired.

Boosters' gratitude to fire's "purifying effects" indicates just how frustrating shaping the project of building an imperial city had become.[80] After the Panic of 1857, Broad and Bedford continued to languish. The provision sheds clung to Market. Railways still scarred major streets. Yet in many ways the decade had sown the seeds for a much more radical postwar reconstruction. Consolidation had created a government with stronger capacity to plan and borrow. Financial crisis had revealed working-class citizens' receptiveness to growth politics. And the vigorous debates over how Philadelphia should look and function had coalesced into a class vision. The problem remained, though, that the bourgeoisie could not build the metropolis on their own. McMichael may have had a Haussmannesque sense of the city as a whole, but the leader columns of his paper hardly had the force of an imperial prefecture. A stronger power was required. Out of the Panic of 1857, indeed, one would emerge committed to consolidation of metropolis and nation. That organization was the Republican Party and from a small spark, it would burn over Philadelphia.

CHAPTER 5

Out of Many, One

Remaking the Polity

If Baron Renfrew hoped for a good night's sleep on October 9, 1860, he had chosen a bad day to arrive in Philadelphia. The English visitor—better known as Queen Victoria's son Albert, the future Edward VII—was the first British royal to visit the land his great-grandfather had lost eight decades before. Having crossed the border from his mother's Canadian provinces, he made his way south via the nation's capital, before being pulled up to Philadelphia by a locomotive called George Washington. At the passenger depot on South Broad Street, a crowd of several hundred onlookers—mostly women, a newspaper slyly reported—had gathered to greet the bachelor prince. But citizens' minds dwelt on other matters. Across the twenty-five wards of the consolidated city, voters were streaming to the polls to pick a governor, congressmen, and a state legislature. The presidential canvass was still several weeks away, but observers were well aware that the results that night would all but determine a critical state's course.[1]

The eighteen-year-old prince hardly rivalled Alexis de Tocqueville as an observer of American democracy, but he must have been staggered by the rough and tumble of electoral politics. His hotel at Ninth and Chestnut Street gave him a fine view of the contest. "No British prince," remarked one observer, "ever before had such an opportunity of examining the working of universal suffrage." Supporters of John Breckinridge—the most ardent pro-slavery candidate in the presidential race—had headquarters one block to the west. Republicans and Douglas Democrats were based a couple of streets to the east. On Chestnut itself, rival factions jostled for territory. By 8 p.m. in the evening, indeed, the street was almost impassable as bonfires and barrels of flaming tar illuminated the sky. As the results poured in, rival paramilitary clubs marched along the thoroughfare. At Seventh, the two parties collided, and only the "density of the crowd" prevented a fight. When marchers passed the prince's hotel, someone recognized the young royal watching from the balcony. A surreal cry of three cheers for Queen Victoria briefly distracted attention from the struggle over the republic's future.[2]

Albert was witnessing a muscular civic culture that Consolidators had tried to abolish. Lines between politics and disorder had blurred in the pre-Consolidation city until the two were all but indistinguishable. Riots had been provoked by political meetings (1844) and borne in the boozy aftermath of elections (1849). With the future of the country at stake in 1860, the threat of bloodshed at the ballot box once more loomed large. Republican mayor Alexander Henry, elected a year after the Panic of 1857, had already received a warning from the South of "murder and destruction of property" in Philadelphia. Election day threatened to drag the city back to the dark days of the 1840s.[3]

That the *North American* would later report the election passing off with "tranquility" says much about the expectations of the time. News of "black eyes and bloody noses" came in from "most of the wards," police wrestled with drunks, and a voter in the southern suburbs was knifed in the thigh. A few blocks north of the historic center, gangs fought with stones and clubs, and on the disputed borderland between Moyamensing and the old city proper, blacks and whites exchanged volleys of bricks and gunfire for half an hour. On each occasion, though, the police broke things up, and despite dozens of arrests and several near misses, the press agreed that the election had gone well. The city had not been embarrassed in front of its royal visitor.[4]

By 10 p.m. the results were in. Morton McMichael, whose paper had switched allegiance from the defunct Whigs to the new Republican Party a few years earlier, declared victory to the crowd outside his newspaper's office. The governorship, state, and four of the city's five congressional districts would all be in the party's hands. Pennsylvania's place in the Republican column made a Lincoln presidency all the more likely. "It is a curious coincidence," a chronicler of the prince's travels wrote, that Albert arrived in Philadelphia "on the very day when the death knell of the slave party rung."[5]

McMichael could be forgiven for having mixed feelings about the result. On the one hand, the Republican triumph ensured that for the first time since the early 1840s, the city's growth coalition would have friends in Washington. Moreover, the party's vision of national consolidation, based on economic expansion, the supremacy of a strong central government, and a commitment to moral and internal improvements writ large Consolidators' designs for Philadelphia. Boosters made much of the links; for them the consolidation of city and nation were entangled projects.

At the same time, though, the election revealed the failure of attempts to bring about a social realignment of politics. Consolidators had hoped to gentrify civic life as well as city streets. Blaming voters, parties, and myopic "small men" in the districts for both social and sectional disintegration, they tried to usher in a host of reforms that would change the rules of metropolitan politics and thrust farsighted "best men" to the fore. Ambitions to build grand avenues, green parks, and a class of citizens whose political horizons took shape in virtuous homes rather than on street corners all seemed to hinge on getting the right people into office; getting the right people into office, meanwhile, seemed to hinge on the reconstruction of the built environment. Consolidation itself here became more than just a state-strengthening measure; it also marked an attempt to change who ruled whom by resculpting the terrain of urban democracy. As the slavery question, which had brought disorder to the Jacksonian metropolis, once more assumed center stage after 1854, however, the movement that had brought about the new city charter fractured.

The Problem with Politics

Projects to consolidate metropolis and nation gathered pace in a democratic age. That age was not to everyone's liking. Sidney George Fisher, the conservative diarist who fought railroad subscription and civic union in the 1840s, offered one of the harshest judgments. In 1844, just days before the militia turned its cannon on the Southwark crowd, he told the British consul of his hope "that the English may learn the true nature" of placing power in the hands of the people before it was too late. Chastised by his friends for his lack of patriotism, he confessed "my hatred of democracy is stronger than my love of country."[6]

For Fisher, democracy led to disintegration across the Union. Ignorant voters, he argued, were "swayed by every radical and dangerous doctrine which designing men put forth." In the 1840s, demagogues had driven Phil-adelphians to mob law, Pennsylvanians to repudiate their state debt, and New Yorkers to reject the landowner's right to rent. Fisher even included the first stirrings of the movement for municipal consolidation—which he saw as an attempt by impoverished suburbs to ransack the wealthy city proper—as part of the "disorganizing and dangerous tendency of the times." By the eve of the Civil War, he was blaming democracy for dis-union. Long before wealthy northerners and southerners turned the tide against democratic rights in the 1870s, Fisher had determined that property and democracy could not peacefully coexist.[7]

The diarist, like his counterparts in Philadelphia's mid-nineteenth-century economic elite, had lived through the throes of democratic trans-formation. In the republic of his youth, he remembered politics as a gentle-man's calling. Voters deferred to their social betters; parties fought their battles in the legislative halls rather than city streets. All that had changed, however, in the age of Jackson. The removal of property restrictions on the franchise, the opening of new offices to election, and the impact of immigration and industrialization provided fertile soil for parties to sow seeds of discord. Even conservative Whigs, he believed, had been forced to pander to the people. Men of property, therefore, found themselves estranged from civic affairs or compromised by their participation. He mulled over the possibility that democratic institutions led to "anarchy, ignorance, [and] brutal violence."[8]

Such a story of the republic's descent into democracy, however selective and self-pitying, spoke to the redistribution of power and authority in Jack-sonian America. Although partisanship had been fierce in early national Philadelphia, there is much to be said for seeing the 1830s and 1840s as a time of immense political upheaval. As specialists tied to new mass-based parties established a foothold, the economic elite either willingly withdrew or reluctantly retreated from city government. Wealthy citizens may have continued to run for offices like Congress or the mayoralty—a position opened to direct election from 1838—but they left much of the legwork of municipal affairs to new men. Fisher deplored the consequences. "The mob is supreme," he wrote on the evening of the 1840 presidential canvass, and "the educated classes are utterly without influence."[9]

In Philadelphia, Fisher stood on the fringe of antidemocratic dissent, but his Burkean pessimism may have been more widely shared than we might think. He certainly claimed his views reflected those of "educated

men and those who have property." Into the 1830s, old Federalists like
Horace Binney indicated a limited monarchy came closer to the republican ideal than a pure democracy, and over the following decades, several
wealthy citizens threw in their lot with nativist parties, which promised
to limit the political rights of the burgeoning immigrant poor, who made
up an ever-growing proportion of Philadelphia's working-class population. Fisher, despite resisting the Know-Nothing siren, saw "excluding
foreigners" as a way to excise "so much democracy . . . from political
power." Vast swathes of the city's working poor—children, women, and
African American men—were after all already deprived of voting rights,
and for some, it was not a leap to disfranchise a few more. Fisher's cousin,
one of Philadelphia's richest men, was an early voice for removing the
vote in municipal elections from non–property holders. Others warned
of the terrors to come without a reassertion of central control. One conservative judge at a Consolidation meeting in 1850 foresaw thousands of
voters at some point in the not too distant future entering the homes of
"the rich citizen" and taking their wealth by force as supine police looked
on.[10]

Doubts about democracy may have been greater in industrializing Philadelphia than any other northern city. The coincidence of democratic
upsurge and urban disorder—Philadelphia's epidemic of street violence
closely corresponded to the rise and fall of the Second Party System—did
not go unnoticed among those who saw "the people" as synonymous with
"the mob." "Our worst riots have been sustained at the time by local popular sympathy," one citizen noted in 1849. "The rowdies," a reformer argued
a few years later, "control our elections."[11]

But such heretical views were hard to express openly in antebellum
America. "Our whole system of government," a Consolidator conceded in
1852, "is so completely mingled with the system of popular elections, that it
appears dangerous to suggest a doubt, or to hazard an argument, unfriendly
to them." Tellingly, Fisher saved his antidemocratic agitation for the dinner
table, and played down hostility to popular sovereignty when he wrote for
the *North American*. That paper tended to decry the effects of a wide suffrage without evincing any enthusiasm for an assault on the principle. "Our
whole body politic," it declared in 1856, "is tainted." Around election time,
though, the daily boasted of Whig support for white male suffrage, and
when it cautiously suggested that a "free republic" required a majority of
freeholders to function, it quickly added, "we do not mean that any should

be disfranchised." Instead of purging voters from the political community, conservatives channeled their energy into rearguard battles against democratization by protecting economic power in private corporations and safeguarding offices from voters' control. Even here though their success was not guaranteed. Pennsylvania Railroad boosters may have managed to secure public money for a corporation largely free from public oversight in 1846, but some of the line's leading supporters failed to stop the opening of judicial office to election four years later. Far more citizens than we might think probably decried in private what one conservative Democrat called the "Blind Credulity of the Multitude," but they had to share the political commons with the swinish herd.[12]

Critics of the new order found themselves on safer ground in attacking politicians and parties rather than voters. Antebellum America may have been the heyday of popular politics—turnout in key elections like 1840 and 1860 approached nine out of ten eligible voters—but plenty perceived an inner malaise. Bourgeois Philadelphians did take sides in party contests, yet they were more vocal than most in voicing opposition to the spirit of partisanship. Frustration with the Second Party System bubbled beneath the surface and occasionally boiled over into antiparty politics.

The sense of politicians as idle and divisive appears in working-class as well as bourgeois reform. Radicals urged producers to resist partisan wiles and associate as workingmen. The politicians of 1849, the socialist George Lippard declared, would be remembered at the end of the century "as we now look back to the grand Inquisitors of the Spanish Inquisition." Even in boisterous Moyamensing, citizens labeled the "low characters" who loafed on street corners "congressmen." When merchants, manufacturers, and professionals assailed party politics, they reasoned from the same republican principles. In pursuing power for its own sake "political adventurers" placed self-preservation ahead of the common good. The cancer of corruption then began to consume the body politic. Critics charged politicians with abusing patronage, forging elections, and trading in votes and offices. When they were not using foul means to stay in power, they simply stirred up trouble. "They aim to *divide* us as a people," one jeremiad declared, so "that they may severally divide the spoils."[13]

To wealthy critics, though, politicians lacked social status as well as republican virtue. Major parties cut across class lines, but divisions existed within the organizations. In antebellum America, middle-class voters were coming to value self-restraint as a manly quality. Evangelical Protestantism and economic calculation often went hand in hand to promote self-cultivation and self-discipline. Citizens sought to bring order not only to their own lives but to the spaces around them: homes, lyceums, and the streets and squares of the city. Party politics, though, seemed to privilege a very different kind of masculinity, one based more on the martial posturing the Prince of Wales witnessed in 1860 than individual improvement. Fist fights were so run of the mill in civic life that an eminent citizen contrasted places of learning to the "brawling of politics." Genteel Philadelphians who participated in party games therefore held their nose when doing so. Fisher, checking voter qualifications as a Whig in the 1840 election, found the atmosphere intoxicating, but complained about "the vulgarity" of his associates. He, like many of his peers, proved far happier mixing with prosperous friends from across the partisan divide than with working-class allies in his own party.[14]

The changing character of the city's representatives appeared to illustrate the coarsening of politics. Jacksonian reform opened opportunities for citizens outside the economic elite to hold office. Wealthy voters felt the problem especially in municipal government. "The truth is," a merchant observed after encountering a blacksmith officeholder in 1839, "the intelligence of this country is excluded from all public stations." Bourgeois citizens either scratched the most distasteful candidates from their ballot papers or held their nose and voted the party ticket. Thomas Pym Cope confessed to feelings of "shame and indignation" in choosing the latter course. Most simply moaned that matters had deteriorated. To the *North American,* the rise of new men signaled a "sad and evil degeneracy" in the city's politicians.[15]

Such lamentations did reflect a real sense of loss. In practice, merchants and manufacturers often lobbied successfully for growth-friendly legislation, and radicals plausibly portrayed an upper class with intimate ties to party leaders. Bourgeois citizens, however, may often have been corrupt themselves, but they were not contented, and their contempt for politicians is too palpable to dismiss as republican platitudes or status anxiety. In their struggles to remove market sheds, build wide boulevards, and create public parks, they had confronted the limits of their power. If they were a ruling class, few were aware of it.

The contrast between political specialists and bourgeois reformers becomes clear whenever the latter imagined a Philadelphia run by men made in their likeness. City-building, as McMichael's paper had argued for

Broad, demanded officers of "social eminence" and "superior energies and talents." Without what one citizen called "strong men, of established reputation, and with a knowledge of the wants of this community" as its representatives, Philadelphia would flounder. The model legislator would transcend the "ignorance, prejudice and passion" of municipal politics and emancipate himself from party feeling. Midcentury "best men" mixed Whig suspicions of uneducated officeholders to a Progressive faith in expertise. "An Uncompromising Whig," for instance, demanded men of "learning and science and intelligence" on the Board of Health instead of pliant tools of "cliques." Fisher found such figures in aristocratic England, but others located them in Second Empire Paris. The "perfection of its municipal system," one Philadelphian argued in 1861, owed much to men from "mercantile ranks" of "the highest personal character," who served as imperial appointees on the council. "The French government," concurred the *North American*, places "men who will see for themselves" at the head of affairs. Closer to home, reformers found an ideal in nonpartisan organizations like the Statistical Society and Board of Trade. With their leadership drawn from the economic elite, and their loyalty lying with city rather than party, they hinted at an alternative to rule by specialists.[16]

Yet it was neither the politician nor the voter that most troubled bourgeois reformers, but rather the relationship between the two. Each succored the other. "The degenerate race," wrote the *North American* of the nation's paupers, "are the slaves of whatever faction will most encourage them." Few would hold back from selling their votes or serving as "hired bullies" to "reckless demagogues." At worst this might stir up class war, as a self-serving politician could stoke envy at the rich. At best it would simply lead to corrupt, ineffectual, and expensive government.[17]

Such fears were explored in Timothy Shay Arthur's 1853 novella, *Before and After the Election*. Arthur, a popular writer for the temperance cause, was more interested in spreading the creed of political nativism than municipal reform, but his story would have rung true for wealthy Philadelphians outside Know Nothing ranks. It charts the career of Patrick Murphy, an ignorant Irishman lured into politics by a wealthy demagogue, who wins over gullible Celtic allies by attacking "capitalists and nabobs," keeping the whiskey flowing at party headquarters, and promising to share the spoils of victory. As a foot soldier in party politics, Murphy works the local taverns, enjoys the campaign barbecue, and drives "drunken vagabonds" to the polls. His patron is eventually elected, but neither man comes out of the relationship well. Murphy's politicking costs him his job, while the candidate finds himself "half-sick with disgust" at having to flatter his Irish "tools."[18]

If Arthur directed his cautionary tale at ordinary voters, he also hinted at the dilemma "best men" faced when entering politics. To remain aloof from the fray entailed all but giving up hopes of high office. Playing by the rules of the new men, however, meant compromising character. To even secure a nomination, one crusading newspaper wrote, a candidate had to "fawn and cringe," "banish all self-respect," and "impose upon himself every degradation." "No gentleman of purity and independence can demean himself by . . . social interchanges with gamesters, drunkards, defaulters, embezzlers, and political vagabonds," a Philadelphian lawyer noted. Those who did so risked ostracism from their peers as class traitors.[19]

The problem posed itself particularly acutely for what one historian has called the "gentleman Democrat." Representing "the union of democracy and wealth," the aristocrat placed himself at the head of the crowd, where he waxed lyrical in the Jacksonian idiom of equal rights. The antebellum archetype was Richard Vaux, a scion of an old Philadelphia family and a man who had danced with Queen Victoria at her coronation. Vaux's popularity among the Democratic faithful and his personal ambition made him a regular candidate for mayor, and during his term in office in the mid-1850s, he became known as "Vaux populi." But his victory owed as much to his command of organizational politics as his family lineage, and he appointed several rowdy backers to the police. "To approach him," one genteel Republican claimed, "you have first to encounter a horde of convicts, ballot-box stuffers and assassins." McMichael, who claimed the mayor as a friend, still accused him of surrounding himself with "the most degrading influences." Politics, it seemed, dragged down even the best of the bourgeoisie. "A very corrupt party," one leader of the Consolidation movement declared, "may place a good man in office, whilst they strip him of all power of doing right, and make him the slave of their most unworthy purposes."[20]

Why, reformers asked, could the best men not govern without the corrupting influence of party? What had happened to the deference of the early national era that the likes of Fisher yearned for? Those honest enough to admit it recognized that its spatial as well as social moorings had been washed away. The walking city of the early nineteenth century provided a suitable terrain for their kind of politics. Its limited scale offered wealthy men plentiful opportunities to demonstrate their fitness for office. Through leadership in crowd action, almsgiving in hard times, and public displays of virtue in fire and militia companies, the old elite cultivated support. The mayor's capacity to enforce the law, as one citizen noted after the Kensington riot of 1844, had once rested on "moral power" as much as physical force. Elements of the old ways persisted into midcentury. A French visitor to Philadelphia in the early 1850s toured the "bad quarters" of the city with a paternalistic chief magistrate who bantered with men he had previously consigned to the county jail. Even into the war years, the mayor used his personal authority to prevent riots.[21]

On a citywide level, though, a politics based on personal presence was hard to sustain. The growth of working-class suburbs separated rich and poor. Private philanthropy proved incapable of dealing with the fallout of financial crisis. And while an eminent citizen like George Cadwalader continued to lead the militia, by 1844, he was training his cannon on the crowd rather than leading the people himself. Meanwhile, the city's political geography came to reflect the Jacksonian principle of local self-government, as districts and boroughs secured charters, and elections once held at the statehouse were outsourced to wards. At a glance, it seems, we have a classic story of modernization as a face-to-face community gives way to a big, bureaucratic society. Party politicians and a professional police proved better equipped than the old elite at governing a big city. While there is great merit in this interpretation, however, it may be better to see city growth as dispersing rather than destroying traditional authority. Urban growth had not led to anarchy, as some contemporaries occasionally implied, but instead to the redistribution of power across the big metropolis. Recentering sovereignty would become one of the principal aims of political reformers.

Sovereignty in the Suburbs

The further removed reformers were from Philadelphia's civilized center, the more foreign its political landscape could seem. As they ventured into the metropolitan frontier, indeed, republican government gave way to something else, which observers addressed with a mix of humor, disgust, and apprehension. Consider for instance Pluck Hill: a reputed resort of "the idle and vicious" with a reputation as the Bedford Street of the northern suburbs. In 1857, police raided the district in search of stolen pigs, a frequent source of conflict between the authorities and poor citizens. The Pluck Hillites, armed with paving stones, an axe, and a gun, "desperately resisted" the officers' invasion. At first glance, newspaper reports suggested the terrain was a stateless wilderness. In a neighborhood in which the "laws of the land, like the laws of morality," were "a perfect dead letter," the "wildest confusion prevailed." Yet at the same time they saw a distinct political order on the urban frontier. The "Queen" of Pluck Hill, a paper claimed, was Kit McCluskey, a tavern keeper who ruled on every disturbance. When the police intervened, she directed the resistance until several "of the rebels . . . were made prisoners of war."[22]

If Pluck Hill had a queen, then Moyamensing had its "King": William McMullen. McMullen, the son of an Irish immigrant, was born in 1824. As a young man, he defended Catholic lives and property in the nativist riots, and some reports placed him in the party that shot the Protestant "martyr" George Shiffler in Kensington. Like other foot soldiers in antebellum politics, McMullen moved easily between street fighting and partisan politics. Around the time of the riots, he became Moyamensing's Democratic bookman, which enabled him to check voters' credentials. After returning from the Mexican War, McMullen acquired a major role in the Democrats' citywide organization, the Keystone Club, though he neither sought nor acquired high office. Before the 1860s he never rose above the rank of alderman, a local magistracy that made him one of the "lesser satellites" of Philadelphia politics, but to his Irish American constituents around Bedford Street, he was the "Squire": a man who commanded the paternalistic respect the best men believed belonged to them. Reformers had little doubt he controlled Moyamensing: a district that the *Public Ledger* suggested in 1849 might need to be placed in the hands of a vigilance committee, if the local authorities continued to neglect their duties.[23]

When reformers surveyed the suburbs, they saw such small sovereigns everywhere. Pig owners ruled over the empire of "porkdom"; volunteer fire companies were a power within the state, an *"imperium in imperio"*; street gangs, "mighty tribes of Philadelphia Indians," flew pirate flags on the Schuylkill. Prior to 1854, these were joined by commissioners in "their high mightiness," who ruled over the "petty local governments" that cut Philadelphia up like the tiny states of the Holy Roman Empire.[24] Legal and extralegal sovereignties reinforced one another. Fire companies, street gangs, and tavern owners not only defended their turf, but also lent a hand to local politicians. McMullen for instance served in the Irish

American Moyamensing Hose, fought among the notorious Killers, and ran a hostelry that served as a base for his political operations. To reformers, these were hard spaces to penetrate, as one policemen found out when he tried to arrest McMullen for election fraud at a tavern in 1850 and found himself threatened with a knife. Contemporaries sensed the importance attached to territory. "MOYAMENSING," a novelist in 1847 has the Killers proclaim, "MUST BE OURS."[25]

Petty sovereignties protected residents from outside influence. Like hill countries or borderlands, they proved resistant to state builders. McCluskey and McMullen's readiness to fight government violence with violence of their own was not uncommon. Over and over again poor suburbanites fought encroachment. Even after Consolidation in 1857, it took nearly a hundred police to dismantle a cluster of piggeries near the Schuylkill.[26] Citizens were adept at the "art of not being governed," or at least not being governed by outsiders. One critic of a citywide police, for example, acknowledged that "rowdies" would have few problems driving off "foreigners and interlopers." Such tactics offered some relief from bourgeois reform and municipal regulation, but we should not romanticize these little fiefdoms. Black neighbors were more likely to be on the receiving end of McMullen's violence than white outsiders, and neighborhoods shielded from the state were often impoverished. But hardship made the defense of an informal economy and community based on the likes of unlicensed taverns, "nuisance" piggeries, and goods appropriated from an urban commons all the more important.[27]

Party politics offered another way to defend territory. While Queen McCluskey, as a woman, had no access to the ballot box, King McMullen complemented his street fighting with Democratic connections. The two indeed bled into one another: the Killers novella probably got it about right when the gang promise to sell the votes they control to the highest party bidder. Violence was certainly an important part of suburban politics. Whig voters in Moyamensing only took their party's ballot "under the apprehension of personal harm," and McMullen's career was littered with brawls, knifings, and assassinations. Such indiscretions were tolerated by higher-ups in the party, though, as McMullen did good work on the ground for gentlemen Democrats like Vaux. McMullen in the antebellum era was not a cog in a citywide political machine, but rather a local chieftain, who made tactical alliances to protect his people. A broad suffrage helped such figures to shield themselves from an aggrandizing state.[28]

Bourgeois reformers mocked suburban sovereigns but envied their power. For figures like McMichael, the best men could see the city as a whole. To them, Philadelphia was a complex but comprehensible totality, and only associated effort across its different parts could lead to uplift. The diminutive scale of the petty sovereignties, though, offered little hope for improvement. The "reign of small men and small measures" held back the metropolis. "They are the great men of their respective localities," the *Sunday Dispatch* remarked, but would "become nobodies" in a united city.[29]

The problem here lay less in democracy itself and more in the confined and decentralized terrain on which it was played out. Philadelphia's destiny, critics implied, took shape in the taverns of Bedford Street rather than the promenades of Broad. A politics spawned miasma-like in the hose houses, gang haunts, and rum shops of the suburbs induced symptoms of myopia. Remedies for the short-sightedness of the "small men" interested more than wealthy reformers. Radicals, whose global perspective jarred with the localism of ward politicians, resented parochialism too. But for bourgeois boosters, the consequences were troubling. When the city needed a Haussmann, it got McMullen.

By the 1850s, suburban sovereigns stood accused of a multitude of sins. Their critics charged them with indulging mobs, wasting money, and impeding grand metropolitan improvements. The small men, after all, had little reason to reconstruct an urban environment that worked for them. Why purify Bedford when they could be "hunting up voters in courts and alleys"? Market Street's provision sheds supposedly provided the most damning evidence in the case for the prosecution. The vendors' stubborn refusal to yield before the march of improvement led one critic to wish "that we had among our prominent citizens . . . *one* that had the prescience to see our future . . . and nerve to do battle for its right direction." By 1858, a wit proposed relocating Bedford Street's residents to the markets, which could then serve as a base for (among other things) "electioneering operations."[30]

The sarcasm belies real concern about the spaces in which city politics took shape. Take for instance the problem of delegate elections, or primary meetings, as they were sometimes known. As the first step in the process of selecting candidates, the meetings marked politics at its most local and democratic. Citizens would attend gatherings in their ward, township, or district to send representatives to their party's citywide nominating convention. For critics, however, the process, which was supposedly dominated by savvy "wire-workers," marked the "incorrigible vice of the American system." Self-styled "best men" in both parties looked to their reform or abolition.[31]

Bourgeois commentators urged their peers to participate, but this was easier said than done, given the city's political geography. "Primary elections," the *North American* complained, had been "abandoned to a very small portion of . . . each ward." "Men of property" needed to start showing up. Residents of the city proper, however, could not simply wander into the delegate elections of independent suburbs. Even those eligible to participate would have found themselves on uncomfortable terrain. Primaries typically took place in hose houses and dram shops, where "respectable citizens" rarely ventured. At some meetings brawling broke out and ballots were destroyed. "The appointed place," McMichael's paper conceded, "may not be one" that a gentlemen of refinement "would habitually visit," and the men he would meet there "may not be of the number that he would daily concert with." But it was better, it argued, "to control them than to be absolutely governed by them."[32] Yet there was no guarantee that bourgeois participation would make any difference at all. Men of McMullen's ilk, Fisher's cousin complained, enjoyed "large influence over a number of humbler inhabitants." And with the help of firemen, gang members, tavern keepers, and even police—"important adjuncts" to meetings, one contemporary observed—they would have little problem getting their way.[33]

The delegate elections distilled the broader challenges self-styled "best men" faced. Urban growth and a broad suffrage, they believed, had made political power decentered and degenerate. What was needed was a program that broke the bond between inept voters and corrupt politicians. The answer, some suggested, lay in the fabric of the city itself. Philadelphia needed retrofitting for republicanism.

Gentrifying Politics

By the early 1850s, bourgeois Philadelphians tended to agree that democracy did not work for them. What though was to be done? Neither restricting voting rights nor mobilizing the "best men" held out much hope of success. The former smacked of aristocratic Federalism; the latter ignored the problems of playing politics on the specialists' terrain. Reformers tried instead to rewrite the rules of the political game. They turned the project of consolidating the city into a program to gentrify city politics.

The Consolidation movement carried the germ of antipartyism from its outset. From the first calls for civic union in the 1840s, support came from across party lines. Consolidators tried to detach their cause from divisive questions in Congress. "What does it matter," asked one citizen in a party paper, "whether Whigs or Democrats govern in a local question?" From 1849, indeed, some reformers were calling for a new charter to stipulate the holding of municipal elections in May, several months removed from distracting state and national races. The metropolitan interest, it seemed, stood between the courts and alleys of Moyamensing and the corridors of power in Washington.[34]

Advocates of a new charter, though, knew they needed political backing. Cities after all were the legal offspring of legislatures. From 1849 to 1850, the Executive Consolidation Committee dispatched "gentlemen of influence and character" to Harrisburg to win representatives over, but instead of a union of city and districts, they had to content themselves with a metropolitan police. Frustrated by the failure, the *Sunday Dispatch*—a muckraking weekly that fired invective at politicians and merchants—suggested asking party nominees in the upcoming state election to pledge themselves to pursuing a new charter, and the idea soon took hold. Pro-Consolidation candidates' subsequent victory in October 1851, the *Evening Bulletin* happily proclaimed, "settles the question of the union of the city and districts."[35]

The *Bulletin*'s triumphalism proved premature. In early 1851, as legislators considered charter revision, opposition began to surface. Petitions poured in from rural townships, and critics in built-up suburbs also condemned the proposed reform. Consolidators dismissed the discontent as the work of small men who would "become much smaller" in a big city, but representatives heard the complaints. They tabled the bill indefinitely just days before the session concluded.[36]

Consolidation's slow strangulation over the first few months of 1851 pushed reformers to ponder seceding from party politics altogether. Advocates of civic union vowed revenge on everyone from party "wire workers" to Philadelphia's Harrisburg slate. Having let the charter die, one citizen warned the pledged legislators, "*they also will be permitted to die*" at the ballot box. Tensions boiled over in September when Consolidators gathered to review their progress. The Executive Consolidation Committee attacked the character and competence of Philadelphia's representatives. Only Edward A. Penniman of the so-called "pledge-breakers" attended the meeting. Penniman—a veteran of the General Trades' Union—symbolized the change in metropolitan politics. Though he backed the Pennsylvania Railroad and worked with Eli Kirk Price on real estate reform, he was, to one journal, an exemplar of the type that had ransacked "the business men of the community."[37] Penniman, the paper argued, should have stuck to his trade rather than sought office; like many regular nominees, he lacked the qualities "to represent a great city." At the meeting, though, he defended his record, and "besprinkled everybody" (as one satirical report put it) "with the pleasant terms 'liars,' 'slanderers,'" and "'villifiers'" Although a few attendees tried to salvage his reputation, the audience responded to his tirade with hisses and boos. Judge Anson V. Parsons wrapped up affairs with a call to "choose a ticket apart from politics" and "sweep the Democratic, the Whig and the Native parties to the winds."[38]

A year and a half later Consolidators did just that. As citizens had done on various occasions over the previous years, including 1849, when a reform ticket had shocked the Whigs in the city proper, reformers turned to anti-party politics. The nationwide sense after midcentury that political parties had outlived their usefulness emboldened the breakaway movement. By 1853, indeed, Whigs and Democrats found themselves fighting an antiparty insurgency across the Union that left the former on the brink of annihilation. Consolidators themselves argued that the "old party lines are almost, if not quite, obliterated."[39]

Consolidation provided a rallying point around which malcontents coalesced. First, often with close ties to Protestant churches, came temperance campaigners. While they strove for total prohibition on the model of a law recently adopted in Maine, some were willing to settle for a stricter system of tavern licensing. Second, headed by the iron manufacturer Stephen Colwell, were friends of the paid fire department. They had organized in late 1852 with a view to replacing unruly volunteer companies with a professional force. Finally came Consolidators who began to organize again in June. Horace Binney, once a fierce opponent of civic union and a man ill at ease with Jacksonian Democracy, told his son that the evils Philadelphia labored under were "intimately connected," and only the projection of "united power" across the city could address them. Alongside other "best men," he began to recruit a Consolidation ticket that could draw support from across the reform spectrum.[40]

Supporters saw the independent ticket of 1853 as an example of how a gentrified political culture might work in Philadelphia. Instead of selecting delegates in boozy primary elections, Consolidators appointed nominating committees, which included prominent boosters, two Pennsylvania Railroad presidents, and leaders in civic institutions like the Board of Trade and Franklin Institute. A few well-known politicians appeared among the names, but men of McMullen's ilk were notably absent. Working alongside advocates of a paid fire department and Maine Law, the committees composed tickets for the city and county bearing "first rate names," which they claimed far surpassed "the average of talent, dignity and efficiency" of a typical party slate. Some of their candidates, including the manufacturer Matthias W. Baldwin, ran as independents. Others had a place on the Whig and Democratic tickets too, though such figures were generally far wealthier than the "political hacks and hangers on of bar-rooms," who supposedly filled out the regular nominations. At the head of the slate stood Price. Binney, convinced that the Consolidation question would "test the virtue of the city," had sought out the attorney for his "general knowledge" and "experience in civil affairs," and Price, who had been involved in the struggle for civic union for nearly half a decade, had good reasons to enlist—not least his large tracts of land in a county crying out for improvement. But he also shared his class's hostility to the city's political culture. "The elective franchise," he wrote in accepting the nomination, had "become almost valueless" under the existing system.[41]

After the election, from which Price, Baldwin, and several other Consolidation candidates emerged victorious, well-heeled reformers extended the experiment in a new style of politics to the making of policy. In their weekly meetings—held in the genteel surroundings of the Board of Trade rather than a lowly tavern—Philadelphia's "most intelligent and discreet citizens" (the North American neglected to add richest) debated the draft of the new charter point by point. McMichael chaired as eminent Whigs and Democrats enjoyed each other's company. The independent representatives helped the measure sail through Harrisburg.[42]

It was easy though to draw misleading lessons from the reform movement. Consolidation, which had failed under party stewardship, succeeded once the best men seized control. "The reign of partizanship is over," the Evening Bulletin declared, "and the rule of patriotism has begun again."[43] Put the right men forward, the argument went, and the people would do their duty. But in actuality the independent ticket benefited from smart compromises and fortunate timing. For all their antiparty rhetoric, Consolidators sought to persuade Philadelphia's politicians that an enlarged city would do little to affect the balance of power. Sometimes this meant working with experienced hands. Joel Batholomew Sutherland, to one historian the prototypical "city boss," joined the reformers' nominating committee, as did other party politicians.[44] Such figures probably realized that as the city grew, so too did the scope for patronage. Their presence, coupled with bourgeois nervousness about what unchecked majorities might do with an enlarged city government, also helps explain the charter's concessions to localism. Provisions for ward representation provided a lifeline for small men like McMullen, who also sought shelter in offices the charter left untouched. In the first post-Consolidation election, for example, the Squire won election as an alderman, a ward-level office protected by the Pennsylvania Constitution. Like state builders from China to Western Europe in the nineteenth century, Philadelphia's reformers had to negotiate with the local powers they set out to undermine.

Consolidators benefited not just from their unlikely alliance with politicians, but also from the widespread revolt against them. In 1853, Whigs and Democrats deserted their parties in droves, but unlike a year later—when the Know Nothings sprung onto the scene—citizens fleeing the major parties lacked a new home. The independent movement, helped by its promise to extend control over Catholic suburbs, provided temporary shelter for these political refugees. Within days of the election, indeed, one nativist reminded reformers that their ticket "would not have been elected" without the assistance of "American Consolidationists."[45] If he was right, then the charter's success owed less to the manner in which it was pursued, and more to the propitious moment it was put before the people. The social realignment of politics threatened to be little more than a blip.

Reformers certainly hoped not. Their design for the city, though compromised by coalition-building, aimed to perpetuate the political style of the reform ticket. Consolidators targeted many of the spaces in which the small men forged power. Hose houses had long been seen as places of electioneering, and the political importance of the firemen was a source of frequent complaint. Price and a fellow senator, for instance, warned of the volunteers "combining together" in the manner of the factions Washington counseled against in his farewell address. A paid system promised to eliminate their influence. Tighter regulation of taverns would likewise weaken the stranglehold of suburban sovereigns while keeping voters away from places that made "bad citizens." If forced to fight delegate elections on unfamiliar terrain and without firemen's muscle, men like McMullen would soon wilt. McMichael's paper went so far as to propose the new city build ward houses so parties no longer needed to meet in places "highly offensive to a large class of voters." Reformers longed to tear up the institutional fabric of party politics and replace it with something more amenable to bourgeois taste and control.[46]

The redrawing of political boundaries also threatened local strongmen. Consolidation's economies of scale, its advocates hoped, would decimate the officeholders who had obstructed reform in the past. Small men will "lose power and influence," an instigator of the independent ticket claimed, "and have to crawl back to their original place of obscurity and insignificance." Abolishing petty sovereignties also promised to reverse the political retreat of Philadelphia's bourgeoisie. The big wards of the new city, Price argued, would induce "men of large experience" to serve in councils. A "dignified office" like the mayor might draw superior candidates eager to serve a city that exceeded in population several states of the Union. Initially, at least, this may have worked. Whig, Democrat, and American merchants and manufacturers—many of whom had never sought office before—sat on the first post-Consolidation common council.[47]

To restore bourgeois influence, Consolidators gave citizens of the city proper a say in suburban governance. Prior to 1853, critics complained, "a man may hold vast and important interests in a district wherein he has no vote." For Thomas M. Pettit, the divisions on the county map tended to "disfranchise men of business," but this hurt suburban commuters as well as city capitalists. The *North American* even saw civic union as a political inducement to suburbanization. "Men," it insisted, "must have a suffrage and control in the government of the particular municipality in which their business and property are situated." Metropolitan growth had divided citizenship and capital, but Consolidation promised to unite them in one metropolis.[48]

Finally Consolidators linked physical reconstruction to political reformation. Midcentury calls for parks and boulevards may have reflected bourgeois ideals of urban refinement, but they often assumed a link between environment and citizenship too. Philadelphia's physical form took on what historians have termed a didactic role: genteel spaces would produce genteel voters. "If the people rule," McMichael's paper remarked, "they must be kept in a condition to fill their office of sovereign." But that required putting them in the proper physical setting.[49]

That setting might be a humble hearth rather than a Haussmannesque avenue. Consolidators' grand designs for parks and boulevards sat alongside schemes to increase Philadelphia's housing stock. Extending the city outward first and foremost met the needs of growth politics: it enriched suburban speculators, occupied the building trades, and countered radical claims that landlords ravaged the urban poor. But political calculations lay behind the project of domesticating Philadelphia's working class too. Consolidators believed that bringing homeownership—or at least a good tenancy—within reach of an ever-greater portion of the population would transform the city's political culture. They were right, but not in the way they necessarily anticipated.

Midcentury reformers frequently tied orderly households to orderly politics. What may appear a relic of premodern patterns of thought here actually had modern roots. The seventeenth-century English philosopher Robert Filmer had argued the patriarchal family provided a model for political authority, and across the Atlantic in the Colonial era such ideas worked to legitimate the power of fathers, husbands, and masters. By the 1850s, though, while elements of Filmerian ideas persisted in the paternalistic defense of slavery, middle-class Philadelphians tended to extol the virtues of domestic life. Responding to the religious and economic upheaval of the first decades of the nineteenth century, domestic ideologues invested the household with sacred significance, casting it as a cathartic refuge from the competitive world beyond its doors. Under women's stewardship, homes had the potential to incubate good citizens and act as a civilizing force. To Henry C. Carey, Philadelphia's eminent political economist, the "moral man" frequented "neither taverns nor gaming-houses. His place is home."[50]

Price, "the father of Consolidation," traced the ties between household and civil authority in more detail than most. As a state senator, he helped write Pennsylvania's married women's property law, and a wartime treatise on the family elaborated his liberal outlook. Home to Price was the "smallest civil institution" yet without it, "government could not live." Nations rose and fell, he claimed, on the strengths of their households. Good "family government" therefore secured the interests of the state, but rather than using this as Filmer did to defend patriarchy, he recommended the "dual reign" of husband and wife. Here, he argued, lay a form of family government peculiarly well-adapted to a republic: one in which women's "power can be made to be most pervasive and useful." That power, though, did not come from voting. Instead, by keeping a good home, women could lure their men away from drinking dens and hose houses. "The city at night would sleep in peace," he declared, for it "is the homeless and traitors to home that cause the chief public charge."[51]

Few middle-class northerners would have found anything controversial in Price's argument, but they were well aware that his republican "family government" did not rule supreme in all the nation's homes. Domesticity remained more ideal than reality. Though Philadelphia served as an important site for its diffusion—workshops produced the furniture that graced genteel homes; publishers churned out periodicals like the nationally renowned *Godey's Lady's Book*—its advocates confronted myriad other ways of organizing households. Beyond the city, utopian socialists, patriarchal slaveholders, and polygamous Mormons provided different models of family authority. And Philadelphia itself hardly looked like a place of domestic bliss. Radical reformers like Lucretia Mott, frustrated at the limited role for women in moral reform, began to demand access to the ballot box after 1848. Men sometimes responded that elections fought in the streets were simply too debased for the gentler sex, while simultaneously condemning the working-class women who played "the Amazonian" in riots.[52] When readers encountered the *Press*'s portrayal of Queen Kit McCluskey's Pluck Hill, they would have seen her violent matriarchy as a stark contrast to their own, supposedly peaceful households. Indeed, the utter absence of a cathartic home life is one of the most striking features in depictions of the Bedford Street neighborhood (see Figure 2). Domesticity had not yet conquered the city, let alone the Union.

And this had troubling implications for men as well as women. "He who acts wickedly in private life," the post-Consolidation mayor Robert T. Conrad argued in 1852, "cannot prove excellent in his public conduct." Without the civilizing influence of a good home, though, what chance did young men have? Reformers complained that they preferred bunking in hose houses or drinking in rum shops to spending time at home. A new generation of voters therefore learned lessons in classrooms unfit for purpose. Fire companies, Consolidators, agreed, were "the worst school for the training of good citizens." One correspondent, writing about suburban gangs, spoke of youth "schooled into anarchy, treason and murder." A prize essay in a collection published by the House of Refuge identified the "street schoolmaster" as Satan himself. Subjecting citizens to the right kind of education required removing them from petty sovereignties like fire companies, neighborhood gangs, and disorderly suburbs.[53]

But Consolidators envisaged using the expanded power of the post-1854 city to strengthen the home: the one petty sovereignty that supported the state. Calls for Consolidation often accompanied demands for stronger parental oversight. Baldwin, for instance, took personal responsibility for his firm's apprenticeship scheme, but combined paternalistic strictures with his active role in the push for a new city charter. A strong home life, though, required more than mere assertiveness on the part of parents or masters: it also needed building. "To brutalize men," a correspondent to the *North American* wrote in 1850, "is not to fit them for their duties as citizens." Yet children, the House of Refuge essayist wrote, were driven onto the street by the "sickening effluvia" in their rickety tenements. Allowing them to grow up in miserable homes pushed them into the hands of men like McMullen. A degraded domestic sphere therefore imperiled the body politic as well as corporeal bodies. "Cage men in mean, uncomfortable habitations," the *Pennsylvanian* asked in 1857, "and what care have they for the institutions of the country in which they live?"[54]

In the years leading up to the Civil War, reformers tried to lay the foundations for good family government. Domestic institutions like workhouses sought to train their inmates in household economy. The consolidated police force turned on street "loafers" and unlicensed tavern keepers. Alternatives to the middle-class home—notably the hose house—came under sustained (though rarely successful) attack. But most importantly, perhaps, some aimed (as one writer put it) to place "decent houses within reach of the poor." With evidence of the consequences of bad homes all around them in riot and disorder, the matter acquired a particular urgency. Even the *North American* printed letters from George Bayne, a doctor who—despite disavowing any affiliation with "agrarians or communists"— suggested that the city build model apartment blocks around common kitchens. Cities, Bayne insisted, were "indebted to the character of their dwellings for the tone of morals and manners," and if Louis Napoleon could provide shelter for Paris's poor, there was no reason a republic should not do likewise. Bayne's plan—which had precedent in feminist domestic design—was less eccentric than it might seem. The *Ledger* urged the city to provide "a proper description of dwellings for those who are unable to procure accommodation through their own efforts."[55]

Above all, municipal reformers tried to prepare the way for a mass migration to the metropolitan frontier; something the *North American* termed by 1859 "the policy of dispersion." Fears that the city had "become too densely peopled" were rife in the years following the riots. Persuaded by the moral environmentalist conviction that cramped confines weakened "the idea of property" and led "human creatures" to "forfeit their character as responsible and respectable beings," McMichael's paper urged Philadelphians "to spread our present population over more space." Consolidation, by extending local government's financial and territorial reach, sped up this suburban exodus. From 1856, horse-drawn passenger railways—privately owned but publicly chartered—abetted the process of outmigration, and just four years later, 18 lines with over 150 miles of track were helping to make "consolidation a tangible fact." By carrying pioneers to cheap land on the metropolitan fringe, they provided the "means of preserving for Philadelphia her well known distinctive character as a city where every family may afford to have a home and a household of its own."[56]

The parallels to national expansion struck contemporaries. The *North American* described the passenger railway's "march of civilization" carrying "law and order" to the suburban frontier, as the "wild youngsters of the borders" acculturated themselves to city norms. Their homogenizing effects "made all sectional distinctions obsolete" and brought "moral and physical blessings." In contrast to pent-up New York, where Manhattan's narrow confines pushed an ill-housed poor into crowded tenements, Philadelphia had the room to grow. By laying "herself out on an imperial scale," the city's "manifest destiny" mirrored the nation's, uplifting both those it encountered and the population it left behind.[57]

The echoes of American empire-building in Consolidators' rhetoric show how they tried to emphasize decentralization's democratic appeal. By claiming "practical consolidation" would open cheap homesteads beyond the built-up limits of the city, boosters localized elements of the land reformers' vision for the West. A few thousand journeymen bought stock in the land companies that promised to turn meadows into lots around Consolidation, and while many of the speculations failed in the Panic of 1857, unemployed laborers had called in the crisis for extending infrastructural improvements to the suburbs. Supporters of passenger railways condemned opponents as "aristocratic charioteers" eager to exclude "plebeian cars" from fashionable promenades. In practice, though, Philadelphia's middle-and upper-classes benefited most from the "bourgeois corridors" created by the streetcars. High fares deterred the white working class, who tended to find shelter close to their workplace. African Americans, meanwhile, were barred from the seats of streetcars and excluded from many of the land companies. But the prospect of an all-white suburban frontier of small property owners enjoyed broad appeal among the electorate.[58]

Like the mass suburbs of post-1945 America, new forms of transportation, access to real estate, and racial exclusion in the antebellum city promised to reorient political sensibilities. Bourgeois Philadelphians could not restore the link between property and voting through antidemocratic reform, but they could make homes easier to acquire. "If a majority of our voters were 'freeholders,'" the North American had argued in 1859, "the country would be in fact what it is in theory—a free republic." It had claimed before that a metropolis built around small houses would reap rewards in the form of less "dependence," "more sound public spirit," and greater "prudence and wholesome conservatism." Advocates of the new city charter—and the practical consolidation that followed its passage—aimed to move Philadelphia closer to the ideal. Yet this was just one aspect of their wider project to reconstruct political culture. The old suburban frontier of Bedford Street sustained the small men. The new suburban frontier of the consolidated city, though, would gentrify city politics. Away from taverns, gangs, and fire companies, and safely ensconced in salubrious homes, voters would begin to see the city as McMichael did: a metropolitan whole.[59]

Consolidators aimed to retrofit Philadelphia for republicanism by moving the classroom of politics from the street to the home. Price indeed concluded his discourse on family government with a lengthy explanation of why his city suited his ideal. Thanks to the prevalence of single homes, he argued, "it is with a pleasing and grateful feeling that we contemplate the expansion of this largest city of our continent." Once "the old parts shall be rebuilt," he continued, "there can be but few confined places to breed physical or moral disease and contagion, or riot and rebellion." In the 1840s, poor family and civil government had been blamed for the chaos, but by the Civil War, Philadelphia's transformation from a city of mobs to a city of homes was well underway.[60]

The Union City

"The destiny of a nation," Conrad had insisted in 1852, "is determined in its homes." Such links between the urban environment and national health became more common as the struggle over slavery intensified. City-building and nation-building proved hard to disentangle. Rewriting the

city's organic law, incorporating new territory, and reconstructing citizenship, all paralleled nation-building projects. Reformers understood the rhetorical value of the comparison. Consolidators rallied to the cry "In Union
There Is Strength, while one proposed "E Pluribus Unum," or "Out of
Many, One," as a motto for the city. At the Consolidation festivities in 1854,
the words hung on a banner from Independence Hall alongside portraits
of Price and Washington.[61]

As the campaign for civic union gathered strength, sectional storms
threatened to tear the federal Union apart. The first effort to consolidate
city and districts in 1844 to 1845 took place amid debates over the annexation of Texas. When the movement for a new charter resumed over the
winter of 1849 to 1850, the threat of southern secession seemed very real.
The armistice hammered out in the Senate staved off the threat of disunion for a time, and in 1853, the reform ticket could suggest (rather
naively) that the slavery question had been settled. Yet as the Consolidation Act wound its way through the Pennsylvania Legislature in early
1854, another bill geared toward encouraging out-migration was under
discussion in Washington. The Kansas-Nebraska Act, introduced by the
Illinois Senator Stephen Douglas, organized territorial governments in
the remainder of Jefferson's Louisiana Purchase. To win over southern
whites, though, Douglas offered to open the two territories—which lay
above the boundary between the social systems of North and South
agreed in the Missouri Compromise of 1820—to slaveholders. Northerners quickly mobilized to halt the imperial designs of a "slave power," and
within a couple of years fighting had broken out in Kansas between pro-
and anti-slavery settlers. The guerrilla conflict marked one of the first
skirmishes of the Civil War.

The links between social and sectional crisis extended beyond rhetorical
appropriation and pure chance. Although they were attentive to the differences between a city and a nation, Consolidators saw the challenges each
confronted as fundamentally alike. No slaveholders stood in the way of
Philadelphia's metropolitan manifest destiny, of course, and while the street
gangs of the suburbs were often compared to "savages," the power required
to subdue them (or civilize them, as reformers would have preferred it)
never approximated anything like the force of the federal government. But
nineteenth-century "bourgeois analysis," Charles Tilly has argued, "posited
an unending race between forces of differentiation and forces of integration." As a way of thinking, this applied to the neighborhood as well as

the nation: "practical people" used the categories to explain "small scale" problems like crime as well as the "large scale" chaos of class conflict. Consolidators, thinking in similar terms, saw the challenge of integrating a divided city and Union as part of the same conundrum. How could they hold both together?[62]

To their critics, integration came through division. Opponents of Consolidation sometimes compared civic union to the centralization of power in Washington. One of William B. Reed's reasons for resigning from the Whig Party in 1855 was his contempt for a new charter he called "wrong and delusive" in principle. By 1862, as a leading figure in Philadelphia's antiwar movement, he spoke of a coming "centralized domination" in the North, and suggested his state's true interests lay with the South. Whether Reed's copperheadism sprang from the same principles that had led him to oppose the 1854 charter is hard to say, but some were more explicit in making comparisons. A writer in the *Ledger,* for instance, had warned at midcentury that the annihilation of local self-government would lead to municipal as well as national dissolution.[63]

Thomas S. Fernon, a Democratic senator from Philadelphia County, made a similar case in his minority report on the proposed 1850 charter, by considering Philadelphia as "a miniature of the Union." He claimed that reformers' eagerness to extend city laws over the outlying district, if applied to the nation as a whole, would "blot out the States" and inspire resistance. For the city too, the measure would arouse a "spirit of secession" and lead to "conflict between the northern and southern wings." Fernon's alternative to the disunionist course of Consolidation must have seemed apposite during the Crisis of 1850: as a grand sectional compromise he proposed leaving the city proper alone, creating a North and South Philadelphia out of the adjacent districts, and leaving open the possibility of enlarging West Philadelphia at some point in the future.[64]

The irrepressible conflict Fernon foresaw between different sections of an enlarged city did not seem so far-fetched given the backdrop of national crisis. Since the early nineteenth century, citizens in the northeastern corner of Philadelphia had been trying to break free from the county. Annexation to the city in 1854 only confirmed their conviction that they had a separate future, and by 1856, efforts were underway to dissolve their ties to the metropolis. A little over a week before the opening shots on Fort Sumter, indeed, they caught the secessionist bug once more and sought confederation with Bucks County.[65]

But Philadelphia's rural environs were too important for Consolidators to concede. Whether as an opportunity for investment or a safety valve for surplus population, they could not be surrendered. Reformers therefore ridiculed Fernon's critique of centralization. Taken to its absurd extremes, the *Sunday Dispatch* argued, it led to an anarchic privatism in which "every man's house is not only his castle, but his municipality." Meanwhile they challenged the conclusions he drew between civic and national government. Rather than an unhealthy aggregation of power, the new city would mirror the checks and balances of the Constitution. "Our wards would constitute the states of the union," the *Dispatch* continued, "and their government the federal government." Others suggested the more apt analogy lay in the district system and the condition of the states prior to 1787. Price contended that "the same paralyzing inefficiency" that forced Americans to abandon the Articles of Confederation now "exists among the city and districts." Fettered by artificial boundaries, Price warned, Philadelphia would meet the same fate as European nations whose "contracted territories" were destined to dwindle in comparison to the United States.[66]

Whether wittingly or not, then, Consolidators found themselves drawn into debates about the terms of national unity. Although the Consolidation coalition excluded African Americans, its leaders reflected the breadth of opinion on slavery. The chair of the first meeting for a union of the city and districts in 1844 had been treasurer of the Pennsylvania Hall Association: the builders of the abolitionist meeting house burnt to the ground in 1838 by a racist mob. Other antislavery agitators, including a Quaker imprisoned for resisting the Fugitive Slave Act of 1850, participated in the movement. Occasionally hints of their influence crept out. When a correspondent to the *Ledger*, in a plea for civic union, wrote the following, he surely knew that he was quoting a popular abolitionist poem:

Lands intersected by a narrow frith abhor each other
And make enemies of men who had else, like kindred drops
Been mingled into one.[67]

Opponents of Consolidation certainly tried to make the link between civic union and national disunion. Price, a regular Whig misleadingly claimed in 1853, was "a notorious abolitionist" and others accused the entire reform ticket of backing the "*isms*" of abolition and women's rights that blighted the prospects of city and nation.[68] Slavery's critics had reason to support Consolidation. What passed for the police forces of the old city and districts proved either incapable or unwilling to protect African Americans and their white allies from mob violence, and the post-1854 force proved much more effective in protecting abolitionists and their property. Moreover, the reform movement broke with parties committed to perpetuating slavery and promised to marginalize white supremacist suburban sovereigns.

Consolidation did hold out some hope to black citizens. The African American elite, despite building their own institutions, had sometimes tried to mitigate the baneful effects of racism by claiming that they belonged alongside Philadelphia's best men. In practice, Philadelphia's white bourgeoisie kept wealthy blacks—who rarely rivaled in riches the city's richest merchants and industrialists—firmly at arm's length, and African Americans were more likely to find a welcome reception in the predominantly white world of midcentury radicalism. But the moral environmentalism that underpinned bourgeois designs for the new city implicitly challenged racial hierarchies. The African American Underground Railroad conductor William Still drew on environmental determinism to challenge segregation. Writing to McMichael's paper in 1859, he contrasted the "genteel colored people" in furnished brick houses to the "degraded" minority in the "ill-fated region" straddling the old boundary between Moyamensing and the city proper. The implication that space rather than race shaped character opened progressive possibilities. One black suburbanite told a white journalist that African Americans "would scatter to remote sections" if given the chance, in search of "cheap rents, cleanliness and comfort." The anonymous source may well have been the abolitionist Robert Purvis, one of the only residents in Philadelphia's northeast to speak out against attempts to secede from the city in the years prior to the Civil War.[69]

But the color line was one boundary few Consolidators wanted to override. Where white voters benefited from public and private support for out-migration, disfranchised blacks found themselves blocked by the racial proscriptions of land companies and horse railways. Black men, excluded from the political community, were given no opportunity to join the campaign to redraw the city charter, and the benefits the new metropolis offered them were meager at best. Even the stronger police could be more of a burden than a blessing for African Americans in the hands of a white supremacist mayor like Richard Vaux. Philadelphia's black population hardly accepted their lot. By 1859, indeed, William Still and others had taken up the fight against streetcar segregation. But Purvis is the only African American I have found to have publicly supported Consolidation prior to 1861. It would take the changes of the war years—and the rise of the Republican Party—to change things.

White Consolidators for their part were generally unionists rather than abolitionists. Few, if any, embraced slavery in the abstract. The likes of the *North American* contrasted the dynamic North to a stagnant South and urged slaveholders to follow their lead by diversifying into industry. But for all their paeans to free labor, Philadelphia's merchants and manufacturers relied on slave goods, and saw the South as a market for their wares. Even Baldwin, who had strong abolitionist sympathies, tried to avoid alienating slaveholding customers.[70]

Still, Baldwin's quiet support for antislavery appears downright heroic when compared to the line taken by other reformers. Few of the city's first families with ties of marriage to the South had been especially active in the campaign for Consolidation. Yet slaveholders found allies among Consolidators too. Price, an active colonizationist and opponent of slavery extension, presents an unlikely example. As the sectional crisis deepened, the father of Consolidation began to sound like a "doughface" southern sympathizer. Days after the body of the executed abolitionist John Brown passed through Philadelphia in 1859, Price joined a huge meeting at Jayne's Hall, where resolutions disavowed any desire to interfere "with the domestic institutions" of sister states, approved of Brown's fate at the hands of the Virginian authorities, and backed the return of fugitive slaves. Price's speech attacked "fanatics of extreme views" and called for rigid adherence to the law. Even the call of another Consolidator at the meeting for the lynching of abolitionists did not lead Price to reconsider. A year later, while confessing "no friendly feelings to the institution of slavery," he claimed nonetheless that "the south alone have the right to deal with it."[71]

Price was in good company, for "citizens who represent in a large degree the wealth, the literature, and the commerce of Philadelphia" joined him at Jayne's Hall, including twenty leaders of the Consolidation movement. Boosters and reformers, indeed, were well-represented in other gatherings that called for compromise in 1850 and in 1859 to 1860. Leading figures in growth politics—Pennsylvania Railroad directors, major factory owners, real estate moguls—turned out in force. Only a few of the more assertive antislavery Consolidators kept clear of the meetings that called for considerable concessions to planters.[72]

Hard though it is to see how a humane man like Price could call for the strengthening of fugitive slave laws as a matter of "peace and conciliation," his actions were entirely in keeping with his unionist principles. Like other Consolidators, Price bemoaned the consequences of jarring jurisdictions in the city, and concluded that only some kind of municipal federation could prevent ceaseless war. The Constitution for him offered the same benefits as Consolidation: it preserved peace, secured property, and won rivals' respect. In his Jayne's Hall speech, Price foresaw states freed from the fetters of the Union raising armies to guard their frontiers. He did not make the analogy directly, but he portrayed a nation reverting to the chaos of Philadelphia prior to 1854. Price's allies in the movement for municipal reform echoed his warning. Judge Edmund King—who had presided over the trials of rioters in 1844—recalled George Washington's desire for "*the consolidation of our Union*" and reminded the post–John Brown meeting that "Border countries have ever been theatres of bloodshed and slaughter." The leader of the campaign to abolish Philadelphia's turbulent fire companies had told a friend in a slave state of the "unending war" that would follow separation.[73]

As the Civil War approached, Consolidators argued that disunion sprang from demagoguery, and claimed patriots who put nation ahead of party would stave off conflict. Reprising their role in the movement for civic union, they implied that only "best men" could prevent disintegration.[74] But the social realignment of politics some reformers had confidently anticipated in 1854 failed to materialize. Instead, the city inched toward sectional politics, and despite the apparent unity on display at mass meetings, the Consolidation coalition threatened to fragment.

In the first municipal election under the new charter, anti-immigrant nativists—in league with Whigs—secured the mayoralty. The Know Nothings, or American Party, were always likely to do well, given Protestant Philadelphia's aversion to Catholicism, and they seized on the antiparty mood. Whigs' support for the Native candidate probably swung the election, but the tactical alliance did little to rejuvenate their party. By 1856, most supporters had abandoned moribund whiggery, and faced a choice between the Americans, Democrats, and Republicans—a new movement founded in the West to check the expansion of slavery. Initially, at least, bourgeois Consolidators tended to opt for one of the first two options. Many old Whigs—Price and Frederick Fraley among them—turned first to the Democrats and then, in 1860, to the Constitutional Unionists. The Republicans after all were easy to portray as a party of abolitionists and agrarians; several radical veterans, including William Elder and William D. Kelley, were among their early backers. McMichael's *North American*, though, had rather reluctantly thrown itself behind the Republican Party, and a handful of wealthy Consolidators campaigned for the party. Their presence proved insufficient as Democrats swept the city, state, and national elections.[75]

Although the Republicans failed in 1856, their efforts lay the groundwork for future success. The party's capacity to draw bourgeois boosters and radicals eager to defend the interests of white labor hinted at a broad appeal. In several industrial suburban wards, indeed, it performed well. Over the following years, party leaders honed their message with great success by exploiting anger at the Dred Scott decision and the financial crisis of 1857.

Like the Consolidation coalition in 1853 to 1854, the Republicans promised political regeneration, economic growth, and outward expansion. The party's readiness to embrace growth politics after the Panic of 1857 sped its ascent. Protectionists such as McMichael and his friend, the political economist Carey, blamed the crash on a low tariff, and argued protection to the American producer would harmonize social and sectional interests. Meanwhile the party's support for free soil, a homestead act, and internal improvements promised to open the West to white workers. Alongside the merchant Alexander Henry at the head of the Republican ticket in 1858 stood a Baldwin machinist, and the union of commerce and industry hinted at the direction the party wanted to go. It is telling, perhaps, that at a Republican rally that year, Henry Clay received more plaudits than any living politician. Clay's vision of sections and classes associated through ties of economic interdependence closely mirrored that of the party.[76]

In their municipal program the Republicans also looked to state-sponsored economic development. The Panic brought to a close the old policy of debt-financed railroad-building—voters across the state amended the Constitution to ban cities from buying stock or lending money to private corporations—but municipal improvements still depended on active government. During the crisis, American Party councilmen—the Republicans had no representatives of their own—proved more receptive than their rivals to heterodox ideas like using city warrants as a circulating currency. Democrats eager to prosecute improvements, such as the Pennsylvania Railroad's lawyer, Theodore Cuyler, found themselves in a minority as their party backed austerity.[77] Although in the spring 1858 campaign, the

Republicans—now allied with the Americans in a fusion People's Party—ran on a platform to curb expenditure, they were forging important alliances. Republican supporters attacked the Democratic administration for failing to provide public works, and the People's Party immediately commenced the work of practical consolidation once it controlled councils. They supported the construction of passenger railways, removed the provision sheds from Market Street, planned the extension of a public park, and backed a program of bridge-building and culverting. "The party in power," McMichael's paper claimed, "has shown that it feels the inspiration of our destiny."[78]

Realizing Philadelphia's prospects allowed the Republicans to forge alliances with voters eager to move out to the metropolitan frontier. "The city is expanding into the county," one of its backers exclaimed, and on the outskirts the party found some of its strongest support. Already by 1858, the People's Party polled best in the fast-improving West End and manufacturing suburbs of the northwest. Democratic loyalists clung on in the rural wards, but wherever the "march of improvement" approached, the Republicans tended to prosper. Party leaders courted aspiring suburbanites. By 1859, four hundred or so building societies—mutual associations formed by working people eager to secure the capital for homes—operated in Philadelphia, and when organizers sought favorable legislation in Harrisburg at a mass meeting, leading Republicans addressed the crowd. The party pushed for homesteads on the suburban frontier as it tried to secure the West for free labor. "Extending our population over a larger area," the *North American* waxed, "will illustrate in the case of our city and its vicinity, what the clear head of Henry Clay desired for the whole country."[79]

When the Prince of Wales visited Philadelphia in 1860, though, the Republicans' position in Philadelphia remained precarious. The party had won over more of the Consolidation coalition, as municipal reformers came to acknowledge that the greater threat to the Union came from southern plantations rather than northern abolitionists. Beyond the compromise meetings, indeed, many Consolidators struck a more bellicose note, refusing to compromise on the further extension of slavery, and questioning the operation of the Fugitive Slave Act. Still, plenty of the city's best men kept their distance, and as tensions mounted, the social solidarities cultivated over the preceding years began to strain. When Price announced his support for the Constitutional Union Party, for example, McMichael's paper printed a sarcastic riposte, which mocked his contribution to reform. For some, the war years exacerbated these divisions and forced McMichael and his friends to beat new paths to class consolidation.[80]

The forked road to Republicanism is especially evident in the case of Fisher. In the mid-1840s, Fisher had warned that the expansion of city and nation would lead to the disintegration of both, and though his hostility to Consolidation appears to have ebbed by 1854, he continued to predict the Union's demise. His sympathies ought to have been with the South, where he saw slaves as naturally servile and planters as an aristocratic counter-weight to northern parvenus. Many of Fisher's family and friends became Copperhead opponents of Abraham Lincoln's administration. Yet in the late 1850s, he inched toward the conclusion that slavery, like democracy, blighted the Union, as he opposed the peculiar institution's march into Kansas, and felt the "slave power" impinging on his own freedom. Even John Brown's raid on Harper's Ferry radicalized him. Fisher had ridden up to Philadelphia on the train carrying Brown's body, and though he condemned the insurrection, he called Brown a "hero," who "has shown that the South is in reality a frightful despotism."[81]

Yet Fisher could not quite bring himself to vote for Lincoln. "The anti-slavery party has become the party of the multitude," he lamented on the eve of the presidential election, and in doing so, it had lost its respectability. Class politics for him won out. Civic life had not been gentrified.[82]

*   *   *

Fisher's aloofness from a political contest that deeply interested him suggests reformers' limited success in reconstructing Philadelphia's political culture. The Republican Party delivered by 1860 much of what a bourgeois-led growth coalition could not. It drew labor and capital into closer union, bound the city with internal improvements, and stimulated growth on the suburban frontier. The *North American* extolled its virtues for the same reason it had backed the Consolidation movement a few years earlier: the party grasped the need to compete with Baltimore, Boston, and New York, and was "resolved to make Philadelphia . . . among the handsomest and finest cities in the world."[83]

Like other insurgent parties in the antebellum era, moreover, it promised to purify politics. McMichael's paper cast the 1858 municipal election as a "simple struggle between vice and virtue" and portrayed the Democrats springing from the "pestiferous atmosphere" of groggeries and gambling dens. But a year later, it conceded that the Republicans themselves "may be defiled by the association of bad men." Few of the names on the party's tickets had any connection with the movement for municipal Consolidation. Many, indeed, had closer ties to fire companies—which had survived reformers' onslaught after 1854—than bourgeois reform.[84]

Meanwhile, Republican leaders, though pursuing a strikingly similar program to Consolidators, used the same policies for different ends. Reformers hoped that building the city upward and outward would weaken the hold of professional politicians. Yet in practice, metropolitan growth sustained party politics, as the enlarged city government provided Republican officials with a vast reservoir of patronage to nourish support.[85] Nor did politics become that much more genteel. No major riots troubled Philadelphia in the years between Consolidation and Civil War, but elections were still won or lost on the street rather than the home, as the Prince of Wales probably realized from his Chestnut Street hotel.

War would divide opinion among Consolidators of how to tie a city and nation together. The circumscription or extension of voting rights, the transformation of political culture, and state-led growth politics all had their advocates. Yet the conflict, though drawing attention away from municipal affairs, made a more radical reconstruction of Philadelphia's society and space possible. It would be harder, however, for a bourgeoisie to lead that reconstruction alone. The merchants, manufacturers, and professionals who had led the struggle to consolidate the city had enjoyed at best limited success in their bid to perpetuate political power. The conflict would test them again.

CHAPTER 6

Consolidating City and Nation

Philadelphia in Civil War and Reconstruction

Charles Godfrey Leland took the consolidationist impulse to its limits. The son of a wealthy merchant, Leland had traveled to Europe after graduating from Princeton, and in 1848 fought on the barricades against France's Orléanist monarchy. Though Leland left Paris when the socialists seemed to be gaining the upper hand, he returned to the United States with new abolitionist convictions. Back in Philadelphia, where he found pro-Southern sentiment repulsively strong, he started work for the crusading *Evening Bulletin*. Leland wrote many of the leaders that condemned the "absolute and uncontrolled rule" of the volunteer firemen and later claimed credit for rousing public indignation against them. After 1861, he went to war with another law unto itself: the plantation household. Leland—one of the earliest Republican converts in the city—claimed in his memoirs that he coined the term "emancipation" as a palatable way to advance abolition.[1]

His 1863 tract *Centralization Versus States Rights* offered his fullest elaboration of consolidation. "In the progressive policy of the nineteenth century," he declared three years after Italian unification, "great schemes of progress and of reform belong to great nations," and "are smothered in small ones, where the narrow limits of the land are reflected in the narrow minds of the people." The Union, then, "*must be united under a firm central policy,*" for "a mass of small independencies" would "soon lead to tyranny." Leland proposed a vast expansion of the federal bureaucracy, not just to meet the wartime emergency, but to encourage "the development of industry," pursue the "general improvement of the people," and confront "the great rising social problems of the age." His ideas bore similarities to radical designs from the 1840s.[2]

But Leland had little time for the utopians. Instead, he argued, the Republican Party now stood as the incarnation of middle-class ideals. Where politics before, he believed, had pitted a radical party of labor (the Democrats) against a conservative party of capital (the Whigs), the Republicans promised to harmonize the interests of contending classes. If the Union had only embraced "a grand system of national development" earlier, slavery would soon have withered. Here, Leland praised the example of his friend, the political economist Henry C. Carey, who helped him revise the pamphlet. Sectional and social conflict would disappear with growth politics directed by a strong state. "We need union, energy, concentration, and consolidation," he insisted.[3]

Few went as far as Leland in advocating centralization after 1861. But as this chapter shows, designs for consolidation moved back and forth between city and nation in the Civil War era, as citizens searched for the means to hold their society together. The extension of civil rights, the renewal of growth politics, and the voluntary efforts of bourgeois citizens all offered possible paths to "practical consolidation." Behind both nation- and city-building projects, moreover, stood a set of ideas about how state power and public borrowing could unite citizens in bonds of association. Leland's friend Carey, despite showing little interest in schemes of urban reconstruction, offered a model here that his followers helped to apply to the city: interests could be harmonized across the metropolis as growth made property-ownership available to an ever larger portion of the population. By the early 1870s, boosters proclaimed Philadelphia a "paradise" for workingmen. Leland's system of national development took a local form, albeit one that would spur fears of financial ruin and political corruption.[4]

Wartime Consolidation

The Civil War threatened metropolis as well as nation. Pennsylvania's border with the South made its cities and railroads an obvious target for Confederate raiders. Northern victories at Antietam and Gettysburg allayed fears of Philadelphia being besieged, but in July 1863, the revolt against conscription in New York—a riot that quickly descended into a racist pogrom—reminded citizens of the threat from within. For the *North American*, the violence may have been "just retribution" on a city sympathetic to treason, but Philadelphia's mobs were too recent a memory to assume that the troubles were unique to Manhattan. Would blood run once more down their streets too?[5]

The answer, it turned out, was no. Consolidators had given the city a government fit for war. Preventative policing proved particularly important. By 1860, the city force exceeded seven hundred officers, who could mobilize quickly thanks to telegraph lines connecting the station houses. No longer would the metropolis suffer, as it had in 1844, for want of speed and men in suffocating a riot. The Republican mayor Alexander Henry used his powers here to good effect, defending abolitionist meetings before the war broke out, and secessionist property after. Attacks on southern sympathizers, free blacks, and even the city itself by Confederate agents were widely anticipated. But the "frequent emergencies" Henry recalled in his farewell address never turned into anything approaching the violence of 1844.[6]

Maintaining cordial relations among the economic elite proved another matter. Either side of midcentury, propertied Philadelphians came together in the campaign for railroad-building and civic union, and many hoped the spirit of cooperation would continue. But slavery and sectionalism split bourgeois society: even firm friends like Eli Kirk Price and Morton Mc-Michael fell out. The conflict strained relations further. Soon after the outbreak of war, the long-running Wistar Party—an "aristocracy" of "social authority"—stopped meeting regularly.[7]

Part of the problem lay in the southern leanings of a portion of the economic elite. Merchants bound by kin and commerce to the Confederacy were lukewarm at best to the Union cause. Genteel residential streets surrounding the old downtown housed southern planters who came to Philadelphia for the summer. They sent their sons to the city's medical colleges, married their daughters to scions of Delaware merchants, and financed the cotton crop through credit drawn on Chestnut Street banks. They had no shortage of friends in Philadelphia, and the city's old money often led to calls for a conciliatory peace. One or two "disloyal talkers" went so far as to suggest Pennsylvania might secede; Unionists accused them of toasting Jefferson Davis. Slavery and war fractured Philadelphia's "upper tenth" and threatened to undo much of the work of the previous fifteen years.[8]

The social fragmentation of the war years spurred new attempts at class consolidation. What began in the parlors of wealthy loyalists soon extended into political action. The Saturday Club, which counted McMichael and leading figures from the commercial and industrial elite among its number, tried to replace the Wistar Party by bringing "the working force of the city" into contact over dinner. Carey meanwhile continued his weekly "Vespers" at which merchants, manufacturers, bankers, intellectuals, and publishers —usually headed by McMichael—discussed "social and industrial problems." Electoral organizing complemented social gatherings. In the summer of 1861, veteran Consolidators formed the No Party party, which married antebellum antipartisanship to wartime nationalism. Though the movement proved short-lived, its insistence in placing nation before party probably eased the migration of prosperous pro-war Democrats to the administration camp. Some of these figures, like attorney Benjamin Harris Brewster, had already left the Democrats once before to back civic union. Now they did so with national consolidation as their goal.[9]

Bourgeois sociability and politics came together in the Union League: a private club pursuing public ends. It grew out of the *North American*'s office, where bourgeois Unionists gathered to hear news from the front. In November 1862, McMichael, Judge Clark Hare, and George H. Boker, angered by the antiwar attitudes they encountered in genteel company, proposed withdrawing "from all social relations with disloyal men." They composed a list of wealthy loyalists, called a meeting, and organized the Union Club, which soon grew into the Union League. The League aimed to shut southern sympathizers "in their own small coteries," and wealthy enemies of the war effort soon retreated to the bookshop of the radical renegade John Campbell, a white supremacist Democrat who became a fierce opponent of the administration. Before long, similar associations had spread to other northern cities, and in 1865 the league's Philadelphia branch boasted over a thousand members. By then pro-Confederate voices were as marginalized as abolitionists had been before the Civil War.[10]

The Union League made loyalty to the Union a test of social respectability. Membership required impeccable patriotism and considerable wealth. Historians of the organization have seen it as either an attempt to resurrect patrician rule or a bid for power on the part of insurgent manufacturers. In Philadelphia, though, the league bore a striking resemblance to the growth coalition of the antebellum era. Industrialists—mostly in the iron and machine trades—slightly outnumbered merchants, but railroad presidents, real estate interests, financiers, publishers, and especially lawyers were also well represented. Leaguers did not shy away from politics, but like their predecessors in the 1850s, they believed a united bourgeoisie could wield influence through character and reputation. As a founder member put it, the club proposed "to accomplish a national and political end by social means." The organization therefore built on prewar traditions of voluntarism, and like the Consolidation Committee, it illustrated bourgeois authority in action, laying the foundations for a postwar politics of class.[11]

The league's composition hints at the ties between civic and national unionism. Few antiwar voices had been significant players in the struggle for metropolitan Consolidation. William B. Reed, one of the loudest critics of the war effort, had left the Whig Party in 1855, partly in protest at its support for the new municipal charter, and other future Copperheads stayed aloof from the campaign. Scions of first families who had supported Consolidation, in contrast, rallied to the national cause. General George Cadwalader—the militia commander in the 1844 riots and perhaps the most energetic municipal reformer among "proper Philadelphians"—quickly joined the Union League. About a fifth of the early membership had played an active role in the Consolidation campaign.[12]

As the Union League mobilized bourgeois Consolidators, it bolstered their flagging democratic convictions. In the antebellum era, wealthy Philadelphians worried about the compatibility of self-government with an enfranchised poor. Yet in 1860 to 1861, it was a powerful propertied class— and not the propertyless—that had brought the republic to the brink of dissolution. Doubts about democracy did not go away entirely and would reappear in Reconstruction. Plenty of critics blamed the war itself on partisan demagogues, and the racial pogrom of the New York Draft Riots led onlookers to ponder the fine line between majorities and mobs. But the Union League nevertheless sold the war as a struggle for the sovereignty of the people: even troublesome suburban "small men" like the Moyamensing boss William McMullen won plaudits when they signed up for military service.[13]

The fight for democracy also became a battle for freedom. War opened opportunities for African Americans. Disenfranchised by the state constitution and chased from the streets, black leaders in the antebellum city turned inward to strengthen their own community, and were given no room to participate in public debates over the likes of Consolidation. A national struggle over slavery, though, opened spaces they had been excluded from. Black associations sprang up to push the case for abolition and enfranchisement. Such institutions, though commonplace in the antebellum city, often had to hide from public view or face violent reprisals. War's approach, however, emboldened black leaders. In 1860, the Underground Railroad conductor William Still helped to establish the Civil, Social, and Statistical Association, which aimed to collect information on the city's black population and push for racial equality. The Pennsylvania Equal Rights League and the Colored People's Union League pursued a similar—and sometimes more assertive—course. Into Reconstruction, these organizations demanded civil rights in southern states and northern cities.[14]

Black loyalism went a long way in a city scarred by white treason. Early calls for African American enlistment were rebuffed, but after the Emancipation Proclamation of 1863, white Unionists and black leaders like Frederick Douglass set about raising colored regiments. Though Democrats blamed "the cowardly conduct of the niggers" for Union defeats, the patriotism and courage of enlisted men won over many whites. When black troops marched through Philadelphia in the second half of 1863, they were met with cheers from streets they had been chased off only a few years before.[15]

The equation of loyalism and respectability raised black hopes of a radical reconstruction of nation and city. In 1862, the land reformer John C. Bowers joined other African Americans in Philadelphia in asking Lincoln to destroy slavery, renounce colonization, and redistribute plantation land. Slaves had "produced much of the wealth of this country," they reminded the president, and masters had "enslaved the world" through monopolizing the fruits of black labor. Concerns closer to home also animated black organizing. On the eve of the Civil War, prominent African Americans had called for an end to segregation on the city's streetcars, but made no headway with the companies. Wartime service subtly shifted the basis of their claims. When making the case for desegregation in the late 1850s, William Still suggested genteel blacks deserved the same treatment as the white bourgeoisie, but by 1864, he and his allies asserted the right of women and children to visit their menfolk in the military. Loyalty to the Union, rather than social respectability, now vindicated claims to civil equality.[16]

Black loyalism prodded bourgeois Philadelphians toward a more egalitarian stance on civil rights. Around midcentury, African Americans struggled to find white allies outside the radical and abolitionist circles. But many of the Consolidators who had lined up to uphold slaveholders' rights in the late 1850s declared slavery a moral and social evil when it led to national dissolution. Years later, the Union Leaguer Leland laughed at the transformation of "dough faces" (a term of abuse for northern allies of the

"slave power") into "hard-baked Abolitionists."[17] Price, having defended
the Fugitive Slave Act even after Lincoln's election, welcomed the destruction of the master's "family government" by 1863; Stephen Colwell, a
Virginia-born iron manufacturer, who once declared the plantation a
school of civilization, became a leading figure in the freedmen's aid movement. Such men now supported streetcar desegregation. By 1865, white
backers included not only antislavery veterans like the industrialist Matthias
W. Baldwin, but also conservative Republicans and Democrats. They argued
in 1865 that the roots of war lay in "the enslavement of the Black Man at
the South and contempt for him at the North": a remarkable position that
placed Philadelphia's racial reconstruction on a par with the work already
underway in the rebel states. Within months of the conflict's end, indeed,
prominent Union Leaguers backed black calls to restore the franchise African American men had been excluded from by the state constitution of
1838.[18]

When slavery and segregation became a barrier to the consolidation of
nation and city, more and more white bourgeois Philadelphians flocked to
the banner of freedom. Emancipation may have been first and foremost
a military necessity for Philadelphia's economic elite, but it promised to
homogenize the nation's social and economic institutions and excise the
tumor of sectional conflict from the body politic. For African Americans,
meanwhile, it opened the opportunity to negotiate a new position in the
city after years of violently enforced exclusion from public debate. The alliance of white Union Leaguers and black activists over the desegregation of
the streetcars and the destruction of slavery, then, brought the latter into
the campaign for practical consolidation in a way growth politics had not.

Reconstruction and Growth

On New Year's Day, 1866, Morton McMichael addressed Philadelphia's
councilmen for the first time as the newly elected mayor of the city. His
victory the previous October marked the apex of a public career that
stretched back to the 1830s. First as a Democrat, then as a Whig, and finally
as a Republican, he had called for the "practical consolidation" of his
metropolis. Philadelphia's spatial and social organization, he believed,
should strengthen bonds of union among a bourgeoisie, between jostling
classes, and across the sectional divisions of a far-reaching metropolis.

His inaugural address restated a formula for urban improvement he had helped to finesse over the previous decades. "The Government of a city of imperial proportions like ours," he argued, "must prove a momentous undertaking, and it is emphatically so now." In a familiar booster vein, he noted Philadelphia's "capacities for illimitable growth," running through advantages bestowed by nature and crafted by labor. Rivers and railroads gave citizens access to the ocean and interior; the vast expanse of the consolidated city meant that before the century was out, it would boast "more people dwelling in more and better houses and spreading over a wider surface, than can be found in any other American metropolis." For Mc-Michael, though, Philadelphians had to take risks to reap rewards: no longer could they afford the "deficiency in combined and concentrated effort" that had hampered them in the past.

The end of the Civil War offered an opportunity to make up for past mistakes. McMichael welcomed the "triumphant close" of a struggle for "national integrity" and the vindication of the "cardinal principles of freedom and humanity." Union victory—and the destruction of slavery with it—had led to "novel and startling commercial consequences." The energies of a "reunited people," he insisted, would soon make up for the drop in demand that came with demobilization.

Here McMichael linked the prospects of free labor to the work of urban promotion. Echoing booster sermons from the 1840s, he predicted that cities would compete for an immense trade, with the best-prepared sure to win the "chiefest prizes." The new mayor recognized the importance of private initiative here but still gave great importance to local government. Its duty lay in perfecting measures to enhance "the wholesomeness of the city," carry light and water "to the furthest boundaries of its built-up portions," and encourage "intercourse between its broadly separated sections." This "shall help forward the grander movements which lie beyond our province." Councils, he declared, should strive to "achieve what is useful and advance what is ornamental."[19]

McMichael found growth politics a friendlier terrain for talking about consolidation than civil rights. During the campaign, indeed, he said nothing on the question of streetcar segregation, despite supporting equal access prior to 1865. Like many of his peers he did come to see black voting as a means to hold the Union together. Even Sidney George Fisher, who railed against the "villainous mumbo jumbo" of universal suffrage, eventually backed a color-blind franchise as the only way to pacify the South. But as in the antebellum city, the "race question" threatened white unity. When northern Republicans backed black voting in their own section, they lost votes, and during a brief Democratic interregnum in Philadelphia, federal troops had to be called in to enforce the Fifteenth Amendment.[20]

The pursuit of urban greatness provided white boosters with a less perilous path to rebuilding. This indeed had been the policy since the 1840s: order would come from expanding upward and outward. The rationale applied to both nation and city. Radical Republican Congressman William D. Kelley—an ardent railroad promoter and a man awakened to the antislavery cause by the burning of Pennsylvania Hall in 1838—argued in 1867 that national development would heal the scars of war. Stimulating "the productive power of the country," he told manufacturers, would "be an important element in the great work of reconstruction," bringing home to white southerners "that they were insisting on poverty" when they could have "wealth and refinement." Kelley, to his credit, never saw economic development as enough in itself; an ally of black leaders like William Still, he advocated equal rights from early in the Civil War. But advocates of growth politics shared his assumption that prosperity meant peace.[21]

Philadelphians looked to benefit from both. Reconstruction witnessed a renewal of civic boosterism on a scale that approached the antebellum heyday of railroad-building (see Figure 3). Although the Panic of 1857 brought an end to municipal railroad funding, and the Civil War reoriented allegiances from city to nation, the course of the conflict gave grounds for wild optimism in the metropolitan future. Disorder in a New York still reeling from the Draft Riots, boosters anticipated, would drive capitalists to the banks of the Delaware. Federal funding for a new naval yard would improve Philadelphia's ocean-borne commerce. And a sympathetic city, state, and federal government—each in Republican hands—would lay the political foundations for fast-paced growth.

Perhaps most importantly, though, mobilization stimulated important sectors of the city's economy. Philadelphia recovered reasonably quickly from the Panic of 1857, but the secession crisis led to another prostration in business. The downturn initially threw thousands out of work, but as a transportation and industrial hub for the Virginian and Mississippi theaters, the city prospered in the "people's contest." Institutions and industries nurtured by boosters came to the fore. The Pennsylvania Railroad—by 1865, the largest private corporation in the world—played a major role in (and profited handsomely from) the Union war effort. Manufacturers too

Figure 3. Postbellum boosterism. The title page to a postbellum guidebook condenses the booster metropolis into a single scene. Ship masts and steam trains show the city's connections; a street railway carries passengers between suburb and center. A large factory, representing Philadelphia's industrial might, is complemented by the grandeur of its neighboring building, Girard College. Source: Reprinted from *Philadelphia Illustrated* (Philadelphia: L. R. Hamersly & Co., 1871). Courtesy of Boston Athenæum.

did well from wartime demands; accounting for inflation, their output increased 70 percent between 1860 and 1870. Factory owners tended to read their success as evidence of the superiority of their social system. "Steam engines" in Philadelphia alone, one paper boasted in 1867, "do more work in a day than all the black slaves of the South ever did in twenty-four hours." But industrialists would need to find peacetime buyers for their wares if they wanted to sustain the wartime boom.[22]

After Appomattox, then, bourgeois Philadelphians looked eagerly to new—or rather renewed—markets. The conquered Confederacy now became an economic battleground as cities readied to fight one another for its business. "The South is becoming the great customer of the North," reported the *Evening Telegraph*, the strongest advocate of a southern policy for Philadelphia. It saw the war-ravaged region as a *terra nullius*, an "almost virgin territory," the paper wrote on another occasion, "as if Japan were freely opened to trade, and America and Europe were competing for the golden prize." The Board of Trade and other commercial and manufacturing interests in the city soon lent their backing to new lines of steamers to ensure Philadelphia did not miss out.[23]

Yet as in the 1840s, it was the West—though this time the Far West rather than the Lakes and Mississippi Valley—that caused the greatest excitement. Wartime Republicans had succeeded where previous politicians had failed in securing federal support for a transcontinental line. Since 1846, Philadelphians had pictured the Pennsylvania Railroad as the first link of an iron chain binding the Atlantic to the Pacific, which they hoped would make their city the main node between Europe and Asia. As the road neared completion, boosters looked forward to the riches to come. By 1867, the Union Leaguer Brewster could declare that his people were "on our way to India," and expected that once the wealth of the Far East coursed along the tracks of the transcontinental highway "the daughters of America shall be clothed as queens ever were not."[24]

Philadelphia's boosters saw Asia through a lens they used to understand other supposedly undeveloped territories. Like riotous Moyamensing before Consolidation, or the South after the Civil War, it was a plague spot awaiting Yankee uplift. The opening of Asia to American capital, the *Press* argued, would be "like the discovery of a continent" that would "shake and readjust the commerce of the world." Railroads and telegraphs would lift the Chinese out of "semi-civilization." But as Philadelphians imagined boarding a train in the Pennsylvania's passenger depot and stepping off in San Francisco, they did not forget the "favourable effect" expansion in the Pacific would have upon "the whole system of American manufactures."[25] Their metropolis stood to benefit more than most.

Boosters therefore tried to annex Southern, Western, and Asian markets for their city in much the same manner they had attempted to claim the

Ohio Valley for Philadelphia in the railroad-building of the 1840s. They needed new allies to do so—the federal government and Pennsylvania Railroad, rather than the municipal authorities—but their aims were strikingly similar. Capturing business for the city's manufacturing wares promised to benefit both commerce and industry. And as Philadelphia grew as the great city of the continent, its real estate owners would reap the rewards.

Routes to Reconstruction

After the Civil War, boosters searched for a method to set their imperial ambitions in stone. Like their antebellum predecessors, they called for the construction of a city adapted to the coming needs of trade and industry. The *Press* urged Philadelphians to "look far into the future" and plan "on a broad and comprehensive scale." Seeing urban "manifest destiny" in the "swampy flats" lying far to the south of the old commercial center, it imagined wharves, warehouses, and railroads humming with the business of a continent and beyond. The "new Philadelphia," it argued, needed to be built in a manner "that shall be our best monument as well as our best investment."[26]

After the conflict, room for urban renewal remained: Philadelphia, as one architect put it, was "*not* a finished city." The war years had arrested most of the municipal improvements proposed around midcentury and promised by the Republican Party in the late 1850s. Coal sheds still scarred Broad Street; Bedford remained a plague spot. Consolidators, the *North American* complained a few months after the Union victory, had planned a city "grand in conception," but what appeared "magnificent on paper" amounted to a mass of "immense unimproved spaces." "We fix our eyes on upon imaginary splendors," it lamented, "and wonder why they do not come of ourselves." The city, like the nation, required uplift.[27]

Peace provided opportunities for reconstruction. Soon after McMichael's inauguration as mayor in 1866, his paper demanded investment in the waterfront and bridges over the Schuylkill as part of a wider program of city planning. But reordering the metropolis around the needs of trade meant more than easing the circulation of goods and people. Great cities required gentility and grandeur to attract capital. "The city which seeks the custom of an empire," the *North American* had argued on the eve of the Civil War, "must be commensurate in its display." After Appomattox, it

Figure 4. North Broad Street. A guidebook in the centennial year could portray north Broad Street as an elegant promenade, but its development
remained uneven. Source: Reprinted from *Philadelphia and Its Environs*
(Philadelphia: J. B. Lippincott, 1876). Courtesy of The Library Company of
Philadelphia.

continued to press for the extension of a public park and the boulevarding
of Broad and Market. Philadelphia "would grow a great deal faster if these
metropolitan avenues were handsomely improved," it wrote in 1867, for
they would provide "conspicuous evidences of prosperity" that the decentralized development of manufacturing tended to hide. Embellishment
could spur on as well as show off metropolitan growth.[28]

Post–Civil War city-building differed from its antebellum predecessor
primarily in scale. By the 1850s, bourgeois Philadelphians broadly agreed
on how their metropolis ought to look and behave (see Figure 4). Space,
light, and air distinguished refined and healthy cities from base and sickly
ones; fine buildings and elegant public spaces, meanwhile, would draw
investment, improve citizens, and consolidate a metropolis across its divisions. Calls for urban reconstruction after Appomattox, though, reflected
the enlarged ambitions of a class emerging triumphantly from war. The
North American continued its relentless campaign for the improvement of
Broad, but by 1870 pictured the thoroughfare as one axis "in a new and
magnificent system of diagonal avenues," which would radiate to all part of

the compass from the Penn Squares. Such aspirations led one cynic, tiring of countless designs for parks, plazas, and avenues, to wonder whether Paris was "not so much of a place after all, compared with Philadelphia." Yet attempts to rein in booster ambitions proved futile, given how important a grand urban form had become to many bourgeois citizens. As one veteran booster declared around 1870, Philadelphia needed a "metropolitan development worthy of the imperial city, which its present condition and future resources warrant us in expecting it to be in the future."[29]

The boulevards and parks of Second Empire Paris provided an example to aspire to here even if only a few boosters dared go so far as to endorse the authoritarian methods used to build them (see Figure 5). Baron Haussmann's city-building had piqued the curiosity of Philadelphians like Mc-Michael in the 1850s. Reading the French capital back then, though, proved difficult. Were the new streets a showy facade masking a broken system or sturdy proof of a modern nation rebuilding from the ruins of the 1848 Revolution? American onlookers never seemed quite sure. By the 1860s, however, the Bonapartist state showed no signs of crumbling, and the reconstruction of Paris continued apace. Moves toward political liberalization even led some Yankee observers to conclude that the emperor had set in stone a physical terrain for self-government superior to any of the cities in their democratic republic. The *Public Ledger* praised the emperor in this vein as "a model reformer to the world." For sure, there were plenty of dissenters too, but even a critic of the new Paris—the newspaperman John W. Forney—found the emperor had made "rich and poor happy" on city streets. He recommended that Philadelphia's municipal authorities dispatch a commission to Paris to study its paving.[30]

Boosters certainly showed a willingness to learn from Paris. The *Ledger*, impressed by Haussmann's ability to turn "nests and quarters" of "vileness and pollution" into "streets of the greatest magnificence," asked in 1866 "whether something similar" should "be studied out and applied" by American cities. A Philadelphian in Paris on the eve of the Franco-Prussian War urged his countrymen to abandon their suspicion of foreign models and apprehend "improvements wonderful even to our own American boastful growth." Haussmann's labors revealed to him "how completely the question of building the city of the nineteenth century has been met."[31]

Remaking Philadelphia on even a fraction of the scale, though, seemed a herculean task, given the difficulties city-builders had faced before the Civil War. "Were the Baron in Philadelphia," a longstanding admirer of the

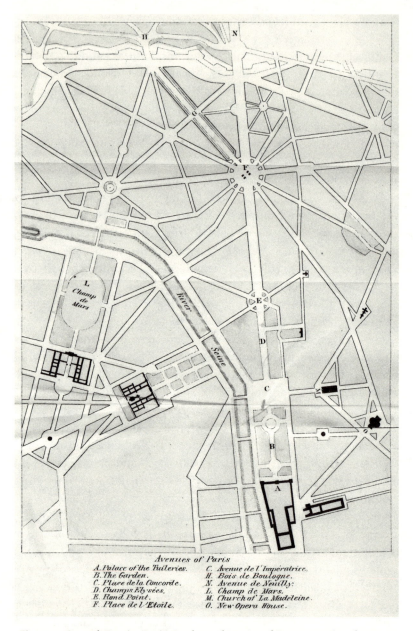

Avenues of Paris

A. Palace of the Tuileries.
B. The Garden.
C. Place de la Concorde.
D. Champs Elysées.
E. Rond Point.
F. Place de l'Étoile.

C. Avenue de l'Impératrice.
H. Bois de Boulogne.
N. Avenue de Neuilly.
L. Champ de Mars.
M. Church of La Madeleine.
O. New Opera House.

Figure 5. Second Empire Paris. In the early years of Reconstruction, boosters turned again to making Philadelphia into the "Paris of America." The earliest design for a boulevard to Fairmount Park, drawn up by the architect William Russell West at the instigation of municipal reformers, included this map of the French capital's avenues. West lauded Napoleon III's city as a model. Source: Reprinted from [William Russell West], *Broad Street, Penn Square, and the Park* (Philadelphia: Jno. Pennington & Son, 1871). Courtesy of The Library Company of Philadelphia.

Second Empire wrote of Haussmann, "he would make short work of Broad Street." But given the absence of a "Louis Napoleon who can order and execute the widening of the streets," citizens needed to look elsewhere. In the 1850s, class discipline, commercial growth, and even state-strengthening had all failed to bring about urban refinement. The grand design of incorporating the likes of Broad and Bedford into an imperial cityscape remained unrealized.[32]

In lieu of a Haussmann, Philadelphia's bourgeoisie sought other ways to assert their authority over urban space. Sometimes they found their interests coincided with those of the city government. Before Consolidation, property had been assessed for taxation by locally elected officials, who predictably undervalued their voters' assets. After 1865, though, Eli Kirk Price helped devise a new system that freed assessment from parochial politics, and the social scientist Thomas Cochran soon became chair of a revamped Board of Revision. By 1867, Philadelphia's real estate shot up four-fold in value.[33]

The consolidated system of tax assessment gave boosters a tool to reshape the metropolis. Stubborn owners, who could no longer rely on friendly local assessors, found themselves "taxed to a degree which they have never experienced." Once forced to sell, their land could be put to its highest and best use. "There is no hope for the laggards," the *Germantown Telegraph*'s correspondent wrote a year later, for "quaint old nests where for so many years forgotten people have roosted must all come into the market by this process." Public power here helped to shape the private market in a manner that advanced the march of improvement.[34]

More often though citizens resorted to the well-established practice of using their economic power and cultural authority to shape the metropolis. Broad Street once more became a focal point for voluntarist efforts. Bourgeois institutions sought to speed the avenue's ascent by locating there. When Union Leaguers looked for a new home at the end of the Civil War, they built their French Renaissance mansion on the boulevard. The masonic order began work on an immense structure on the street on the northern side of the Market intersection. Price, in alliance with what one paper derisively called the "respectability" of Philadelphia, meanwhile spearheaded a campaign to grant the Penn Squares to the city's learned institutions. Supporters argued that the scheme would bring "architectural symmetry and beauty" to a spot that before the Civil War had been eyed by the Pennsylvania Railroad as a freight depot. Ultimately, though, the state legislature—which retained jurisdiction over the land—rejected their application.[35]

Boosters also lobbied for the improvement of Broad itself, as they sought to make it, as the Consolidator Henry C. Townsend put it, "the only rival on this side of the water of . . . the Avenue de l'Imperatrice." In 1866, owners from the northern end of the avenue gathered to call for the replacement of the cobblestones. Four years later, after a long struggle to remove rail tracks from the center of the street, citizens organized the Broad Street Improvement League (BSIL) to make the case for a boulevard. Real estate owners on Broad were well represented at the meeting, and perhaps not coincidentally, a pamphlet published that year by speculators pushed development of the southern portion of the avenue as one of the most "desirable localities" for those of "wealth and taste." But the league drew plenty of wealthy citizens with no immediate financial interest in the boulevard. Merchants, manufacturers, attorneys, and financiers—many of them active in the Consolidation movement two decades before—raised the cry for a grand metropolitan thoroughfare to rival the Rue de Rivoli.[36]

Associated efforts to transform the built environment sometimes combined philanthropy with profit. Much like the northern planters who migrated to the vanquished South to show the economic and social superiority of free labor, moral regeneration and personal gain went hand in hand.[37] Not far from Broad Street, in the courts and alleys of the Bedford Street neighborhood, the Beneficent Building Association (BBA) approached the work of reconstruction with these twin goals in mind. Attempting to strip the street of its unfavorable associations, the city renamed it after the recently purchased Alaska territory in 1867, but the new title only emphasized its frontier status. It sat within the bounds of a metropolis, yet remained wild, remote, and unproductive.

Founded in 1869, with Price among its backers, the BBA wove together antebellum ideas about home, environment, and dispersal to transform the "Alaska District." Through private subscription, the association bought blighted properties, razed them to the ground, and erected single family homes in their stead. These were set back further in their lots and leased to carefully vetted tenants. Bourgeois voluntarism promised a host of benefits. Though devoid of the drama of Haussmannization, the slow work of rebuilding would gradually widen the street, leaving room for light, air, and virtue to penetrate. The better class of residents in BBA-owned homes would soon start to influence longstanding inhabitants of the vicinity. And the bad sorts displaced by the demolitions would be forced to seek shelter in better suburban neighborhoods, where, as a Bedford Street missionary put it, "shame begins to be possible" to the resident "because not *every* thing now about him is vile." Religious tutelage alone, the association itself argued, could not save the inhabitants. Salvation instead lay in the "*the physical reformation of the street*": the "harbors and breeders" of Alaska's "iniquity" needed excising. Price, who had led calls for environmental uplift since the 1850s, called the remedy "radically curative."[38]

But investors in the BBA may have had a broader point to prove about real estate and refinement. Both before and after the Civil War, bourgeois critics had noted the riches to be gained from renting overcrowded properties in Bedford Street's environs. Now they tried to show that slumlords were not the only ones who could make money from the district. Putting in $1,000 each, they had poured $56,000 into rebuilding the street by 1876, and were getting a return of around 3 percent per annum. As Gilded Age investments went, this hardly amounted to the most remunerative use of capital, but it seemed to vindicate the longstanding claim that private interests and public wants could combine to improve the city.[39]

Established in 1869 by fifty bourgeois reformers, the Philadelphia Fountain Society (PFS) had less interest in profits than the BBA, but still linked virtuous behavior to urban improvement. Its founder, the Union Leaguer Dr. Wilson C. Swann, saw himself leading a movement for "good government" and a "virtuous life." The organization aimed to provide fountains in the streets to give thirsty citizens an alternative to the city's taverns and to usher in a "new era in the moral condition of the people." Many of its backers, though, saw it as a vehicle to embellish the city. At early meetings, they praised "foreign countries where both in ancient and in modern times fountains have been made objects of adornment," while Swann reminded members that European cities like Paris owed their reputation to such ornamentation. By 1874, the PFS had erected seventy fountains, with Broad and Bedford the focal points for their efforts.[40]

The associations that sprang up after the Civil War to transform Philadelphia's space and people may have differed in their aims and methods, but they had much in common. Where the BSIL lobbied government, the BBA mobilized capital, and the PFS relied on a mixture of private philanthropy and municipal cooperation. Yet supporters often came from the coalition that had fought for the consolidation of city and Union, and figures like Price and McMichael moved between the various organizations.

For them, voluntarism had its advantages, by bringing "best men" together to exert pressure on politicians and establish cultural authority over the built environment.

Their work also linked the consolidation of city and Union. During and after the Civil War, boosters surveyed spaces like Bedford and Broad in a nationalist cartography. They mapped the former as a "plague spot" or wild frontier in need of the same civilizing hand as the South or West. They mapped the latter as unionist terrain. Broad, the *North American* argued during debates over the Kansas-Nebraska Act, could not afford to be a "sectional avenue" in a consolidated Philadelphia. Although in 1854 the paper had a divided metropolis rather than nation in mind, the street's monumental proportions elevated its importance in the conflict, as it became a staging ground for patriotic display. Federal troops, torchlit parades, and Lincoln's hearse passed over its cobbles. Union Leaguers chose the street for their home and purchased a house for General Ulysses S. Grant—eager no doubt to benefit from his celebrity—nearby in the fashionable West End. A supporter of the BSIL pictured another military hero—the victor at Gettysburg, George Gordon Meade—leading a march along its length to mark the hundredth anniversary of American independence.[41]

As well as commemorating wartime valor, though, the avenue foretold the glorious future of the United States in a way humble Independence Hall could not. In the age of Haussmann, after all, wide thoroughfares offered a ready measure of national as well as metropolitan progress. What "would France be without Paris?" one improver of Broad asked in 1867, and "what would Paris be without its boulevards?" Henry M. Watts, a Consolidator who had begun the bourgeois migration to Broad in the 1850s, agreed. In 1870, he had just returned from a diplomatic posting in Vienna, where he would have witnessed the building of the Haussmannesque Ringstrasse at first hand. Watts now spoke of the "necessity" for "magnificent avenues" in America too. But in asking for assistance from municipal and state government, the BSIL acknowledged that even when directed by a well-organized bourgeoisie, the city's real estate market could not bring about urban refinement. Something more was required.[42]

The Practical Consolidation of City and Nation

Somewhere near Watts at the inaugural meeting of the BSIL sat the forty-eight-year-old banker Jay Cooke, a man who knew a thing or two about nation-making. Five years earlier, in the final months of the war, a New York reporter observed the practical consolidation of the Union in Cooke's Chestnut Street offices. Cooke—the financier of the Civil War—was selling thirty-year federal bonds as telegraph boys relayed news of buyers from across the North and West. Many of the takers, though, came from beyond the ranks of big banks and insurance companies. Cooke looked on approvingly as a commander of African American troops invested some of his men's savings. "I am glad to have black soldiers take the Government loan," he told the New Yorker, for the "subscription should run like a core through the whole country, tying it together . . . and solidifying the nation." "Its general diffusion," a Cooke ally wrote of the debt, "will bind us together with a common interest."[43]

Cooke's marketing of the national debt marked a departure in American statecraft. The novelty lay less in borrowing to fight—every war the United States had waged since its inception had been financed in part by loans—and more in the methods he used to raise cash. Cooke—no more than a minor player in Philadelphia's money market at the start of the Civil War—had successfully lobbied Secretary of the Treasury Salmon P. Chase for the right to sell bonds on commission. Rather than looking to sell solely to financial institutions and foreign governments, though, Cooke turned instead to the northern people. A national debt, he and his allies argued in Hamiltonian terms, was a blessing, not least as it gave bondholders a vested interest in the preservation of the state. The farther the federal loans traveled, he reasoned, the faster loyalism would spread: debt could hold the Union together by giving Americans a financial stake in the security of their country. Hundreds of thousands of citizens took up his offer as federal borrowing ballooned from $65 million at the start of the conflict to $2.6 billion by 1865.[44]

Whether Cooke remembered similar arguments about a consolidated municipal debt in 1853 to 1854 is unclear, but he learned more than we might expect in the antebellum city. The banker has been cast as the poster child for postwar privatism: a man whose national orientation gave him little reason to care about his hometown. But Cooke's associational nationalism probably had roots in the pre–Civil War city. In 1855, Cooke had joined the leadership of the charity consolidation movement, an ecumenical scheme led by municipal Consolidators and evangelical Christians that sought to unite public and private welfare under the auspices of the economic elite. After the conflict, the devout Presbyterian helped

establish the Pennsylvania Citizens' Association, an organization dominated by moral environmentalists, which set out to investigate the causes
of crime and poverty, open employment offices, and house the intemper-
ate in cathartic villages. One newspaper compared the scale of its ambitions for social reconstruction in the North to that of the Freedmen's
Bureau in the South. Cooke's reforming zeal may have been borne more
in a tradition of Christian communitarianism than the secular consolida-
tionism of his friend McMichael, but the institutions they both championed saw the city as an interdependent but fragile whole. And if debt
could bind a nation together, then what could it do for Philadelphia? At
the BSIL meeting, indeed, Cooke had joined the chorus of bourgeois
voices calling for the municipal authorities to borrow to fund the boulevarding of Broad.[45]

The links Cooke drew between debt and union replayed on a larger
stage antebellum debates over urban political economy. Massive municipal borrowing between 1846 and 1854 had built Philadelphia's railroad
empire. Consolidators hoped to use the fiscal might of the new city to
enlarge and embellish their metropolis. Though debt-financing often
drew fierce criticism, its defenders saw it as a binding agent for the
metropolis, whether through mingling the finances of the districts in what
a reformer called "one consolidated loan," or through funding what
McMichael called the "practical consolidation" of infrastructural
improvements. Between 1858 and 1860, the People's Party—a coalition
of Republicans and Natives—began to put the principle into practice by
spending on suburban development.[46]

War pushed city borrowing to new levels. Although the federal government bore the brunt of expense for defending the Union, the onus fell
on states, counties, and cities to bolster their defenses and fill the ranks.
Philadelphia's councils helped to fortify the city and fund the bounties that
kept draft agents—and with them the prospect of draft resistance—at bay.
The costs soon mounted. By April 1865, the funded debt stood at almost
$29 million, an increase of $4.2 million over the course of a single year, and
nearly double the amount owed at Consolidation.[47]

Whether the debt was a blessing, though, remained up for debate. The
conservative Republican mayor Alexander Henry continually urged councils to rein in nonessential expenditure and reminded them of the generation to come who would have to pay off the principal. Henry here echoed
warnings from the 1840s about a city living beyond its means. Yet investors

themselves showed confidence in the city's ability to pay. In March 1864, the municipal authorities raised over $2.5 million in a single day with purchasers paying a 6 percent premium. The straitened circumstances of the early postwar era saw Democrats, who found the debt "too portentous in its prospective proportions," agitate for austerity, but the municipality continued to find willing buyers. City loans, unlike their national equivalent, were held by wealthy individuals and financial institutions, and consequently lacked the democratic, nationalist character of Cooke's notes. But like the national debt, the city's credit signaled an expression of confidence in the future.[48]

McMichael's *North American*, which had pushed for expansive metropolitan government prior to the 1840s and 1850s, proved the most forthright bourgeois defender of debt-financed growth. National borrowing may have been vast, it counseled in 1867, but "our resources were found fully equal to such a burden." A similar logic now underpinned the case for spending on Philadelphia. "The cost of keeping up a city home," it argued in a critique of a Cincinnati tax revolt, required farsightedness on the part of municipal governments. Investing in the future, the paper explained, spurred the development that in turn diminished the original debt. It contrasted individuals' pursuit of short-term profits to the "wider and broader and more enduring foundation" of communities that required long-term planning. There was no "odiousness" to debt.[49]

McMichael had not convinced everyone that a great debt was a great blessing in the late 1860s, but he had good reason for optimism. Although limited in his powers as mayor, he could use the position as a bully pulpit to push for improvement, and could expect support from councilmen and state legislators of his party. In this regard, the capacity to borrow on a large scale may have been the most important bequest of antebellum reformers. Reflecting on the 1854 Consolidation Act from a postbellum perch, Price remembered his allies' desire to ensure "the enlarged City should in her united strength be enabled to achieve great things."[50] They succeeded. Between 1865 and 1875, the debt increased from $29 million to $55 million, with urban improvements taking up a sizeable chunk of the spending. "Haussmann," a despairing citizen complained in 1871, "must have emigrated to Philadelphia." But that spending did not always come about as a result of decisions taken in the mayor's office or council chambers. Instead, many of the bigger schemes sprang from legislators in Harrisburg, who then ordered the city to raise the money.[51]

By the early 1870s, then, the combination of bourgeois association and debt-financing had begun the work of reconstructing the city. Broad Street improvers, at the urging of the BSIL, secured support for boulevarding parts of the avenue. Fairmount Park—established in the antebellum era— was extended in the late 1860s to become (as it remains today) the largest of its kind in the nation. On the Penn Squares, meanwhile, the foundations were set for Philadelphia's immense Second Empire city hall, projected at its inception to be the tallest structure in the Union and still the largest nonsteel building in the world. Not all of these projects enjoyed universal popularity among the city's bourgeoisie—the new public buildings, as we will see in the next chapter, split the economic elite—but each realized antebellum ambitions for a grand and genteel cityscape. And as long as citizens remained optimistic about urban growth, each could seem afford- able. "The one great object," as Forney's *Press* put it, lay in creating "the Philadelphia of the future."[52]

Such optimism chimed with the views of Henry C. Carey. Carey—son of the eminent publisher and political economist Matthew—by the 1850s was the favorite intellectual of Philadelphia's bourgeoisie. Merchants, man- ufacturers, and professionals feted him for his defense of American industry against British free trade. But Carey's renown extended beyond his native city. Karl Marx called him the only political economist of note in the New World, though grudging respect did not prevent him from tearing Careyite theory to pieces.[53]

Carey's appeal lay in part in his rejection of the pessimism of the British Classical School. The likes of David Ricardo and Thomas Malthus, taking the Old World as a model, assumed that resources were scarce, and that any increase of earnings for labor would mean less for capital. In the United Kingdom, their ideas were put to use by opponents of trade unions and factory reform, but American radicals such as George Lippard used similar reasoning to make the case for radical reform. Carey tried to refute both cases. The potential for growth, he argued, was infinite, but it required the association of labor and capital. Marx, who dismissed Carey as a "harmo- nizer" for his attempts to reconcile the irreconcilable, nevertheless acknowl- edged that his model had some merits in a rapidly expanding North American economy.

Like Cooke, moreover, Carey saw political economy as a path to national consolidation. In his early career, he had rejected the economic nationalism of his father in favor of free trade, but by the end of the 1840s, he had become an ardent protectionist. Over the following years, he blamed low tariffs for sectional and social disharmony. Cotton exports may have made plenty of planters rich, he and his followers argued, but they discouraged diversification, reduced the region to a colonial dependency on Britain, and deepened the rift between North and South. Pennsylvania's nurturing of home industry provided a more worthy example to emulate. Rather than rely on imports, manufacturers had endeavored to build a strong home market, which ensured wealth remained in the state. Where white southerners had become dependent on decisions taken thousands of miles away, then, Pennsylvanians had strengthened ties of interdependence to the benefit of merchants, manufacturers, and farmers. But a tariff also promised to reduce social tension in a city that had witnessed plenty of battles over the rights of labor. Protection from foreign competition, Carey and his followers insisted, would give industrialists the confidence to expand production, raise wages, and ensure their workers had the purchasing power to stimulate demand; one historical sociologist has even seen Careyism as a forerunner of Fordism. Careyite political economy therefore rejected the disaggregating tendencies of both free trade and the radical critique of capitalism.[54]

Carey insisted he had an alternative to disintegration. Like Cooke's debt, indeed, his tariff would weave together the nation in a web of economic interdependence. As a model for nation-building, it enjoyed wide influence. One of Carey's admirers, the Prussian Friedrich List, was among the architects of the Zollverein, the customs union of German states that preceded unification. Philadelphians after the foundation of the Second Reich in 1870 boasted that the seeds of German unification had been sown in their city. If Americans had learned their lessons as well as List, Kelley claimed, they might have avoided Civil War. Carey, an early Republican and Union Leaguer, certainly placed himself in the nationalist camp.[55]

Careyite thought marked one manifestation of the broader consolidationist impulse in Philadelphia. Carey himself counted municipal reformers like McMichael, Colwell, and Kelley among his most devoted disciples. In part, of course, his popularity came from how closely his theories corresponded to the wants of manufacturers. But Carey's preoccupation with the forces of integration and disintegration—the process of practical consolidation—seem to have mattered too. Economic relationships rather than debt, railroads, or urban space wove his web of interdependence, and without the protective hand of the state, he insisted, entire regions and classes would find themselves exposed to exploitation. In a city renowned for its privatism, he condemned individualism and argued the association of means rather than the atomization of market forces provided a path to prosperity. The mouthpiece of a manufacturing bourgeoisie could sometimes sound like a midcentury critic of capitalism. When applied to the built environment, such associationist principles would leave their mark.[56]

Building "the Metropolis of Labor"

Carey's search for harmony mattered in a city with a long tradition of labor militancy. His father's *Plea for the Poor*, an analysis of poverty in the hard times of the 1830s, marked an early attempt to understand the structural roots of inequality, and lent weight to his call for a high wage economy.[57] That decade, both Careys witnessed the growth of working-class organization. Over the following years, the younger Carey grappled with the problem of class conflict long before the subject became fashionable elsewhere, and his followers, applying their master's associationist logic to the city itself, sought to enlist working people in building a metropolis of labor. In doing so, they helped to fashion a powerful defense of consolidationist growth politics.

After 1861, wartime pressures threatened to expose the tensions in Carey's "harmony of interests" doctrine. Although jobs were plentiful after the secession crisis, inflation depressed real wages by around a fifth.[58] The city's journeymen organized from a sturdy base. Unlike the Panic of 1837, the economic collapse of 1857 had brought unemployed workers together across lines of craft and culture, and as the hard times receded, they rebuilt unions and sought to claw back what they had conceded in the crisis.

Although radicals did not always succeed, they struck at the heart of growth politics. Well-organized printers staged a series of stoppages in the years before the Civil War that targeted booster papers like the *Evening Bulletin*. Mechanics in the city's locomotive works, meanwhile, formed a union in 1858, which launched a strike at Matthias W. Baldwin's large factory two years later. Baldwin, who after pushing Consolidation through the state capitol in 1854 had become an early Republican convert, paid reasonably well, but discontent had festered since the Panic, when two hundred men were laid off and others paid in depreciated railroad bonds. The locomotive builder offered workers Careyite homilies on the "association" of "capital and labor," refused to recognize the union, and sought replacements elsewhere. After four months the strikers gave up.[59]

One of the leaders in the Baldwin dispute—Jonathan C. Fincher—tried to learn lessons from defeat by building a movement culture to rival mid-century radicalism. At its heart stood his newspaper, *Fincher's Trades' Review*, which from 1863, turned its columns over to furthering the cause of a peaceful "social revolution." Though neither as utopian nor internationalist as George Lippard's earlier *Quaker City* weekly, *Fincher's* articulated similar ideas, upholding the right of the worker to the fruits of his toil, rejecting "the dogmas of sectarian pigmies," and urging working-class consolidation. It called itself "an Organization paper," and like Lippard's predecessor, saw "combination" as "the Engine of Civilization," driving nations, capital, and labor forward. From mid-1863 onward, workers seemed to be paying heed. New unions won a series of strikes for higher wages, regulated entry into their trades, and linked up with locals elsewhere in the nation. A new citywide trades' assembly drew up plans for a library and an annual ball. Cooperative ventures, with the midcentury land reformer John Shedden among the leaders, tried to establish stores through the city, corresponding with Britain's Rochdale Pioneers in the process.[60]

Fincher's focused on what united white workers. Talk of the "domestic institutions of this country"—the usual euphemism for slavery—barely appeared in its pages, and while it lauded the efforts of white female operatives to organize, it had (in contrast to George Lippard and the land reformers who saw links between the labor question in the North and South) little to say to the city's African Americans. The paper also proved hostile to party politics, warning workingmen against wasting their time in "ward meetings" and "torchlight processions," and prodding them to pursue an independent course at the polls. Only a minority of Philadelphia's working people read *Fincher's*—the paper was in perennial dire straits—but it provides a window onto the war within a war across the workshops of the city.[61]

Wartime radicals battled growth politics as well as party politics. Countering the city's Careyite orthodoxy, *Fincher's* held that labor and capital were "in the natural course of things, opposed to each other." Capitalists who professed "to be our protectors," Fincher, Shedden, and William D. Young wrote, presided in practice over "undressed wrongs." Boosters' eagerness to "see in each mountain a gold mine" met derision.[62]

Workingmen found evidence of growth politics' failings in the fabric of the city itself. Both bourgeois reformers and radical critics recognized in the 1850s that Philadelphia had "insoluble housing problems." Consolidation's land grab and the People's Party's suburban improvements both aimed to address the issue, but in a decade in which the population grew by 38 percent, the building work could not keep up. Immigrants continued to seek shelter in overcrowded wards that lined the border of the old city proper, and most working-class suburbanites located near their place of work, rather than commuting to the city on streetcars. War then slowed the speed of construction while raising the price of rent. *Fincher's* even blamed the cost of "living in cities" for strikes.[63]

What troubled radicals, though, was the process rather than pace of growth. Echoing their midcentury predecessors, they reminded working people that though their labor had built up the city, producers were forced to rent as the wealthy "accumulated great blocks of houses." Poor tenants shared insalubrious "alleys and by-ways" with nuisances like slaughterhouses, which "seldom shock the nasal sensibilities of those who occupy brown and marble stone fronts." "Capitalists and speculators," *Fincher's* complained in 1865, "are gradually monopolizing all the wide and airy thoroughfares." When middle-class residents too found themselves pushed out to the suburbs by rising real estate values, they displaced the working people they encountered. "The poor must keep their distance, and seek the more cheap and obscure dwellings," the paper noted, as it attacked gentrification. "The march of improvement," it concluded, "ejects the workers from their homes."[64]

Radicals differed from their bourgeois counterparts on the causes rather than consequences of bad housing. Both agreed that overcrowding amounted to a "social evil." When *Fincher's* reprinted a piece that argued good homes made for "a good husband, a kind father, and an exemplary citizen," it could have been lifted from Price's sermon on family government. To Price, though, the remedy for metropolitan woes lay in orderly outward expansion. His antebellum reforms therefore strengthened city government and liberalized property markets, while his work with the BBA aimed to secure private profit and moral uplift. The weekly, in contrast, blamed the "crimes of Capital" for forcing labor into "dirty haunts."[65]

As construction slowed and rents rose toward the end of the Civil War, Fincher suggested that the housing question could serve as a foundation for working-class politics. "No two interests," his weekly wrote of landlord and tenant, "clash as frequently." Wherever capitalists erected "wretched tumble-down shanties," it argued, responsibility lay with them for the evils that ensued. When capital drove labor into "putrid dens," it became "its murderer." If working people united, though, they could claim "the indefeasible right to good dwellings." The paper proposed a host of practical reforms, including better protection of tenants' personal property, boards of arbitration to determine disputes, the factoring of rising rent into wage claims, and the decentralization of manufacturing to small towns. By early 1866, some "laboring people," angry at the continued increase in the cost of housing, were calling for meetings to organize tenants. Such concerns were reflected in the platform of the postwar National Labor Union (NLU)—the first nationwide trades' congress—which blamed landlords for pushing workingmen into "illy-ventilated dwellings" and "poor houses in the suburbs" as they sought to make real estate pay like other investments.[66]

Although formed in Baltimore, the NLU had a heavy Philadelphia contingent, and the iron molder and *Fincher's* correspondent William H. Sylvis served as its first president. Under his leadership, the NLU urged women and African Americans to organize, while remaining noncommittal on Reconstruction. Back in his native city, Sylvis proved more willing to involve himself in politics. In the 1865 mayoral election, he and fellow craft unionists canvassed the two candidates on their "views upon the labor question." The committee were more interested in the eight-hour day than in the housing question, but both played into the quality of life beyond the workplace, and the Democrats' candidate, Daniel M. Fox, backed a policy that would allow the workingman to become an "intelligent citizen" and "a good head of family." McMichael, on the other hand, provided no assurances. Sylvis and his allies rejected McMichael, reminded supporters that the *North American*'s editor had "ever been opposed to the labor reform movement," and urged journeymen to join "in striking down the man who has had his feet upon our necks." The NLU leader sought to make the 1865 election into a battle that pitted growth politics against white working-class radicalism.[67]

Philadelphia's boosters and businessmen had been busy organizing themselves over the previous years. For them, strikers posed a threat to growth. In 1859, for example, the *North American* made the study of labor relations part of its analysis of the real estate market. When Cincinnati workshop owners visited Philadelphia in June 1863 to see how employers "successfully resisted the tyranny" of craft unions, McMichael's paper explained how taking on apprentices ensured a steady supply of strike-breakers, and hoped the midwesterners would return to Ohio aware that those who wanted to be "free themselves must strike the blow." McMichael, who did not dare try to emancipate himself from the printers on his own fully unionized shop floor, reputedly rejected requests to insert strike notices from other trades in his advertising columns. Others simply refused to recognize claims to bargaining rights. With inflation rising in 1864, Fincher's machinists' union formed a committee to negotiate with owners across the city, but most employers, including municipal Consolidators Baldwin and Samuel Vaughan Merrick, turned the men away. Owners turned the power of the city's police on strikers too.[68]

By Reconstruction, though, the "labor question" involved questions over space as well as wages. The destruction of slavery, as Eric Foner has shown, threatened to expose contradictions in free labor ideology that the likes of Lippard had endeavored to reveal a few years before.[69] As *Fincher's* attests, radicals saw those contradictions taking form in the city itself, where workers wanted cheap, clean housing in place of the courts and alleys to which rising rents often confined them. If there was, as Carey insisted, a "harmony of interests" between labor and capital, then could it take expression in metropolitan geography? Consolidators before the war had suggested that might be the case, given Philadelphia's vast territory and reputation as a city of homes. Associational enterprise and municipal debt here had the potential to build up a democratic periphery as well as an imperial center.

In the aftermath of the Civil War, working-class loyalty seemed up for grabs. Careyites like McMichael insisted they stood on labor's side. The head of the Board of Trade and a leading Consolidator, Frederick Fraley, declared that protection provided work, spurred consumption, and made people "happy, contented and prosperous." The pro-tariff Industrial League, which he helped to establish in 1865 with McMichael, Cooke, and leading manufacturers, had 1,200 workingmen from around the Union on its roster by the end of the decade. Protectionism's appeal to Philadelphia's working people is open to debate. Industrial wards that benefited from the tariff were among the first to turn to the Republican Party in the late 1850s, and though after the conflict Sylvis rejected the harmony of interests doctrine, he acknowledged Carey as the "ablest writer of the age." Many mid-century radicals, however, including the land reformer Shedden, continued to search for alternatives to industrial capitalism, and Philadelphians appeared in the ranks of the socialist First International as well as native-born movements like the Knights of Labor, which took root in the city in the early 1870s.[70]

A handful, though, moved toward Careyism. William D. Kelley, who had joined the journeymen's movement in the 1830s and remained a friend to radical groups up to midcentury, became Carey's closest ally in Congress after the Civil War. "When he goes into society," one wag put it, "he backs women into corners and asks them their opinion of the duty on steel rails." Another Carey disciple to migrate from radical ranks was William Elder. A native Pittsburgher, he trained in medicine and law, before entering politics in 1839 as a candidate of a fusion anti-Mason/Whig ticket. His hostility to slavery, however, led him to the political abolitionism of the Liberty Party. By the mid-1840s, Elder was rallying workingmen to the Liberty banner with some success, and when he moved to Philadelphia, he found a home among utopians, land reformers, and craft unionists. He proved particularly active in the Fourierist Philadelphia Union of Associationists, which he joined in 1848, and served as its sinister sounding "Chief of the Group of Indoctrination." But around 1850—disillusioned with the failure of third parties, the collapse of the 1848 Revolutions, and the racism of radicals like John Campbell—he called for a new movement that would unite labor reform and antislavery. He found it in Carey's brand of Republicanism, and in 1859, toured Pennsylvania with the political economist to extol the benefits of protection. During the Civil War, Carey helped him find a position in the Treasury Department, where Elder joined up with Cooke to show how the nation's extraordinary ratios of growth would soon write off the national debt.[71]

These radical Careyites saw in the association of labor and capital an alternative to social disintegration. Both Kelley and Elder—like another protectionist, the municipal Consolidator and iron manufacturer Stephen Colwell—had warned of a coming conflict between rich and poor around midcentury. But by the Civil War, they had concluded that interdependence could be harnessed to stave off the threat. Association—which a Carey biographer has called the "cooperative tendency among small units"—stood at the center of harmony of interests theory, but it borrowed significantly from the utopian thought off the 1840s. In radical vocabulary, the term had a precise meaning. Labor should associate, radicals argued, until "every worker is a capitalist." The associative logic underpinned schemes for communal living and cooperative enterprise. For Elder, it signaled "a power"—a force multiplier—which produced "Samson strength." When association was fused with radical ideology, the machine could work toward reconstruction. Labor, the pacific and antislavery Elder argued, needed to learn the "corporative principle" from "armies, cotton plantations and cotton factories." Then the world would see "the realized fraternity of the race" in the form of "labor emancipated, labor associated." Association here was a cry for modernization and solidarity.[72]

Elder's associationist thought resonated after the combined efforts of the war years. His first collection of postbellum essays began with the claim that "association with his fellow-men is the first and greatest necessity of man's life." Indeed, it was to Elder what class conflict was to Marx: the driving force of human history. He charted a dialectic in which the "unityism" of ancient and medieval despotism brought into being the rights-based individualism (he termed it "civilization") that had led to religious reformation and social revolution over the preceding centuries. But that individualism in turn had been found wanting—the war between labor and capital offered ample proof—so the "present epoch" marked the "renascence of the associative movement." The evidence was everywhere: the rise of the business corporation, the consolidation of national states, and the "guarantyism" that led to the formation of secret societies, savings banks, and craft unions.[73]

Associationist idealism ran through Elder's thought, but after his migration to the Careyite camp, it subtly shifted in emphasis. Aspects of the utopian socialism remained in the language. When in 1871 he talked about "repellant individualism," "fraternity with industry," and the "brotherhood of man," the author might have been conversing with his younger self. Certainly the old faith in human potential had not deserted him: he celebrated the granting of black suffrage and continued to laud worker-owned cooperatives that had flickered briefly in the late 1840s. Yet writing with class conflict in Europe and America on his mind, he assailed "Unions of resistance," which in substituting "reformation" for "revolution" had undermined the true cause of cooperation.[74]

Like Carey, however, Elder stripped association of the meaning radicals had given it in the 1840s. While it might still legitimately describe a worker-owned cooperative or a revolutionary secret society, it could just as well apply to the union of labor and capital in a business enterprise. Association was amoral; whether its power was used for good or evil depended on who wielded it. Here, then, lay part of the appeal of Careyite thought to figures like Elder and Kelley. The eclipse of radicalism and the Second Party System around midcentury had left them looking for new models of association. Economic interdependence, national union, and equal citizenship became their consolidationist cry.

One of the finest expressions of association in action, for Elder and others, lay in the urban form itself. They lauded Philadelphia's building societies as superior forms of working-class association to trade unions. The societies had sprung up in the antebellum city as a safer place for journeymen and their families to secure capital and property than speculative land companies. Their operations rested on a simple principle. Stockholders would pay a small sum—typically a dollar a week—to meet the cost of what was usually a $200 share. As the association built up its balance, investors could bid for loans. The mortgage, secured against the shareholder's newly purchased property, would be paid off over a period of a few years. When the association wound up, the profits would be distributed evenly. The societies made working-class borrowing to buy property— hitherto near impossible given the difficulty of acquiring mortgages—a real possibility. They proved wildly popular, and after Republicans backed a general incorporation law in the late 1850s that removed obstacles to their establishment, hundreds secured charters. As early as 1856, Kelley had used them to demonstrate the superiority of the northern social system.[75]

By the late 1860s, building associations were helping to push the city outward at a rate of around three thousand new dwellings—mostly small two-story houses—a year. In 1872 incorporators had established the Union of Building Associations (UBA), and estimates a few years later indicated the city boasted anywhere between five hundred and eight hundred active organizations with about seventy thousand investors. Journals and books explained their operation to the uninitiated. The Social Science Association—led by Carey and dominated by his followers—made them a particular object of study. And for the city's working-class, they offered relief from rising rents and security for their savings. Tenancy remained the norm—despite some estimates of close to half of Philadelphia's heads of household owning property as late as 1890, just 22.8 percent of houses were owner occupied—but the building societies held out a realistic hope of homeownership.[76]

For bourgeois Philadelphians too, the building associations offered a way to strengthen the city's domestic sphere: an ambition of antebellum reformers. Though they rarely admitted as much, they shared many of Fincher's concerns about the city's "wretched tenement homes." The ill effects were social and economic. A year after the Draft Riots, the *Evening Bulletin* blamed Gotham's housing for its "huge 'dangerous class,'" while a Philadelphia medical journal, reasoning that the "lives and health of . . . [the]

laboring classes constitute an important part of the capital of our cities,"
warned that sickly neighborhoods like Bedford Street did not "contribute
their quota" to metropolitan wealth.[77]

Given the causal links between urban decay and disorder, early postbellum reformers welcomed any association that could advance the work of
rebuilding, and wealthy citizens paid close attention to plans for model
housing. When McMichael's friend John Forney—a newspaper publisher
and wartime Republican convert—went to Europe in late 1860s, he devoted
a chapter of his travelogue to George Peabody's model lodgings in London,
which he suggested imitating in American cities. As the work of reconstructing plantation households began in the South, then, bourgeois northerners looked to put their own laborers' homes in order.[78]

Ambitions for municipal and national reconstruction here occasionally
overlapped. George Bayne, who had advocated communal housing in the
North American before the Civil War, now tried to persuade the Freedmen's
Bureau that the "orthodox municipal panacea" of relief for ex-slaves would
not work. Building on his earlier designs for Philadelphia, he proposed
borrowing from a powerful, paternal government to fund communities of
two thousand freedpeople, who would live in family units. Each community
would boast a diverse industrial base and share a scrip currency. Citizens
fearful of further social and sectional conflict tended to pay heed to such
designs. Even the arch-pessimist Fisher suggested model housing might
work in both the North and the South, while the inventor William F. Channing told social scientists that as the "first step toward social order is to
secure the independent existence of the individual or family in a home,"
mutual organizations might build vast federative homesteads, in a form of
"scientific cooperation" that countered the anarchic tendencies of communism and individualism.[79]

Building associations offered a more practical path to physical and
moral renewal. Good homes, reformers had argued since the 1840s,
removed citizens from the dangerous terrain of tavern and street, and provided a superior setting for "family government." As tenants became taxpayers, they would pay more heed to municipal politics, and vote out
careless and corrupt officers. Housing, social scientists insisted in this vein,
would elevate occupants to a "higher civilization" by providing the space
required to ensure "responsibility as individual elements of society."
Working-class association appeared to be accelerating the transformation
of the city of mobs into the city of homes.[80]

Philadelphia's growth therefore made it safe for democracy: a stark contrast to the 1840s. "To the common form of building associations," one citizen claimed in 1867, the metropolis owes "blessings which she enjoys beyond any other large city in the world." To some, it offered a heaven on earth: a "millennial" cure for social conflict and sickly tenements. To one Careyite, for instance, housing a large population was a "social question of the highest character," but he found in his hometown a "building system for the great cities" that united labor, capital, and landowner in a web of interdependence.[81] To him, then, the question of the nineteenth-century city had been answered not by a Haussmann, but by the associated power of Philadelphia's free laborers.

The building associations also channeled capital into the built environment. Boosters had sought to mobilize the savings of small investors since the 1840s, encouraging workers to pour money into railroads, real estate, and the national loans. Working people's participation in growth politics lent credibility to bourgeois claims that the common good rather than class interest was the end they had in mind. Money on a different magnitude, though, went into the building associations. In 1874, the UBA claimed the organizations they represented had poured $100 million into Pennsylvania, and three years later, a social scientist estimated $30 million had gone into Philadelphia's real estate market alone. Such a scale of investment, in Careyite terms, strengthened the home market necessary for a manufacturing metropolis to live off "the wants and desires of its own population." Certainly it stimulated a boom in the building trades: the number of carpenters and builders in Philadelphia increased from 878 in 1860 to 4,454 a decade later. At least 20,000 citizens worked in construction-related trades by 1870, with many more in related occupations like the horse railways. Moreover, as Elder indicated in his analysis of the associations, working-class shareholders were borrowing against their future earnings, building the city outward with confidence in their own upward mobility. Debt-financed urban expansion then did not just rest on municipal borrowing, it also came from the consolidated power of the city's artisans and laborers.[82]

*   *   *

On July 4, 1876—the United States' hundredth birthday—the Centennial Exposition opened its doors in Philadelphia. Over the following months, nearly ten million people came through the gates. The Centennial, despite being a national celebration, condensed the strengths and weaknesses of Consolidators' metropolitan achievements into a single event. Veterans of the battle for municipal union played prominent roles in the exposition's planning, and Fraley—an architect of the 1854 Act and an ardent nationalist—served as the Board of Finance's secretary.

The proposal to hold a centennial celebration in the Union birthplace came from a Midwestern academic after the Civil War, but Philadelphia boosters, with Fraley's Franklin Institute at the helm, soon took up the call. By 1871, Congress had got on board, and over the following years, a mixture of city, state, and federal money helped organizers fund the world's fair. However, the bulk of the investment came from the tradition of urban voluntarism, as the Board of Finance—led by bourgeois Philadelphians, building on the experience of the wartime Sanitary Fair, and supported by the likes of the Union League—went about raising money. The Fairmount Park Commission set aside a portion of its grounds, which were laid out according to a plan that, while mirroring Philadelphia's grid, also borrowed from designs in Vienna and Paris. Thus, dreams of what Broad Street might become began to take shape on a blank canvas a few miles west of the old downtown. The exposition was both a product of and a chance to display growth politics at work: railroads—both horse-drawn and steam-powered—brought visitors to and fro, while the industrial might on display in the buildings proved the wisdom of a tariff. In the collaboration between public and private power brokers, the grandeur of the design, and the evocation of Philadelphia's productive power, the Centennial presented to the world a city boosters hoped Consolidation would create. All that was missing in their ensemble was the row home, though at the Columbian Exposition in Chicago seventeen years later, a "model Philadelphia house" did appear among the exhibits.[83]

By the Centennial, Philadelphia's status as a "city of homes" had become a standard boast of civic boosters. Suburban rows constructed with building association capital, the likes of the North American argued over and over again, provided a stronger foundation for urban greatness than New York's overcrowded tenements. The city's decentered residential geography helped to explain its loyal service in the war and its peaceful development since. Its grand center and domestic periphery absorbed labor, improved citizens, and developed industry. Carey's harmony of interests doctrine had been urbanized; Philadelphia's "practical consolidation," if not complete, seemed well on course to create a metropolis imperial in scale but republican in form. Public and private power, underpinned by a vast debt, and extending over the immense terrain of the consolidated metropolis, was reconstructing the city of the 1840s. Then, Philadelphia's political and social geography had succored rioters and threatened growth. Now it did precisely the opposite.

Yet the imperial republican city was never as stable as boosters suggested. Consolidated Philadelphia rested on the power of local government, the availability of public and private credit, and economic expansion driven in part by the growth politics of the national government. The Republican Party, bourgeois unionists, and black and white voters provided the bricks; the Careyite vision of associated capitalism, the mortar. In an unstable world, Philadelphia could seem a model of solidity: a structure neither Civil War nor social strife could bring down. But the metropolis had design flaws too. After 1865, and particularly in the harder economic climate of the 1870s, cracks in the edifice between party politicians and "best men," suburban expansionists and critics of outward growth, and friends and foes of democracy began to widen. Even the Centennial raised doubts: the event was costly, consigned nonwhites to the margins, and strained the city's capacity to provide services. The former mayor Alexander Henry warned organizers that "security for person and property" at the event "can only be had through the 'one man power' in its almost absolute exercise." Philadelphia's union could sometimes seem more fragile than sanguine boosters liked to concede. Leland may have extolled the principle of consolidation, but it could divide as well as unite.[84]

CHAPTER 7

Philadelphia Redeemed

In June 1871, bourgeois boosters gathered at the Commercial Exchange to hear the Radical Republican Congressman William D. Kelley extol the prospects of the Northern Pacific Railroad, a route projected to run from Duluth, Minnesota, to the Puget Sound. The meeting's officers amounted to a who's who of civic promoters. Prominent among the dozens of vice presidents were Morton McMichael, municipal Consolidators, presidents of the Pennsylvania Railroad, and Kelley's friend and ally, Henry C. Carey. Behind the enterprise, though, stood Jay Cooke, who had taken control of financing the venture the previous summer, and had borrowed from the methods he had used to fund the war effort by appealing to small investors. In terms Cooke would have approved of, Kelley explained how the Northern Pacific would open up the resources of the Far West and the stagnant empires beyond, adding "inconceivably to the wealth, power and influence of the nation." Philadelphia stood to benefit more than most as the line gave energy to labor, capital, and real estate.[1]

But Kelley, an old ally of the Hungarian nationalist Louis Kossuth and Philadelphia's utopian socialists, had grander aims. Probably with contemporary urban upheavals in mind—the Paris Commune and the first of New York's sectarian Orange riots were recent events—he reprised an argument he had made amid conflict over immigration in 1840s Philadelphia. The road to the Pacific, Kelley insisted, would draw population out from the overcrowded nations of Europe and the teeming cities of the eastern seaboard. The "tide of immigration will continue," he declared, "until regenerated Europe shall give the labourer political power and social consideration." Railroad-building and outward migration could renew Philadelphia, the Old World, and the New.[2]

The builder Charles M. Leslie did not share Kelley's global ambitions, but he tried to show too how boosterism, finance, and out-migration could leave its mark on Philadelphia. Eager in the real estate boom of the late 1860s to erect a series of streets "worthy of a poet's pen," Leslie obtained ground to the southwest of the old city proper near the Schuylkill, where he planned a genteel alternative to the crowded alleys of the inner suburbs. Probably influenced by his friend Eli Kirk Price, who had proposed something similar around midcentury, he followed the plan of the urban grid, but replaced cobblestone paving with elegant gardens, which he lined with small homes "designed for the masses." Leslie expected members of building associations to occupy the garden blocks and joined several of the organizations himself to fund the speculative venture. In wondering what "a marvelous influence . . . hundreds of such streets and parks" would have across the urban form, he tried to add "a little to the reputation of Philadelphia as a 'City of homes.'" His design brought the urban refinement of genteel districts within reach of working-class citizens (see Figure 6).[3]

Kelley's plea for the Northern Pacific Railroad and Leslie's projected garden blocks marked attempts to harmonize interests by building a city imperial in scale and republican in form. Each depended on mobilizing capital and labor; each promised to reap rewards for both rich and poor Philadelphians. And one made the other possible, as western extension, a consolidated national market, and the promise of overseas riches gave citizens the confidence that their city would continue to grow peacefully. Both rested on borrowing in anticipation of that future—whether through building societies or bond issues—and both came crashing down in 1873. Cooke's Northern Pacific (which probably to Kelley's ignorance had done nothing to organize the vast system of emigration he promised) went bankrupt, bringing down its financier's bank and beginning the first financial crisis of the Gilded Age.[4] An overextended Leslie was among the victims, and overwhelmed by claims from creditors and mechanics for money, he fled to Brazil. The economic catastrophe—which compounded growing concerns about the expansion of debt and democracy—tested Philadelphia's growth politics. It lent weight to calls for rethinking the wisdom of urban reconstruction.

Historians of the Civil War era have often seen the Panic of 1873 as speeding a "retreat from Reconstruction," in which Republicans backed away from support for the use of strong state power. In confronting militant workers, bourgeois northerners realized they had more in common with southern planters than landless blacks, and joined a nationwide

Figure 6. Madison Square garden block. Funded by building association stock, Charles Leslie's Madison Square promised to bring gentility within reach of the city's white working-class housing by supplanting combustible street life with cathartic garden blocks. Leslie's building empire collapsed in the Panic of 1873, and he fled to Rio de Janeiro, but booster publications used his development to showcase Philadelphia as the "city of homes." Source: Reprinted from *Philadelphia and Its Environs* (Philadelphia: J. B. Lippincott, 1876). Courtesy of The Library Company of Philadelphia.

"counterrevolution of property." The rapid democratization that followed the end of the Civil War gave way to a longer period of retrenchment.[5] Philadelphia felt the effects of this wider American Thermidor. The Panic heightened social tensions, and led plenty of wealthy citizens to conclude that local reconstruction had progressed too far and too fast. The power wielded by the city's poor and the cost of urban improvements each needed curbing. And these two could seem—not without reason—increasingly interlinked given the connections between democracy, debt, and a commitment to upward and outward metropolitan growth.

Doubts about the city's postwar course, though, preceded 1873. Even in the early postwar years, which witnessed the most ambitious attempts at urban reconstruction, critics had questioned the wisdom of growth politics. Consolidators' failure to purge the city's politics of partisan operators left bourgeois citizens with the same ambivalence toward municipal government as their counterparts in Boss Tweed's New York—impressed by the growth and peace but often disgusted with the kind of people it thrust to the fore. Various events contributed to growing unease. These ranged from local decisions over taxation via national developments like Tweed's fall in New York to the international upheaval of the Paris Commune. Each ate away at bourgeois support for the local vision of the Republican Party and led to a reassertion of the kind of penny-pinching ideas about urban growth that had been rejected in the debate over railroad subscriptions and municipal Consolidation between 1846 and 1854. For some, especially after 1873, it led to questioning of the logic of civic union itself.

This chapter explores growing concerns about growth politics over the course of Reconstruction. Designed to find a way out of the social crisis the city faced in the antebellum era, growth politics had produced problems of its own, in the form of powerful corporations, an industrial proletariat, and an expensive and corrupt city government locked into a program of outward expansion. Philadelphia's redeemers—to borrow a term usually applied to the South—struggled to form a majority (even among their own class), but like national renegades from the Republican Party, they weakened the capacity for the radical reconstruction of metropolitan space and society that the likes of Kelley and Leslie envisaged.

Routes to Redemption

Lessons from home and abroad weakened support for Philadelphia's physical reconstruction. Admiration for Second Empire urbanism had peaked in the years after the Civil War when the likes of the *Public Ledger* called Napoleon III "the model reformer to the world," and citizens claimed he had all but "solved" the "question of building the city of the nineteenth century." But concerns about the wisdom of the emperor's course lingered. Carey, for instance, condemned Paris as a vast centralized city concentrating dangerous wealth and power, while others wondered what would

happen if the public works stopped. "There is a wealth of statues and fountains," argued the *North American* in 1869, "but the people wonder where
the poor are to live." McMichael's friend John W. Forney offered a similar
assessment. On a visit to the French capital, he saw the "old faubourgs
where Revolution plotted . . . being torn out by the roots, like so many
poisonous fangs." But the question of what the laboring classes might do if
cut loose from construction work was a "terrible one" for Napoleon III,
and the absence of the means or will for most of the capital's residents to
acquire a house of their own only compounded the risk. Philadelphia's
"city of homes"—more reminiscent of decentralized London than imperial
Paris—provided a sounder model.[6]

Bourgeois Philadelphians, though, were often more concerned by the
cost of reconstruction in Paris than the consequences. In 1868, the full
extent of Paris's debt became clear, and Napoleon III soon dismissed Haussmann from office. Meanwhile in New York, reformers fired the opening
salvoes against William Tweed's spendthrift Tammany Hall machine. In
this climate, the arguments made by Cooke and McMichael that rapid
growth would diminish vast debts seemed harder to sustain. Even Mc-
Michael's *North American*, which had often praised Paris, expressed horror
at the "confused and outrageous system of financial management." Americans, it counseled, often saw the "splendid city as a model of imitation in
the way of public works and improvements," but few would accept the
"frightful municipal debt" and "appalling taxation" that came with it. The
Germantown Telegraph, a suburban newspaper that had initially welcomed
Consolidation as a boon to rural landowners, took the critique further. In
the spring of 1871, it blamed Philadelphia's vast borrowing on well-traveled
citizens "infatuated with the splendors of the European capitals," who
proved "willing to run into almost any extravagance . . . in order to imitate
what they have seen abroad." Calls for retrenchment were growing louder.[7]

That the *Telegraph*'s words appeared just a week or so after the inauguration of the short-lived Paris Commune may have been no coincidence,
for events in the French capital undermined bourgeois faith in urban reconstruction. In 1870, defeat to Bismarck's Prussia forced Napoleon III's abdi-
cation, and led to the proclamation of the Third Republic. Prussian troops
besieged Paris, and when the new French authorities tried to surrender,
citizens seized the city government and adopted a raft of radical measures.
The Second Empire became the first French government since that of
Napoleon I to be brought down by military defeat rather than revolutionary

upheaval, but if Haussmann's rebuilding had served its purpose of barricade-proofing Paris, communards' readiness to reclaim control suggested the poor had been temporarily pacified rather than permanently placated.

Communards' hostility to private property and traditional authority horrified bourgeois Philadelphia. They were cast as "lawless men and women who everywhere cloak their 'agrarianism,' their 'free love,' their hatred of all family ties and all social order, under the banner of the 'social republic.'" Price called them "not only the enemies of all rights of property, but the enemies of mankind," and argued they must be "treated as such by all governments that preserve social order." When republican troops reclaimed the city and executed thousands of its Red defenders, the *Inquirer* welcomed the bloodshed as something "the world in general" could look on with approval.[8]

The ruin of Paris served as a spur to the ongoing reappraisal of Bonapartist urbanism. Instead of stabilizing a society susceptible to revolution, which almost all of Napoleon III's American admirers saw as his greatest success, the Second Empire, in its death throes, had given birth to the world's first communist government, and as some critics predicted in the 1850s, the displaced poor (if only for a short time) had retaken the metropolis. Architectural admiration for Haussmann's Paris persisted, shaping plans for Philadelphia and other American cities into the twentieth century, but the sense that Napoleon III had found a way to hold together an interdependent, turbulent polity withered. The Third Republic's brutal suppression of the Commune, indeed, rather than the Second Empire's city-building, now provided an example for bourgeois citizens to ponder as they confronted their own striking workers.[9]

Yet the roots of retrenchment lay at home as well as abroad. By the early 1870s, consolidators knew full well that the 1854 charter had failed to bring about an end to partisan rule, as so-called "party hacks" found ways to prosper in the enlarged city. Nor had a ballooning municipal debt—which doubled over the course of the 1860s to almost $40 million—necessarily improved people's perception of municipal administration: complaints about filthy streets and expensive services filled the columns of postbellum newspapers (see Figure 7). Citizens, as they had in the antebellum era, searched for the source of misgovernment. Those with doubts about democracy, troubled by the national turn toward extending voting rights in Reconstruction, continued to blame a widespread suffrage. Clark Hare,

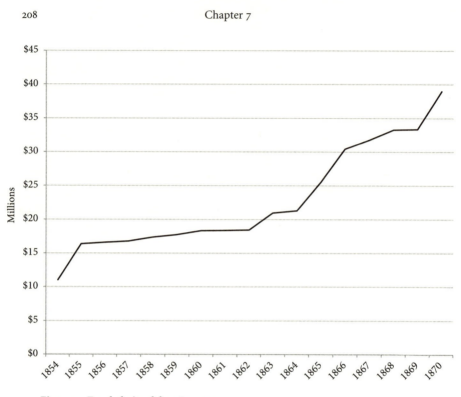

Figure 7. Funded city debt, 1854–70.

a veteran of the struggle to suppress the 1844 riots and a founder of the Union League, believed the "criminal classes" organized as a "political body" to sway elections, while Sidney George Fisher, who had often questioned the compatibility of democracy and property, privately admitted his preference for a monarchy. Fisher's record of conversations with friends indicates his views on the "hopelessness of finding a remedy under universal suffrage" were not uncommon among the economic elite even before 1873.[10]

More often, though, wealthy citizens bemoaned the absence of "best men" from office. McMichael's stint in city hall (1866–1869) stood as a rare exception that proved hard to repeat. As one paper hinted, his "dinner-table witticisms and well-turned sentences" were all very well, but party managers who "cordially and frequently mix with the masses" enjoyed better prospects. McMichael only served one term in city hall, and the next Republican chief magistrate, William S. Stokely, bore more of the hallmarks of the postbellum politician. A journeyman confectioner, volunteer

fireman, and Civil War–era councilman, Stokely built a strong ward operation, and used it as a springboard for citywide power. The genteel Union
League rejected Stokely's membership in 1871.[11]

If Stokely's rise through the ranks of ward politics suggests the survival
of the localism reformers had targeted in 1854, however, postbellum politics
differed from its antebellum predecessor. Power now flowed from the
"small men" to city bosses rather than remaining splendidly isolated in
petty sovereignties. After 1854, councils claimed executive control over
departments, while state legislators continually intervened in matters of
municipal concern like the regulation of street railways. Alliances between
councilmen, department heads, and Harrisburg politicians enabled a handful of bosses to build metropolitan-wide rings, which they sustained
through sharing out contracts and jobs. Stokely himself proved adept at the
new style of ring rule through his roles in the Highways Department and
Public Buildings Commission.[12]

When mixed with white supremacy, the old localism could still wreak
havoc as the 1871 slaying of Octavius Catto revealed. William McMullen,
the "Squire" of Moyamensing, had adapted easily enough to post-
Consolidation politics, and allied his mostly Irish American followers in the
Fourth Ward to Democratic politicians seeking higher office. Passage of the
Fifteenth Amendment in his racially diverse district, though, threatened his
authority, and during a brief period of Democratic rule in 1870, federal
troops were called in to protect black voting rights, given the unwillingness
of the police to do likewise. A year later on election day, with troops absent,
a fireman in McMullen's Moyamensing Hose shot the African American
civil rights leader Catto along the South Street corridor that before 1854 had
marked the contested border between the southern suburbs and the city
proper. Unlike in New York, where civil strife between Protestants and
Catholics the same year weakened support for a wide suffrage, Catto's
assassination briefly bolstered the democratic commitments of a white
Republican bourgeoisie. Yet as reformers began to organize over the following years, they showed more concern with reining in the power of ring
leaders than small men like McMullen. Only successful campaigns to pro-
fessionalize the fire department and abolish the ward office of aldermen
hint at enduring concerns about localism; Reformers' increasingly directed
their fire against ring rule instead.[13]

It would be too schematic to suggest that political reformers around
1870 switched from a concern with remaking space to protecting taxpayers,

but there is a discernible shift in emphasis that paralleled the national retreat from Reconstruction. The power councilmen and department heads exerted over the public purse troubled investors in taxable real estate. In the 1850s, bourgeois Consolidators had hoped metropolitan annexation would restrain men like McMullen, whom they expected to sink into insignificance in a vast city of homes. Expansion, though, actually enlarged the terrain of a different kind of boss, whose power came less from personal authority and more from mastery of aspects of city government. In response to ring rule, bourgeois citizens could try to shield power in appointive bodies like the Fairmount Park Commission, established by legislative fiat in 1867 with reforming stalwarts like McMichael and Price at the helm. But such powerful public institutions became vulnerable prey for politicians, and according to Price, the board, which in 1871 had been joined by the leader of the Republican Gas ring, risked becoming a "body ruled by the party lash." Cutting spending offered a way to starve patronage-thirsty bosses.[14]

Consolidators' attempts to forge a new style of politics through redrawing Philadelphia's city's political space seemed to have failed, and they were left unsure how to proceed. When reformers in the Union League pushed for a new state constitution in 1872, they made limiting municipal debt a major aim. Price, who in the 1854 charter had envisaged creating a government with greater powers to spend, initially backed the idea in principle, though when the proposal made it through the convention, he attacked it for leaving citizens "fettered and powerless." If it passed, he warned, Pennsylvanians would never again be able to build parks, centennial halls, or asylums for soldiers' widows. Price accepted reformers' diagnosis of municipal ills but recoiled from the remedy prescribed. He doubted with good reason that reform and reconstruction could go hand in hand.[15]

A Retreat from Urban Reconstruction

Two questions dominated debates over urban reconstruction in the early 1870s: who should direct the process and who should pay? Even the strongest advocates of growth politics found themselves torn as they tried to formulate a response. In 1869, for instance, they divided over a Pennsylvania Supreme Court decision that left the bill for boulevarding parts of Broad Street in the hands of taxpayers, rather than, as the city had stipulated, the property owners on the avenue who stood to benefit most from the improvement.[16]

The court's decision in *Hammett v. the City of Philadelphia*, confirmed just a few days after the inaugural meeting of the bourgeois-dominated Broad Street Improvement League, vindicated the claims of promoters who had just gathered at the Academy of Music. Judge George Sharswood accepted the principle of "local taxation for local purposes" but argued the project was not "for the advantage and comfort of those who live upon it." Instead, he concluded, the objective was "to make a great public drive." With "monuments, statuary, and fountains" sure to go up on the boulevard in "the natural course of things," forcing immediate property owners to pay would establish a dangerous precedent that could extend to all manner of public improvements. Sharswood's argument, which made the future of Broad squarely a matter for the public purse, affirmed city-building principles articulated over and over again by the *North American* throughout the preceding two decades and repeated once more by McMichael's son at the Broad Street Improvement League's inaugural meeting. By asserting that a monumental street was a matter of public rather than private interest, the ruling appeared to open the door for further projects of urban embellishment.[17]

But in the minority opinion, Justice John Read—a strong supporter of Consolidation and railroad subscriptions—argued that residents ought to pay for the boulevarding themselves, given how rapidly their property would augment in value. Read won support in segments of the press, which lambasted the selfishness of the "magnates who inhabit the brown stone palaces of North Broad." An unlikelier ally, though, appeared in the guise of the *North American*, which, fearing the city could not afford a $500,000 loan, claimed the ruling contradicted "common justice." Although the paper reluctantly accepted the decision and urged the work to begin soon, McMichael's long-standing insistence that the improvement of Broad was a matter for the common welfare of Philadelphia seemed to have evaporated in the face of the parlous condition of the municipal treasury.[18]

Condemnation of the Hammett decision by long-term supporters of an activist local state suggested that given the condition of the municipal coffers around 1870, many boosters no longer saw government as the best agent to make an imperial metropolis. Indeed, as Robin L. Einhorn has pointed out, the "segmented system" of local taxation devolved responsibility for city-building onto owners of private property themselves, leaving little room for planning but real capacity for neighborhood control.[19] This was not quite what happened on Broad. Councils, rather than property owners, decided on the repaving, but required the latter to foot the bill. As an approach to urban embellishment, it was contradictory. Boulevarding the avenue, bourgeois commentators agreed, was in the public interest— even Read accepted this—but only a handful of property holders could be charged for the finished work. City government could decree improvements in the common good, but compel private owners to pay for them; the price of embellishment would be paid in the present, and not deferred for posterity to meet. By shifting the burden of improvement from the metropolis to the locality and from the future to the here and now, Read's logic threatened to undermine support for reconstruction.

More conservative voices began to find a receptive audience when they pleaded for efficient rather than expansionist government. One of their mouthpieces was the Citizens' Association, established in early 1870 to reform the urban environment and "relieve from their exhaustive duties the gentlemen who now make politics a business." Prominent Consolidators—including Price, who chaired the first meeting—stood at the fore, and activists compared Philadelphia unfavorably to European cities like Paris. In calling for transforming Broad into a "grand highway," the association provided impetus to the later BSIL, and its members did not shy away from using state power. Edward Shippen, for instance, argued the street's development "would have to be done under lash and spur."[20]

But the principal objective of the organization lay in pressuring municipal government to perform its most basic functions—especially remedying the problem of the city's "filthy streets"—properly. Calling for value for money in taxation, while attacking what it saw as incompetent public bodies like the Board of Health, the association enjoyed a series of minor successes, as the city unblocked drains and cleared away long-standing nuisances in response to its lobbying. But support for grander construction projects appeared a dangerous distraction for members, not to mention another way to increase the burden of debt on metropolitan real estate. As in 1860, when Carey's nephew Henry Charles Lea had warned against lavishing "millions on ornamentation" in Philadelphia, when "many improvements indispensable to the health & comfort of the citizens" had been postponed, there was a sense that city government had to return to its limited, municipal roots.[21]

Boosters, like their counterparts in New York, faced a dilemma: hold their noses, back ring rule, and build the city up or else raise the standard of reform, starve the municipal beast, and see the metropolis stagnate. Party loyalists too sometimes liked to invoke what one ward politician called "great ideas of cities" to justify straightening crooked streets, and if they profited a little in the process, did it matter if the greater good had been served? The allegiance of "best men" to the Republican Party's growth politics complicated matters further. Most identified closely with the Republicans' developmental program at local and national level—both high tariffs and construction work helped maintain a "harmony of interests"—and they feared that bolting from the regular ticket would let in disloyal (and worse, perhaps, pro–free trade) Democrats.[22]

Yet few found local Republican leaders anything more than necessary evils. The *North American* especially struggled to balance the interests of party, class, and city. Despite its criticism of the Hammett decision, McMichael's paper remained for the most part a staunch defender of debt-financing to fund construction, but even it conceded by 1875 that the municipal finances would soon render "great works" impossible. Organizations like the BSIL, meanwhile, tried to mediate between bourgeois citizens and professional politicians to advance their pet projects. But others—more sensitive to their pockets and manners—refused to muddy their hands, preferring to exert influence through genteel institutions sheltered from partisan politics. The Citizens' Association, a critic noted, carried "the odor of fast horsemanship."[23]

Bourgeois divisions—which mirrored on a metropolitan level the national split in the Republican Party between stalwarts and liberals—placed limits on the urban ambitions of city-builders. After 1870, indeed, some boosters decried the enlargement of an already remote and "overgrown" park as an unnecessary expense. One paper called demands for another $3 million loan in 1872 "so extravagant that it should be resisted to the utmost" and mocked McMichael's pleas on behalf of the "toiling masses," who were rarely seen on Fairmount's grounds. Reform associations in the wards sometimes joined the opposition, which became so strong that John Jay Smith—Andrew Jackson Downing's successor as the editor of the *Horticulturalist*—worried that the result would be the park's "neglect" and "decay."[24]

It is against this backdrop of anxiety over misgovernment and debt that we need to understand the fierce debate in the early 1870s over locating public buildings at Penn Square. The construction of a new city hall proved especially contentious on account of the role of Stokely's Republican ring. With construction vested in an unelected commission composed of party leaders and major contractors, questions were soon asked over whether the body could be trusted, and once contracts started to go to associates of the appointees, these concerns only increased. The unlimited taxing power invested in the commission proved especially unpopular, especially when the project—which would eventually cost over $23 million—started to run hopelessly over budget. To critics, indeed, the whole affair reeked of the political "jobs" polluting city government on a scale McMullen—with only the miniscule resources of a poor district behind him—could never have contemplated prior to Consolidation. Opponents organized, turning to political campaigns, legislative lobbying, and the legal system to try to block the scheme.[25]

Anger at the creation of the Public Buildings Commission (PBC) led to the establishment of the genteel Citizens Municipal Reform Association (CMRA) in 1871. The CMRA, often in conjunction with the bourgeois Union League and Social Science Association, pushed for retrenchment, probity, and the election of the "best men." By 1873, they had succeeded in bringing into being a constitutional convention that restrained the state's influence in city affairs, placed limits on the contraction of municipal debt, and abolished the Board of Aldermen that had long been a springboard to power for the likes of McMullen. After their victory, however, the movement ran out of steam, and Republican regulars proved adept at bypassing the new limits on their power. But reformers still came close to electing an independent candidate for mayor in 1874. The CMRA's influence forced booster publications like the *North American* to continually address the charge that the city could ill-afford the political and financial costs of bold projects. Postwar enthusiasm for a strong local government was giving way to the belief that its powers needed reining in.[26]

Property and Postbellum Reform

After 1870, schemes like City Hall seemed to many of Philadelphia's economic elite distortions of their urban vision. They reflected not so much the power of bourgeois enterprise and culture, as they did the political machinations of corrupt officeholders. As Howard Gillette Jr. has argued, the new public buildings stood as a "symbol" of the Republican machine, and in spite of the monumental proportions of the Penn Squares project, represented to many wealthy citizens a challenge to their ideal of a grand, refined, and orderly city.[27] Such qualms, however, did not stop at the monuments of the center, but extended to the furthest reaches of the urban frontier. Even Philadelphia's row homes—supposedly the guarantors of sound government—came under critical scrutiny in the straitened circumstances of the 1870s. Yet reformers continued to cling to the idea of a relationship between space, property, and political virtue fashioned before the Civil War. It was after all from the taverns, alleys, and up to 1871, the engine houses of the Fourth Ward that McMullen continued to draw his strength, and wherever domestic mores were absent, partisan politicians seemed to flourish. Private property in the city of homes here became the basis of a bid to broaden the reform coalition and embrace the growing working class.

Although municipal reformers directed their efforts to debt and taxes, they had ideas about how the city ought to look. One telling argument against placing city hall on Broad Street rested on the claim that the metropolitan avenue had to be kept free of the "haunts of vice" that followed barroom politicians. CMRA leaders, in fact, commissioned the eminent architect William Russell West to draw up an alternative plan for Penn Squares, which, drawing inspiration from Paris, proposed turning the Broad-Market intersection into a plaza linked to Fairmount Park by a new diagonal boulevard: the first iteration of what would eventually become the Benjamin Franklin Parkway (see Figure 5).[28]

Neither did reformers dissent from the dogma that the row home could safeguard good government and social peace. Nothing illustrated the belief more clearly than a rebellion against an 1871 attempt by Harrisburg Republicans to create appointive commissions akin to the PBC to run the city's police, streets, and waterworks. At a well-attended protest meeting that counted McMichael and other Republican "best men" among the officers, speakers assailed the plans as an affront to the principles of self-government and a recipe for financial catastrophe. It fell to the post-Consolidation mayor and "gentleman Democrat" Richard Vaux, though, to appeal on behalf of the "artisans and mechanics" who had made Philadelphia the city of homes. He warned of the "tears, weeping, distress and despair" among this class if rising taxes kept them from acquiring property.[29]

Vaux's sentimental appeal was echoed by another reformist Democrat, the attorney John O'Byrne, who pointed to New York's stark divide between tenements and mansions. The source of such inequality, he insisted, lay in Albany-appointed commissions, and Philadelphians risked a similar fate unless they found the means to resist ring rule. "It is you who will be made to suffer," O'Byrne told the city's workingmen, although his picture of a society in which the "rich capitalist and the very poor laborer" lived in utterly contrasting conditions may have been more worrying for the prosperous officers in attendance. "Class distinction and social war will follow," he counseled—the Paris Commune doubtless fresh in his mind—if workers found their access to good homes denied.[30]

By returning to the old radical contrast between the upper tenth and lower million, reformers tried to draw working- and middle-class property owners to the ranks of retrenchment. Even a critic of suburban expansion acknowledged that growth on the urban frontier "multiplies the number of those interested in keeping down taxes," while during the Centennial, the Social Science Association heard a paper praising building associations for drawing the worker away from the "empty theories of the 'poisoner' and demagogue.'" Well into the 1870s, then, bourgeois Philadelphians continued to weave home and housing into the city's "social fabric," and the CMRA—arguing their stockholders had "a more vital interest than any other class of citizens in the reform of our municipal affairs"—wrote directly to the building societies to ask for a list of their members. In their address to investors, they stuck to the familiar claim that widespread property ownership was "the most satisfactory outgrowth of our social system," leading to "thrift and comfort," "self-respecting independence and domestic morality," and the "surest guarantee of the preservation" of the city's republican institutions. "If our present system of universal householding is to continue and expand," reformers argued, taxes needed reducing, or else "the time is not far distant when the wealthy alone will be able to own or occupy entire houses."[31]

The CMRA's attempt to broaden its base through appealing to working people marked the first time the relationship between domestic expansion and political preference had been tested. Given in the judgment of the organization's historian, it "failed miserably in the electoral arena," the results were not promising. Reformers faced two obstacles. First, as part of an overwhelmingly bourgeois movement—more than one paper referred to them disparagingly as "brown-stoners" after the expensive facades of their West End homes—they had difficulty attracting poorer voters for exactly the same reasons aloof politicians had struggled in the antebellum era. Ill at ease in the realm of popular politics, reformers were easy to portray as aristocrats in campaign season, and lost out in elections where a muscular presence proved vital. One Republican officer said of reformers in the early 1870s that he would "rather have one good worker round the polls on election day" than "all the League put together."[32]

The second difficulty reformers had to overcome lay in the links between metropolitan expansion, suburban voters, and machine politicians. Rolling back the urban frontier—a policy Consolidators assumed would weaken the hold of party loyalties—in practice boosted Republican rule. Demands for services like lighting, police, and paved streets emanating from suburban wards, Gillette has shown, bound the pioneers to the major party in councils, while votes from the fast-growing periphery helped to settle major questions like the location of the new city hall. Meanwhile, Republican councilmen and department heads often made handy profits from real estate speculation, ensuring city money was employed to secure improvements on land they or their allies held. Thus developers—not one of whom can be identified among the manufacturers, bankers, merchants, and attorneys who founded the CMRA—increasingly gravitated to politicians rather than the economic elite, while suburban voters punished Republican regulars, in the hard times of the mid to late 1870s, when they too curbed expenditure. Decentralization bound voters and politicians in ties that may have been less personal than in the case of an old suburban sovereign like McMullen, but proved no less hard to break. In looking to the building societies to broaden their base, reformers were going to be disappointed.[33]

If homeownership in itself did not lead citizens to enlist in crusades against corruption, then elements of the economic elite began to rethink their faith in Philadelphia's expansive residential geography. Even the *North American*, usually a steadfast supporter of metropolitan out-migration, sometimes expressed its discomfort at the consequences of outward growth. Its critique rested on finance as much as politics. Localizing the logic of the late Carey—one of the few antebellum critics of rapid westward emigration—the paper showed how rapid decentralization discouraged interdependence. "There is a certain limit north and south to our growth," it argued when the economy began to falter in 1871, as it called for families to abandon the suburbs and "reside near the centre of business and amusements." A little later that year, the daily even wished suburban expansion could be "arrested for five years" to boost demand for downtown property and increase the density of street railway traffic. The "mistaken policy" of "shifting population from the centre to the circumference" needed to stop.[34]

For the *North American* to speak of a "manifestly overbuilt" Philadelphia represented a remarkable about-turn, given the paper's long-standing support for the "manifest destiny" of suburban expansion, but it was not alone as profits from real estate began to decline with the economic slowdown. Thomas Cochran, a friend of Price who foresaw Philadelphia outstripping "all the cities of the world," agreed with the journal. Cochran's position as the chair of the Board of Revision of Taxes gave him a synoptic vision of both the city's real estate market and its finances, and in an address to social scientists in 1871, he dwelt on the usual moral virtues of the city of homes. But decentralization came at a cost. The "increased surface improvements" needed in a metropolis of two-story row homes led to "increased surface expenses" for the municipality, and here—even more than political abuses—lay the root of the tax burden borne by property holders. Cochran's address won the approbation of the *North American*, which found the "sprawling process" worryingly "expensive to the city."[35]

Although these ideas verged on the heretical, their appearance in the early 1870s reflected increasing doubts about urban growth. Up to 1870, almost all boosters agreed that rolling back the urban frontier represented the best way to save the city from corruption and high taxation. Now, to a minority at least, the opposite was actually the case. But the class conflict O'Byrne had predicted, alongside the dangers overcrowded districts still said to be harboring "worse savages" than the "tribes of the west" continued to present, ensured the policy of dispersal remained a social imperative. Perhaps more significantly, however, it could not be stopped. The nexus of building societies, machine politics, and real estate speculation combined to thrust the city outward, irrespective of the wishes of the economic elite. Bourgeois Philadelphians might have continued to profit in this process, as owners of suburban lots and "men of wealth" regularly "besieged" councils to lobby for improvements beyond the built-up limits of the city. But their capacity to control the process of expansion had limits. Around Consolidation, there was a palpable belief that a consolidated local state, marshaled by the "best men," might be able to exert a guiding hand over the way the city grew. The sense such figures could do this now through public power—as the struggle over the new public buildings had already shown in the center—diminished in the face of the financial and political problems growth politics had generated. For some, the price of an expanding urban empire had become prohibitively high.[36]

The Limits of Private Enterprise

By the 1870s, then, the notion that the state had to take the lead in transforming Philadelphia was losing bourgeois support. But that public vision of an active municipality had only been one aspect of booster political economy in the Civil War era. Instead, it was more common to see government purely as a facilitator—a means to unleash private energies in the property market—than an end in itself. The city might pave Broad, Mc-Michael's son argued, but the "costly and elegant structures" that would then be erected "must be the part of private enterprise." Here railroads rather than a Haussmannesque state assumed center stage. Their role was to bring the metropolis the bounty of the West, pour the profits into the built environment, and transform merchant and industrial capital into a physical embodiment of wealth and power. But even though they had been funded in part with public money, they remained private corporations.[37]

If railroads reaching into the West drove boosters' imperial ambitions, then urban growth rested on the local application of the same technology. The street railway system, with close to fifty lines and three hundred miles of track by 1874, became crucial to building the city outward. Tying the residential periphery to the fashion and commerce of the center, the companies hastened the process of practical consolidation. Like the railroads, though, their public role could not disguise the fact they were privately owned. Chartered by the legislature and barely subject to any jurisdiction by the city, their loyalties lay with stockholders rather than citizens.

Even as private corporations, however, the notion of the city's railways building up an imperial metropolis seemed perfectly plausible. By annihilating distance across the city, horse cars transformed farms and meadows into building lots within easy commuting distance of the center for the army of clerks who staffed the business houses around the Exchange. Meanwhile the Pennsylvania Railroad drew capital to the real estate market that might otherwise have gone to Baltimore or New York. The fine warehouses that lined Market Street, the grain elevator the railroad purchased for the

Delaware Front, and the growth around its depot in West Philadelphia all offered evidence of the line's success.

Railways served too as symbols of metropolitan greatness. Boosters proudly pointed to Philadelphia as the street railway capital of the world, and saw in the adoption of the horse cars by "every city of any size in the land" a vindication of the policy of dispersal fashioned on the Delaware. As the Pennsylvania became one of the biggest corporations on the planet, meanwhile, promoters reminded citizens of its local roots. To the *North American* in 1871, it was "now perfectly understood everywhere that Philadelphia is the home of the strongest, the most powerful, the best organized and the grandest railway corporations in the world." Yet for all the successes of the city's internal and external lines, the link between commercial dynamism, railway expansion, and the prestige of a grand urban form actually proved far from straightforward.[38]

The difficulties began with the street railways. After 1856, the companies had cemented their position in the city through a series of alliances with local and state politicians. Their friends in high places made public regulation difficult. As early as 1858, Mayor Alexander Henry worried owners of the horse car network might, like volunteer fire companies, "acquire undue ascendancy" in politics. By the postbellum era, companies had purchased legislation that all but freed them from municipal regulation, and they had the power to influence the location of the new city hall.[39]

These railways disturbed an economic elite that wanted authority for itself over public space. The Citizens' Association received over six hundred complaints about streets that came under the responsibilities of the corporations. Its members probably concurred with the *Sunday Morning Times* when it argued the "city is blessed and cursed with too many passenger railway companies," but the problems they generated to some seemed increasingly to be outweighing the benefits. With their power, one reform tract claimed, "private corporations had vested rights in our streets, while property owners and taxpayers had none." Street railways, then, had come to threaten both the politics and the space of the city, the very objects of metropolitan life that boosters pushing them in the 1850s had argued they would improve.[40]

Similar charges could be leveled against the city's biggest railroads, especially the Pennsylvania, which by the postbellum era had risen to the rank of the world's largest corporation. Well before the Civil War, boosters had begun to realize that the transformation of railroad profits into the symbolic capital of a grand urban form was not a straightforward process. The Pennsylvania's attempt to secure the Penn Squares as a freight station had united the city's bourgeoisie in opposition in 1851. Freight tracks running down Market and Broad continued to debase the two avenues most central to urban embellishment. And the depots the Pennsylvania erected—in stark contrast here to the vaulted arches of London's Paddington or the neo-Gothic spires of St. Pancras—were put up in a manner the *North American* found "utterly unworthy" of the "capital, business or dignity" of the line. By the end of the 1850s, indeed, it was clear that the railroads and the trade they brought in were making massive demands on city space that rarely led in the direction of metropolitan grandeur.[41]

Simmering tensions boiled over again in 1874, when the Pennsylvania announced plans to use its land on the western side of the Schuylkill for a stockyard capable of processing over twenty-five thousand animals a day. The location of the abattoir stirred controversy. Hitherto slaughterhouses had been dispersed through poorer neighborhoods, which disgusted working-class radicals, but made them largely invisible to Philadelphia's middle class. The new centralized site, however, was positioned between the three bourgeois enclaves of Spring Garden, West Philadelphia, and the West End of the old city proper. Residents of these districts sought an injunction to prevent the development from going ahead. Westerly winds in summer, petitioners warned, "will carry the offensive effluvia to the handsomest improvements and most highly taxed dwellings in the city." Property would "greatly depreciate"—perhaps by as much as half, according to one conveyancer—in what would soon be, a series of witnesses predicted in familiar terms, the coming "center of population."[42]

Bourgeois Philadelphians mobilized to fight the corporation. The equity suit was spearheaded by the CMRA and shaped by their social outlook. Witnesses who testified on behalf of the Pennsylvania about slaughterhouses in their neighborhoods had a "Celtic twang about them," the Consolidator William Henry Rawle told the court, and given such people were accustomed to "filthy work," it did not surprise him that they could deal with unpleasant smells. "I presume," the attorney told the judges in a revealing analogy, "that a negro minstrel does not much mind blacking his face every night, but it is a sort of thing that your Honors or ourselves would not take kindly to." Thus while the racially degraded poor could cope with the stench, those whose "senses have not been so hardened, and who by their education and habits of life retain the sensitiveness of their

natural organization, are entitled to enjoy life in comfort as they are consti-
tuted." The decision of the Pennsylvania Railroad to turn the coming heart
of a great metropolis over to a slaughterhouse troubled boosters for the
same reasons they had worried about trade on the Market Street freight
line. In both cases the wealth of a corporation they had worked to bring
into being threatened to undermine their genteel ideal of urban space.[43]

Part of the problem for boosters clinging to the creed of antebellum
growth politics was that the Pennsylvania Railroad had outgrown its
municipal parent. Even before the Civil War, the road controlled a route to
Chicago, and its president would be appointed to run the Union Pacific
after the conflict. But as the road consolidated what one servant would call
an "imperial federation" in the West, it was also empire-building in the
East, securing an outlet in New York in the early 1870s.[44] The Pennsylvania's
foothold on the Hudson allowed it to take full advantage of the road it
constructed during the Civil War across an unbuilt portion of northern
Philadelphia. Goods could now pass from Chicago to Gotham on the network without stopping in William Penn's metropolis. And with the city no
longer exerting any control on the board, little could be done to stop it
from acting in the fiduciary interests of its stockholders. Boosters, then,
could draw on Jacksonian anti-corporate rhetoric to attack the Pennsylvania as much as they liked. But they could not change the legal fact that the
road was a private corporation.

Contrary to the expectations of boosters at Consolidation, then, the
Pennsylvania Railroad, and not the city, had grown to imperial proportions.
In the Civil War, its president Colonel Thomas Alexander Scott had helped
coordinate the Union war effort, even ferrying troops from Gettysburg to
suppress the New York draft riots. After the conflict, Scott, a man contemporaries compared to Alexander, Caesar, and Napoleon, become so important in national affairs that he helped break the impasse in the contested
presidential election of 1876. Scott (whose policy, an admiring employee
recalled, ensured "local magnates" were "dispensed with") was not be-
holden to the city. Many boosters had hoped their own metropolis would
acquire the power Scott enjoyed, but the private corporation could now
cross a continent, shape elections, and hold together a nation. Bourgeois
citizens, though proud of the Pennsylvania's achievements, wondered
whether the smell of offal and manure wafting into their parlors from the
Schuylkill abattoir was a just reward.[45]

The private power of the railroads—both within the city and without—had been as central to the project of antebellum boosterism as the public power of the state. By the 1870s, though, both the streetcar network and corporate behemoths like the Pennsylvania had offered only mixed blessings. Enriched for sure as investors, Philadelphians from the economic elite were nevertheless concerned at the environmental impact of the lines on their vision of a refined and well-ordered city. While degradation caused by the roads had been limited to working-class wards, it could be tolerated, but the impact on wealthy suburbs and the metropolitan center proved difficult to ignore. However, in abandoning the idea of the railway as an agent for improving urban space, boosters—having already been scared off using government by ring rule and spiraling debt—were left without the means to transform Philadelphia. Both the public and the private city had failed them. Like their attitude to the state itself, some now began to call for limits too on corporate power—the demand for action against the abattoir here might be seen as analogous to campaigns at the national level against rate fixing and other railroad misdemeanors—but they made little headway. Meanwhile, just a year after the Centennial had papered over cracks in the alliance between the city's economic elite and the Pennsylvania Railroad, the line became the focal point in a crisis that some feared would reduce Philadelphia to the condition of Paris under the Communards.

The Great Railroad Strike of 1877 and the Geography of Urban Disorder

Amid the strikes and riots of the Jacksonian era boosters had cast the Pennsylvania Railroad as the cornerstone of a growth coalition that would build Philadelphia upward and outward, while providing employment for a turbulent population. That model of urban growth by the 1850s hinged on a social cartography that made the family home the dividing line between the respectable and the dangerous classes. The city's decentralized residential geography—a product in part of the business the Pennsylvania Railroad brought in—therefore served not only as an index of urban greatness, but also a guarantor of civic peace. Growth had turned Philadelphia, boosters boasted, into the "Paradise of Workingmen."[46]

These assumptions faced a severe test in the summer of 1877. From the Civil War onward, working-class movements had gained ground in the city. Their progress proved uneven, but after the wartime mobilization led by the likes of Jonathan Fincher, new organizations like the secretive Knights of Labor—founded in Philadelphia's textile districts and owing much of its ritual to George Lippard's earlier Brotherhood of the Union—built a solid foundation. In aiming for higher wages, an eight-hour day, and better housing, they were reformist rather than revolutionary, but their assertive stance revealed the increasing strength of organized workers.[47]

Orthodox Careyites sometimes met these claims with the pessimistic pronouncements of English political economy their master had rejected. Rising wages, they warned, would only lead to a rise in prices, meaning workingmen would find themselves no better off. The bourgeois press especially proved hostile to striking and suggested solidarities should be expressed elsewhere. As the *Inquirer* argued, building associations—"labor societies in the strictest sense"—were a far better alternative to walkouts that tended "to perpetuate class distinctions which it is the object of American society to remove." William Elder, one of the radical converts to Careyite political economy in the 1850s, defended labor unions but suggested the true form of "guarantyism" lay in working-class support for tariffs and homes.[48]

As in 1837 and 1857, the economic downturn of 1873 weakened the labor movement—only nine of the thirty national unions in existence at the outset of the depression were still around four years later—but increasing radicalism among both organized and unorganized workers led to anxieties about the Commune crossing the Atlantic. Radicals used the fears to their advantage. A year after the Panic, one former carpenter warned of an uprising of the unemployed, and claimed that without urgent reform, July 4, 1876, might mark "the inauguration of the bloodiest and most sanguinary revolution that ever occurred in the history of the world." By March 1877, a speaker at a workingmen's meeting tried to "prove that the country was upon the verge of a revolution" and though such prospects seem unlikely with hindsight, they resonated at the time. "The Red Spectre that has been the terror of France," counseled one paper that same year, "affrights the conservative portion of the community in every riotous parade of labor societies."[49]

Railroads stood at the fulcrum of these struggles. The Pennsylvania, as in 1857, had weathered the lean times, but in May 1877, its managers, in league with the nation's other major lines, tried to impose a pay cut of 10 percent across its workforce. Scott initially appeased angry workers, but elsewhere resentment at the move spurred opposition. On the Pennsylvania's line from Pittsburgh and Chicago, a new industrial union began to pick up support. By mid-June, with membership extending over the country, it threatened a general strike. When the Baltimore and Ohio tried to cut wages again on July 16, the walkout began. Within three days, the stoppage spread to the Pennsylvania at Pittsburgh, where Philadelphia militiamen killed over forty citizens in suppressing the disturbances. Inside seventy-two hours, engineers struck on the banks of the Schuylkill, effectively shutting down the city's communication with the West.[50]

On the evening of July 22, with police charging at strikers in the vicinity of the West Philadelphia depot, Mayor William S. Stokely met with Scott and McMichael to discuss how to maintain order. At 10:30 pm, the *North American* publisher emerged to tell a waiting journalist that he had expected to find "tumult, disorder and excitement" and was relieved the city remained relatively calm. Nevertheless, he continued, Philadelphia faced a "very bad condition of affairs," one "worse, indeed, than I have before seen here in the course of all my long life." McMichael had seen civil commotion before as sheriff during the upheavals of the early 1840s, and he confronted militant workingmen on Philadelphia's streets and his own establishment. Ever since, he had used his paper as a bully pulpit to push for the construction of an imperial city that could avoid the social tensions of the likes of London, Paris, and New York. In 1877, though, that project seemed to be coming apart.[51]

For a few days, Philadelphia stood on edge. A hundred leading citizens met in an attempt to find a way to keep the peace, but even many of them must have thought their efforts would be in vein. On Saturday night, a crowd entered the offices of *Sunday Dispatch* to publish a call for a meeting in support of the strikers. More than a thousand sympathizers gathered outside the Pennsylvania's West Philadelphia depot with others stationed nearby. Near the line's roundhouse, police charged some four hundred workers as shots rang out. An attempt to torch railroad property was narrowly thwarted by the civic authorities. Against a backdrop, then, that "vividly recalled the stirring times of the war," there seemed little doubt to the *North American* "that the scenes of carnage and riot that are disgracing the cities of Baltimore and Pittsburg will be transferred to Philadelphia before many hours have fled."[52]

In confronting the crisis, boosters turned to the platitudes of growth politics. Some claimed the railroads were the best source of employment in the city and that workers were hurting themselves in fighting them. Others, following the lead of the CMRA, appealed to the conservatism of property owners. Mayor Stokely, for example, calling Philadelphia a metropolis in which people's "earnings are invested in their dwelling houses," warned "the humblest would suffer with the wealthiest" if rioters gained control. The *Evening Star* pointed to the "immediate personal interest" of holders of "building association stock" in "maintaining the peace of the city and protecting property from destruction." And the press blamed tramps— homeless vagrants uprooted by the economic slump—for the troubles rather than well-housed workers. The extent to which these pleas to the old building blocks of the growth coalition had any impact is difficult to gauge, but the strike in Philadelphia did attract less popular support than in Pittsburgh, Baltimore, and other major cities. The city's decentralized policy of urban growth may have offered the Pennsylvania a modicum of security.[53]

But bourgeois Philadelphia relied less on its houses than its police in the strike. Here, Benjamin Harris Brewster later suggested, the Consolidation of 1854 had saved the city from the violence that ravaged other metropolises. Although Scott and Stokely were nervous enough to ask the federal government for troops, the resources of the local state proved sufficient to subdue working-class agitation. On the first day of the disturbance, the city mobilized six hundred policemen inside half an hour to reach the Pennsylvania's depot, a stark contrast to the mayor of Pittsburgh, who had less than a dozen officers at his disposal. The authorities were also able to enforce a ban on public meetings, a measure that inhibited coordination among agitators, and ensured that unlike every other major city in the state, there could be no major public statement of support for the strikers. Meanwhile, the infrastructure of streets, bridges, and railways proved an ideal terrain for moving forces into and through the city.[54]

Among the economic elite, few objected to suppressing the strike. The reaction to the disorder in many respects echoed the response to the riots of 1844. Then, the leading attorney Horace Binney had quickly organized a meeting to endorse the action of the militia in firing on the Southwark crowd. By 1877, both the Board of Trade and the Commercial Exchange called for the use of the army if the need arose, and the *North American* demanded the establishment of a permanent national force for the suppression of civil disturbances. Such voices wanted the didactic pedagogy of the bayonet rather than the gentler education of a cathartic environment. "The method of tuition is brutal and bloody," McMichael's paper concluded, "but the lessons are all the more effective." "If this railroad war is an American form of French Communism," argued the *Evening Bulletin*, "we may at least adopt the Paris fashion of knocking it in the head."[55]

This desire for order—present from the very beginning in the movement to consolidate Philadelphia—weathered the strike rather better than midcentury reformers' broader associational vision. Having seen their faith in urban reconstruction questioned by debt and corruption, boosters now had to ask whether their designs to rebuild the urban environment had really made the city any more secure than it had been in the 1840s. The neighborhoods worst afflicted were prosperous manufacturing suburbs like Spring Garden and West Philadelphia, the very places in which domestic piety had been expected to tame the so-called barbarism of the city's inner frontier. Those sympathetic to the strikers might have pointed out here that with unemployment nationwide at five million, railroad employees and their neighbors were driven by desperation to rebel. But finding food, work, and good housing for the poor now seemed less pressing a concern than suppressing what Scott insisted was a war against the United States.[56]

In 1877, the Great Strike revealed a new geography of disorder. The area around Bedford Street, which came to be called the Alaska District in the postbellum era, had long been seen as the main source of the miasmas plaguing the city. Yet that "plague spot" now appeared less threatening than factory suburbs. Catto's assassination had marked the last major disturbance in the borderland that had produced so many of the riots of the antebellum era. Farther out in industrial districts, though, the roots of the strike seemed to lie less in degraded streets or poor family government than tension between workers and management on the very corporation that since 1846 had been the cornerstone of growth politics. Just as the Pennsylvania Railroad had drawn the economic elite together at its inception, the strike against it united those who had fallen out over questions like the Park Loan and the new public buildings. As in the 1840s, taming the dangerous classes remained the objective, but the focus of concern had shifted from the metropolitan form to the shop floor. The connections between the "labor question" and the urban question no longer seemed self-evident.

Danger now lay in a social rather than spatial organization. The militant laborer rather than the Moyamensing rowdy became the object of concern. Interviews with radicals in the bourgeois press underscored the growing preoccupation. One leader's (presumably satirical) exposition of the "law of generally progressive unfoldment as it applies to the second octave of the diametric scale of economic science" perhaps provides as good an answer as any to the question of why there is no socialism in the United States, but the mixture of fascination and horror such figures provoked among the economic elite suggests the changing mood. This is not to say that the goal of remaking the urban environment and its people had been forgotten. Praise for the splendor of Paris or the domestic comforts of Penn's metropolis still figured prominently in booster discourse. Urban reform too would come to the forefront again after a series of public health crises over the ensuing two decades, and found new life in the City Beautiful movement of the Progressive Era. But the troubles of 1877 seemed to imply to wealthy Philadelphians that the real danger came from the radicalized worker rather than what Price had called "traitors to home." Environmental improvement as a solution to social evils was beginning to give way to a determination to crush communism.[57]

A year after the strike, members of Philadelphia's American Philosophical Society heard the judge and ex-Republican congressman Martin Russell Thayer outline the best way to reclaim a metropolis under control of rioters. Noting how "occasions have arisen in the recent past, and may occur in the future" when the civil authorities prove unable to cope, he prescribed ways for dealing with the "mob" using infantry, cavalry, and artillery. Thayer reassured his audience that "a city which has a system of parallel streets" would be easier to recapture though he warned that each house might need to be taken in turn. If a pitched battle arose, he suggested, troops needed to wait till a crowd got to within a hundred yards then "pour upon it a fire that will destroy it." His speech suggested he had learned from the suppression of the Commune, but the railroad disturbances of the previous year were surely foremost in his mind.[58]

To disarm the people might also mean disfranchising them. Ideas once confined to the private conversations of Fisher and his friends became increasingly mainstream in bourgeois circles after 1877. In New York, a commission led by Samuel J. Tilden had proposed removing the voting rights of non-tax paying New Yorkers in municipal elections, while some Philadelphians too began to openly avow a similar measure. Weeks after the Great Strike, McMichael's paper called "the large body of voters" without property the "greatest disability a city has to contend with." The "physical balance of power" in a metropolis, it argued, lay with an idle and corruptible poor, and it suggested that sensible opinion was inching toward the position "that something more than residence is necessary to qualify a man for voting for Councilman." Commission government, chosen by property owners, marked the paper's preferred option. When the Pennsylvania legislature investigated the matter in 1878 via a municipal commission, Lea proposed that taxpayers alone might choose the upper chamber of the bicameral councils, which would retain a veto power over financial decisions. He warned that "universal suffrage and popular government must be pronounced incompatible with municipal prosperity and good order" without reform.[59]

Lea's recommendation did not win over the commissioners who saw greater profligacy outside the ranks of the poor. They warned that to apply Tilden's design to Philadelphia would mean removing the voting rights of thousands of industrious citizens living in good homes. For them, indeed, the problems with city debt owed less to an "irresponsible class" of operatives than they did to the suburban speculators who lobbied councilmen and legislators for improvements where they were not needed. "Owners of property," they concluded curtly, "need more protection against themselves than against the non–property holding class."[60]

The municipal commission of 1878 may have checked Philadelphia's counterrevolution of property, but in a manner reminiscent of their predecessors' response to the 1844 riots, genteel Philadelphians had reacted to disorder by calling for the use of force or the curbing of democratic rights. Out of the earlier riots though had come creative ideas about how to reconcile urban growth, wage labor, and a widespread suffrage, which coalesced into the midcentury movement to consolidate an interdependent city across its social and spatial boundaries. By the retreat from Reconstruction in the late 1870s, that consolidationist impulse proved harder to locate.

The "Unnatural Union" of City and Suburb

In the 1830s and 1840s, many of the civic elite believed strikes and rioting had threatened Philadelphia's ascent as a metropolitan center. After 1877, with talk of socialism in the air, the city's urban empire once more seemed threatened from within. The bourgeoisie, both before and after the Civil War, had steadfastly supported militia companies and police forces in their battles with the disorderly. But in other respects, the responses to disorder in the two eras were subtly different. Reformers of the antebellum years saw building Philadelphia upward and outward as a vaccine against epidemic violence. Only a few, like the Germantown exile Fisher, had fled to romantic suburbs miles beyond the urban frontier. Even before the strike of 1877, though, the prospect of escaping the metropolis had begun to appeal to the Gilded Age bourgeoisie. Having failed to reclaim control of the consolidated city, they began to retreat beyond its expansive borders.

Elite migration outside Philadelphia's metropolitan limits gathered pace in the 1870s. Midway through the decade, the Pennsylvania Railroad—noting how the "tendency of population in the centres of civilization is to follow the sun"—begun to market mansions and hotels in romantically named suburbs on its "Main Line" west of the city border. Two CMRA leaders—Clement C. Biddle and Charles Wheeler—were among the first to flee what they saw as a corrupted and conflict-ridden city. By 1876, the *North American* reported a growing "exodus" of residents to homes beyond the corporate boundaries.[61]

Suburban out-migration in the 1850s had not necessarily implied a rejection of the city. Boosters talked of growth on the metropolitan frontier as "tributary" to the greatness of the center, and property owners on Philadelphia's rural fringe craved access to the kind of urban services that had become commonplace in densely built-up neighborhoods. The interdependence of city and suburb underpinned the Consolidation Act and helped entice remote villages like Germantown into the enlarged metropolis. Price, the architect of the 1854 reform, expected suburbs left beyond the new bounds to eventually follow Germantown's lead. His prediction that Fairmount Park, far to the West of the commercial district, would one day stand at the center of a great metropolis suggested his faith in the onward march of Philadelphia's manifest destiny, and he anticipated that the Main Line suburbs would soon "be asked to let some of their townships become wards of the great City."[62]

Price's prophecy of further consolidation, though, would not come to pass. The Philadelphians who moved out to Montgomery County probably had no intention of reuniting with the city they had left behind. A few years before the 1877 strike, Brookline, adjacent to Boston, had become one of the first suburban districts in the country to resist incorporation into a larger city, a decision aided by technological advances that made infrastructural improvements easier for suburbs to manage on their own. The bourgeois commuters able to afford the railroad fares to take them into the city each day from the Main Line were more than likely to follow Brookliners' lead, given the equation of the city with corruption, high taxation, and social conflict. Even as early as 1855, a citizen beyond the municipal limits had wondered why any of his neighbors would be "so insane" as to advocate a union with a metropolis notorious as "a nest of rottenness, riot and rabid intolerance." The *Germantown Telegraph*, which had helped to bring the borough into Philadelphia in 1854, sometimes called for secession after the Civil War. Germantown had "lost everything and gained nothing by consolidation," it concluded.[63]

The paper was displaying more than a hint of ingratitude. Property owners in the district, after all, had benefited tremendously from the improvements Consolidation ushered in, and in other, less prosperous suburbs, the call was often for more support for development from the center and not less. But Germantown's links to the downtown—via horse-drawn cars and a commuter railroad—were in private hands. Its prosperous residents could pay for their own improvements through local property taxes and bond issues. And despite the growth of manufactures in the district, the carefully cultivated image of a romantic retreat meant few were willing to see it as part of a large industrial metropolis, especially when a significant portion of the municipal budget went on a police force designed for densely populated districts. The journal's call for a dissolution of the "unnatural union of country and city under one government" signaled a shift in the relationship between parts of the suburban periphery and the metropolitan core. Such separatist sentiments—more in keeping with twentieth-century suburbanites than their mid-nineteenth-century antecedents—challenged consolidators' faith that in union lay strength. Germantown, the *Telegraph* implied, could manage quite comfortably on its own.[64]

Although suburban separatism remained a minority position through the 1870s, its appearance hinted at growing doubts among the bourgeoisie about the wider logic of consolidation. Social scientists like Robert Ellis Thompson, impressed by the midcentury wave of national and metropolitan unifications, could continue to put forward the case that interdependence made association in larger units inevitable. But by the Gilded Age, that interdependence was becoming harder to see. The late nineteenth century accelerated Philadelphia's compartmentalization into socially segregated spaces. Street railways funneled passengers from one neighborhood to the next in a manner that ensured bourgeois Philadelphians experienced the city without ever having to leave their own enclaves.[65] Like Friedrich Engels's Manchester, commerce lining the main thoroughfares shielded

wealthy citizens from the hardship on the streets behind, while the migration of social threat from a street like Bedford on the edge of the center to
distant industrial suburbs made the "labor question" harder to locate than
it had been to midcentury reformers and radicals. Even as social scientists
made the metropolis better known to the bourgeoisie, then, the understanding (however flawed) that came from everyday interaction across
social boundaries weakened. The sorting of urban space into distinct neighborhoods differentiated by social class and land use—the process of "functional specialization"—enabled wealthy Philadelphians to turn their backs
on other parts of the city as did a turn inward to the private sphere of the
home. Place continued to matter for an economic elite with cultural and
financial investment in the city, and labor strife and mass immigration
offered plenty of opportunities for reformers to intervene, but social relations on the shop floor now seemed more important than the spatial organization of the city. Contrary to Price's predictions, then, Philadelphia
would not extend its boundaries again: the Consolidation Act of 1854 fixed
the borders of the twentieth-century city.

*   *   *

At the end of the 1870s, Philadelphia remained a divided metropolis. While
better known, better controlled, and much larger than it had been in the
pre-Consolidation era, the hostilities that had led to fighting in the 1840s
had given way to different patterns of conflict. Attempts to answer the labor
question had enjoyed some success: some midcentury radicals, indeed, had
become ardent champions of a harmony of interests doctrine that promised
to distribute the fruits of industry more fairly. Philadelphia's economy had
expanded rapidly thanks to industry, railroads, and real estate, and even
spectacular failures like Cooke's Northern Pacific and Leslie's garden blocks
in 1873 did not shake faith in growth. But that growth was less value-free
than historians have sometimes implied. Rather, it hinged on assumptions
about the organization of urban space that divided the city into an imposing center and residential periphery. Philadelphia's monuments ranged
from the vast city hall to the humble row home. Each, boosters believed,
owed its existence to wider networks of trade, finance, and state power
forged from the 1840s onward by railroad builders, working people, and
municipal reformers. And each had the capacity to leave its imprint on
citizens, turning the disorderly residents of the riot era into the disciplined,

productive, and frugal occupants of a city of homes. At times—not least after the Great Strike of 1877 left the city relatively unscathed—bourgeois citizens could congratulate themselves on some success.

Yet the crisis of confidence in the 1870s, with its roots in doubts about debt, disorder, and democracy at home and abroad, shook growth politics. By 1877, it is harder to find traces of the almost utopian belief of midcentury reformers in the capacity of urban expansion to reconstruct the metropolis. Coming to the fore instead, we see another strand in bourgeois thought already evident in antebellum debates about rioting and reform but devoid of the wider possibilities consolidationist ideas opened up. This discourse stressed the use of state power primarily as a way of maintaining order and protecting industry. It questioned the legitimacy of government intervention in other arenas, not least borrowing "for posterity to pay," which the state municipal commission decried as "evil, and only evil."[66] And it saw the separation of classes—and for that matter cities and suburbs—rather than their interdependence as inevitable and perhaps even necessary. Not every bourgeois reformer embraced such ideas enthusiastically, but by 1877, with ring rule and class conflict rife, it made intuitive sense to many wealthy citizens. In accepting the inevitability of social tension, however, Consolidators implicitly admitted their failure to harmonize interests through growth politics.

"Though the limits of the City expanded at a bound," Price recorded in remembering the Consolidation Act, "the minds of the citizens could not be so suddenly enlarged."[67] His words suggest the relationship advocates of annexation had drawn between space and society from midcentury onward no longer seemed so clear amid the power struggles of the Gilded Age. Consolidators had set out to remake a city and its people. The outcome was not always what they had imagined.

CONCLUSION

Between the 1830s and 1870s, Philadelphians—in common with urban Americans up and down the major metropolises of the East Coast— confronted social and sectional crises. The phenomenal growth of their city and republic, many citizens believed, threatened to tear both apart. Finding a way to channel that growth in a way that tended toward consolidation rather than disunion preoccupied citizens. Recognizing they lived in an interdependent and complex society, many of the figures I have focused on over the preceding pages found in growth politics, urban reconstruction, and national unification the tools to hold their world together. The ideas they forged, which migrated easily between metropolis and nation, suggest the boundaries we tend to draw between the urban and national history of the Civil War-era United States are themselves permeable. As the social scientist Robert Ellis Thompson observed in 1880, consolidation seemed a hallmark of the era, a law as evident in the coming together of Italy or the defeat of the South as it was in the empire-building of the Pennsylvania Railroad and the redrawing of Philadelphia's municipal borders.[1] City and nation here can fruitfully be studied together.

Consolidators in Philadelphia were ardent modernizers, mocking the "fogyism" that held the city back, and urging citizens to embrace the progressive "spirit of the age." Although they sometimes feared what the future held, they believed that under the right leadership, metropolis and nation could advance in wealth and grandeur. Even after the Civil War, more than we might expect believed that Philadelphia's immense terrain, productive might, and links to the West gave it the potential to surpass New York as the central city of the continent, and almost all expected their republic to outpace the monarchies over the Atlantic in the race for global supremacy. Understanding their urban and national vision requires us to see their world with that sense of possibility, and to question the view of residents as bound by an inward-looking privatism. Consolidators styled themselves as cosmopolitans at odds with the parochialism of suburban districts and state sovereignty, hostile to the disintegrative tendencies of individualism, and in harmony with the associational spirit of the age.

By the 1870s, their achievement seemed complete. Although New York remained ascendant, merchants, manufacturers, and professionals along the Delaware had come together as a class, built the biggest public and private corporations in the world, and enlisted in a successful struggle to unite the nation under a social and economic order given the imprimatur of legitimacy by Philadelphia's political economists. The markers of a modern metropolis and republic had been put in place. Railroads crisscrossed the continent; railways linked the downtown to remote suburbs. The fruits of metropolitan industry flowed across an enlarged city and outward to a protected national market. A powerful municipal government provided stimulus for growth and services for residents. And in a grand center and expanding frontier, Philadelphia's "manifest destiny" appeared to mirror the nation's: wide access to property on the periphery marked a kind of capitalism with American characteristics. As a "city of homes," indeed, the metropolis became a model to emulate in an era of fraught class conflict. By the Progressive Era, at least thirty cities—ranging from big metropolitan centers like Detroit, Indianapolis, and San Francisco to small towns—adopted the "city of homes" moniker, as they sought to stimulate growth and secure themselves against social conflict.

Such outcomes can sometimes seem the products of unthinking decisions, the inevitable workings out of a privatist tradition, or the logical consequences of a process of modernization. What I have tried to suggest here, though, is that the reconstruction of a gridironed American city did not proceed along a straight line. To understand what the city became requires focusing on the conflicts that drove its development as well as the consensus that superficially characterized its late nineteenth-century condition. In a struggle over power, citizens articulated very different designs for what their metropolis—and their nation—might be, and while the urban visions of utopian socialists or admirers of Bonapartist Paris are easily forgotten, they played their part in shaping Philadelphia. Seeing the era through the prism of consolidation here allows us to glimpse the heretical ideas that fed into city-building: ideas that sometimes promised to upend the building blocks of an American liberal tradition of private property and a small state. And it helps us to understand how the urban form—much like the nation in the same period—became an object of struggle around which social classes and political movements coalesced.

Whatever the politics of their modernizing instincts, the midcentury consolidators bridged the gap between Early National and Progressive reform, reflecting as they did the republican civic culture of the former and the preference for large-scale organizational solutions of the other. A radical like George Lippard could hymn the virtues of his namesake Washington while looking forward to a socialist future; a conservative like Stephen Colwell could lament the poison of political corruption while imagining a society in which states' rights had ceased to exist. Their late nineteenth-century heirs took up the baton. The radical turned Careyite Republican William D. Kelley's daughter Florence translated her friend Friedrich Engel's *Condition of the English Working Class*—first published in German in 1844—for an American audience. When she returned to the United States, she became a radical urban reformer. Eli Kirk Price's grandson, meanwhile, put into practice midcentury designs for boulevards when he led the campaign to build the City Beautiful–inspired Benjamin Franklin Parkway from the new city hall out to Fairmount Park. Battles between party operatives and the "best men," which had first surfaced before municipal Consolidation in 1854, continued. The latter thought they had won a great victory with a revision to the city charter—the Bullitt Bill—in 1885, though as was the case after the new state constitution of 1873, their success proved short-lived. A "corrupt but contented" metropolis, as the muckraking journalist Lincoln Steffens famously put it, was another legacy of the midcentury generation, who had ultimately ceded control of growth politics to Republican bosses and big corporations.[2]

Such similarities were not necessarily obvious at the turn of the century. To Progressives the city of 1854 seemed a world away from their industrial metropolis. Sixty years later Sam Bass Warner Jr. went so far as to suggest that "the Philadelphia of one generation barely resembled its predecessor."[3] This might be the case if we look at transportation or architecture. But the preoccupation of Progressive Era urbanists with combustible social relations and tumultuous economic and spatial change was not so novel. The solutions they fashioned—slum reform, parks, and boulevards—were born in the leader columns of the *North American* and the *Public Ledger* half a century before.

Yet in other respects, early twentieth-century Philadelphia was not the city the earlier generation of boosters had imagined. Where industry had once been encouraged to locate near the center of the metropolis, advocates of the Parkway now tried to force it out. And with finance capital increasingly centered around the big houses of Wall Street, the city's hopes of attaining metropolitan supremacy were gone. Even the directors of the Pennsylvania Railroad relisted their corporation on the New York Stock Exchange. Midcentury Americans could still imagine an eastern city superseding Manhattan; the consolidation of the national economy over the course of the Gilded Age made such a prospect improbable.

Perhaps above all, Civil War-era consolidators shared an elastic notion of municipal boundaries that allowed the city to extend its border outward to encompass future growth. For the first half century of the consolidated city, the prospects of further enlargement rarely came up: so much land had been incorporated into the new metropolis in 1854 that another round of expansion appeared decades away. By the early 1900s, however, the growth of the Main Line commuter towns to the northwest of Fairmount Park meant that for the first time since Consolidation, sizeable suburbs on the Pennsylvania side of the Delaware sprung up beyond the metropolitan border. But suburbanites blessed with the technology to provide their own infrastructure and wary of the big city's machine politics rarely wanted incorporation. The problem this presented—one that now plagues many older American urban centers—was evident in 1922: "Philadelphia emigrants," an antiquarian wrote, "pay no taxes to the city where they earn their living."[4]

Today's metropolis is an inheritance of this earlier project of bordermaking; the challenges its citizens face will be familiar in cities up and down the East Coast and Midwest. Industry might have largely gone from the center. Suburbs that lie beyond the city boundaries are more diverse than the early Main Line. And the gap in wealth between core and periphery has increased markedly as economic decline and white flight have weakened the city's tax base. Race as much as class is the fundamental divide. As in the earlier era, however, private and public investment is poured into the center and gentrifying residential neighborhoods. In parts of the city where thousands of building societies once prospered, it is difficult to find a bank. Growth remains a panacea, with convention centers, riverside casinos, and new airport termini, the twenty-first century successors to the Pennsylvania Railroad.[5]

With decline, a veil of mystique has once again shrouded poor neighborhoods. Few whites venture into supposed "no-go" areas of North Philadelphia. Yesterday's Seventh and Bedford is today's Fifth and Indiana: the degraded poor of Moyamensing transformed into today's racialized "underclass." The urban frontier now is not so much the built-up periphery than the ever-changing borderline between "improving," mostly white, middle-class neighborhoods radiating outward from the center, and poor, predominantly black ones. The remark of a Civil War-era reformer that the "'march of improvement' ejects the workers from their homes" resonates today in grassroots campaigns against gentrification.[6] Policing, incarceration, and welfare reform—all tactics tried by an earlier generation either side of Civil War—keep the better-off residents who have returned to the city safe from the new "dangerous classes." In some respects, then, the contemporary city resembles in its social geography the riot-era metropolis. An expanding bourgeois core, pushed outward by gentrifiers, presses up against dangerous, turbulent neighborhoods. The advantage of consolidation lies only in its capacity to provide security for wealth.

Calls for some form of new consolidation a century and a half after the first are not without their critics. In Philadelphia's northeast—where secessionist sentiment found expression soon after the 1854 annexation— white neighborhoods in the 1980s tried to detach themselves from the predominantly black parts of the city. One academic, arguing the 1854 reform has "outlived its usefulness," has even suggested that breaking the city up into smaller, self-governing districts would lead to a civic renaissance. The big bureaucratic metropolis, he argues, has grown too large and unwieldy for its citizens to love. Dissolving it would allow the likes of Kensington and Southwark to exploit their competitive advantages and renew a grassroots democratic culture.[7] But this return to localism would hardly address many of the problems the city faces. Cutting off wealthier portions of the city from the poorer tax districts does not seem an especially useful way of providing services to communities that badly need them. Finding a way to broaden the tax base and persuade residents of the region they live in an interdependent metropolis, as Price and his allies realized long ago, perhaps offers a better way forward for the city.

"It should not be," Price had argued in 1854, "that the city should sink to be an appendage to her own colonies."[8] As his words suggest, Consolidation was ultimately a question of the distribution of power in the metropolis, about who should control whom? The answer bourgeois Philadelphians forged between the 1840s and 1870s focused unsurprisingly on the capacity of their class to radiate power outward from an imperial center. It was a project shaped by social and racial prejudices and tied to the process of continental conquest. And partly as a result, the consolidated city—like the consolidated nation that emerged from the Civil War—did not suddenly become a harmonious whole.

As I write this though, just days after my country, the United Kingdom, voted to cut its ties from a larger union, I am ever more forcibly struck by the coherence of consolidators' understanding of interdependence. "An epidemic having its rise among a neglected population is not confined to its source," the *Inquirer* wrote about public health during the secession crisis of 1860 to 1861, "but spreads in every direction, attacking those who flatter themselves that they are far removed even from the appearance of danger."[9] What applied to disease could also apply to disorder and destitution. Few citizens in an age of consolidation could afford to shut themselves off from what lay beyond their psychological and political borders. Whatever the limitations of figures like Morton McMichael or George Lippard, their realization is something we could do well to remember today. Strength for them lay in union, and not in isolation.

NOTES

Introduction

1. Robert Ellis Thompson, "Lessons for Social Science from the Streets of Philadelphia," *Penn Monthly* 11 (Dec. 1880): 922–23, 934. On the decline of civic space, see Sam Bass Warner Jr., *The Private City: Philadelphia in Three Periods of Its Growth* (Philadelphia: University of Pennsylvania Press, 1968), 54, 56; Mary P. Ryan, *Civic Wars: Democracy and Public Life in the American City During the Nineteenth Century* (Berkeley: University of California Press, 1997), 309; Richard Sennett, *The Fall of Public Man* (New York: Knopf, 1976).

2. Thompson, "Streets of Philadelphia," 929–31. On Philadelphia's Consolidation, see Howard Gillette Jr., "The Emergence of the Modern Metropolis: Philadelphia in the Age of Its Consolidation," in *The Divided Metropolis: Social and Spatial Dimensions of Philadelphia, 1800–1975*, ed. William W. Cutler and Howard Gillette Jr. (Westport, Conn.: Greenwood Press, 1980), 3–25; Michael P. McCarthy, "The Philadelphia Consolidation of 1854: A Reappraisal," *PMHB* 110 (1986): 531–48; Warner, *Private City*, 125–57; Michael Feldberg, *The Philadelphia Riots of 1844: A Study of Ethnic Conflict* (Westport, Conn.: Greenwood Press, 1975), 178–94; *North American*, Mar. 14, 1855; *Commercial List*, Dec. 24, 1853.

3. On consolidation in the era, see John Higham, *From Boundlessness to Consolidation: The Transformation of American Culture, 1848–1860* (Ann Arbor, Mich.: William L. Clements Library, 1969); Iver Bernstein, *The New York City Draft Riots: Their Significance for American Society and Politics in the Age of the Civil War* (Oxford: Oxford University Press, 1990), 76; Sven Beckert, *The Monied Metropolis: New York City and the Consolidation of the American Bourgeoisie, 1850–1896* (Cambridge: Cambridge University Press, 2001). The best overview of municipal consolidation in the period is Kenneth T. Jackson, *Crabgrass Frontier: The Suburbanization of the United States* (Oxford: Oxford University Press, 1985), 138–56. See also Jon C. Teaford, *City and Suburb: The Political Fragmentation of Metropolitan America, 1850–1970* (Baltimore: John Hopkins University Press, 1979). For talk of urban manifest destiny, see for example *Commercial List*, Dec. 24, 1853.

4. My reading of city-builders' imperial ambitions is indebted to David M. Scobey, *Empire City: The Making and Meaning of the New York City Landscape* (Philadelphia: Temple University Press, 2002); William Cronon, *Nature's Metropolis: Chicago and the Great West* (New York: Norton, 1991). On urban violence, see especially Michael Feldberg, *The Turbulent Era: Riot and Disorder in Jacksonian America* (Oxford: Oxford University Press, 1980). *North American*, July 31, 1860; George Lippard, *The Quaker City, or, the Monks of Monk Hall*, ed. David Reynolds (Amherst: University of Massachusetts Press, [1845] 1995), 372–93.

5. The only full treatment of McMichael's career is Robert L. Bloom, "The Philadelphia North American: A History, 1839–1925," PhD diss., Columbia University, 1952.

6. [John Bell Bouton], *The Life and Choice Writings of George Lippard* (New York: H. H. Randall, 1855); *George Lippard, Prophet of Protest: Writings of an American Radical*, ed. David S. Reynolds (New York: P. Lang, 1986).

7. On alternative designs for modernity in the 1850s, see for instance, Adam-Max Tuchinsky, *Horace Greeley's New York Tribune: Civil War-Era Socialism and the Crisis of Free Labor* (Ithaca, N.Y.: Cornell University Press, 2009); Walter Johnson, *River of Dark Dreams: Slavery and Empire in the Cotton Kingdom* (Cambridge, Mass.: Harvard University Press, 2012); Dolores Hayden, *The Grand Domestic Revolution: A History of Feminist Designs for American Homes, Neighborhoods, and Cities* (Cambridge, Mass.: MIT Press, 1981).

8. Lewis Mumford, *The City in History* (New York: Harcourt, 1961), 453.

9. Warner, *Private City*, 102, 156–57; Bruce M. Stave, "A Conversation with Sam Bass Warner, Jr," *JUH* 1 (1974): 85–110; John D. Fairfield, "Private City, Public City: Power and Vision in American Cities," *JUH* 29 (2003): 437–62.

10. For a sharp assessment of Consolidation that emphasizes the modernizing thrust of the movement, see Gillette, "Modern Metropolis." On Gilded Age liberalism, see for instance, Eric Foner, *Reconstruction: America's Unfinished Revolution, 1863–1877* (New York: Harper & Row, 1988), 488–511.

11. On the subordination of city to nation, albeit for different reasons, see Charles Tilly, *Coercion, Capital, and European States, A.D. 990–1990* (Cambridge, Mass.: Blackwell, 1990); Warner, *Private City*, 84–85. For an American perspective, see Mark A. Peterson, *The City-State of Boston: The Rise and Fall of an Atlantic Power, 1630–1865* (Princeton, N.J.: Princeton University Press, forthcoming 2019). On links between city-building and nation-making, see for instance, Scobey, *Empire City*; Robin L. Einhorn, *Property Rules: Political Economy in Chicago, 1833–1872* (Chicago: University of Chicago Press, 1991), xvi; Bruce Dorsey, *Reforming Men and Women: Gender in the Antebellum City* (Ithaca, N.Y.: Cornell University Press, 2002), 8; Adam Arenson, *The Great Heart of the Republic: St. Louis and the Cultural Civil War* (Cambridge, Mass.: Harvard University Press, 2011), 2; Barbara Berglund, *Making San Francisco American: Cultural Frontiers in the Urban West, 1846–1906* (Lawrence: University Press of Kansas, 2007); Adam Smith, *The Stormy Present: Conservatism and the Problem of Slavery in Northern Politics, 1846–1865* (Chapel Hill: University of North Carolina Press, 2017), 25–26.

12. On the idea of an urban commons, see Catherine McNeur, *Taming Manhattan: Environmental Battles in the Antebellum City* (Cambridge, Mass.: Harvard University Press, 2014), 3. *Finchers' Trades' Review*, Mar. 25, 1865; David Schuyler, *The New Urban Landscape: The Redefinition of City Form in Nineteenth-Century America* (Baltimore: Johns Hopkins University Press, 1986), 6–8; *Press*, June 23, 1867.

13. On "common referents" and transnational history, see Daniel T. Rodgers, *Atlantic Crossings: Social Politics in a Progressive Age* (Cambridge, Mass.: Harvard University Press, 1998), 3–4. On Philadelphia's global positioning, see Jerome I. Hodos, *Second Cities: Globalization and Local Politics in Manchester and Philadelphia* (Philadelphia: Temple University Press, 2011).

14. On localism in Philadelphia, see Allen Steinberg, *The Transformation of Criminal Justice: Philadelphia, 1800–1880* (Chapel Hill: University of North Carolina Press, 1989); Harry C. Silcox, *Philadelphia Politics from the Bottom Up: The Life of Irishman William McMullen, 1824–1901* (Philadelphia: Balch Institute Press, 1989). On "fogyism" as a booster slur elsewhere, see Mark V. Wetherington, *The New South Comes to Wiregrass, Georgia, 1860–1910* (Knoxville: University of Tennessee Press, 1994), 40.

15. Jessica C. Roney, *Governed by a Spirit of Opposition: The Origins of American Political Practice in Colonial Philadelphia* (Baltimore: Johns Hopkins University Press, 2014); Albrecht Koschnik, *"Let a Common Interest Bind Us Together": Associations, Partisanship, and Culture in Philadelphia, 1775–1840* (Charlottesville: University of Virginia Press, 2007). On civil society in the Early Republic, see Johann N. Neem, *Creating a Nation of Joiners: Democracy and Civil Society in Early National Massachusetts* (Cambridge, Mass.: Harvard University Press, 2008).

16. Daniel Walker Howe, *The Political Culture of the American Whigs* (Chicago: University of Chicago Press, 1979), 115; Jeffrey P. Sklansky, *The Soul's Economy: Market Society and Selfhood in American Thought, 1820–1920* (Chapel Hill: University of North Carolina Press, 2002), 91–92; *Spirit of the Times*, Jan. 12, 1849; A City Voter, letter to *Public Ledger*, July 22, 1851.

17. Johann N. Neem, *Creating a Nation of Joiners: Democracy and Civil Society in Early National Massachusetts* (Cambridge, Mass.: Harvard University Press, 2008), 82; William Elder, *Questions of the Day: Economic and Social* (Philadelphia: Henry Carey Baird, 1871), 248–52.

18. Warner, *Private City*, 3–4.

19. Eli Kirk Price journal (#3589), Historical Society of Philadelphia (HSP), Philadelphia. My thoughts on power and the city have been shaped by David C. Hammack, "Problems in the Historical Study of Power in the Cities and Towns of the United States, 1800–1960," *AHR* 83 (1978): 323–49; Thomas Bender, "Wholes and Parts: The Need for Synthesis in American History," *JAH* 73 (1986): 120–36.

20. Lewis Mumford, *The Culture of Cities* (New York: Harcourt Brace, 1938), 3; William J. Novak, "The Myth of the 'Weak' American State," *AHR* 113 (2008): 752–72. The decentered nature of power in Philadelphia is explored in J. Matthew Gallman, *Mastering Wartime: A Social History of Philadelphia During the Civil War* (Philadelphia: University of Pennsylvania Press, 1990). For contrasting responses to the question of who ruled nineteenth-century cities, see Edward Pessen, "Who Governed the Nation's Cities in the 'Era of the Common Man'?" *Political Science Quarterly* 87 (1972): 591–614; Warner, *Private City*, 79–98. Most historians have tended to concur with Warner, who argued the economic elite withdrew from civic leadership.

21. Jürgen Osterhammel, *The Transformation of the World: A Global History of the Nineteenth Century*, trans. Patrick Camiller (Princeton, N.J.: Princeton University Press, 2014), 573–74; James C. Scott, *Seeing Like a State: How Certain Schemes to Improve the Human Condition Have Failed* (New Haven, Conn.: Yale University Press, 1998).

22. On parsimony and municipal finance, see Terence J. McDonald, *The Parameters of Fiscal Policy* (Berkeley: University of California Press, 1986), 122–43.

23. On class formation in midcentury Philadelphia, see for instance, Bruce Laurie, *Working People of Philadelphia, 1800–1850* (Philadelphia: Temple University Press, 1980); Stuart M. Blumin, *The Emergence of the Middle Class: Social Experience in the American City, 1760–1900* (Cambridge: Cambridge University Press, 1989); John Henry Hepp, *The Middle-Class City: Transforming Space and Time in Philadelphia, 1876–1926* (Philadelphia: University of Pennsylvania Press, 2003). My discussion of growth regimes is influenced by John R. Logan and Harvey L. Molotch, *Urban Fortunes: The Political Economy of Place* (Berkeley: University of California Press, 1987).

24. Although many histories of city planning begin in the late nineteenth century, a number of historians have explored behavior, culture, and the built environment in an earlier

period. See for example, Dell Upton, *Another City: Urban Life and Urban Spaces in the New American Republic* (New Haven, Conn.: Yale University Press, 2008); Mona Domosh, *Invented Cities: The Creation of Landscape in Nineteenth-Century New York and Boston* (New Haven, Conn.: Yale University Press, 1996); Schuyler, *New Urban Landscape*; Thomas Bender, *Toward an Urban Vision: Ideas and Institutions in Nineteenth Century America* (Baltimore: John Hopkins University Press, 1975); Paul S. Boyer, *Urban Masses and Moral Order in America, 1820– 1920* (Cambridge, Mass.: Harvard University Press, 1978); Scobey, *Empire City*. On urban planning more broadly, see John William Reps, *The Making of Urban America: A History of City Planning in the United States* (Princeton, N.J.: Princeton University Press, 1965).

25. *North American*, July 31, 1860; Lippard, *Quaker City*, 372–93.

Chapter 1

1. *North American*, Sept. 14, 1854.

2. Asa Briggs, *Victorian Cities* (London: Penguin, 1990), 96; Andrew Lees, *Cities Perceived: Urban Society in European and American Thought, 1820–1940* (Manchester: Manchester University Press, 1985), 63, 67; Osterhammel, *Transformation of the World*, 273; John Todd, *The Moral Influence, Dangers and Duties, Connected with Great Cities* (Philadelphia: Smith & Peck, 1841), 22; Edgar Allan Poe, *Tales of Mystery and Imagination* (London: J. M. Dent and Sons, 1912), 101–9. On Poe in Philadelphia, see, Samuel Otter, *Philadelphia Stories: America's Literature of Race and Freedom* (Oxford: Oxford University Press, 2010), 170.

3. Scott, *Seeing Like a State*, 53–83; Richard Dennis, *Cities in Modernity: Representations and Productions of Metropolitan Space, 1840–1930* (Cambridge: Cambridge University Press, 2008), 52–53.

4. On the city as a frontier, see Dennis, *Cities in Modernity*, 52; John Marriott, *The Other Empire: Metropolis, India and Progress in the Colonial Imagination* (Manchester: Manchester University Press, 2003). On the quest to understand the city, see for instance, Stuart M. Blumin, "Explaining the New Metropolis: Perception, Depiction, and Analysis in Mid-Nineteenth-Century New York City," *JUH* 11 (1984): 9–38. *North American*, Sept. 14, 1854.

5. *North American*, Sept. 14, 1854. The "search for order" is usually seen as a postbellum phenomenon, but it can be dated much earlier. See Robert H. Wiebe, *The Search for Order, 1877–1920* (New York: Hill and Wang, 1967). My understanding of the relationship between prophecy and politics draws on Cronon, *Nature's Metropolis*, 31; Johnson, *River of Dark Dreams*, 310, 312.

6. J. C. Sydney, *Map of the City of Philadelphia, Together with All the Surrounding Districts* (Philadelphia: Smith & Wistar, 1849); Emma Jones Lapsansky, "South Street Philadelphia, 1762–1854: 'A Haven for Those Low in the World,' " PhD diss., University of Pennsylvania, 1975, 37.

7. For an overview of Philadelphia in this period, see Nicholas B. Wainwright, "The Age of Nicholas Biddle," and Elizabeth Geffen, "Industrial Development and Social Crisis," in *Philadelphia: A 300-Year History,* ed. Russell F. Weigley (New York: Norton, 1982), 258–362.

8. See for example, *North American*, July 25, 1844; *Ledger*, Sept. 17, 1850; *Sunday Dispatch*, July 2, 1854.

9. Warner, *Private City*, 21, 50.

10. On economic development, see Diane Lindstrom, *Economic Development in the Philadelphia Region, 1810–1850* (New York: Columbia University Press, 1978). On the decline of the city as a financial center, see especially, Robert E. Wright, *The First Wall Street: Chestnut Street,*

Philadelphia, and the Birth of American Finance (Chicago: University of Chicago Press, 2005), 131–63; Job. R. Tyson, *Mr. Tyson's Letters to the British Consul on the Commerce of Philadelphia* (Philadelphia: Inquirer Job Press, 1851), 3, 15.

11. Warner, *Private City*, 63–78; Geffen, "Industrial Development and Social Crisis," 307–62; Philip Scranton, *Proprietary Capitalism: The Textile Manufacture at Philadelphia, 1800–1885* (Cambridge: Cambridge University Press, 1983), 75–134; Lindstrom, *Economic Development*, 23; David Montgomery, "The Shuttle and the Cross: Weavers and Artisans in the Kensington Riots of 1844," *Journal of Social History* 5 (1972): 411–46; Scranton, *Proprietary Capitalism*, 177–223; Feldberg, *Philadelphia Riots of 1844*, 32; Laurie, *Working People of Philadelphia*, 127.

12. John K. Brown, *The Baldwin Locomotive Works, 1831–1915* (Baltimore: Johns Hopkins University Press, 1995), 2; Wolcott Calkins, Daniel S. Miller, and Joseph R. Chandler, *Memorial of Matthias W. Baldwin* (Philadelphia: n.p., 1867), 16.

13. Brown, *Baldwin Locomotive Works*, 21.

14. A similar point is made about Samuel Smedley's 1860 *Atlas* in Adam Levine, "The Grid Versus Nature: The History and Legacy of Topographical Change in Philadelphia," in *Nature's Entrepôt: Philadelphia's Urban Sphere and Its Environmental Thresholds*, ed. Brian Black and Michael J. Chiarappa (Pittsburgh, Pa.: University of Pittsburgh Press, 2012), 156.

15. Frances Milton Trollope, *Domestic Manners of the Americans*, vol. 2 (London: Whittaker, Treacher & Co., 1832), 73.

16. Scott, *Seeing Like a State*, 56.

17. John William Reps, *The Making of Urban America: A History of City Planning in the United States* (Princeton, N.J.: Princeton University Press, 1965), 161–74; Warner, *Private City*, 50, 52; Lapsansky, "South Street," 45; Geffen, "Industrial Development and Social Crisis," 315; *North American*, Apr. 7, 1857.

18. Geffen, "Industrial Development and Social Crisis," 349; Laurie, *Working People of Philadelphia*, 110; Silcox, *William McMullen*, 34; James J. Connolly, *An Elusive Unity: Urban Democracy and Machine Politics in Industrializing America* (Ithaca, N.Y.: Cornell University Press, 2011), 11; Frank Gerrity, "The Disruption of the Philadelphia Whigocracy: Joseph R. Chandler, Anti-Catholicism, and the Congressional Election of 1854," *PMHB* 111 (1987): 163.

19. Timothy J. Gilfoyle, *City of Eros: New York City, Prostitution, and the Commercialization of Sex, 1790–1920* (New York: Norton, 1992), 81–84; Bruce Laurie, "Fire Companies and Gangs in Southwark: The 1840s," in *The Peoples of Philadelphia: A History of Ethnic Groups and Lower-Class Life, 1740–1940*, ed. Allen F. Davis and Mark H. Haller (Philadelphia: Temple University Press, 1973), 71–87.

20. Eric Hobsbawm, *Primitive Rebels: Studies in Archaic Forms of Social Movements in the 19th and 20th Centuries* (New York: Norton, 1959), 110–11; Otter, *Philadelphia Stories*, 135; Geffen, "Industrial Development and Social Crisis," 343; Leonard L. Richards, *Gentlemen of Property and Standing: Anti-Abolition Mobs in Jacksonian America* (Oxford: Oxford University Press, 1970).

21. On the wider turn against mob action, see Kimberley K. Smith, *The Dominion of Voice: Riot, Reason, and Romance in Antebellum Politics* (Lawrence: University Press of Kansas, 1999), 50; On the Kensington riot, see Feldberg, *Philadelphia Riots of 1844*, 99–119, and the forthcoming study by Zachary Schrag.

22. Noel Ignatiev, *How the Irish Became White*, (New York: Routledge, 1995), 151–53.

23. *A Full and Complete Account of the Late Awful Riots in Philadelphia* (Philadelphia: John B. Perry, 1844), 20; *The Olive Branch, or, an Earnest Appeal in Behalf of Religion, the Supremacy of Law, and Social Order* (Philadelphia: M. Fithian, 1844), 4; A Protestant and Native Philadelphian, *The Truth Unveiled; Or, A Calm and Impartial Exposition of the Origin and Immediate Cause of the Terrible Riots in Philadelphia* (Philadelphia: M. Fithian, 1844), 24. On the novelty of the Southwark riot especially, see Ignatiev, *How the Irish Became White*, 152; Feldberg, *Philadelphia Riots of 1844*, 162.

24. Sidney George Fisher diary (#1462), May 12, 1844, HSP (hereafter cited as Fisher diary).

25. On the Philadelphia press, see Robinson, "Ledger," 43–55; Elwyn B. Robinson, "The North American: Advocate of Protection," *PMHB* 64 (1940): 345–55; J. Thomas Scharf and Thompson Westcott, *History of Philadelphia, 1609–1884*, vol. 3 (Philadelphia: L. H. Everts, 1884), 1958–2062; *Ledger*, June 13, 1854.

26. *Boston Evening Transcript*, May 15, 1854.

27. *Ledger*, Apr. 27, 1849.

28. See for example, Washington, letter to *Ledger*, July 25, 1851; *Evening Bulletin*, June 14, 1853.

29. Anderson, *Imagined Communities*, 36.

30. See for example, *North American*, Apr. 6, 1852.

31. E. Digby Baltzell, *Philadelphia Gentlemen: The Making of a National Upper Class* (New Brunswick, N.J.: Transaction Publishers, 1989), 81; Daniel R. Goodwin, "Obituary Notice of Samuel Vaughan Merrick, Esq.," *Proceedings of the American Philosophical Society* 11 (1869): 586.

32. Fisher diary, Nov. 19, 1843. See Daniel Kilbride, *An American Aristocracy: Southern Planters in Antebellum Philadelphia* (Columbia: University of South Carolina Press, 2006), 3; Andrew Dawson, *Lives of the Philadelphia Engineers: Capital, Class, and Revolution, 1830–1890* (Burlington, Vt.: Ashgate, 2004), 1; Baltzell, *Philadelphia Gentlemen*, 397; Nathaniel Burt, *The Perennial Philadelphians: The Anatomy of an American Aristocracy* (Philadelphia: University of Pennsylvania Press, [1963] 1999), 23–32.

33. Beckert, *Monied Metropolis*, 78; Iver Bernstein, *The New York City Draft Riots: Their Significance for American Society and Politics in the Age of the Civil War* (Oxford: Oxford University Press, 1990), 125–92.

34. On McMichael, see Bloom, "The Philadelphia North American." See also Robert L. Bloom, "Morton McMichael's *North American*," *PMHB* 77 (1953): 164–80; Howard Gillette, "Corrupt and Contented: Philadelphia's Political Machine, 1865–1887," PhD diss., Yale University, 1970, 18–26; Edwin N. Benson, *In Memoriam: Henry Armitt Brown, J. Gillingham Fell, Morton McMichael* (Philadelphia: Henry B. Ashmead, 1879), 11–15.

35. "Edgar Allan Poe, "A Chapter on Autography [part II]," *Graham's Magazine* 19 (Dec. 1841), 278.

36. John W. Forney, *Anecdotes of Public Men*, vol. 2 (Washington, D.C.: Harper & Brothers, 1881), 116, 119.

37. On McMichael's balancing of antipartyism and Whiggery, see Steinberg, *Transformation of Criminal Justice*, 105. On his interaction with Democrats, see Forney, *Anecdotes of Public Men*, vol. 2, 117.

38. *North American*, Apr. 6, 1852; Aug. 16, 1853; Candidus, letter to *North American*, Mar. 12, 1857.

39. *North American*, Apr. 6, 1852; *Fincher's Trades' Review*, June 6, 1863; Julianna Randolph Wood, *Biographical Sketch of Richard D. Wood*, vol. 2 (Philadelphia: Lippincott's Press, 1871), 45, 180.

40. An Old Citizen, letter to *Ledger*, May 16, 1844; "To His Excellency the Governor of Pennsylvania," Cadwalader Family Papers (#1454), Series VII, Box 431, Folder 5, HSP.

41. Fisher diary, July 24, 1844.

42. Ibid., May 12, 1844.

43. Thomas P. Cope diary, vol. 7, July 7, 1844, http://triptych.brynmawr.edu/ (hereafter cited as Cope diary).

44. Fisher diary, May 26, July 24, 1844.

45. *North American*, Aug. 21, 1849; T., letter to *North American*, Nov. 13, 1849.

46. Cope diary, vol. 7, May 8, 1844; Fisher diary, July 24, 1844; *North American*, Mar. 2, 1852; Feb. 22, Apr. 12, 18, 1854; *New York Herald*, Nov. 13, 1844; *Pennsylvanian*, Nov. 11, 1857; Mechanic, letter to *Spirit of the Times*, Dec. 22, 1849; C., letter to *North American*, Oct. 3, 1849. On the use of foreign terms to make sense of the American city in the period, see Elizabeth Kelly Gray, "The World by Gaslight: Urban-Gothic Literature and Moral Reform in New York City, 1845–1860," *American Nineteenth Century History* 10 (2009): 137–61.

47. The term "common referents" is borrowed from Rodgers, *Atlantic Crossings*, 3–4, though he dates them to later in the century.

48. *Bulletin*, Mar. 25, 1851; *Prize Essays on Juvenile Delinquency, Published Under the Direction of the Board of Managers of the House of Refuge, Philadelphia* (Philadelphia: Edward C. & John Biddle, 1855), 117. On fears of Jacobinism in the Early Republic, see Rachel Hope Cleves, *The Reign of Terror in America: Visions of Violence from Anti-Jacobinism to Antislavery* (Cambridge: Cambridge University Press, 2009).

49. T., letter to *North American*, Nov. 13, 1849; *Ledger*, Nov. 15, 1849; *Awful Riots in Philadelphia*, 55–60; *The Particulars of the Late Riots, With a View of the Burning of the Catholic Churches, St. Michaels & St. Augustines* (Philadelphia: 23 N. Second Street, 1844), 24.

50. Cope diary, vol. 7, May 9, 15, July 10, 17, 1844.

51. *Awful Riots in Philadelphia*, 60.

52. *North American*, July 13, 1844; Ibid., 16.

53. *Ledger*, July 26, 1844.

54. Bruce Sinclair, *Philadelphia's Philosopher Mechanics: A History of the Franklin Institute, 1824–1865* (Baltimore: Johns Hopkins University Press, 1975), 58; Philadelphia Board of Trade, Annual Report, 1844, p. 1, HSP.

55. Philadelphia Board of Trade, Annual Report, 1844, 1850, p. 13, HSP. See also Edwin Wolf II, "The Origins of Philadelphia's Self-Depreciation, 1820–1920," *PMHB* 104 (1980): 58–73.

56. William Wordsworth, *The Poems of William Wordsworth* (London: Edward Moxon, 1847), 387; *North American*, Aug. 30, 1853; Edwin T. Freedley, *Philadelphia and Its Manufactures: A Handbook Exhibiting the Development, Variety, and Statistics of the Manufacturing Industry of Philadelphia in 1857* (Philadelphia: Edward Young, 1858), 17. On the marketing plans, see San., letter to *North American*, July 21, 1849; E. F. letter to *Ledger*, Jan. 21, 1851; Board of Trade, Minutes, 1833–1852, Dec. 15, 1851; Jan. 19, 1852, Philadelphia Board of Trade Records, 1801–1942 (#1791), HSP.

57. Freedley, *Philadelphia*, 17; Patricia C. Cohen, *A Calculating People: The Spread of Numeracy in Early America* (Chicago: University of Chicago Press, 1982), 154–55; *North American*, May 8, 1854.

58. *United States Gazette*, Mar. 12, 1846; Statistical Society of Pennsylvania, *Constitution and By-Laws of the Statistical Society of Pennsylvania* (Philadelphia: Crissy and Markley, 1847); Statistical Society of Pennsylvania, *Circular* (Philadelphia: n.p., 1847); Tyson, *Commerce of Philadelphia*, 11–12; *North American*, Dec. 29, 1846; Apr. 22, 1854; *Ledger*, Aug. 27, 1847; Philadelphia Board of Trade, Annual Report, 1854, pp. 11–12; 1855, pp. 6–7, HSP.

59. Philadelphia Corn Exchange Association. *Fifth Annual Report* (Philadelphia: Commercial List Office, 1859), 7; Edwin T. Freedley, *A Practical Treatise on Business: Or How to Get, Save, Spend, Give, Lend, and Bequeath Money* (Philadelphia: Lippincott, Grambo & Co., 1853); Freedley, *Philadelphia*, 18, 139–40.

60. Freedley, *Philadelphia*, 17, 56–57, 89; William D. Kelley, *Address Delivered Before the Franklin Institute of the State of Pennsylvania at the Close of the Twenty-Second Exhibition of American Manufacturers* (Philadelphia: n.p., 1852), 6, 10; *North American*, Feb. 15, 1853; "Philadelphia and Her Prospects," Feb. 14, 1859, Poulson Scrap Books, vol. 1, p. 35, LCP.

61. Philadelphia Board of Trade, Annual Report, 1857, p. 5; 1858, p. 6, HSP; *North American*, Mar. 3, 23, 31, 1853; Mar. 12, 1857; E., letter to *North American*, Apr. 2, 1852.

62. Fisher diary, July 24, 1844.

63. See for instance, E. P. Thompson, *The Making of the English Working Class* (London: V. Gollancz, 1963); Herbert G. Gutman, *Work, Culture, and Society in Industrializing America: Essays in American Working-Class and Social History* (New York: Vintage Books, 1977); Bruce Laurie, *Artisans into Workers: Labor in Nineteenth-Century America* (New York: Hill and Wang, 1989). In Philadelphia, the best treatment is Laurie, *Working People of Philadelphia*, 54–56.

64. See for instance, Brown, *Baldwin Locomotive Works*, 20–21; Domenic Vitiello, *Engineering Philadelphia: The Sellers Family and the Industrial Metropolis* (Ithaca, N.Y.: Cornell University Press, 2013), 108–9.

65. *The Olive Branch, or, an Earnest Appeal in Behalf of Religion, the Supremacy of Law, and Social Order* (Philadelphia: M. Fithian, 1844), 9; Todd, *Great Cities*, 204.

66. *Awful Riots in Philadelphia*, 46; Daniel R. Biddle and Murray Dubin, *Tasting Freedom: Octavius Catto and the Battle for Equality in America* (Philadelphia: Temple University Press, 2010), 136; *Prize Essays on Juvenile Delinquency*, 38.

67. Wood, *Richard D. Wood*, vol. 2, 43; Calkins, Miller, and Chandler, *Matthias W. Baldwin*, 114–38. For donors and managers, see PSEIP, *Report of the Managers*, 1848, 12–14; 1849, 7; 1851, 3. On Mullen and the Moyamensing Workhouse, see Steinberg, *Transformation of Criminal Justice*, 160–62; Priscilla Ferguson Clement, *Welfare and the Poor in Nineteenth-Century Philadelphia, 1800–1854* (Rutherford, N.J.: Farleigh Dickinson University Press, 1985), 156–57; J. Matthew Gallman, *Receiving Erin's Children: Philadelphia, Liverpool, and the Irish Famine Migration, 1845–1855* (Chapel Hill: University of North Carolina Press, 2000), 76–77. On the New York Association for Improving the Condition of the Poor, see Bernstein, *New York City Draft Riots*, 179–84.

68. PSEIP, *Constitution* (Philadelphia: n.p., 1847), 5, 9; A Citizen, letter to *North American*, Jan. 19, 1855. On the retreat from outdoor relief, see Clement, *Welfare and the Poor*, 67; Dorsey, *Reforming Men and Women*, 51.

69. PSEIP, *Constitution*, 9; PSEIP, *Report of the Managers*, 1851, 8, 10; *Friends' Review*, Oct. 14, 1848, 62.

70. Benjamin T. Sewell, *Sorrow's Circuit, or Five Years' Experience in the Bedford Street Mission* (Philadelphia: Published for the Support of the Gospel in the Bedford Street Mission,

1859), 41. Clement, *Welfare and the Poor*, 156; Kenneth W. Milano, *The History of the Kensington Soup Society* (Charleston, S.C.: History Press, 2009); *General Organization for the Relief of the Poor: A Plan for the Consolidation of Charities* (Philadelphia: King & Baird, 1855); *North American*, Jan. 2, 4, Feb. 26; Mar. 9, 1855.

71. *North American*, Mar. 6, 1855; *Consolidation of Charities*, 6, 12.

72. PSEIP, *Report of the Managers*, 1851, 6; *North American*, Jan. 24, 1855.

73. *Inquirer*, Dec. 18, 1861; *Dispatch*, Dec. 2, 1866.

74. Sewell, *Sorrow's Circuit*, 37, 42, 331; *North American*, June 1, 1847; An Old Amateur, *Mysteries of Philadelphia, or: Scenes of Real Life in the Quaker City* (Philadelphia: n.p., 1848), 65.

75. Steinberg, *Transformation of Criminal Justice*, 160–61; *Ledger*, Oct. 4, 1848; Sewell, *Sorrow's Circuit*, 44; *Dispatch*, Jan. 19, 1851. My reading of resistance to enclosure is shaped by James C. Scott, *The Art of Not Being Governed: An Anarchist History of Upland Southeast Asia* (New Haven, Conn.: Yale University Press, 2009), 4–9.

76. George Rogers Taylor, ed., "'Philadelphia in Slices' by George G. Foster," *PMHB* 93 (1969): 38–42; An Old Amateur, *Mysteries of Philadelphia*, 65; *North American*, Mar. 10, 1854. On mysteries fiction, see Paul Joseph Erickson, "Welcome to Sodom: The Cultural Work of City-Mysteries Fiction in Antebellum America," PhD diss., University of Texas at Austin, 2005; Michael Denning, *Mechanic Accents: Dime Novels and Working-Class Culture in America* (London: Verso, 1987), 85–91; James Rees, *Mysteries of City Life; or, Stray Leaves from the World's Book* (Philadelphia: J. W. Moore, 1849), 26.

77. *North American*, June 1, 1847; *Bulletin*, Mar. 25, 1851; Amy Kaplan, "Manifest Domesticity," *American Literature* 70 (1998), 581–606.

78. *North American*, Feb. 22, 1854.

79. Ibid., Feb. 22, 1854; May 28, 1845; Laurie, *Working People of Philadelphia*, 119–21; William J. Mullen, *An Appeal to Tax-Payers in Opposition to the Existing Law for the Sale of Intoxicating Liquors* (Philadelphia: Jared Craig, 1852), 30, 32. On temperance reform in Philadelphia, see Dorsey, *Reforming Men and Women*, 90–135.

80. Philadelphia, Board of Health, *Report of the Sanitary Committee of the Board of Health of Philadelphia on the Subject of the Asiatic Cholera* (Philadelphia: Crissy and Markley, 1848), 5; Sam Alewitz, *Filthy Dirty: A Social History of Unsanitary Philadelphia in the Late Nineteenth Century*, (New York: Garland, 1989), 27; Isaac Parrish, *The Sanitary Condition of Philadelphia: From the Report of the Committee on Public Hygiene of the American Medical Association* (Philadelphia: T. K. and P. G. Collins, 1849), 9–13; Philadelphia, Board of Health, *Asiatic Cholera*, 5–6; Edward T. Morman, "Guarding Against Alien Impurities: The Philadelphia Lazaretto 1854–1893," *PMHB* 108 (1984): 132–33.

81. Drew R. McCoy, *The Elusive Republic: Political Economy in Jeffersonian America* (Chapel Hill: University of North Carolina Press, 1980), 127; Upton, *Another City*, 134; Peter Thompson, *Rum, Punch, and Revolution*, (Philadelphia: University of Pennsylvania Press, 1999), 185; *Bulletin*, Mar. 7, 1855.

82. *Prize Essays on Juvenile Delinquency*, 113–14. Despite the similar premise and setting, there is no indication that this inspired the plot of the 1983 Philadelphia comedy *Trading Places*.

83. *Pennsylvanian*, Oct. 2, 1857; George Bayne, letter to *North American*, Aug. 29, 1851. On interdependence, see for example, Harold L. Platt, *Shock Cities: The Environmental Transformation and Reform of Manchester and Chicago*, (Chicago: University of Chicago Press, 2005),

10; Scobey, *Empire City*, 159; Schuyler, *New Urban Landscape*, 6; Stanley K. Schultz, *Constructing Urban Culture: American Cities and City Planning, 1800–1920* (Philadelphia: Temple University Press, 1989), 112; Paul S. Boyer, *Urban Masses and Moral Order in America, 1820–1920* (Cambridge, Mass.: Harvard University Press, 1978), 89.

84. PSEIP, *Report of the Managers*, 1848, 7; Michael Meranze, *Laboratories of Virtue: Punishment, Revolution, and Authority in Philadelphia, 1760–1835* (Chapel Hill: University of North Carolina Press, 1996), 295; William D. Kelley, *Address Delivered at the Colored Department of the House of Refuge* (Philadelphia: T. K. and P. G. Collins, 1850), 6.

85. A. J. Pleasonton diary (#Am.1242), June 11, 1838, HSP; Thomas Bradford to George Cadwalader, July 8, 1844, Cadwalader Family Papers (#1454), Series VII, Box 431, Folder 5, HSP; Feldberg, *Philadelphia Riots of 1844*, 10; *Street Talk About an Ordinance of Councils, Passed the 11th July, 1844 Organizing a Military Force for the Government of Philadelphia* (Philadelphia: n.p., 1844); Cope diary, vol. 7, Dec. 5, 1844.

86. *History of Pennsylvania Hall, Which Was Destroyed by a Mob, on the 17th of May, 1838* (Philadelphia: Merrihew and Gunn, 1838), 4, 25; *United States Gazette*, Nov. 11, 1844. On the Consolidation movement in 1844, see Feldberg, *Philadelphia Riots of 1844*, 186–88.

87. Scott, *Seeing Like a State*, 61; *United States Gazette*, Nov. 12, 1844; *Ledger*, July 25, Aug. 20, Nov. 13, 1844; *North American*, July 25, 1844.

88. *United States Gazette*, Dec. 30, 1844; *North American*, Jan. 2, 1845; *Pennsylvanian*, Jan. 4, 1845; letter to *United States Gazette*, Dec. 28, 1844; Cope diary, vol. 7, Nov. 20, 1844.

89. Fisher diary, Feb. 1845.

90. Citizen, letter to *Pennsylvanian*, Dec. 30, 1844; *United States Gazette*, Dec. 30, 1844; A. B., letter to *Ledger*, Feb. 4, 1851.

91. *Pennsylvanian*, Jan. 4, 1845; Feldberg, *Philadelphia Riots of 1844*, 187–88.

92. S. [Sidney George Fisher], letter to *United States Gazette*, Jan. 30, 1845.

93. Fisher diary, Apr. 28. 1844.

Chapter 2

1. *Ledger*, Nov. 12, 1844; *New York Herald*, Nov. 13, 1844. On the book's popularity and the Mercer case, see David S. Reynolds, introduction to Lippard, *Quaker City*, vii, xii–xiii.

2. *New York Herald*, Nov. 13, 1844; George Lippard, letter to *Ledger*, Nov. 28, 1846.

3. Friedrich Engels, *Die Lage der Arbeitenden Klasse in England* (Leipzig: Otto Wigand, 1845). When an English edition appeared in 1887, the translator was Engels's friend Florence Kelley, the daughter of another Philadelphia radical of the 1840s, William D. Kelley.

4. On Philadelphia's radical tradition, see Eric Foner, *Tom Paine and Revolutionary America* (Oxford: Oxford University Press, 1976); Laurie, *Working People of Philadelphia*, especially, 68–83. Historians have tended to focus on radical critiques of wage labor, rather than the production of space. For exceptions, see Joel Schwartz, " 'To Every Man's Door': Railroads and Use of the Streets in Jacksonian Philadelphia," *PMHB* 128 (2004): 35–61; Elizabeth Blackmar, *Manhattan for Rent, 1785–1850* (Ithaca, N.Y.: Cornell University Press, 1989). On Lippard and the negotiation of class boundaries, see Shelley Streeby, "Opening up the Story: George Lippard and the Construction of Class," *Boundary 2* 24 (1997): 177–203.

5. See for instance, Norman Ware, *The Industrial Worker, 1840–1860: The Reaction of American Industrial Society to the Advance of the Industrial Revolution* (New York: Houghton Mifflin, 1924).

6. Laurie, *Working People of Philadelphia*, 54–56, 68, 85–87.

7. Wainwright, "The Age of Nicholas Biddle," 279; Lewis H. Arky, "The Mechanic's Union of Trade Associations and the Formation of the Philadelphia Working-Men's Movement," *PMHB* 76 (1952): 142–76. The critique of urban space is noted in Edward Pessen, *Most Uncommon Jacksonians: The Radical Leaders of the Early Labor Movement* (Albany: State University of New York Press, 1967), 21.

8. Montgomery, "The Shuttle and the Cross," 419. On the GTU and its aftermath, see Laurie, *Working People of Philadelphia*, 87–103.

9. Laurie, *Working People of Philadelphia*, 124–25; Geffen, "Industrial Development and Social Crisis," 337; Feldberg, *The Turbulent Era*, 64; *North American*, Mar. 29, 1844; Feldberg, *Philadelphia Riots of 1844*, 14; *Ledger*, Mar. 12, 1844.

10. A Protestant and Native Philadelphian, *The Truth Unveiled*, 6; Cope diary, vol. 7, May 11, 1844.

11. Montgomery, "The Shuttle and the Cross," 433–34. For press reports of weavers' strikes in Kensington, see *Inquirer*, Jan. 12, 13, 14, 1843; *Ledger*, Jan. 20, 23, 1844; Philadelphia Board of Trade, Annual Report, 1844, HSP.

12. On George Lippard's life, see [Bouton], *Life and Choice Writings of George Lippard*; Joseph Jackson, "George Lippard: Misunderstood Man of Letters," *PMHB* 59 (1935): 376–91; Roger Butterfield, "George Lippard and His Secret Brotherhood," *PMHB* 79 (1955): 285–304; Joseph Jablonski, "George Lippard," in *The American Radical*, ed. Mari Jo Buhle, Paul Buhle, and Harvey J. Kaye (New York: Routledge, 1994), 33–39. For different takes on the class audience for mysteries fiction, and a broader discussion of the genre, see Denning, *Mechanic Accents*; Erickson, "Welcome to Sodom."

13. Erickson, "Welcome to Sodom," 13, 15, chapter 4. On the relationship between Lippard as a critic of capitalism and a popular writer, see Gary Ashwill, "The Mysteries of Capitalism in George Lippard's City Novels," *ESQ* 40 (1994): 313.

14. David S. Reynolds, "Introduction: George Lippard in His Times," in *George Lippard, Prophet of Protest: Writings of an American Radical*, ed. David S. Reynolds (New York: P. Lang, 1986), 6, 21.

15. Lippard, *The Quaker City*, 2; Streeby, "George Lippard," 182. Lippard's "producerism" and conspiracy theory both place him in the tradition of populist politics. See Michael Kazin, *The Populist Persuasion: An American History* (Ithaca, N.Y.: Cornell University Press, 1998).

16. Denning, *Mechanic Accents*, 85; Hal Draper, *Karl Marx's Theory of Revolution*, vol. 1, *State and Bureaucracy* (New York: Monthly Review Press, 1977), 227–29; Edward S. Cutler, *Recovering the New: Transatlantic Roots of Modernism* (Hanover: University of New Hampshire Press, 2003), 11; Reynolds, introduction to *Quaker City*, by Lippard, xiv. At least one author argues Lippard was an "urban gothic" writer rather than a scribe of "city mysteries." See Janis P. Stout, *Sodoms in Eden: The City in American Fiction before 1860* (Westport, Conn.: Greenwood Press, 1976), 44–45. On the politics of mysteries novelists, see Erickson, "Welcome to Sodom," 54, 60, 378–419.

17. Erickson, "Welcome to Sodom," 51; An Old Amateur, *Mysteries of Philadelphia*, i, 9, 52–53.

18. George Lippard, *The Nazarene, or, the Last of the Washingtons* (Philadelphia: T. B. Peterson, 1854), 166. Samuel Otter argues that Lippard's "realistic narrative" in depicting industrial Kensington contrasts with his "gothic" depiction of Moyamensing. The former stands in for the North, while the latter served as the South. See Otter, *Philadelphia Stories*, 186.

19. *George Lippard, Prophet of Protest*, 64–68. Lippard's shifting perspectives are discussed in Otter, *Philadelphia Stories*, 177–78.

20. Denning, *Mechanic Accents*, 92; Lippard, *Quaker City*, 50, 53; Unger, "Dens of Iniquity," 319.

21. Lippard, *Quaker City*, 55–56.

22. Ibid., 379; William Elder, *Periscopics; or, Current Subjects Extemporaneously Treated* (New York: J. C. Darby, 1854), 129.

23. Lippard's "social constructivist" take on character is discussed in Ashwill, "Mysteries of Capitalism," 309.

24. George Lippard, *Life and Adventures of Charles Anderson Chester, the Notorious Leader of the Philadelphia "Killers"* (Philadelphia: Yates & Smith, 1850), 11; *Quaker City*, Dec. 1, 1849.

25. [Bouton], *Life and Choice Writings of George Lippard*, 22; Lippard, *Quaker City*, 106, 477–78.

26. Lippard, *Quaker City*, 372–93.

27. Ibid., 385, 389.

28. On Lippard's use of utopia and dystopia, see Nathaniel Williams, "George Lippard's Fragile Utopian Future and 1840s American Economic Turmoil," *Utopian Studies* 24 (2013): 166–83.

29. Laurie, *Working People of Philadelphia*, 165; *Ledger*, Apr. 24, 1844; Feb. 19, June 27, 1848; Nov. 16, 1850; *Spirit of the Times and Daily Keystone*, Jan. 12, 1849. On association, see Warner, *Private City*, 61.

30. John Campbell, letter to *New York Tribune*, Nov. 29, 1850; *Quaker City*, Apr. 14, 1849.

31. Laurie, *Working People of Philadelphia*, 163. On Shedden, see Reynolds, "Introduction," 35; Steve Leikin, "Sovereigns of Industry," in *Encyclopedia of United States Labor and Working-Class History*, vol. 3, ed. Eric Arneson (New York: Routledge, 2007), 1310; Timothy Messer-Kruse, *The Yankee International: Marxism and the American Reform Tradition, 1848–1876* (Chapel Hill: University of North Carolina Press, 1998), 136, 239, 288. On Campbell's career as a Chartist, see Ray Boston, *British Chartists in America, 1839–1900* (Manchester: Manchester University Press, 1971), 58; Paul A. Pickering, *Chartism and the Chartists in Manchester and Salford* (London: Macmillan, 1995), 44–45, 48, 53, 66–67; Andrew Heath, "'The Producers on the One Side, and the Capitalists on the Other': Labor Reform, Slavery, and the Career of a Transatlantic Radical," *American Nineteenth Century History* 13 (2012): 199–227. One Hungarian revolutionary, who visited with Louis Kossuth in 1852, reputedly married an African American and lived on the notorious Bedford Street. *North American*, Aug. 9, 1859.

32. Timothy Mason Roberts, *Distant Revolutions: 1848 and the Challenge to American Exceptionalism* (Charlottesville: University of Virginia Press, 2009), 57; *Ledger*, Apr. 25, 1848.

33. *Ledger*, Apr. 25, 1848. The speaker is recorded as Francis J. Grand, but this was probably the German immigrant, mathematician, journalist, and political commentator Francis J. Grund.

34. *Quaker City*, Mar. 3, 1849. On Lippard and 1848, see Roberts, *Distant Revolutions*, 58; G. G. Foster and Thomas Dunn English, *The French Revolution of 1848: Its Causes, Actors, Events and Influences* (Philadelphia: G. B. Zieber & Co., 1848), 12, 44, 115.

35. Foster and English, *French Revolution*, 9–11, 17.

36. Ibid., 177–78.

37. Taylor, "Philadelphia in Slices," 26, 34–41. On the *Tribune* as a radical paper in this period, see Adam-Max Tuchinsky, "'The Bourgeoisie Will Fall and Fall Forever': The *New-York Tribune*, the 1848 French Revolution, and American Social Democratic Discourse," *JAH* 92 (2005): 470–97.

38. Taylor, "Philadelphia in Slices," 38, 70.

39. *The Almighty Dollar; or, the Brilliant Exploits of a Killer: A Thrilling Romance of Quakerdelphia* (Philadelphia: Zieber & Co., 1847), 15. The novella receives a brief mention in Matt Cohen and Edlie L. Wong, introduction to *The Killers: A Narrative of Real Life in Philadelphia*, by George Lippard (Philadelphia: University of Pennsylvania Press, 2014), 30, 34. George B. Zieber, the publisher, also printed Lippard's *Quaker City* and Foster and English's account of the 1848 Revolution. Campbell published a lost book, *Lectures upon the Great French Revolution*, sometime before 1851, but he defended the Jacobins in other settings too. John Campbell, *A Theory of Equality; or, The Way to Make Every Man Act Honestly* (Philadelphia: John B. Perry, 1848), 92; W. Brotherhead, *Forty Years Among the Old Booksellers of Philadelphia* (Philadelphia: A. P. Brotherhead, 1891), 37; John Campbell, letter to *New York Tribune*, Nov. 1, 1850.

40. Campbell, *Theory of Equality*, iii–iv, 193; Elder, *Periscopics*, 279–80.

41. *Ledger*, Apr. 25, 1848; *North American*, Apr. 25, 1848; *Inquirer*, May 18, 1848.

42. Timothy Mason Roberts, "'Revolutions Have Become the Bloody Toy of the Multitude': European Revolutions, the South, and the Crisis of 1850," *Journal of the Early Republic* 25 (2005): 259–83; Andre M. Fleche, *The Revolution of 1861: The American Civil War in the Age of Nationalist Conflict* (Chapel Hill: University of North Carolina Press, 2012), 17; *North American*, July 17, 1848; Oct. 30, 1852; *Quaker City*, Sept. 22, 29, 1849.

43. Laurie, *Working People of Philadelphia*, 180.

44. *Quaker City*, Aug. 25, Sept. 22, Nov. 24, Dec. 29, 1849; Roberts, *Distant Revolutions*, 87. George Lippard to William MacFarlane, Mar. 3, 1851, Brotherhood of Union Collection, LCP; Roberts, *Distant Revolutions*, 87; *North American*, June 14, 1848.

45. *Ledger*, Feb. 7, 1849; Laurie, *Working People of Philadelphia*, 180; *Quaker City*, Nov. 24, 1849.

46. Campbell, *Theory of Equality*, iii; Foster and English, *French Revolution*, 160–61; *Quaker City*, Oct. 20, 1849; Lippard, *Quaker City*, 164.

47. On Campbell, see *Ledger*, June 27, 1848; *Spirit of the Times*, Jan. 12, 1849; John Campbell, letters to *New York Tribune*, Aug. 6, Sept. 28, Nov. 1, 1850; Brotherhood of Union Circular, Jan. 1, 1852, Brotherhood of Union Collection, LCP.

48. John Campbell to *New York Tribune*, Apr. 26, 1851; *Ledger*, Nov. 1, 1850; William D. Kelley, *Characteristics of the Age: An Address Delivered Before the Linnaean Association of Pennsylvania College* (Philadelphia: Campbell & Power, 1850), 8.

49. Paola Gemme, *Domesticating Foreign Struggles: The Italian Risorgimento and Antebellum American Identity* (Athens: University of Georgia Press, 2005).

50. *North American*, May 5, 1848.

51. Leonard Syd Wallach, "Chapel, Custom, Craft: The Transformation of the Struggle to Control the Labor Process Among the Journeymen Printers of Philadelphia, 1850–1886," PhD diss., Columbia University, 1984, 307; *Ledger*, July 16, 1851.

52. Michael F. Conlin, "The Dangerous Isms and the Fanatical Ists: Antebellum Conservatives in the South and North Confront the Modernity Conspiracy," *Journal of the Civil*

War Era 4 (2014): 215; Stephen Colwell, *New Themes for the Protestant Clergy* (Philadelphia: Lippincott, Grambo & Co., 1851), 359. On Colwell and Rush in the Consolidation movement, see Eli Kirk Price, *The History of the Consolidation of the City of Philadelphia* (Philadelphia: J. B. Lippincott, 1873), 29–30. Fisher diary, Aug. 8, Oct. 3, Nov. 13, 1858; Apr. 7, Oct. 16, 1867; Apr. 20, 1869.

53. *Ledger*, May 31, 1851.

54. Feldberg, *Philadelphia Riots of 1844*, 164–65; Laurie, *Working People of Philadelphia*, 174–76.

55. One author, for instance, argues Lippard employed anti-Catholic tropes without embracing nativism. See Dorsey, *Reforming Men and Women*, 239; Shelley Streeby, *American Sensations: Class, Empire, and the Production of Popular Culture* (Berkeley: University of California Press, 2002), 23.

56. George Lippard, *The Nazarene, or, the Last of the Washingtons* (Philadelphia: T. B. Peterson, 1854), 130; Lippard, *Quaker City*, 262, 269; *Quaker City*, Aug. 25, 1849; John Campbell, letter to *New York Tribune*, Nov. 29, 1850.

57. *Ledger*, May 6, 1848; Nov. 16, Dec. 7, 14, 21, 1850; *Almighty Dollar*, 16.

58. Lippard, *The Killers*, 118. For critical work, see Cohen and Wong's introduction, and Otter, *Philadelphia Stories*, 187–90. On the riot, see Elizabeth M. Geffen, "Violence in Philadelphia in the 1840s and 1850s," *Pennsylvania History* 36 (1969): 388; Gallman, *Erin's Children*, 196.

59. Geffen, "Industrial Development and Social Crisis," 353.

60. On Elder, see Reinhard O. Johnson, *The Liberty Party, 1840–1848: Antislavery Third-Party Politics in the United States* (Baton Rouge: Louisiana State University Press, 2009), 158, 230, 265; *Ledger*, Dec. 7, 1850; June 25, 1851; John Campbell, *Negro-Mania, Being an Examination of the Falsely Assumed Equality of the Various Races of Men* (Philadelphia: Campbell & Power, 1851), 4.

61. *Quaker City*, Apr. 7, 1849; Campbell, *Theory of Equality*, 16, 25; *Quaker City*, Mar. 3, 1849.

62. Lippard's support for the Whig candidate Zachary Taylor rested almost entirely on the latter's "no-party-ism." *See Quaker City*, Sept. 29, 1849.

63. *Ledger*, Nov. 16, 23, 30, 1850; Campbell, *Negro-Mania*, 4. Lippard joined John Shedden and others to campaign for the repeal of the Fugitive Slave Law and other reforms in advance of the 1852 election. See *Washington National Era*, July 15, 1852. On Lippard's final work, and his treatment of race more broadly, see Otter, *Philadelphia Stories*, 187–90; Timothy Helwig, "Denying the Wages of Whiteness: The Racial Politics of George Lippard's Working-Class Protest," *American Studies* 47 (2006): 87–111.

64. *Ledger*, Oct. 29, Nov. 1, 1850; Laurie, *Working People of Philadelphia*, 191.

65. *Ledger*, June 2, 17, Sept. 20, Oct. 3, 1851. See also Laurie, *Working People of Philadelphia*, 194–95. On Kelley's politics in this period, see Michael Robert Greco, "William Darrah Kelley: The Ante-Bellum Years," PhD diss., Johns Hopkins University, 1974.

66. William T. Risler, *A Triumphant Refutation of John Campbell's Book, Which He Calls Negro-Mania* (Philadelphia: n.p., 1851), 3; John Campbell, letter to *New York Herald*, June 7, 1851.

67. John Campbell, letter to *New York Herald*, June 7, 1851. On Campbell's fight against British abolitionists that summer, see too, *New York Tribune*, June 16, 1851; *Pennsylvania Freeman*, June 19, 1851; *Ledger*, June 21, 1851; Henry C. Wright, letter to *The Liberator* (Boston), July 4, 1851.

68. Campbell, *Negro-Mania*, 459, 544.

69. One abolitionist paper called *Negro-Mania* "the most wasteful expenditure of paper, ink, binding materials, and labor, we remember to have seen." *Pennsylvania Freeman*, Sept. 25, 1851. For other reactions, see *Inquirer*, Sept. 1, 1851; *Pittsburgh Daily Morning Post*, Dec. 2, 1851; *Boston Investigator*, Sept. 10, 1851; An American Democrat, letter to *Boston Investigator*, Oct. 1, 1851; Risler, *Triumphant Refutation*. In the South, the work was received more favorably. See for instance, L. S. M., "Negro-Mania," *De Bow's Review* 2 (May 1852), 507.

70. William Elder, *Third Parties: The Duty of Anti-Slavery Voters* (Philadelphia: Merrihew and Thompson, 1851), 10, 13; On Elder's migration to the Republicans, see *Washington Daily National Era*, Mar. 11, 1854; *Boston Daily Atlas*, Feb. 15, 1856; *North American*, June 17, 1856.

71. "Lippard's Diary," June 2, 1853, MS vol. 1, Brotherhood of Union Collection, LCP.

72. *Quaker City*, Dec. 22, 1849.

73. Ibid., Apr. 7, Oct. 20, Sept. 29, 1849.

74. For reports of the meeting, see *Ledger*, Nov. 17, 1849; *North American*, Nov. 17, 1849.

75. *Ledger*, Oct. 3, 1851; Laurie, *Working People of Philadelphia*, 194.

76. *Quaker City*, Aug. 11, 1849; Butterfield, "George Lippard," 299; Jablonski, "George Lippard," 38.

Chapter 3

1. *Commercial List*, Dec. 24, 1853.

2. On ties between empire- and city-building in the nineteenth century, see Scobey, *Empire City*, 43–52; Cronon, *Nature's Metropolis*, 41–46; Gary Brechin, *Imperial San Francisco: Urban Power, Earthly Ruin* (Berkeley: University of California Press, 1999); Eugene P. Moehring, *Urbanism and Empire in the Far West, 1840–1890* (Reno: University of Nevada Press, 2004); Jonathan Schneer, *London 1900: The Imperial Metropolis* (New Haven, Conn.: Yale University Press, 1999). The best history of the early Pennsylvania is Albert J. Churella, *The Pennsylvania Railroad: Building an Empire, 1846–1917* (Philadelphia: University of Pennsylvania Press, 2013).

3. Thomas R. Hietala, *Manifest Design: Anxious Aggrandizement in Late Jacksonian America* (Ithaca, N.Y.: Cornell University Press, 1985). The term "urban imperialism" comes from Arthur M. Schlesinger, "The City in American History," *Mississippi Valley Historical Review* 27 (1940): 43–66. "Urban mercantilism" and "municipal foreign policy" offer alternatives. See Leonard P. Curry, *The Corporate City: The American City as a Political Entity, 1800–1850* (Westport, Conn.: Greenwood Press, 1997), 223–29; Hodos, *Second Cities*, 121–46.

4. My understanding of "growth politics" is shaped by Harvey Molotch, "The City as a Growth Machine: Toward a Political Economy of Place," *American Journal of Sociology* 82 (1976): 309–32; Logan and Molotch, *Urban Fortunes*; Hodos, *Second Cities*, 125. On a growth regime in Philadelphia, see Andrew M. Schocket, *Founding Corporate Power in Early National Philadelphia* (De Kalb: Northern Illinois University Press, 2007), 211.

5. *North American*, June 6, 12, 1846; Cope diary, vol. 10, Aug. 3, 1850. On Cope, see Warner, *Private City*, 80–81.

6. James Weston Livingood, *The Philadelphia-Baltimore Trade Rivalry, 1780–1860* (Harrisburg: Pennsylvania Historical and Museum Commission, 1947); Churella, *Pennsylvania Railroad*, 36–58, 64–74.

7. *North American*, Sept. 17, 1853.

8. Committee of Nine, letter to *United States Gazette*, Dec. 25, 1845; *United States Gazette*, Dec. 11, 1845; Feb. 27, Apr. 28, 1846.

9. Philadelphia Board of Trade, Annual Report, 1846, p. 8, HSP; *North American*, Apr. 14, 1846. See also Cronon, *Nature's Metropolis*, 43–44; Johnson, *River of Dark Dreams*, 257. Boosterism, Scobey writes, "offered a fable of destiny that invested entrepreneurial will with inevitability." Scobey, *Empire City*, 49.

10. Morton McMichael, *An Address Delivered Before the Northern Lyceum of the City and County of Philadelphia* (Philadelphia: Charles Alexander, 1839), 28; *Ledger*, Oct. 19, 1846.

11. *North American*, Apr. 14, 1846.

12. Cope diary, vol. 8, July 13, 1846.

13. Churella, *Pennsylvania Railroad*, 92; Taylor, "Philadelphia in Slices," 30; *Ledger*, Aug. 18, 1847; *Address of the Committee of Seven to the Citizens of Philadelphia, and of Pennsylvania* (Philadelphia: Jesper Harding, 1846), 13.

14. *Ledger*, Sept. 24, 1847; David Harvey, *The Urbanization of Capital: Studies in the History and Theory of Capitalist Urbanization* (Baltimore: John Hopkins University Press, 1985), 6–7, 16, and *The Urban Experience* (Baltimore: Johns Hopkins University Press, 1989), 65.

15. Many Voters, letter to *United States Gazette*, June 13, 1846; Louis Hartz, *Economic Policy and Democratic Thought: Pennsylvania, 1776–1860* (Cambridge, Mass.: Harvard University Press, 1948), 4; Churella, *Pennsylvania Railroad*, 100; Schocket, *Founding Corporate Power*, 212–13.

16. Seventy-Six, letter to *United States Gazette*, June 4, 1846.

17. *United States Gazette*, Dec. 6, 11, 1845.

18. Of the 29 industrialists listed as canvassers for subscriptions in late 1846, six were iron and steel manufacturers, one was the locomotive builder Matthias W. Baldwin, and another made steam engines.

19. On the legal argument, see Horace Binney, *Opinion of Horace Binney, Esq.: Upon the Right of the City Councils to Subscribe for Stock in the Pennsylvania Rail-Road Company* (Philadelphia: C. Sherman, 1846), 20. On the question of why public funding was needed for a profit-making corporation, see Horace Binney et al., letter to *United States Gazette*, Oct. 9, 1846. Binney probably wrote A Voter, letters to *United States Gazette*, May 29, June 4, 5, 17, July 8, 14, 1846. The Nile analogy was used by an early president of the Pennsylvania Railroad, William C. Patterson. See *North American*, Jan. 13, 1851.

20. A Whig, letter to *United States Gazette*, June 24, 1846; A Member of the Philadelphia Bar, *Wealth and Biography of Wealthy Citizens of Philadelphia* (Philadelphia: G. B. Zieber, 1845), 6. On bondholding among wealthy Philadelphians, see Schocket, *Founding Corporate Power*, 123–26.

21. Justice, letter to *Pennsylvanian*, Jan. 1, 1845; Another Tax Payer, letter to *United States Gazette*, July 16, 1846.

22. *United States Gazette*, June 18, 1846; A Voter, letter to *United States Gazette*, May 29, 1846; "Remonstrance of the Citizens," printed in *United States Gazette*, June 18, 1846.

23. Another Tax Payer, letters to *United States Gazette*, July 3, 16, 1846; Binney et al., letter to *United States Gazette*, Oct. 9, 1846.

24. Thomas Pym Cope, letter to *United States Gazette*, July 4, 1846. On the safety of railroad debt, see Another Voter, letter to United States Gazette, June 4, 1846; A Freeholder of the City of Philadelphia, letter to *United State Gazette*, June 18, 1846; *United States Gazette*,

June 23, July 4, 1846. For similar debates about debt in New York, see Scobey, *Empire City*, 203.

25. *United States Gazette,* Dec. 6, 1845; An Old Citizen, letter to *United States Gazette*, June 4, 1846; Many Voters, letter to *United States Gazette*, June 13, 1846; A Freeholder of the City of Philadelphia, letter to *United States Gazette*, June 18, 1846. See also letter to *United States Gazette*, June 1, 1846; Real Estate, letter to *North American*, June 2, 1846; A Philadelphian, letter to *North American*, June 4, 1846; *Pennsylvania Rail Road: Its Necessity and Advantages to Philadelphia* (Philadelphia, n.p.: 1846), 1.

26. *Address of the Committee of Seven*, 37; *North American*, June 23, 1846.

27. Ledger, May 2, 1849; *United States Gazette*, Apr. 28, 1846; Seventy-Six, letter to *United States Gazette*, June 9, 1846; letter to *Ledger*, June 29, 1846; *North American*, June 18, 30, July 3, 1846; Ecce, letter to *United States Gazette*, Nov. 4, 1846.

28. United States Gazette, Nov. 10, 1846; *Report of the Committee on Railroads of the City of Philadelphia* (Philadelphia: Crissey and Markley, 1854). The political and legal battles over the municipal subscription is given comprehensive treatment in Churella, *Pennsylvania Railroad*, 93–100.

29. *Address of the Committee of Seven*, 27, 37.

30. *Ledger*, Oct. 15, 1851; Taylor, "Philadelphia in Slices," 30; *Commercial List*, Feb. 11, 1854; Tyson, *Commerce of Philadelphia*, 26.

31. A Merchant of Philadelphia, *Memoirs and Autobiographies of Some of the Wealthy Citizens of Philadelphia* (Philadelphia: Published by the Booksellers, 1846), 20, 22, 41–42; Wood, *Richard D. Wood*, vol. 2, pp. 42, 75, 109, 126, 129, 171, 174; Cadwalader Family Papers (#1454), Series VII, Box 432, Folder 6, HSP; Eli Kirk Price journal (#3589), p. 1, HSP; Stephen N. Winslow, *Biographies of the Successful Philadelphia Merchants* (Philadelphia: James K. Simon, 1864), 98, 127; For contemporary assessments of investment practices, see *Ledger*, Sept. 24, 1857; *North American*, Sept. 29, 1865. See also Robert E. Wright's persuasive analysis of property markets. Robert E. Wright, "Ground Rents Against Populist Historiography: Mid-Atlantic Land Tenure, 1750–1820," *Journal of Interdisciplinary History* 29 (1998): 23–42.

32. *North American*, June 9, 1860; Winslow, *Philadelphia Merchants*, 98; Freedley, *Philadelphia*, 128. On profits from speculation, see Geffen, "Industrial Development and Social Crisis," 311–12.

33. *North American*, Dec. 20, 1854; Seventy-Six, letter to *United States Gazette*, June 9, 1846; Ecce, letter to *United States Gazette*, Nov. 4, 1846.

34. *Commercial List*, Apr. 8, 1854; *Bulletin*, Apr. 22, 1851; *North American*, Aug. 28, 1854; Apr. 18, 1857; Mar. 12, Aug. 10, 1859. On "creative destruction" in New York, see Scobey, *Empire City*, 66–70, 78–79.

35. The idea of a city molded by thousands of tiny decisions is developed in Sam Bass Warner Jr., *Streetcar Suburbs: The Process of Growth in Boston, 1870–1900* (Cambridge, Mass.: Harvard University Press, 1962). See also Diane Shaw, *City Building on the Eastern Frontier: Sorting the New Nineteenth-Century City*, (Baltimore: Johns Hopkins University Press, 2004).

36. *North American*, May 22, 1849; Nov. 25, 1858.

37. *Dispatch*, Mar. 17, 1850; *North American*, Jan. 19, 1854. On the grid and real estate, see Warner, *Private City*, 52; Carolyn Teich Adams, *Philadelphia: Neighborhoods, Division, and Conflict in a Postindustrial City* (Philadelphia: Temple University Press, 1991), 4. On the street numbering issue, see Russell F. Weigley, "The Border City in the City War," in *Philadelphia*,

ed. Weigley, 375. My discussion of land surveys, gridirons, and the commodification of land is influenced by Andro Linklater, *Owning the Earth: The Transforming History of Land Ownership* (London: Bloomsbury, 2014), 219; Johnson, *River of Dark Dreams*, 36.

38. *North American*, Nov. 8, 1853; *Dispatch*, May 3, Dec. 27, 1857.

39. *North American*, Nov. 25, 1858; Aug. 10, 1859. On parallel developments in New York, see Scobey, *Empire City*, 5, 92–93, 110–11.

40. *United States Gazette*, Dec. 7, 1846; McCarthy, "Consolidation of 1854," 540; *North American*, Apr. 26, 1844. On Price and real estate, see for instance, Charles M. S. Leslie to Roland Seegar (#1995), 1873, p. 62, HSP; Fisher diary, Mar. 17, 1858; Benjamin H. Brewster, "Address on the Late Eli Kirk Price," 1886, p. 7, Box 1, Folder 23, MC 1999.13, Eli Kirk Price Collection, Archives and Special Collections, Dickinson College.

41. Eli Kirk Price, *Of the Limitations of Actions and of Liens Against Real Estate in Pennsylvania* (Philadelphia: Kay & Brother, 1857), vii; Eli Kirk Price, *Some Objections to the Proposed Constitution* (Philadelphia: King & Baird, 1873), 18. Howard Gillette Jr. sees Price as "secular and cosmopolitan" in his support for reform. Gillette Jr., "Modern Metropolis," 9–10.

42. Brewster, "Price," 14–15; *The Liberator* (Boston), May 20, 1859. Price later played a minor role in the Reconstruction-era "Peace Policy."

43. "Revival of Saxon Laws in Pennsylvania," *Olwine's Law Journal* 1 (1850): 41; Eli Kirk Price, *The Act for the Sale of Real Estate* (Philadelphia: Kay & Brother, 1874), 9–10; Brewster, "Eli Kirk Price," 12.

44. Price, *Act for the Sale of Real Estate*, 1–2, 62, 180, 182; Brewster, "Eli Kirk Price," 12.

45. Stephen Simpson, *The Working Man's Manual: A New Theory of Political Economy* (Philadelphia Thomas L. Bonsal, 1831), 86, 89, 127; George Lippard, *Prophet of Protest*, 51; Lippard, *Quaker City*, 389.

46. Churella, *Pennsylvania Railroad*, 79, 99; *Ledger*, Oct. 8, 1850; *Quaker City*, Apr. 14, 1849; Andrew M. Schocket, *Founding Corporate Power in Early National Philadelphia* (DeKalb: Northern Illinois University Press, 2007).

47. Elder, *Periscopics*, 285, 314.

48. *New York Tribune*, June 13, 1848; *Ledger*, Oct. 5, 1850; June 17, 25, 1851; *Quaker City*, Nov. 24, 1849.

49. Stuart M. Blumin, "Residential Mobility Within the Nineteenth-Century City," in *Peoples of Philadelphia*, ed. Davis and Haller, 45; Mechanic, letter to *Spirit of the Times and Daily Keystone*, Dec. 22, 1849.

50. Campbell, *Theory of Equality*, 80, 105–6; *Quaker City,* Dec. 29, 1849.

51. *Quaker City*, Mar. 3, 1849; Richard J. Williams, *The Law of Landlord and Tenant in Pennsylvania* (Philadelphia: T. & J. W. Johnson & Co., 1901), 120. On other struggles against rent, see for instance, Reeve Huston, *Land and Freedom: Rural Society, Popular Protest, and Party Politics in Antebellum New York* (Oxford: Oxford University Press, 2000).

52. Cope diary, vol. 8, Dec. 11, 1845; *Ledger,* Apr. 28, 1846; L. W. S., letter to *North American*, June 18, 1846.

53. A Freeholder of the City of Philadelphia, letter to *United States Gazette*, June 18, 1846; James C. Fisher et al., *Town Meeting* (n.p., 1838); *Pennsylvania Inquirer*, Mar. 31, 1838; John Gilder et al., *Town Meeting* (n.p., 1838). The estimate on employment in the building trades comes from Donna J. Rilling, *Making Houses, Crafting Capitalism: Builders in Philadelphia, 1790–1850* (Philadelphia: University of Pennsylvania Press, 2001), viii.

54. *Bulletin*, March 4, 1853; *North American*, June 25, 1846; *Ledger*, June 26, 1846; Sept. 26, 1851.

55. *Bulletin*, Aug. 23, 1855; *North American*, Nov. 25, 1858. On ground rent, see Wright, "Ground Rents," 23–42; Rilling, *Making Houses*, 43–48. The first reference I have found to Philadelphia as a "city of homes" appears in the *Ledger*, Feb. 10, 1846. By the postbellum era it had become commonplace, as chapter 6 explores.

56. Broad Street Homestead Association, *Articles of Association* (Philadelphia: G. S. Harris, 1849); *Spirit of the Times*, Nov. 19, 1849; Edmund Wrigley, *The Working Man's Way to Wealth: A Practical Treatise on Building Associations, What They Are and How to Use Them* (Philadelphia: James K. Simon, 1869), 18; *The Union Land and Homestead Association* (Philadelphia: Duross Printers, 1854), 2; Lansdown Land Company, *Constitution* (Philadelphia: n.p., 1855), 4; Wrigley, *Way to Wealth*, 17; *Ledger*, Oct. 8, 1852; West Philadelphia Homestead Association, *Opinions of the Public Press*, 14; *Dispatch*, July 30, 1854. My estimate on participation is based on subscription records in the Walnut Street Land Company, Minute Book, 1854–1870, HSP.

57. West Philadelphia Homestead Association, *Economy Is Wealth: Every Man, Woman and Child a Freeholder* (Philadelphia: n.p., 1855), 5–6; West Philadelphia Homestead Association, *Opinions of the Public Press* (Philadelphia: n.p., 1855), 3–4, 24.

58. West Philadelphia Homestead Association, *Economy is Wealth*, 5–6; West Philadelphia Homestead Association, *Public Press*, 3–4, 17, 24; *North American*, Mar. 14, 1853. For promises of a quick profit, see *Passyunk and Mifflin Land Association* (Philadelphia: n.p., 1855), 2; Lansdown Land Company, *Constitution*, 4; *Pennsylvanian*, Dec. 15, 1855.

59. *Spirit of the Times*, Nov. 19, 1849; Washington Retreat Land and Building Association, *Charter, Constitution, and By-Laws* (Philadelphia: T. K. and P. G. Collins, 1854), 5; West Philadelphia Homestead Association, *Economy is Wealth*, 7; *Pennsylvanian*, Dec. 15, 1855; July 18, 1857; *Spirit of the Times*, Nov. 28, 1849.

60. *Union Land and Homestead Association*, 3; Broad Street Homestead Association, *Articles of Association*, 5; Lansdown Land Company, *Constitution*, 3; *Spirit of the Times*, Nov. 28, 1849; *George Lippard, Prophet of Protest*, 191; West Philadelphia Homestead Association, *Economy is Wealth*, 5.

61. Wrigley, *Way to Wealth*, 18.

62. *Ledger*, Aug. 4, 1851; *Spirit of the Times*, Jan. 3, 11, Apr. 13, Oct. 5, Nov. 19, 1849.

63. William D. Kelley, *Characteristics of the Age* (Philadelphia: Campbell & Power, 1850), 8; William D. Kelley, *Address Delivered Before the Franklin Institute of the State of Pennsylvania* (Philadelphia: The Institute, 1852), 13–14.

64. *Ledger*, Oct. 21, 1850; William D. Kelley, *The New Northwest* (n.p., 1871), 8–9.

65. *North American*, Jan. 28, 1854; Tecumseh, letter to *Ledger*, July 28, 1853; *Ledger*, Mar. 10, 1852.

66. *Pennsylvanian*, Oct. 28, Nov. 4, 1853; *North American*, Nov. 10, 12, 1853.

67. Price, *Consolidation*, 19.

68. Pennsylvania Senate, *Minority Report of the Select Committee on the Subject of the Consolidation of the City of Philadelphia*, (Harrisburg: n.p., 1851), 24; *Pennsylvanian*, Dec. 7, 1853; *Germantown Telegraph*, Jan. 4, 1854; *North American*, Dec. 7, 1853.

69. Franklin [pseud.], letter to *Ledger*, Nov. 19, 1850; *North American*, Mar. 26, 1852; T. O'N., letter to *Dispatch*, Jan. 1, 1854.

70. *Dispatch,* Feb. 20, 1853.

71. *Bulletin,* Feb. 1, 1854.

72. Tecumseh, letter to *Ledger,* July 28, 1853; *North American,* Nov. 25, 1858; A Genuine Democrat, letter to *Ledger,* Oct. 8, 1853; Anti-Aristocracy, letter to *Ledger,* Oct. 11, 1853.

73. Pennsylvania Senate, *Consolidation of the City of Philadelphia: Report of the Select Committee* (Philadelphia: n.p., 1854), 2–4; *North American,* July 30, Nov. 19, 1853; *Pennsylvanian,* Dec. 7, 1853.

74. *North American,* Nov. 19, 1853; Walnut Street Land Company, Minute Book, Nov. 11, 1856; June 9, 1857, HSP; *Germantown Telegraph,* Jan. 4, 11, 1854; *Pennsylvanian,* Dec. 7, 1853. See for example.

75. *Ledger,* Nov. 17, 1849; Otter, *Philadelphia Stories,* 186.

76. *Spirit of the Times,* Feb. 10, 13, 14, 1849.

77. *Ledger,* Nov. 17, 1849; Mar. 10, 1852. *North American,* Nov. 9, 1853.

78. Fellow Citizen, letter to *Ledger,* Aug. 29, 1850; *North American,* Nov. 12, 1853.

79. Pro Bono Publico, letter to *Ledger,* Mar. 1, 1854; *North American,* Mar. 13, 1854.

80. *North American,* Mar. 13, 1854.

Chapter 4

1. *Ledger,* July 6, 1854; *North American,* July 6, 1854.

2. *North American,* July 29, Nov. 14, 1854; Nov. 26, 1858; Karen Sawislak, *Smoldering City: Chicagoans and the Great Fire, 1871–1874* (Chicago: University of Chicago Press, 1995), 2.

3. *North American,* Oct. 4, 1861; R., letter to *Ledger,* Feb. 12, 1852.

4. On the reconstruction of Paris, see for instance, David P. Jordan, *Transforming Paris: The Life and Labors of Baron Haussmann* (New York: Free Press, 1995). On American interest in Haussmann in the Progressive Era, see Rodgers, *Atlantic Crossings,* 166–73. On interest in the Civil War era, see Scobey, *Empire City,* 189–216; Michael Wallace and Edwin Burrows, *Gotham: A History of New York City to 1898* (Oxford: Oxford University Press, 2001), 829; Alan Lessoff, *The Nation and Its City: Politics, "Corruption," and Progress in Washington, D.C., 1861–1902* (Baltimore: Johns Hopkins University Press, 1994), 1; Mona Domosh, *Invented Cities: The Creation of Landscape in Nineteenth-Century New York & Boston* (New Haven, Conn.: Yale University Press, 1996), 110.

5. G., letter to *Bulletin,* Nov. 23, 1853; *Address of the Committee of Seven to the Citizens of Philadelphia* (Philadelphia: Jesper Harding, 1846), 28; *North American,* Dec. 22, 1852; *Ledger,* Apr. 5, 1856.

6. See for instance, John R. Kellett, *The Impact of Railways on Victorian Cities* (London: Routledge, 1969), 68; Dennis, *Cities in Modernity,* 115–16.

7. Civis, letter to *North American,* Feb. 24, 1853; *Ledger,* Aug. 10, 1847; Jan. 11, 1851; Dec. 5, 1855; A Friend to Health, letter to *Ledger,* Apr. 25, 1844.

8. A Citizen, letter to *Ledger,* Aug. 4, 1852.

9. Ibid.; *North American,* May 5, Dec. 22, 1852.

10. Board of Trade, Minutes, Feb. 21, 1853, Philadelphia Board of Trade Records, 1801–1942 (#1791), HSP.

11. Agnes Addison Gilchrist, "Market Houses in High Street," *Transactions of the American Philosophical Society* 43 (1953): 304; Candice L. Harrison, "The Contest of Exchange: Space, Power, and Politics in Philadelphia's Public Markets, 1770–1859," PhD diss., Emory University, 2008, 217–19.

12. Mayor of Philadelphia, Annual Report, 1856, 230; A Constituent, letter to *North American*, Mar. 29, 1852; *North American*, Jan. 17, 1853.

13. Gilchrist, "Market Houses," 306; Senex, letter to *North American*, Feb. 24, 1853; L. W. G., letter to *Bulletin*, Jan. 20, 1853; Americus, letter to *North American*, Mar. 3, 1853.

14. Richard L. Bushman, *The Refinement of America: Persons, Houses, Cities* (New York: Alfred A. Knopf, 1992), xiii, 368–70. On midcentury urban space and class formation, see Gunther Paul Barth, *City People: The Rise of Modern City Culture in Nineteenth-Century America* (Oxford: Oxford University Press, 1980); Scobey, *Empire City*; Stuart M. Blumin, *The Emergence of the Middle Class: Social Experience in the American City, 1760–1900* (Cambridge: Cambridge University Press, 1989), 163–79; Edward Pessen, *Riches, Class and Power Before the Civil War* (Lexington, Mass.: D. C. Heath and Company, 1973), 169–204.

15. *Ledger*, Sept. 6, 1848; *North American*, Feb. 6, 1854; Charles E. Peterson, "Ante-Bellum Skyscraper," *Journal of the Society of Architectural Historians* 9 (1950): 27; Fry, letter to *Bulletin*, June 24, 1856.

16. See for instance, E. K. P. [Eli Kirk Price], letter to *North American*, Oct. 28, 1851; R., letter to *Ledger*, Feb. 12, 1852.

17. Scobey, *Empire City*, 145; Rachel Weber, "Extracting Value from the City: Neoliberalism and Urban Redevelopment," *Antipode* 34 (July 2002), 521–22.

18. See for instance, *Dispatch*, Feb. 20, 1853; Citizen, letter to *Ledger*, Aug. 23, 1854.

19. *Bulletin*, Apr. 3, 1855.

20. *Ledger*, Jan. 28, 1850; Wolcott Calkins et al., *Memorial of Matthias W. Baldwin* (Philadelphia: n.p., 1867), 114–38.

21. *Pittsfield Sun*, Dec. 9, 1858; "Real Estate Book," Joseph Harrison Inventories, 1859, HSP; *Baltimore Sun*, Mar. 21, 1859; Joseph Harrison Jr., *The Iron Worker and King Solomon, with a Memoir and Appendix* (Philadelphia: J. B. Lippincott, 1869), 36; *North American*, Nov. 22, 1856; Nov. 26, 1858; *Ledger*, Nov. 21, 1856. On Harrison, see Sue Himelick Nutty, "John Sartain and Joseph Harrison, Jr.," in *Philadelphia's Cultural Landscape: The Sartain Family Legacy*, ed. Katherine Martinez and Page Talbott (Philadelphia: Temple University Press, 2000), 51–61; Dawson, *Philadelphia Engineers*, 98–99; Baltzell, *Philadelphia Gentlemen*, 183–84.

22. See for example, Health, letter to *North American*, Nov. 21, 1849. *Ledger*, June 18, 1851; W., letter to *North American*, Sept. 9, 1851; *North American*, Jan. 14, 1859; Baltzell, *Philadelphia Gentlemen*, 183–84.

23. *North American*, Sept. 14, 1854; *Ledger*, Apr. 28, 1853.

24. *Ledger*, Sept. 3, 1852; M. D., letter to *Pennsylvania Inquirer*, Oct. 31, 1838; *Pennsylvania Inquirer*, Nov. 10, 1838; Nicholas B. Wainwright, ed.,"The Diary of Samuel Breck, 1839–1840," *PMHB* 103 (1979): 501–2.

25. *Bulletin*, May 10, 1851; *North American*, Feb. 6, 28, Aug. 28, 1854; May 20, 1856; Oct. 11, 1861.

26. *North American*, Apr. 30, 1853; Dec. 16, 1852. On trees and Broad, see also A., letter to *Ledger*, Nov. 13, 1850; X., letter to *Bulletin*, May 5, 1853; Spirit of Penn, letter to *Ledger*, Apr. 28, 1861. On fountains, see A Philadelphian, letter to *Ledger*, May 27, 1851.

27. Schuyler, *New Urban Landscape*; *North American*, Jan. 26, 1854.

28. Anthrax, letter to *Ledger*, Dec. 18, 1851; *Charter, Supplements, and By-Laws of the Point Breeze Park Association* (Philadelphia: Crissy & Markley, 1856), 5, 19–20, 22–23; *North American*, Oct. 2, 1854; June 23, 1855; *Ledger*, Apr. 28, 1853; David Scobey, "Anatomy of a Promenade:

The Politics of Bourgeois Sociability in Nineteenth-Century New York," *Social History* 17 (1992): 203–27.

29. *North American*, Feb. 28, 1854.

30. Ibid., May 28, 1853; Scobey, *Empire City*, 10. See also Chris Otter, "Making Liberalism Durable: Vision and Civility in the Late Victorian City," *Social History* 27 (2002): 6.

31. W., letter to *North American*, Sept. 9, 1851; *Ledger*, June 18, 1851; Improvement, letter to *North American*, July 26, 1851; Mencus, letter to *North American*, May 19, 1851; *North American*, July 16, 1851; Health, letter to *Bulletin*, July 22, 1851; County Medical Society, letter to *North American*, Oct. 25, 1851; *North American*, July 1, 1853; Anthrax, letter to *Ledger*, Dec. 18, 1851. On the development of Philadelphia's parks, see Elizabeth Milroy, *The Grid and the River: Philadelphia's Green Places, 1682–1876* (University Park: Pennsylvania State University Press, 2016).

32. E. K. P. [Eli Kirk Price], letter to *North American*, Oct. 28, 1851; *North American*, May 28, 1853; Jan. 13, 1854; Scobey, *Empire City*, 216. On checkerboard design, see John William Reps, *The Making of Urban America*, 314–22.

33. Harrison, "Philadelphia's Public Markets," 197; E. K. P. [Eli Kirk Price], letter to *North American*, Oct. 28, 1851; J. B. O., letter to *North American*, Mar. 12, 1852.

34. Harrison, "Philadelphia's Public Markets," 196, 208; "Progress in Philadelphia," Poulson Scrap Books, vol. 10, p. 70; L. W. G., letter to *Bulletin*, Jan. 20, 1853; *North American*, Feb. 24, 1853; J. B. O., letter to *North American*, Mar. 12, 1852. On "fogyism," see, for instance, *Bulletin*, Apr. 13, 1853; "Progress vs. Fogyism," [1858?], Poulson Scrap Books, vol. 10, p. 19.

35. *Evening Telegraph*, Dec. 1, 1870; *North American*, Feb. 22, Apr. 18, 1854. For descriptions of the Bedford Street neighborhood as a frontier, see for instance, *North American*, June 1, 1847; Feb. 22, 1854; *Evening Journal*, Apr. 23, 1857.

36. *Inquirer*, Nov. 24, 1860. See also *Sixth Annual Report of the Northern Home for Friendless Children* (Philadelphia: Henry B. Ashmead, 1859), 9–10, which counted Harrison and several Consolidators among its life members.

37. *North American*, Apr. 18, 1854. See also John, the Outcast, *The Homeless Heir, Or, Life in Bedford Street: A Mystery of Philadelphia* (Philadelphia: J. H. C. Whiting, 1856), 4.

38. *Inquirer*, Nov. 24, 1860; *North American*, Apr. 18, 1854; Philanthropos, letter to *North American*, July 31, 1858. See also John, the Outcast, *The Homeless Heir*, 4; *Sixth Annual Report of the Northern Home for Friendless Children*, 9–10.

39. *North American*, Jan. 3, 1853.

40. Upton, *Another City*, 105. On names, see *North American*, May 28, 1845; *Ledger*, Jan. 25, 1853; *Bulletin*, Jan, 29, 1853.

41. *Bulletin*, Jan. 29, 1853; Sewell, *Sorrow's Circuit*, 260, 324–25; Philadelphia Society of Friends, *A Statistical Inquiry into the Condition of the People of Color of the City and Districts of Philadelphia*, (Philadelphia: Kite & Walton, 1849), 38; *Bulletin*, Mar. 7, 1855.

42. *Evening Journal*, Apr. 23, 1857; Dec. 1, 1870; *Dispatch*, Dec. 2, 1866; *Evening Telegraph*, Dec. 1, 1870; July 29, 1873; *Press*, July 21, 1867; *North American*, Apr. 24, 1854.

43. Michael Feldberg, *The Turbulent Era*, 65–70; *United States Gazette*, Aug. 6, 1840; Cope diary, vol. 7, May 7, 1844, 35; Wainwright, "Samuel Breck," 517–18. See also *Dispatch*, Jan. 1, 1854.

44. Schwartz, "To Every Man's Door," 38–39; *North American*, Apr. 6, June 21, Oct. 25, 1854; *Pennsylvanian*, Dec. 18, 1854.

45. *North American*, Dec. 16, 1852; Jan. 30, 1854; May 20, 1856; Hexamer and Locher, Maps of the City of Philadelphia, 1858 to 1860, vol., 3, plate 34 [Greater Philadelphia GeoHistory Network].

46. Notebooks, Cephas Grier Childs Collection (#127), Box 1, vols., 5, 7, HSP.

47. *North American*, June 22, 1846; Prudence, letter to *North American*, May 14, 1852; *North American*, Jan. 25, 1855.

48. A Citizen, letter to *Bulletin*, Mar. 5, 1866; *Commercial List*, Jan. 14, 1854; Scobey, *Empire City*, 136. See also A Philadelphian, letter to *North American*, June 16, 1859.

49. Bushman, *Refinement of America*, 398.

50. Depot, letter to *Commercial List*, May 3, 1851; A Poor Man, letter to *Ledger*, May 7, 1851; Progress, letter to *Ledger*, May 7, 1851; *Ledger*, Dec. 9, 1850; *Dispatch*, May 11, 1851.

51. Letter to *Bulletin*, Mar. 1, 1856; *Dispatch*, Feb. 3, 1850.

52. Solomon K. Hoxie, letters to North American, May 26, June 28, 1859; *A Few Facts and Consideration for Business Men Upon a Delaware Terminus for the Pennsylvania Railroad* (Philadelphia, U.S. Steam-Power and Job Printing Office: 1859), 30.

53. *North American*, May 26, June 28, Aug. 4, 1859; Joseph Harrison, letter to *North American*, June 11, 1859; Coleman Sellers, "An Obituary Notice of Mr. Joseph Harrison, Jr.," *Proceedings of the American Philosophical Society* 14 (1875): 350; *Delaware Terminus for the Pennsylvania Railroad*, 27, 30.

54. Kneass, *Report*, 15; Pennsylvania Railroad, *Thirteenth Annual Report* (Philadelphia: Crissy & Markley, 1860), 12–13; Sellers, "Joseph Harrison," 350.

55. X., letter to *Bulletin*, May 5, 1853.

56. Samuel H. Kneass, *Report on Drainage and Sewerage Made to the Select and Common Councils* (Philadelphia: Crissy & Markley, 1853), 5, 7.

57. See for instance, *Ordinances and Joint Resolutions of the Select and Common Councils of the City of Philadelphia* (Philadelphia: Bicking & Guilbert, 1858). On local government, see William J. Novak, *The People's Welfare: Law and Regulation in Nineteenth-Century America* (Chapel Hill: University of North Carolina Press, 1996); Jon C. Teaford, *The Municipal Revolution in America: Origins of Modern Urban Government, 1650–1825* (Chicago: University of Chicago Press, 1975). On antebellum city debt, see Eric H. Monkkonen, *The Local State: Public Money and American Cities* (Palo Alto, Calif.: Stanford University Press, 1995), 36–37.

58. *Ledger*, Oct. 17, 1848; Nov. 11, 1853.

59. Ibid., May 14, 1847; Aug. 30, 1854; *North American*, May 28, Dec. 20, 1853.

60. *A Further Supplement to an Act Entitled an Act to Incorporate the City of Philadelphia* (Philadelphia: n.p., 1854), 11, 14; *A Further Supplement to an Act Entitled An Act to Incorporate the City of Philadelphia, Passed Jan. 31, 1854, with Further Acts in Relation to the City of Philadelphia* (Philadelphia: Crissy & Markley, 1859), 42, 51–58.

61. *North American*, Dec. 22, 1851; Nov. 8, 1853; July 27, Nov. 21, 1860.

62. Horace Howard Furness to William Henry Furness, Nov. 1, 1855, Furness-Bullitt Family Papers (#1903), Box 1, Folder 2, HSP; Fisher diary, Nov. 28, 1857; Lambda, letter to *North American*, Dec. 30, 1859; David Harvey, *Paris: Capital of Modernity* (London: Routledge, 2003).

63. R. B., "Paris, with American Eyes," *Penn Monthly* 1 (July 1870): 278; *North American*, July 27, 1860; *Press*, June 23, 1863; Fisher diary, Nov. 28, 1857; *Bulletin*, July 16, 1863.

64. C., letters to *North American*, Oct. 3, Oct. 23, 1849; July 27, 1853; *Inquirer*, Apr. 17, 1861; *Ledger*, Aug. 12, 1868. Given the similarities between the letters, it seems likely that "C." was the same writer.

65. *North American*, July 16, 1860.

66. On the affair, see ibid., Sept. 16, 20, 1854; Lorenzo Sabine, *Notes on Duels and Duelling* (London Sampson Low, Son, & Co., 1855), 317–19.

67. Eli Kirk Price, letter to *North American*, May 24, 1855; letter to North American, Oct. 6, 1856.

68. James L. Huston, *The Panic of 1857 and the Coming of the Civil War* (Baton Rouge: Louisiana State University Press, 1987), 17, 23; Fisher diary, Oct. 1, 1857; John C. Bullitt to Mildred Bullitt, Oct. 19, 1857, Furness-Bullitt Family Papers (#1903), Box 2, Folder 17, HSP.

69. For reports of the incident, see *North American*, Nov. 7, 1857, and *Pennsylvanian*, Nov. 7, 1857.

70. Wallach, "Journeymen Printers of Philadelphia," 336.

71. *North American*, Oct. 26, Nov. 10, 11, 13, 1857; The Committee, letter to *Ledger*, Oct. 28, 1857; *Pennsylvanian*, Nov. 10, 1857; *Press*, Nov. 10, 13, 1857.

72. R. J. B., letter to *Press*, Oct. 21, 1857; *North American*, Nov. 13, 1857; Wallach, "Journeymen Printers of Philadelphia," 268; *Pennsylvanian*, Nov. 10, 11, 1857; *Press*, Nov. 13, Dec. 5, 1857.

73. The Committee, letter to *Ledger*, Oct. 28, 1857; *Pennsylvanian*, Nov. 10, 1857. On calls elsewhere, see James L. Huston, *The Panic of 1857 and the Coming of the Civil War* (Baton Rouge: Louisiana State University Press, 1987), 26–27; Wallace and Burrows, *Gotham*, 849–50; Scobey, *Empire City*, 199–200.

74. *Pennsylvanian*, Nov. 11, 1857; *North American*, Nov. 12, 1857.

75. *North American*, Nov. 12, 1857; *Press*, Nov. 11, 1857.

76. *Pennsylvanian*, Nov. 10, 11, 14, 1857; *North American*, Oct. 28, Nov. 14, 1857; Appendix to the *Journal of Select Council*, Nov. 19, 1857 to May 7, 1858, 31; Benjamin J. Klebaner, "Poor Relief and Public Works During the Depression of 1857," *Historian* 22 (1960): 271.

77. *North American*, Oct. 26, 1857; *New York Times*, Oct. 27, 1857; *Press*, Nov. 14, 1857; *Ledger*, Nov. 6, 1857; *Dispatch*, Nov. 15, 1857.

78. Appendix to the *Journal of the Common Council*, May to Nov., 1857, 400–406; *Pennsylvanian*, Nov. 6, 1857.

79. *Press*, Nov. 20, Dec. 5, 1857; *Dispatch*, Nov. 15, Dec. 6, 1857.

80. "City Architecture," *Architectural Review* 1 (Mar. 1869): 596–97.

Chapter 5

1. *Ledger*, Oct. 8, 1860.

2. Robert Cellem, *Visit of His Royal Highness the Prince of Wales to the British North American Provinces and United States* (Toronto: Henry Rowsell, 1861), 378; *Ledger*, Oct. 10, 1860; *Press*, Oct. 10, 1860.

3. K. G. C. [Knights of the Golden Circle?], letter to Alexander Henry, Apr. 17, 1860, Alexander Henry Papers (#278), Box 1, Folder 3, HSP.

4. *North American*, Oct. 10, 1860. See also on the election *Ledger*, Oct. 10, 1860; *Press*, Oct. 10, 1860.

5. Cellem, *Visit of His Royal Highness*, 378.

6. Fisher diary, June 30, 1844; Jan. 7, 1844.

7. Ibid., Jan. 5, 1845; Jan. 13, 1860.

8. Ibid., June, 1844.

9. Ibid., Oct. 31, 1840. On the transformation of politics, see Warner, *Private City*, 79–98; Peter McCaffery, *When Bosses Ruled Philadelphia: The Emergence of the Republican Machine, 1867–1933* (State College, Penn.: Pennsylvania State University Press, 1993), 1–3, 5.

10. Fisher diary, Oct. 21, 1844; Jan. 5, 1845; Alan M. Zachary, "Social Thought in the Philadelphia Leadership Community, 1800–1848," PhD diss., Northwestern University, 1974, 170, 224; J. Francis Fisher, *Reform in Our Municipal Elections: A Plan Suggested to the Tax Payers of Philadelphia and New York* (Philadelphia: William P. Kildare, 1866), 8; J. Francis Fisher, *The Degradation of Our Representative System and Its Reform* (Philadelphia: C. Sherman, Son & Co., 1863); *Ledger*, Sept. 17, 1850. On nativism as a bourgeois antidemocratic movement, see Bruce Levine, "Conservatism, Nativism, and Slavery: Thomas R. Whitney and the Origins of the Know-Nothing Party," *JAH* 88 (2001): 455–88.

11. T., letter to *North American*, Nov. 13, 1849; *Prize Essays on Juvenile Delinquency*, 155.

12. Stephen Colwell, *Politics for American Christians* (Philadelphia: Lippincott, Grambo & Co., 1852), 57; *North American*, June 19, 1847; Mar. 8, 1856; Feb. 10, 1859; Andrew M. Schocket, *Founding Corporate Power in Early National Philadelphia* (DeKalb: Northern Illinois University Press, 2007), 10–11; Cope diary, vol. 10, Oct. 7, 1850; *Ledger*, Oct. 8, 1850; Francis E. Brewster, *The Philosophy of Human Nature* (Philadelphia: Getz & Buck, 1851), 443.

13. *Quaker City*, Sept. 29, 1849; *Fincher's*, July 25, 1863; *Contested Election Between Horn R. Kneass and William B. Reed for the Office of District Attorney of the County of Philadelphia* (Philadelphia: n.p., 1851), 65, 83; Colwell, *Politics for American Christians*, 53; Brewster, *Philosophy of Human Nature*, 381; John F. Watson, *Annals of Philadelphia in the Olden Time* (Philadelphia: Elijah Thomas, 1857), 596.

14. Thomas L. Wharton, *Address Delivered at the Opening of the New Hall of the Athenaeum of Philadelphia* (Philadelphia: John C. Clark, 1847), 13.

15. Wainwright, "Samuel Breck," 501; Regular Ticket, letter to *Bulletin*, Oct 6, 1853; Cope diary, vol. 10, Oct. 7, 1850; *North American*, July 29, 1853.

16. *North American*, Aug. 24, 1853; Jan. 14, 1859; Dec. 16, 1852; Civis, letter to *Bulletin*, Oct. 7, 1853; J. B. O., letter to *North American*, Mar. 12, 1852; An Uncompromising Whig, letter to *Ledger*, Dec. 23, 1852; Ajax, letter to *Inquirer*, Jan. 12, 1861.

17. *North American*, Feb. 19, 1857.

18. Timothy Shay Arthur, *Before and After the Election, or, the Political Experience of Mr. Patrick Murphy* (Philadelphia: J. W. Bradley, 1853), 5, 7, 9, 11–12, 14, 25–32.

19. *Dispatch*, Sept. 9, 1849; Brewster, *Philosophy of Human Nature*, 381.

20. Charles Godfrey Leland, *Memoirs* (London: William Heinemann, 1894), 219; *North American*, May 3, 1858; Colwell, *Politics for American Christians*, 54. On Vaux, see Warner, *Private City*, 91–98.

21. An Old Citizen, letter to Ledger, May 16, 1844; J. J. Ampère, *Promenade En Amérique, Etats-Unis, Cuba, Mexique* (Paris: Michel Lévy Frères, 1860), 412–13; Gallman, *Mastering Wartime*, 171.

22. *Press*, Sept. 25, 1857, in Poulson Scrap Books, vol. 9, p. 75.

23. *Dispatch*, Apr. 11, 1858; W. R. Dickerson, *The Letters of Junius* (Philadelphia: n.p., 1850), 42; *Ledger*, Oct. 25, 1849. On McMullen, see Silcox, *William McMullen*, 34; Ignatiev, *How the Irish Became White*, 160–62.

24. *Press*, Aug. 8, 1857; *Bulletin*, May 27, 1853; *North American*, June 1, 1847; *Ledger*, Sept. 25, 1850; Sept. 28, 1857; Kensington, letter to *Ledger*, Jan. 14, 1851. On the firemen as a political force, see McCaffery, *When Bosses Ruled Philadelphia*, 12.

25. *North American*, Sept. 2, 1850; *Almighty Dollar*, 15.

26. *Press*, Aug. 8, 1857.

27. Ibid.; A Citizen, letter to *Ledger*, Aug. 21, 1850. My reading here is shaped by McNeur, *Taming Manhattan*, 2–3, and Scott, *The Art of Not Being Governed*.

28. *Almighty Dollar*, 15; *Contested Election Between Horn R. Kneass and William B. Reed*, 2; McCaffery, *When Bosses Ruled Philadelphia*, 15.

29. *North American*, Oct. 7, 1853; Apr. 11, 1854; *Dispatch*, June 9, 1850.

30. *North American*, Feb. 21, 1856; J. B. O., letter to *North American*, Mar. 12, 1852; Philanthropos, letter to *North American*, July 31, 1858.

31. Fisher, *Reform in Our Municipal Elections*, 4; A. B., letter to *Pennsylvanian*, May 20, 1858; *Bulletin*, July 16, Sept. 23, 1851. On the process of electing delegates, see *Spirit of the Times*, Dec. 3, 1849; *Ledger*, Aug. 25, 1852. On reform designs, see, for instance, Samuel P. Dinsmore, *Suggestions Touching the Municipal Government of New York* (New York: Hilton & Co., 1860); Fisher, *Reform in Our Municipal Elections*, 22–25.

32. *North American*, July 29, Aug. 9, 16, 1853; Sept. 10, 1859; *Pennsylvania Inquirer*, Aug. 2, 1843; Mullen, *An Appeal to Tax-Payers*, 31. On violence at the meetings, see *New York Times*, Mar. 2, 1852; Brewster, *Philosophy of Human Nature*, 384.

33. Fisher, *Degradation of Our Representative System*, 19–20; *North American*, Sept. 10, 1859; *Dispatch*, Sept. 28, 1851.

34. A Citizen, letter to *Pennsylvanian*, Oct. 31, 1849; *Ledger*, Nov. 17, 1849; *Dispatch*, Jan. 20, 1850.

35. Penn, letter to *Ledger*, Mar. 25, 1850; *Dispatch*, June 9, 1850; *Ledger*, Aug. 26, 1850; *Bulletin*, Oct. 9, 1850.

36. *Germantown Telegraph*, Feb. 12, 1851. On the bill's fate, see *Dispatch*, Apr. 13, 1851; Ingles, letter to *Ledger*, Apr. 14, 1851.

37. *Bulletin*, Oct. 1, 4, 1853.

38. A Ledger Man, letter to *Ledger*, Apr. 4, 1851; *Bulletin*, Oct. 1, 4, 1853; *Dispatch*, Sept. 21, 1851; *Ledger*, Sept. 18, 1851. On Penniman, see Laurie, *Working People of Philadelphia*, 111, 114.

39. *Bulletin*, Oct. 1, 1853.

40. *North American*, June 28, 1853; *Ledger*, July 6, 1853; Report of the Committee Appointed to Devise a Plan for the Better Organization of the Fire Department," Box 1, Folder 23, MC 1999.13, Eli Kirk Price Collection, Archives and Special Collections, Dickinson College; Wood, *Richard D. Wood*, vol. 2, p. 65; Price, *Consolidation*, 18–19.

41. *North American*, Aug. 11, Oct. 7, 1853; *Bulletin*, Sept. 20, Oct. 1, 1853; Price, *Consolidation*, 20, 23.

42. *North American*, Dec. 30, 1853.

43. *Bulletin*, Oct. 15, 1853.

44. Warner, *Private City*, 86–87.

45. American Consolidationists, letter to *Ledger*, Oct. 15, 1853.

46. Eli Kirk Price and Levi Foulkrod, letter to *North American*, May 1, 1854; *Ledger*, Mar. 28, 1844; *North American*, Mar. 1, 1854.

47. J. S. P. [Jacob S. Price?], letter to *North American*, Nov. 26, 1853. Pennsylvania Senate, *Consolidation*, 12; [Thomas M. Coleman], *Daguerreotype Sketches of the Members of First Common Council, After Consolidation, for 1854 and 1855* (Philadelphia: W. H. Sickels, 1855), 36, 110.

48. Franklin, letter to *Ledger*, Mar. 14, 1851; *Ledger*, Sept. 17, 1850; *North American*, Nov. 19, 1853.

49. *North American*, Mar. 8, 1856.

50. Henry C. Carey, *The Harmony of Interests: Agricultural, Manufacturing, and Commercial* (Philadelphia: Henry Carey Baird, 1865), 202.

51. Eli Kirk Price, "The Family as an Element of Government," *Proceedings of the American Philosophical Society* 9 (June, 1863): 306–9, 315–18.

52. *North American*, June 10, 1846.

53. Robert T. Conrad, *An Address Delivered Before the Literary Societies of Pennsylvania College, Gettysburg, September 15, 1852* (Philadelphia: Crissy & Markley, 1852), 27; *Bulletin*, Feb. 5, 1853; Eli K. Price and Levi Foulkrod, letter to *North American*, May 1, 1854; T. S., letter to *Ledger*, Apr. 19, 1849; *Prize Essays on Juvenile Delinquency*, 110.

54. Brown, *Baldwin Locomotive Works*, 136–37; E., letter to *North American*, Mar. 26, 1850; *Prize Essays on Juvenile Delinquency*, 112; *Pennsylvanian*, Oct. 2, 1857.

55. *North American*, Sept. 21, 1854; *Prize Essays on Juvenile Delinquency*, 122; Geo. Bayne, letters to *North American*, Aug. 29, 1851; Feb. 16, 1852; *Ledger*, Aug. 30, 1854. McMichael's paper endorsed a similar design to Bayne's but proposed that "public spirited capitalists" should build it. See *North American*, Jan. 3, 1854. On feminist designs from the period, see Dolores Hayden, *The Grand Domestic Revolution: A History of Feminist Designs for American Homes, Neighborhoods, and Cities* (Cambridge, Mass.: MIT Press, 1981), 68–79.

56. *North American*, Apr. 29, 1854; July 10, 1854; Sept. 4, 1857; July 8, 1859; George Francis Train, *Observations on Street Railways* (London: Sampson Low, Son, & Co., 1860), 74.

57. *North American*, Mar. 22, June 16, 1859; Nov. 8, 1862; Jacob Dewees, *Pennsylvania in Self-Defence: An Appeal to the Legislature and the People Upon the Rights of Labor* (Philadelphia: H. Orr, 1859), 43.

58. *A Consideration of the Subject of the Central Passenger Railway* (Philadelphia: W. B. Zieber, 1858), 5; Hepp, *Middle-Class City*, 25.

59. *North American*, July 4, 1856; Feb. 10, 1859.

60. Price, "Family," 319–20.

61. Conrad, *Address*, 27; A City Voter, letter to *Ledger*, June 24, 1851; *North American*, Mar. 13, 1854.

62. Charles Tilly, *Big Structures, Large Processes, Huge Comparisons* (New York: Russell Sage Foundation, 1984), 2–4.

63. William B. Reed, letter to *North American*, Aug. 10, 1855; William B. Reed, *A Paper Containing a Statement and Vindication of Certain Political Opinions* (Philadelphia: John Campbell, 1862), 21; A. B., letter to *Ledger*, Feb. 4, 1851. One historian argues that mercantile opposition to centralization blocked Consolidation. See Dawson, *Philadelphia Engineers*, 131.

64. Pennsylvania Senate, *Minority Report of the Select Committee on the Subject of the Consolidation of the City of Philadelphia*, 3, 20–21.

65. Joseph C. Martindale, *A History of the Townships of Byberry and Moreland* (Philadelphia: George W. Jacobs, 1901), 183; letter to *Germantown Telegraph*, Feb. 7, 1855; Tax-Payer, letter to *Germantown Telegraph*, Feb. 27, 1856; *Inquirer*, Apr. 5, 1861. See also *North American*, Jan. 19, 1861.

66. *Dispatch*, Mar. 30, 1851; *Bulletin*, Nov. 11, 1849; Mar. 27, 1851; Pennsylvania Senate, *Minority Report*, 5–7.

67. A City Voter, letters to *Ledger*, July 22, Aug. 30, 1851.

68. Anti-Aristocracy, letter to *Ledger*, Oct. 11, 1853; *Ledger*, Oct. 10, 11, 1853.

69. W. S. [William Still], letter to *North American*, Aug. 31, 1859; *Press*, Sept. 4, 1860; Martindale, *Byberry and Moreland*, 183. On African Americans and bourgeois respectability, see for example, Julie Winch, ed., *The Elite of Our People: Joseph Willson's Sketches of Upper-Class Life in Antebellum Philadelphia* (University Park: Pennsylvania State University Press, 2000).

70. *North American*, Sept. 12, 1848; Jan, 25, 1850; Aug. 17, 1853; *Bulletin*, Nov. 30, 1855; [Stephen Colwell], *The South: A Letter From a Friend in the North With Special Reference to the Effects of Disunion Upon Slavery* (Philadelphia: C. Sherman and Son, 1856), 11–12; Calkins, Miller, and Chandler, *Matthias W. Baldwin*, 147–49.

71. *North American*, Dec. 8, 1859; Eli Kirk Price, letter to *North American*, Oct. 11, 1860.

72. *North American*, Dec. 8, 1859; Dec. 14, 1860; *Inquirer*, Dec. 14, 1860.

73. E. K. P. [Eli Kirk Price], letter to *North American*, Dec. 10, 1860; *North American*, Dec. 8, 1859; [Colwell], *Effects of Disunion*, 27.

74. [Colwell], *Effects of Disunion*, 43.

75. *North American*, June 17, 1856.

76. Rodney J. Morrison, "Henry C. Carey and American Economic Development," *Transactions of the American Philosophical Society* 76 (1986): 44; *Dispatch*, Mar. 21, 1858; *North American*, May 3, 1858. On the Republicans' early appeal in Philadelphia, see McCaffery, *When Bosses Ruled Philadelphia*, 7–9.

77. See for instance, reports of councils in *Press*, Oct. 7, 1857; *North American*, Oct. 9, 16, 1857; *Pennsylvanian*, Oct. 20, Dec. 4, 1857.

78. *North American*, May 3, 1858; Apr. 5, 1859; Apr. 19, 1860; *Pennsylvanian*, June 7, 1858; *Sunday Atlas*, Dec. 5, 1858.

79. Observer, letter to *North American*, June 4, 1859; *North American*, Mar. 24, Apr. 15, 1859; *Ledger*, Mar. 24, 1859; *Pennsylvanian*, Mar. 31, 1859.

80. Eli Kirk Price, letter to *North American*, Oct. 11, 1860; *North American*, Oct. 9, 1860.

81. Kilbride, *American Aristocracy*, 50–52, 155; Fisher diary, Dec. 3, 1859; Jan. 1, 1860.

82. Fisher diary, Nov. 6, 1860.

83. *North American*, Apr. 19, 1860.

84. Ibid., May 4, 1858; Apr. 5, 1859; McCaffery, *When Bosses Ruled Philadelphia*, 15.

85. On the persistence of localism after Consolidation, see Steinberg, *Transformation of Criminal Justice*, 150.

Chapter 6

1. Leland, *Memoirs*, 136, 170–83, 216–20, 229, 237, 242–43.

2. Charles Godfrey Leland, *Centralization or "States Rights"* (New York: C. T. Evans, 1863), 4–7, 10.

3. Leland, *Memoirs*, 213; Leland, *Centralization*, 2–4, 6, 10.

4. *North American*, Mar. 14, 1855; *Inquirer*, July 2, 1872.

5. *North American*, July 16, Oct. 16, 1863. For a comparison that tried to distinguish between the Draft Riots and violence in Philadelphia, see *Bulletin*, July 16, 1863.

6. Weigley, "Border City," 372, 390; *Appendix to Journal of Common Council* (Philadelphia: King & Baird, 1861), 154; Untitled, Dec. 1860?, Alexander Henry Papers, Box 1, Folder 5, HSP; Gallman, *Mastering Wartime*, 170–92; *Evening Telegraph*, Jan. 1, 1866.

7. *Chronicle of the Union League of Philadelphia, 1862–1902* (Philadelphia: n.p., 1902), 51; Hampton L. Carson, *The Centenary of the Wistar Party: An Historical Address* (Philadelphia: Printed for the Wistar Association, 1918), 23.

8. Charles Ingersoll, *A Letter to a Friend in a Slave State* (Philadelphia: J. Campbell, 1862); Gary B. Nash, *First City: Philadelphia and the Forging of Historical Memory* (Philadelphia: University of Pennsylvania Press, 2002), 231; Kilbride, *American Aristocracy*, 5; Russell F. Weigley, "'A Peaceful City': Public Order in Philadelphia from Consolidation through the Civil War," in *Peoples of Philadelphia*, ed. Davis and Haller, 160–64; Dawson, *Philadelphia Engineers*, 145; *Chronicle of the Union League*, 38. On Philadelphia's southern sympathies, see for instance, Kilbride, *American Aristocracy*, 153–55.

9. Domenic Vitiello, "Engineering the Metropolis: The Sellers Family and Industrial Philadelphia," PhD diss., University of Pennsylvania, 2004, 214; *Evening Telegraph*, May 8, 1871; *North American*, Aug. 2, 20, 1861. On antiparty nationalism, see Adam I. P. Smith, *No Party Now: Politics in the Civil War North* (Oxford: Oxford University Press, 2006).

10. *Chronicle of the Union League*, 39, 44; Weigley, "'A Peaceful City,'" 167–69.

11. Melinda Lawson, "'A Profound National Devotion': The Civil War Union Leagues and the Construction of a New National Patriotism," *Civil War History* 48 (2002): 338–62; Dawson, *Philadelphia Engineers*, 142; *Chronicle of the Union League*, 373; Gallman, *Mastering Wartime*, 9.

12. William B. Reed, letter to *North American*, Aug. 10, 1855. Membership data come from *Proceedings of a Meeting of the Union Club of Philadelphia* (Philadelphia: J. B. Lippincott, 1871); *Chronicle of the Union League*, 461–524.

13. *North American*, Aug. 13, 1861.

14. Andrew Diemer, "Reconstructing Philadelphia: African Americans and Politics in the Post-Civil War North," *PMHB* 133 (2009): 33–34. On Philadelphia's African American population, see Gary B. Nash, *Forging Freedom: The Formation of Philadelphia's Black Community, 1720–1840* (Cambridge, Mass.: Harvard University Press, 1988); Winch, *Elite of Our People*; Roger Lane, *William Dorsey's Philadelphia and Ours: On the Past and Future of the Black City in America* (Oxford: Oxford University Press, 1991); Theodore Hershberg, Alan N. Burstein, Eugene P. Ericksen, Stephanie W. Greenberg, and William L. Yancey, "A Tale of Three Cities: Blacks, Immigrants, and Opportunity in Philadelphia, 1850–1880, 1930, 1970," in *Philadelphia: Work, Space, Family, and Group Experience in the Nineteenth Century: Essays Toward an Interdisciplinary History of the City*, ed. Theodore Hershberg (Oxford: Oxford University Press, 1981), 461–85.

15. Gallman, *Mastering Wartime*, 45–46; Isaac Leach to John Campbell, Aug. 16, 1864, Box 3a, Subseries 3.1, William J. Campbell Bookstore Records (SCRC 167), Temple University; *Christian Recorder*, Oct. 10. 1863.

16. J. C. Davis et al., *An Appeal from the Colored Men of Philadelphia to the President of the United States* (Philadelphia: n.p., 1862), 5–6; W. S. [William Still], letter to *North American*, Aug. 31, 1859; William Still, *Still's Underground Rail Road Records* (Philadelphia: William Still, 1886), lv–lvii.

17. Leland, *Memoirs*, 137.

18. *At a Meeting Held at Concert Hall, on Friday Evening, the 13th Instant, the Following Resolutions Were Unanimously Adopted* (Philadelphia: n.p., 1865). See also William Still et al., "Petition for the Colored People of Philadelphia to Ride in the Cars," June 10, 1862, Box 3A,

folder Oversize 73, HSP Miscellaneous Collection (#425). In the 1862 petition, Price and McMichael are among the signatories. On calls for voting rights, see the speech of Charles Gibbons in *Proceedings of the Union League of Philadelphia, in Commemoration of the Eighty-Ninth Anniversary of American Independence* (Philadelphia: King & Baird, 1865), 30–31.

19. *Evening Telegraph*, Jan. 1, 1866.

20. Fisher diary, Jan. 20, 1866; July 4, 1869; Diemer, "Reconstructing Philadelphia," 62–63.

21. *Proceedings of the National Convention of Manufacturers Held at Cleveland, Ohio* (Cleveland, Ohio: Sanford & Hayward, 1867), 14; William D. Kelley, *The Safeguards of Personal Liberty* (Philadelphia: Merrihew & Son, 1865).

22. Walter Licht, "Civil Wars, 1850–1900," in *Pennsylvania: A History of the Commonwealth*, ed. Randall M. Miller and William Pencak (State College, Pa.: Pennsylvania State University Press, 2002), 232; Gallman, *Mastering Wartime*, 255; *Press*, May 21, 1867.

23. *Evening Telegraph*, Jan. 2, 15, 1866; Philadelphia Board of Trade, Annual Report, 1865, pp. 19–20, HSP.

24. Benjamin Harris Brewster, *Address of the Hon. Benj. Harris Brewster at a Meeting of Excursionists Near Fort Harker, Kansas* (Philadelphia: Review Printing House, 1867), 13, 15.

25. *Press*, June 21, 1867; *Evening Telegraph*, Jan. 25, 1866; *North American*, Mar. 27, 1867.

26. *Press*, May 21, 1867.

27. [William Russell West], *Broad Street, Penn Square, and the Park* (Philadelphia: Jno. Pennington & Son, 1871), 3; *North American*, Aug. 10, 1865.

28. *North American*, Aug 9, 1859; Mar. 30, 1866; Apr. 1, 1867.

29. *North American*, Oct. 29, 1870; Penn, letter to *Telegraph*, Mar. 29, 1871; Henry C. Townsend to Public Buildings Commission, PBC: History (160.32), vol. 1, 87.

30. *Ledger*, Mar. 22, 1866; John W. Forney, *Letters from Europe* (Philadelphia: T. B. Peterson & Brothers, 1867), 129.

31. *Ledger*, Mar. 22, 1866; R. B., "Paris with American Eyes," 273, 278, 288, 291, 292.

32. C., letter to *Ledger*, Aug. 12, 1868; *Bulletin*, July 26, 1867.

33. *Inquirer*, Sept. 25, 1867. On valuation, see *North American*, Mar. 24, 1854; *Inquirer*, Jan. 12, 1867. On the Board in city government, see Edward P. Allinson and Boies Penrose, *Philadelphia, 1681–1887: A History of Municipal Development* (Baltimore: Johns Hopkins University Press, 1887), 237–38; J. T. Rothrock, "Biographical Memoir of the Late Honorable Eli K. Price, LL.D.," *Proceedings of the American Philosophical Society* 23 (1886): 591.

34. Penn, letter to *Germantown Telegraph*, July 12, 1871.

35. *Dispatch*, Apr. 5, 1867; R., letter to *North American*, July 12, 1867.

36. Henry C. Townsend to Public Buildings Commission, PBC: History (160.32), vol. 1, 87; *South Broad Street, Philadelphia*, (Philadelphia: n.p., 1870). Details of the meeting are drawn from the *North American*, July 1, 1870; *Morning Post*, July 1, 1870; *Age*, July 1, 1870; *Press*, July 1, 1870; *Ledger*, July 2, 1870; *Dispatch*, July 3, 1870; *Sunday Morning Times*, July 3, 1870.

37. See for example, Lawrence N. Powell, *New Masters: Northern Planters During the Civil War and Reconstruction* (New York: Fordham University Press, 1999).

38. Beneficent Building Association, *Second Annual Report of the Board of Managers*, (Philadelphia: William F. Kildare, 1871), 3, 8; Eli Kirk Price, "The Plague Spot," May 1879, in Price Family Papers (#3690), HSP.

39. Beneficent Building Association, *Seventh Annual Report of the Board of Managers*, (Philadelphia: n.p., 1876), 2.

40. *Press*, Nov. 14, 1874; Philadelphia Fountain Society, Annual Reports, 7, 11, 15, 22; "Philadelphia Fountain Society," Fairmont Park Art Association Records (#2045), HSP.

41. *Morning Post*, July 1, 1870; *North American*, Feb. 28, 1854; Dan Rottenberg, *The Man Who Made Wall Street: Anthony J. Drexel and the Rise of Modern Finance* (Philadelphia: University of Pennsylvania Press, 2001), 78. Grant never occupied the house. Two days after it was presented to him, Lincoln's assassination forced him to return to Washington.

42. *North American*, Mar. 21, 1867; *Age*, July 1, 1870; *Ledger*, July 1, 1870.

43. *Press*, Mar. 13, 1865; "Wherein the National Debt May Be Made a National Blessing," Jay Cooke Papers (#0148), HSP, Box 99, Folder 3.

44. Melinda Lawson, *Patriot Fires: Forging a New American Nationalism in the Civil War North* (Lawrence: University Press of Kansas, 2002), 42–43, 58.

45. Warner, *Private City*, 84; *General Organization for the Relief of the Poor: A Plan for the Consolidation of Charities* (Philadelphia: King & Baird, 1855); Citizens Association of Pennsylvania, *An Address to the People with Act of Incorporation* (Philadelphia: Henry B. Ashmead, 1866); Citizens Association of Pennsylvania, *First Annual Report* (Philadelphia: Henry B. Ashmead, 1867); *North American*, May 3, 1866; Sarah W. Tracy, *Alcoholism in America: From Reconstruction to Prohibition* (Baltimore: Johns Hopkins University Press, 2005), 111; *Dispatch*, July 15, 1866.

46. Pennsylvania Senate, *Consolidation*, 13.

47. Gallman, *Mastering Wartime*, 28; Mayor of Philadelphia, Annual Report, 1864, p. 5. On Civil War recruitment, see James W. Geary, *We Need Men: The Union Draft in the Civil War* (DeKalb: Northern Illinois University Press, 1991); 85, 113. On Philadelphia in particular, see William Dusinberre, *Civil War Issues in Philadelphia* (Philadelphia: University of Pennsylvania Press, 1965), 160–61.

48. "Office of the Mayor of Philadelphia, Mar. 30, 1864," Box 1, Folder 13, Alexander Henry Papers (#278), HSP; *Age*, Mar. 29. 1865; *Common Sense About Taxes, no. 2* (Philadelphia: n.p., 1867), 2.

49. *North American*, Apr. 24, June 25, 1867.

50. "Act of Aug, 1870, P. Law 1548," Eli Kirk Price journal (#3589), HSP.

51. Mayor of Philadelphia, Annual Report, 1864, pp. vi, 5; Penn, letter to *Germantown Telegraph*, Mar. 29, 1871.

52. *Sunday Morning Times*, Dec. 29, 1872; Milroy, *Grid and the River*, 270–303; "New Public Buildings," *Centennial* (Dec. 1875): 1; *Press*, Nov. 6, 1874.

53. *North American*, Apr. 28, 1859. On Carey, see Paul K. Conkin, *Prophets of Prosperity: America's First Political Economists* (Bloomington: Indiana University Press, 1980), 261–312; Andrew Dawson, "Reassessing Henry Carey: The Problems of Writing Political Economy in Nineteenth-Century America," *Journal of American Studies* 34 (2000): 465–85.

54. [Colwell], *Effects of Disunion*, 11–12; Burt, *Perennial Philadelphians*, 407.

55. William H. Goetzmann, *Beyond the Revolution: A History of American Thought from Paine to Pragmatism* (New York: Basic Books, 2009), 77–78; William D. Kelley, *Letters from Europe* (Philadelphia: Porter and Coates, 1879), 4–5.

56. *North American*, Apr. 28, 1859. On Carey, interdependence, and association, see Howe, *Political Culture of the American Whigs*, 115; Sklansky, *Soul's Economy*, 91–92. On Carey, as the voice of Philadelphia's industrialists, see Dawson, "Reassessing Henry Carey," 465–85.

57. [Matthew Carey], *Plea for the Poor* (Philadelphia: L. R. Bailey, 1837).

58. Gallman, *Mastering Wartime*, 225.

59. NTU Minutes, Feb. 6, 1858; Jan. 25, 1860 (#2076), HSP; Brown, *Baldwin Locomotive Works*, 22–24; Dawson, *Philadelphia Engineers*, 137; *Ledger*, Mar. 10, 1860; N. B. Thayer and Samuel Blakeley, letter to *Fincher's*, Sept. 24, 1864; *Press*, Mar. 9, 1860.

60. *Fincher's*, June 6, Nov. 7, Dec. 5, 1863; W. D. Robinson, letter to *Fincher's*, May 7, 1864; William Abels, letter to *Fincher's*, Apr. 16, 1864; Journeymen Morocco Finishers' Association, letter to *Fincher's*, June 18, 1864; Charles H. Schurch, letters to *Fincher's*, Aug. 6, Oct. 15, 1864; John Shedden et al., letter to *Fincher's*, Oct. 31, 1863; Worker, letter to *Fincher's*, July 4, 1863; William H. Sylvis, letter to *Fincher's*, Aug. 17, 1863; Gallman, *Mastering Wartime*, 234–35; Dawson, *Philadelphia Engineers*, 138.

61. *Fincher's*, Aug. 1, 8, 1863; June 18, 1864; W. H. S. [William H. Sylvis], letter to *Fincher's*, May 14, 1863.

62. *Fincher's*, June 20, 1863; July 9, 1864; Shedden et al., letter to *Fincher's*, Oct. 31, 1863.

63. Weigley, "Border City," 373; *Fincher's*, Nov. 7, 1863.

64. S. B., letter to *Fincher's*, Jan. 9, Feb. 6, 1864; *Fincher's*, July 11, Sept. 19, 1863; Jan. 21, 1865.

65. *Fincher's*, Apr. 1, Mar. 25, 1865.

66. *Fincher's*, Feb. 6, 27, Nov. 19, 1864; Mar. 25, 1865; letter to *Evening Telegraph*, Apr. 6, 1866; John R. Commons et al., ed., *A Documentary History of American Industrial Society*, vol. 9 (Cleveland: The Arthur H. Clark Company, 1910), 139, 150–51.

67. William H. Sylvis, *Fellow Workingmen of Philadelphia* (1865), Hagley Library Collection.

68. *North American*, July 28, 1858; Aug. 26, 1859; *Fincher's*, June 6, July 18, 1863; Gallman, *Mastering Wartime*, 232, 237–38; N. B. Thayer, letter to *Fincher's*, Aug. 27, 1864; *Dispatch*, Feb. 20, 1858.

69. Foner, *Reconstruction*, xxiv.

70. *Bulletin*, Nov. 30, 1865; Feb. 7, 1867; Apr. 29, 1869; James C. Sylvis, *The Life, Speeches, Labors and Essays of William H. Sylvis* (Philadelphia: Claxton, Remsen & Haffelfinger, 1872), 105, 161.

71. Ira V. Brown, "William D. Kelley and Radical Reconstruction," *PMHB* 75 (1961): 316; Reinhard O. Johnson, *The Liberty Party, 1840–1848: Antislavery Third-Party Politics in the United States* (Baton Rouge: Louisiana State University Press, 2009), 63–64, 158; Carl J. Guarneri, *The Utopian Alternative: Fourierism in Nineteenth-Century America* (Ithaca, N.Y.: Cornell University Press, 1994), 245, 468; Elder, *Periscopics*, 242–46; Elder, *Third Parties*; William Elder, *How Our National Debt Can Be Paid: The Wealth, Resources, and Power of the People of the United States* (Philadelphia: Sherman & Co., 1865), 5, 8–12.

72. Morrison, "Henry C. Carey," 61; *Quaker City*, Apr. 14, 1849; Elder, *Periscopics*, 234.

73. Elder, *Questions of the Day*, 9, 248–51.

74. Ibid., 260, 297, 313, 326, 328.

75. William D. Kelley, *An Address Delivered by Hon. William D. Kelley at Girard Avenue, Above Eleventh St., on October 3, 1856* (Philadelphia: Sunday Morning Times, 1856), 10.

76. *Inquirer*, Apr. 11, Nov. 25, 1872; Lorin Blodget, "A Building System for the Great Cities," *Penn Monthly* 8 (Apr. 1877): 285–304; *Dispatch*, Aug. 22, 1875; William F. Channing, "Organized Homesteads and Households," *The Popular Science Monthly* (Oct. 1876), 733–38; Walter Licht, *Getting Work: Philadelphia, 1840–1950* (Cambridge, Mass.: Harvard University

Press, 1992), 249; Richard N. Juliani, "The Origin and the Development of the Italian Community in Philadelphia," in *The Ethnic Experience in Pennsylvania*, ed. John E. Bodnar (Lewisburg, Pa.: Bucknell University Press, 1973), 249. On guidance for their use, see for instance, discussion of the monthly *Building Association Journal* in the *Inquirer*, Nov. 25, 1872; Edmund Wrigley, *How to Manage Building Associations* (Philadelphia: James K. Simon, 1873).

77. *North American*, Aug. 28, 1860; *Inquirer*, Feb. 25, 1861; *Bulletin*, Sept. 14, 1864; "Dwellings for the Poor," *The Medical and Surgical Reporter* 6 (Apr. 1861): 51.

78. Forney, *Letters from Europe*, 62–69.

79. George Bayne, letters to *North American*, Aug. 29, 1851; Feb. 16, 1852; George Bayne to Oliver Otis Howard, June 1, 1865, Register and Letters Received by the Commissioner, 1865–1872, M752, roll 13, images 683–86, Records of Bureau of Refugees, Freedman and Abandoned Lands and Freedman's Saving, National Archives, Record Group 105, [accessed via Family Search Online]; Julie Saville, *The Work of Reconstruction: From Slave to Wage Laborer in South Carolina, 1860–1870* (Cambridge: Cambridge University Press, 1994), 46; Fisher diary, Nov. 28, 1865; Channing, "Homesteads and Households," 737.

80. Blodget, "Building System," 286, 294. The importance of housing to the SSA is pointed out in Alewitz, *Filthy Dirty*, 25.

81. Jackson, letter to *Evening Star*, Aug. 13, 1867; Joseph I. Doran, "The Operations of Our Building Associations," Philadelphia Social Science Association, *Papers*, Van Pelt Library, University of Pennsylvania, Philadelphia; Blodget, "Building System," 291. Historians have sometimes offered qualified support for claims the associations ameliorated social tensions. See for instance, Nash, *First City*, 287; George E. Thomas, *William L. Price: Arts and Crafts to Modern Design* (New York: Princeton Architectural Press, 2000), 16.

82. *Inquirer*, Oct. 26, 1874; Blodget, "Building System," 297; *Dispatch*, Aug. 22, 1875; *North American*, Aug. 9, 1859; Gallman, *Mastering Wartime*, 228; Elder, *Questions of the Day*, 323. My estimate of employment in building-related trades is based on figures from the 1870 Census of Manufactures.

83. Bruno Giberti, *Designing the Centennial: A History of the 1876 International Exhibition in Philadelphia* (Lexington: University Press of Kentucky, 2002), 76; Hodos, *Second Cities*, 157, 159; Milroy, *Grid and the River*, 322–30; Nash, *First City*, 287; Amanda Casper, "Row Houses," *Encyclopedia of Greater Philadelphia* (Philadelphia: University of Pennsylvania Press, 2016), online edition, http://philadelphiaencyclopedia.org/archive/row-houses/.

84. Robert W. Rydell, *All the World's a Fair: Visions of Empire at American International Expositions, 1876–1916* (Chicago: University of Chicago Press, 1984), 27–29, 34–35; Alexander Henry to John Welsh (1876?), Alexander Henry Papers (#278), Box 2, Folder 2, HSP.

Chapter 7

1. William D. Kelley, *The New Northwest* (n.p., 1871), 13, 29–30.

2. Ibid., 28.

3. Charles M. S. Leslie to Roland Seegar, 1873, (#1995), HSP.

4. Richard White, *Railroaded: The Transcontinentals and the Making of Modern America* (New York: W. W. Norton & Co., 2011), 74.

5. W. E. B. Du Bois, *Black Reconstruction in America: An Essay Toward a History of the Part Which Black Folk Played in the Attempt to Reconstruct Democracy in America, 1860–1880* (London: Cass, 1966); Foner, *Reconstruction*; Heather Cox Richardson, *The Death of Reconstruction: Race, Labor, and Politics in the Post-Civil War North, 1865–1901* (Cambridge, Mass.:

Harvard University Press, 2001). For an interpretation of the Panic particularly attentive to political dynamics, see Nicolas Barreyre, *Gold and Freedom: The Political Economy of Recon-struction* (Charlottesville: University of Virginia Press, 2016). On antidemocratic thought in the 1870s North, see Alexander Keyssar, *The Right to Vote: The Contested History of Democracy in the United States* (New York: Basic Books, 2000), 94–138.

6. *Ledger*, Mar. 22, 1866; R. B., "Paris, With American Eyes," 278; Henry C. Carey, *Review of the Decade, 1857–1867* (Philadelphia: Collins, Printer, 1867), 21–24; John Forney, letter to *Press*, July 8, 1867; *North American*, June 29, 1869; Forney, *Letters from Europe*, 126–28.

7. *North American*, July 2, 1868; June 29, 1869; *Germantown Telegraph*, Mar. 29, 1871.

8. *Inquirer*, May 15, 24, 1871; *Ledger*, May 30, 1871; Price, *Act for the Sale of Real Estate*, 182. The Philadelphia pattern was replicated elsewhere in the United States. See for instance, Philip Mark Katz, *From Appomattox to Montmartre: Americans and the Paris Commune* (Cambridge, Mass.: Harvard University Press, 1998); Beckert, *Monied Metropolis*, 179–81.

9. On the translation of Haussmann's ideas elsewhere in the 1870s, see Lessoff, *The Nation and Its City*, 68–71.

10. *Sunday Morning Times*, Nov. 20, 1870; Fisher diary, Apr. 7, 1867; Apr. 16, May 16, June 12, July 18, 1869; Mar. 1, 1870.

11. *Dispatch*, Mar. 1, 1867; Gillette, "Corrupt and Contented," 143–44.

12. McCaffery, *When Bosses Ruled Philadelphia*, xx.

13. Nash, *First City*, 253.

14. McCaffery, *When Bosses Ruled Philadelphia*, 5; Eli Kirk Price, letter to *North American*, June 17, 1874. On the PFC, see Milroy, *Grid and the River*, 274, 316.

15. Gillette, "Corrupt and Contented," 71–72; Price, *Objections to the Proposed Constitution*, 14, 16.

16. On the funding of local improvements, see Robin L. Einhorn, *Property Rules: Political Economy in Chicago, 1833–1872* (Chicago: University of Chicago Press, 2001), xv. For the case, see *Hammett v. Philadelphia*, May 11, 1869, 65 Pa. 146; 1869 Pa. LEXIS 274.

17. *Morning Post*, July 1, 1870.

18. *Sunday Morning Times*, July 10, 1870; *North American*, July 19, 1871.

19. Einhorn, *Property Rules*, xvi.

20. *Inquirer*, Jan. 18, 19, 1870; *North American*, June 17, 1870.

21. *Inquirer*, Jan. 19, 1870; *North American*, Feb. 7, 1871; *Sunday Morning Times*, May 29, 1870; Citizens' Association for the Improvement of the Streets and Roads of Philadelphia, *First Annual Report* (Philadelphia: J. Moore & Sons, 1871), 4; Instructions for R. S. Randall from Henry Charles Lea (1860–1861), 1, Henry Charles Lea Papers, Kislak Center for Special Collections, Rare Books and Manuscripts, University of Pennsylvania (hereafter cited as Lea Papers).

22. Scobey, *Empire City*, 204–9; Girard College, *In the Matter of the Opening of Girard Avenue and Twenty-Second Street Through the Grounds of Girard College* (Philadelphia: G. V. Town & Son, 1874), 12.

23. *North American*, Jan. 23, 1875; *Dispatch*, Jan. 30, 1870.

24. *Sunday Morning Times*, Mar. 17, Apr. 21, Oct. 20, 1872; John Jay Smith, *Recollections of John Jay Smith*, (Philadelphia: Lippincott, 1892), 295–96.

25. "Fifty Reasons for Abolishing the Building Commission," p. 1, Lea Papers.

26. On the CMRA and the wider culture of bourgeois reform, see McCaffery, *When Bosses Ruled Philadelphia*, 48–59.

27. Howard Gillette Jr., "Philadelphia's City Hall: Monument to a New Political Machine," *PMHB* 97 (1973): 233–49.

28. *Bulletin*, Sept. 20, 1870; [West], *Broad Street, Penn Square, and the Park*. The copy of the pamphlet in the Henry Charles Lea collection in Van Pelt Library, University of Pennsylvania, includes a handwritten preamble by Thomas Webster, explaining the design's role in the reform movement. See Lea Papers, Box 164, Folder 2101.

29. *Inquirer*, Mar. 15, 1871.

30. Ibid.

31. Citizen, letter to *Inquirer*, Nov. 20, 1871; Doran, "Operations of Our Building Associations," 16; "Citizens' Municipal Reform Association to the Building Associations of the City," Lea Papers, Box 165, Folder 2109; Citizens' Municipal Reform Association, "To the Householders and Members of Building Associations of Philadelphia," 1–2, Lea Papers, Box 165, Folder 2109.

32. McCaffery, *When Bosses Ruled Philadelphia*, 53; *Sunday Morning Times*, Sept. 24, 1871.

33. Gillette, "Corrupt and Contented," 20–26, 244, 256.

34. *North American*, Mar. 23, May 24, 1871.

35. Thomas Cochran to Eli Kirk Price, n.d., Society Collection, HSP; Thomas Cochran, "Local Taxation," *Penn Monthly* 2 (May 1871): 228; *North American*, June 2, 1871.

36. *North American*, Apr. 15, 1874; Robert P. Porter, *Local Government: At Home and Abroad* (n.p., 1879), 191.

37. *Morning Post*, July 1, 1870.

38. *North American*, July 6, 1871; June 19, 1873.

39. Mayor of Philadelphia, Annual Report, 1858, 31; Gillette, "Corrupt and Contented," 187–88.

40. Citizens' Association, *First Annual Report*, 17; *Sunday Morning Times*, Mar. 3, 1872; CMRA, *Passenger Railways*, (Philadelphia: n.p., 1874), 3.

41. *North American*, July 4, 1860.

42. "To the President and Directors of the Pennsylvania R. R. Co.," p. 58, Lea Papers, Box 165, Folder 2115; *North American*, Sept. 24, 1874. For a slightly different reading of the stockyard question and the place of manufactures in the city, see Vitiello, "Engineering the Metropolis," 312–15.

43. "Sellers et al. vs. The Pennsylvania Railroad Company et al.: Opening Argument of Wm. Henry Rawle, Esq., on Motion for Injunction to Restrain Slaughter-House," pp. 38–41, Lea Papers, Box 165, Folder 2119.

44. Pennsylvania Railroad Company, *Fiftieth Anniversary of the Incorporation of the Pennsylvania Railroad Company* (Philadelphia: Allen, Lane & Scott, 1896), 58.

45. Pennsylvania Railroad Company, *Fiftieth Anniversary of the Incorporation*, 59; C. Vann Woodward, *Reunion and Reaction: The Compromise of 1877 and the End of Reconstruction* (Oxford: Oxford University Press, 1991), 68–121. Scott, perhaps, is a more fitting figure than Jay Cooke to symbolize what Warner argued was the reorientation of businessmen's horizons from the city to the nation after the Civil War. Warner, *Private City*, 84–85.

46. *Inquirer*, July 2, 1872.

47. David Montgomery, *Beyond Equality: Labor and the Radical Republicans, 1862–1872*, (Urbana: University of Illinois Press, 1967), 176–85, 230–37.

48. *Inquirer*, Apr. 5, 1877; Elder, *Questions of the Day*, 5, 264, 321–29.

49. R. R. Jackaway, *The Great Approaching Conflict Between Capital and Labor* (n.p., 1874), 22–23; *Inquirer*, Mar. 13, Apr. 5, 1877.

50. Philip S. Foner, *The Great Labor Uprising of 1877* (New York: Monrad Press, 1977).

51. *Inquirer*, July 23, 1877.

52. *North American*, July 26, 1877.

53. *Evening Star*, July 24, 26, 1877.

54. Brewster, "Eli Kirk Price," 19–21; Foner, *Great Labor Uprising*, 58, 70; Gallman, *Mastering Wartime*, 338–39.

55. *North American*, July 23, 1877; *Bulletin*, July 25, 1877.

56. Michael A. Bellesiles, *1877: America's Year of Living Violently* (New York: The New Press, 2010), 159.

57. *Inquirer*, July 26, Aug. 3, 1877; Price, "Family as an Element of Government," 318.

58. M. Russell Thayer, "Movements of Troops in Cities in Cases of Riot or Insurrection," *Proceedings of the American Philosophical Society* 18 (July 1878), 89–95.

59. *North American*, Aug. 11, Nov. 16, 1877; B. B. Strang et al., *Report of the Commission to Devise a Plan for the Government of Cities of the State of Pennsylvania* (Harrisburg, Pa.: Lane S. Hart, 1878), 167, 170.

60. Strang et al., *Plan for the Government of Cities of the State of Pennsylvania*, 6.

61. Pennsylvania Railroad, *Suburban Stations and Rural Homes of the Pennsylvania Railroad* (Philadelphia: Pennsylvania Railroad, 1875), 3; *North American*, Apr. 26, 1876.

62. Price, "Our Unknown City Laws," (Philadelphia: n.p., 1884), 6.

63. J. W., letter to *Germantown Telegraph*, Aug. 15, 1855; *Germantown Telegraph*, Feb. 7, Mar. 14, 1855; Mar. 3, 1869. On the turn away from annexation, see Richardson Dilworth, *The Urban Origins of Suburban Autonomy* (Cambridge, Mass.: Harvard University Press, 2005), 3; Jackson, *Crabgrass Frontier*, 150–56.

64. *Germantown Telegraph*, Mar. 3, 1869.

65. Hepp, *Middle-Class City*, 47.

66. Strang, *Plan for the Government of Cities of the State of Pennsylvania*, 7.

67. Price, *Consolidation*, 120.

Conclusion

1. Thompson, "Streets of Philadelphia," 919–41.

2. Kathryn Kish Sklar, *Florence Kelley and the Nation's Work* (New Haven, Conn.: Yale University Press, 1995); David Bruce Brownlee, *Building the City Beautiful: The Benjamin Franklin Parkway and the Philadelphia Museum of Art* (Philadelphia: Philadelphia Museum of Art, 1989); McCaffery, *When Bosses Ruled Philadelphia*.

3. Warner, *Private City*, xi.

4. J. W. Townsend, *The Old Main Line* (Philadelphia: n.p., 1922), 8. On suburban autonomy, see Dilworth, *Suburban Autonomy*, 3; Jackson, *Crabgrass Frontier*, 150–56.

5. On twentieth- and twenty-first century Philadelphia and attempts to attract global trade and investment, see for example Hodos, *Second Cities*, 19.

6. *Fincher's*, Jan. 21, 1865.

7. On the campaign for secession, a bill for which passed the State Senate in 1988, see *Inquirer*, Nov. 16, 1983; Feb. 10, 1988; Mar. 13, 1991. On the attempt to break up the consolidated city, see *Daily News*, July 25, 2000.

8. Pennsylvania Senate, *Consolidation*, 4.

9. *Inquirer*, Feb. 25, 1861.

INDEX

Page numbers in italics represent illustrations.

ACKNOWLEDGMENTS

The intellectual debts I have racked up in writing this book would bring a blush to the face of even the most spendthrift booster. At the University of Pennsylvania, Walter Licht's enthusiasm for Philadelphia and its industrial heritage proved inspiring. Classes and discussions with Steve Hahn, Tom Sugrue, and Kathy Peiss introduced me to new ideas and unexpected perspectives. Amy Hillier inducted me into the world of Geographic Information Systems and provided a great deal of assistance with mapmaking. And like so many works on urban America, the work first took shape under the late Michael Katz, who helped to convince me that there might be something worth saying about the making of a nineteenth-century city charter. The financial help I received in the form of a Benjamin Franklin scholarship and a Dolores Quinn foundation fellowship enabled me to pursue my research.

I was lucky enough at Penn to find myself among a supportive and brilliant cohort of graduate students. For the mix of ideas, camaraderie, and couches to sleep on, I'm especially grateful to John Kenney, Rene Luis-Alvarez, Ben Mercer, Sarah Van Beurden, Nicole Maurantonio, Jo Cohen, Erik Mathisen, Matt Karp, Kyle Roberts, Dan Amsterdam, Daniel Stedman-Jones, and Domenic Vitiello, whose own knowledge of Philadelphia is unsurpassed.

Philadelphia's research libraries must be among the best in the world, and librarians at the City Archives, Kislak Center, Historical Society of Pennsylvania (HSP), and Library Company of Philadelphia (LCP) all proved especially helpful. My particular gratitude goes to Connie King and her colleagues at LCP who proved so patient as I worked my way through bound volumes of dusty nineteenth-century newspapers. That HSP and LCP were kind enough to award me a fellowship as I began to revise the manuscript speaks volumes for their patience.

In Sheffield, I've had the good fortune to encounter generous colleagues, and whatever regulatory obstacles line our path, there's a commitment in the department to scholarly endeavor that has made it a wonderful place to work. My fellow Americanists Dan Scroop, Simon Middleton, and Sarah Miller-Davenport have all helped me to hone my ideas, as have historians working on other areas: not least Simon Loseby, James Shaw, Charles West, Caroline Pennock, and all the staff who have contributed to our Cities class. Bob Moore, Mary Vincent, and Phil Withington have each been supportive heads of department, while members past and present of the Los Companeros writing group have pushed me to commit pen to paper and offered noisy constructive criticism washed down with ample local ale. Our undergraduate students—not least veterans of the special subject HST3105, Reconstructing America, who amaze me every year with their research and insights—have kept me on course with the project. Conversations with recently minted PhDs in nineteenth-century American history who came out of that seminar—Belle Grenville-Mathers, Charlie Thompson, Alex Page, and James Williamson—prodded me to think about questions over centralized power in the period. And Pete David, alongside the members of the Payroll Union, provided me with an utterly different way of thinking about antebellum Philadelphia. Their album on the subject, *Paris of America*, is well worth checking out (and comes with free footnotes).

Scholars on both sides of the Atlantic have also offered more assistance than I could rightfully expect. In Europe, Dan Peart, Marc Palen, Bruce Baker, Cristina Bon, and other members of the British American Nineteenth Century Historians association have always been willing to share ideas and advice. Adam I. P. Smith at University College London meanwhile has been continually supportive and has kindly read sections of the manuscript. I am grateful for the opportunity to present portions of the work at Leicester, Oxford, Cambridge, Leeds Met, and the Catholic University of Milan. In the United States, Aaron Wunsch was generous enough to share his own research on Eli Kirk Price, while encouraging me to think through the links between Consolidation and association. I look forward to seeing his outstanding work on rural cemeteries in print soon. Zachary Schrag, who is writing an exciting book on the 1844 riots, read the entire manuscript, and has pushed me to strengthen the framing and argument in myriad ways. Whatever virtues there might be in the book owe much to his efforts. I've benefited too from correspondence and conversations with other scholars—among them Howard Gillette Jr., Adam Arenson, Elizabeth Milroy, Bruce Dorsey, Daniel Kilbride, Tyler Anbinder, and the late C. Dallett Hemphill—who have taken the time to offer help and advice to a historian working on Civil War-era America from afar. At Penn Press, meanwhile, Bob Lockhart has proved a careful reader and a far more patient editor than I've deserved. I'd heard good things from every author I'd encountered who had worked with him, and the encouragement and feedback he has provided from our initial email exchange has helped to keep me moving forward.

Mum and Dad stopped asking when the book was coming out some time ago but their support, along with that of my in-laws Warren and Jessie in Pittsburgh, made my research possible. So too has the companionship of Tehyun Ma. My love of American cities came from wandering the streets of Philadelphia with her. Next time we visit, we can finally give the nineteenth-century landmarks a miss.